The Phoenix Principle, Vol. 1

Messiah in The Making

Born of Ritual and Revolution

Stephen H. Provost

All material © 2012, 2018 Stephen H. Provost

Previously published by the author as a single work, "The Phoenix Principle," under the name Stifyn Emrys.

Cover artwork: Public domain images
Cover concept and design: Stephen H. Provost
All interior images are in the public domain.

No part of this book may be reproduced, or stored in a retrieval system, or transmitted in any form or by any means, electronic, mechanical, photocopying, recording, or otherwise, without the express written permission of the publisher.

Dragon Crown Books 2018
All rights reserved.

ISBN: 978-1-948594-07-3

For Samaire, who had faith in me
when I no longer believe

Contents

1	Dragon Ladies	5
2	Abomination	37
3	Rainmaker	57
4	The Man Who Would Not Die	63
5	Eclipse	113
6	The Idumean	143
7	A Child is Born	163
8	The Galilean	203
9	Voice in the Wilderness	213
10	The Prefect and the Poor	227
11	Parting the Waters	239
12	The Bridegroom	253
13	The Bethsaida Incident	271
14	The Seeds of Revolution	285
15	Sponsors and Spies	307
16	Hosanna in the Highest	335
17	Betrayal	347
18	King of the Jews	377
19	Another Voice from Ramah	419
20	The Sorcerer	445
21	Showdown in Jerusalem	463
	Appendix: Timeline	482
	Bibliography	485
	Notes	493

I

Dragon Ladies

Patterns are key in deciphering ancient myth. These patterns, based on ancient archetypes, occur with regularity.

One such pattern involves the story of the sacred yet tragic union of a noble prince and harlot priestess. Throughout the Hebrew scriptures, this tale resurfaces, with slight variation, time and again. It is not always immediately apparent, but once one learns to recognize it, the signs are hard to miss.

One story of particular note is the so-called rape of Dinah, a tale that surfaces in the *Genesis* account immediately after the story of Jacob's conflict with Esau. It is the story of Jacob's daughter, who was propositioned by a prince named Shechem — a man who subsequently sought to have her for his wife. Shechem was the son of a king named Hamor, whose realm seems to have abutted that of Jacob and who fell desperately in love with Dinah.

Though the story has come to be known as the "rape" of Dinah, the scribes never actually say that the young prince raped her. Instead, they report that he defiled or violated her. In a modern context, this would seem to denote a rape, and there is some indication that Shechem took the woman forcibly to his bed. But the ancients were probably engaging in a form of wordplay that their audience would have recognized, even though modern readers are unlikely to notice it. The Hebrew word they use to denote defilement is *innah*, a term that bears a resemblance to that of the story's heroine, but one which even more so recalls the divine name of the goddess Inanna, mistress of the great ziggurat.

At her temple, it was customary for women to act as prostitutes in service to the goddess once in their lifetime. Herodotus describes the practice as follows:

"The following is the most shameful practice in Babylon. Every woman born of the country must sit in the temple of Aphrodite and associate once in her life with a strange man." The historian, who associates Inanna with the Greek goddess Aphrodite, goes on to describe this practice in some detail. "They sit with a wreath of braids around their head in the holy precinct. There are many women, some coming and others going away. Straight paths are made between them in every direction, along which the strangers can walk to make their choice.

"When a woman sits there, she may not go home until one of the strangers has thrown money in her lap and associated with her outside the holy place," he continues. He then comments ruefully that such a practice worked fine for the more comely maidens but proved to be a burden for the less attractive: "All those who are beautiful and well-made return quickly home, but the ugly ones must wait a long time until they can satisfy the custom — many having to wait three or four years." [1]

Was Dinah taking part in such a ritual with Shechem?

It seems entirely possible.

The ritual described by Herodotus seems like a common man's version of that practiced at the temple of Luxor. This was the site of the mystical union between the hidden god Amen (in the guise of the king) and the queen, who served as the wife of god. As with the rites of Inanna, it took place in a temple and was considered a sanctified act of piety. It differed, however, in that it involved only the royal couple and was not extended to involve the masses.

In this sense, the Luxor ritual provided an even closer counterpart to the union of Dinah and Shechem, both of whom were of royal blood. Dinah was the daughter of Jacob, who was in fact the Hyksos pharaoh Yakob-har; Shechem was the prince of a neighboring land. It was clearly not an Egyptian kingdom, for it disdained the practice of circumcision that was the order of the day in Egypt. And this posed a problem for Shechem.

The defilement mentioned in the text probably referred to the fact that he was an uncircumcised prince who had violated Dinah in the sense that he had robbed her of her virginity. Here, the observations of Herodotus on Inanna's temple are again worth quoting.

Referring to the woman obliged to serve as a temple prostitute, he records this stipulation: "When she has given herself, she has fulfilled her holy duty to the goddess and returns home, and however much she is offered thereafter, she is not to be won." [2]

Because she was no longer a virgin, she was now unfit for the sacred act. This was a principle that extended from the temple courts into everyday life, where men shunned women who were no longer virgins as "damaged goods" unfit for marriage because they had been defiled. This might have occurred during a rape, but it could just as easily have occurred through a consensual act. Regardless, consent was not the issue to the ancient mind, which viewed any such violation as a heinous crime against the woman and her family.

Why would Shechem commit such a crime?

The answer is simple: As a foreign, uncircumcised prince, he would not have been allowed to marry Dinah under normal circumstances, and he therefore had to stack the deck in his favor.

He appears to have done so by breaking the law.

The punishment for violating a virgin was simple. To begin with, the guilty party had to pay the woman's father fifty shekels, which would have been a simple matter for a prince with a national treasury at his disposal. But there was another consequence, as well: "He must marry the girl, for he has violated her." [3] This was exactly what

Shechem wanted to do. The marriage sanction was imposed to ensure that a woman would be cared for, despite the fact that she was no longer a virgin and therefore less likely to win a husband. As an uncircumcised alien, Shechem would have had no chance of marrying Dinah; as someone who had violated her, he was *required* to marry her.

It was an ingenious attempt to circumvent the culture of the day by using the Hebrews' (actually the Hyksos') own laws against them.

Hamor agreed to his son's request, apparently seeing such a marriage as a means of forging a dynastic alliance with his powerful neighbors. In the hope of strengthening this link, however, he upped the ante. In addition to asking that Dinah be allowed to marry Shechem, he proposed that *all* the daughters of the leading Hebrew men be betrothed to the men of his kingdom.

This was an unprecedented step, and Jacob's sons were understandably wary. They insisted that Shechem and the other would-be grooms first undergo the rite of circumcision, so they might be worthy to take Hebrew wives. This, it turned out, was nothing more than a ruse — for they had no intention of going forward with the arrangement at all. The Shechemites kept their part of the bargain, allowing themselves to undergo the painful rite demanded of them. But while they were still sore from the operation, they suddenly found themselves under siege from the Hebrew army: "While all of them were still in pain ... Dinah's brothers took their swords and attacked the unsuspecting city, killing every male. They put Hamor and his son Shechem to the sword, and they took Dinah from Shechem's house and left." [4]

The story is a clear variation on the story of Danaus' fifty daughters, who fled Egypt aboard a ship bound for the city of Argo. According to this story, they were pledged to marry the sons of Danaus' twin brother Aegyptus but stabbed their would-be husbands on their wedding night.

The same fate awaits Shechem and his countrymen, who are substituted in the Hebrew legend for the "sons of Aegyptus" — an archetypal king of Egypt. This pharaoh's counterpart in the story of Dinah is Shechem's father, who is likewise a king and is identified ethnically as a Hivite. Such a designation in the Hebrew text does not serve to shed any appreciable light on the tale. But thankfully, an alternate translation does. In the Greek version known as the Septuagint, the king is identified not as a Hivite but a *Horite* — someone associated with the Egyptian god Horus. He was therefore a king of Egypt, a scion of the royal Theban house, just as the mythical Aegyptus was. Dinah's name, meanwhile, certainly recalls that of Danaus.

The name Shechem, furthermore, is based on the Hebrew word for "shoulder" — a baffling and seemingly insignificant bit of information that nonetheless would have implications for future storytellers.

More about that later.

For now it is enough to say that Shechem was not the only prince to find himself enmeshed in sexual controversy during the period in question, and that Dinah was not the only woman in the Hebrew scriptures to be at the center of such a scandal. Indeed, several other incidents of note are recorded in the Hebrew scriptures, and two of these involve different women with the same name. Pure coincidence? Hardly. For the name in question has been encountered before in quite a different context.

Tamar.

This was, of course, the Hebrew word for date palm, the benu tree that was the nesting place of the phoenix and the inspiration behind the Osirian *djed* column. Just as the apple tree was the tree of life in Greek and Celtic legend, the date palm performed the same function in the ancient Near East, particularly in Egypt. But it was important in Hebrew tradition as well, where it served a symbol of the "just" or "righteous" man destined to partake of heaven's riches.[5]

Repeatedly, members of the high priestly family are referred to as "the just." And with good reason. The Hebrew word for this concept was *tsedeq* or *zadok*, and the dynasty of priests that included the slain hero Onias traced its lineage back to a man named Zadok. This particular priest had served as high priest during the reign of David and had set a standard for righteousness that his sons were sworn to uphold. To be righteous meant to be upright, but the moral dimension was only one facet of this concept. The Zadokite high priests, as they came to be called, were guardians of the temple's inner sanctuary, the shrine of the ark that carried the dead king to the heavens so that he might become the new Osiris.

Osiris was first encased in an ark, then in a tree.

A tamarisk or palm.

And just as the cherub with the flaming sword had guarded this sacred tree of life in the garden known as Eden, so the *kher heb* priests of the Zadokite line stood watch over the ark in the sanctuary. The ark was the tree. The tree was the ark. And the temple itself was but a symbol of the ancient garden. For many years, it apparently contained its own *djed* column in the form of an Asherah pole, the tree of Osiris set upright to signify the god-king's resurrection. This process of raising the pillar was part of the ceremony known as the opening of the mouth, in which the Egyptian *kher heb* priest played such a crucial role. And just as the god himself was "upright" and living, so too were the Zadokite priests who were keepers of his shrine. They were morally pure and therefore fit to partake of the resurrection by eating the fruit of the date palm, the tree of life. (They were, quite literally, pillars of the community — a phrase that may well derive from these priests' association with the pillar of Osiris.)

All of which brings us back to Tamar.

The palm lady.

How does she fit in? The palm tree as the model for the *djed* column is obviously a symbol of the male god Osiris, yet the tree itself is identified as *tamar* in the Hebrew texts — a decidedly feminine name consistently worn by a woman. What is going on here? This apparent incongruity is reminiscent of that involving the Asherah pole. An artificial phallic pillar or tree, it plainly symbolized the masculine Osiris yet was associated even more closely with a certain goddess. The obvious explanation is that goddess was the consort of the dead king and mistress of the garden, so intimately connected with the tree that she came to be identified with it. This is the role played by Diana as keeper of the sacred grove, and by Mary Magdalene in standing vigil at Jesus' garden tomb. They and the other women of the garden (Morgan, Nimue, Circe and so on) were performing the same function initiated by the Asherah goddess at the beginning of time. When she was known as Eve.

The Temptress

She would be forever linked, like the others, to a single tree — the tree of knowledge in the ancient garden. This was the same garden that served as a model for the temple at Jerusalem, which for centuries housed the Asherah pole or divine "tree." It is therefore hardly surprising to find a certain affinity between the character of Eve and the goddess of the Asherah.

Eve is actually given two names in the Hebrew scriptures. The first is *issa*, which simply means "woman" and bears a noticeable likeness to the name Isis. More commonly, however, she is referred to using the word that came to be identified as her proper name, *hawwa*. This particular word may be taken from the Phoenician word *hwy*, meaning "life." Eve was, after all, depicted by the Hebrew scribes as the mother of all living.[6] And it appears that the Asherah goddess had a similar role, being named in some texts as the mother and nurse of the great gods.

But there is an even more interesting possibility to consider — it has been suggested that the name is derived instead from the Aramaic *hewya* or *hwah*, variants of the same root which have the meaning "serpent." [7]

In one Sumerian tale, the famed hero Gilgamesh fights a loud and arrogant beast described as so ferocious that its teeth are the teeth of a dragon.[8] This description of the creature's teeth provides a clue as to his nature, but it is the beast's name that truly gives him away: Hawawa. The resemblance of this name to the Aramaic word for serpent, *hwah*, is not to be missed. It is a resemblance that makes clear the nature of the beast: Hawawa is obviously a serpent or dragon, and Gilgamesh is the knight in shining armor destined to destroy him.

This particular legend of Gilgamesh involves the hero's attempt to enter a paradisiacal realm known as the Land of the Living and cut down a tree guarded by Hawawa.

And here we find a clear connection with the Eden myth.

It recalls Eve's close association with the serpent who guards the sacred tree in the garden. And her name, *hawwa*, is virtually identical to that of the serpent in the Gilgamesh story. If this association is correct, it would make the true meaning of her name something like "serpent lady" (or to use a phrase that has acquired something of a pejorative meaning over the centuries, dragon lady).

A temptress.

The tree itself was a *djed* column, or the pole of the Asherah goddess. This particular goddess wore several titles, including "she who treads on the sea." [9] This would identify her as a mermaid or sea goddess in the mold of Isis. And Asherah is further identified with the queen of the Egyptian pantheon in her association with Isis' star, Sirius. According to Phoenician myth, Asherah had seventy children — one for each day the bright star tarried beneath the horizon.[10] She is also the grail bearer, the temptress with the dish of plenty and the golden cup who invites her companions to eat, drink and be merry, much as Inanna invited Enki to imbibe the fruit of the vine so she could obtain his tablets of wisdom:

Why has the lady of the sea arrived?
Why has the mother of the gods come?

Are you hungry ...
Or thirsty ...?
Have something to eat or drink!

Eat some food from the table;
Drink some wine from the goblet –
Blood of the vine from the golden cup [11]

The impression that some sort of proto-Eucharist is being conducted is inescapable. Further references in this ancient passage make it clear that more than drunkenness is involved: The sexual overtones are quite apparent. No sooner has he finished talking of this great feast, than the narrator turns his attention to Asherah's consort, the venerable bull god named El: "Does El the king's passion excite you?" he asks the goddess. "Does the love of the bull (god) arouse you?"

There immediately follows a reference, placed on the lips of Asherah, to this god's unsurpassed wisdom. There can be no doubt that we are once again in the realm of the sacred coupling, during which wisdom was supposedly conveyed between male and female — and thence to their progeny in the sacred bloodline.

This was the function of the woman as grail bearer and keeper of the bloodline. She passed on to her sons the wisdom of their fathers. Or their folly, as the case may be. This is perhaps why the sins of the fathers were held against their descendants by the ancient Hebrews: "For I, Yahweh your god, am a jealous god, punishing the children for the sin of their fathers to the third and fourth generation of those who hate me." [12]

It may well also be the source of the so-called doctrine of original sin, which punishes all the descendants of Adam for his indiscretion in the garden. The bloodline was a powerful thing, it seemed, for good or ill.

And this was especially so for the bloodline of kings, who wielded the greatest power and were also expected to have the greatest wisdom. Among the Hebrews, these kings would come from the bloodline of Judah, one of the twelve sons of Jacob, who was described in the following terms:

You are a lion's cub, O Judah
You return from the prey, my son
Like a lion, he crouches and lies down
Like a lioness, who dares to rouse him?

The scepter will not depart from Judah
Nor the ruler's staff from between his feet
Until he comes to whom it belongs
And the obedience of the nations is his

He will wash his garments in wine
His robes in the blood of grapes [13]

This final reference to the wine is an obvious reference Judah's identity as a scion of the royal bloodline, as symbolized by the scepter he is destined to retain. The language is incredibly similar to that of the passage involving Asherah, a goddess whose sons were described as "her pride of lions." [14] Judah, as a lion's cub, would have been one of her children — which only makes sense in light of her role as the mother of the gods, matriarch of the sacred bloodline.

From Judah would come all the kings destined to reign in Jerusalem, or so the legend went.

David.

Solomon.

Even Jesus.

And they would be born, fittingly, from a bloodline that began with a woman named Tamar.

The Tamar Chronicles

Tamar was not just anybody. She was, in fact, Judah's own daughter-in-law. He had arranged for her to marry his eldest son, in the hope that she would bear a child to him and thus continue the bloodline. Unfortunately, however, the boy died young before he was able to conceive a son with Tamar, and Judah was left to look for other options. The most obvious of these was to marry another of his sons to Tamar, a course of action that would in fact be codified under the Mosaic law. This custom was known as a levirate marriage, so named for the Hebrew word *levir*, meaning "brother-in-law." Under this law, as detailed previously, a man whose brother died without an heir was obligated to marry his widow and raise up children in his name.

The purpose of this mandate was quite clear: It ensured the continuance of the sacred bloodline through the priestess serving as the "wife of god." This was the nature of the ancient Egyptian custom. And for whatever reason (the text is not explicit), Tamar had been chosen to serve in this capacity. Judah knew it was imperative that she bear his family's offspring if they were to continue on the throne. He therefore ordered his second son to take Tamar as his wife, telling him in no uncertain terms: "Produce offspring for your brother." [15]

The youth, however, balked at this idea. He knew that the child he produced would not be counted as his, and he was not happy at the prospect of providing a sort of stud service for his dead brother. He therefore determined to keep from impregnating Tamar by failing to complete the sex act and spilling his semen out on the ground. For this act of defiance, he was sentenced to death — a punishment the writer attributes to Yahweh, but which was probably carried out by Judah himself. He would not have taken kindly to such an act of disobedience, news of which was doubtless conveyed to him by Tamar herself.

But having carried out his vengeance, he was left with a quandary: His third son was still a child, incapable of shouldering the levirate burden because of his youth. Judah was therefore left with no choice but to tell Tamar she must wait until he had grown old enough to father a child. In the meantime, he told her, she would have to live as a widow in her father's house.

This was not the sort of thing Tamar had been hoping to hear. Distraught at the prospect of waiting years for Judah's youngest son to grow up, she devised a plan whereby she might expedite the process — by seducing Judah himself. When, at length, his wife died, she knew her opportunity had come. Having been deprived of his mate's company, Judah would be eager for female companionship, and Tamar knew she was just the person to provide it. She therefore disguised herself as a prostitute and sat down at city gates about the time she knew Judah was scheduled to pass by.

The ploy worked. Aroused at the sight of her, Judah approached Tamar and propositioned her, not realizing she was his own daughter-in-law. But Tamar would not be so easily swayed. She knew that if she were to become pregnant, she would be branded a whore and suffer the consequences — and severe consequences they were. Under Mosaic law, the daughter of a priest who was found to have engaged in harlotry was burned to death.[16]

The word for prostitution here is important.

The Hebrews had two separate words for this act, which in fact referred to entirely different concepts. The distinction between them, however, has been lost on modern translators, who insist on lumping them together under a single heading called harlotry. The first term, *zanah*, stems from a word meaning "to commit adultery" and indeed refers to a common street harlot. The second word, however, has nothing to do with this concept. It is *qadeshah*, a feminine form of the word *qadesh*, which means simply "the holy."

The law's proscription against a harlotry applied only to the daughter of a priest playing the part of a common prostitute or *zanah*. There was good reason for this. The daughter of a priest carried the sacred priestly bloodline and was therefore not prohibited from, but in fact expected to act as a *qadeshah*. She was the holy temple virgin prostitute or "wife of god," who was destined to conceive the future priest-king. But if she defiled herself by committing adultery as a *zanah*, she not only disqualified herself from meeting her holy obligation, she also brought shame on the family of the king. Such an act on the part of a priest's daughter was an embarrassment and an outrage.

When Tamar sat down by the city gates, she was playing the part of a common *zanah*. And she knew the risks of doing so. She therefore asked payment from Judah in the form of his seal, cord and staff — providing her with the necessary proof that, if she conceived a child, he was its father.

Of course, she did conceive.

And of course, Judah found out about her pregnancy when the child's presence in her womb became apparent "about three months later."

In a fury, he accused her of common harlotry and invoked the Mosaic law against her. (The fact that no such law existed until centuries later did not seem to bother the scribes, who apparently had no qualms about applying it retroactively to their tale.) "Bring her out and have her burned to death!" he demanded.[17]

That's when Tamar produced her ace in the hole. She still held the cord and seal of the man who had lain with her.

"I am pregnant by the man who owns these," she taunted, producing the items. "See if you recognize whose cord and seal these are."[18] Her question was, of course, not intended to elicit an answer per se. Of course, Judah knew the items in question belonged to him, and so did everyone else present. He had been hoodwinked and therefore had no choice but to accept Tamar into his household.

In time, she gave birth to twins, one of whom would carry on the bloodline down through David and, eventually (it was asserted), Jesus. She is one of only four women mentioned in the genealogy of Jesus as recorded by the author of *Matthew*, each of them known as a harlot or seductress:

- Tamar, who seduced Judah.
- Rahab, a harlot who helped Joshua's forces capture Jericho.
- Ruth, who seduced her kinsman Boaz and became the grandmother of David.

- Bath-Sheba, who tempted David into an adulterous affair.

The Scarlet Cord

The only one of these four women not involved in a sexual tryst of some sort was Rahab, who was nonetheless described as a harlot. According to legend, she sheltered Joshua's scouts when they entered Jericho on a mission of espionage, then hung a scarlet cord from her window so they could escape and flee into the hills. There, she told them, they were to wait three days until the enemy had stopped looking for them before continuing on their way.

Though there is no overt reference to an act of ritual intercourse, erotic and mythic imagery abounds. Not only is Rahab a harlot, she allows the spies to enter in her house. There, the text explicitly says, they are hidden. All this is reminiscent of the Egyptian ritual in which the sacred priestess allows the god Amen, in the guise of the king, to enter *her* house — the temple at Luxor — and share her marriage bed. The name Amen, it is worth recalling, means "hidden one." The pharaoh is disguised as the god, and his identity thus remains hidden, just as the spies are hidden in the story of Rahab. By the time he has left the temple at Luxor, he will have fathered a child upon his priestess, thus continuing the sacred bloodline that is symbolized quite effectively in the legend of Rahab.

By the scarlet cord.

This is not the first appearance of the scarlet cord or thread in this capacity. Indeed, it makes its first appearance in the legend of Tamar and Judah when the former stands ready to give birth. Knowing that her mistress is pregnant with twin sons by her father-in-law, the quick-thinking midwife stands ready with a scarlet thread in case one of the sons should begin to emerge from the womb and then return for a moment. By tying the thread to this child's finger or toe, she could identify him as the truly first-born son and keeper of the bloodline.

This tactic worked as it was supposed to, and the midwife tied the thread to the finger of the first-born, which subsequently disappeared back inside the birth canal. When the two children were actually born, the second son broke out first. As it turned out, despite the midwife's diligence, the messianic line passed through the second child in any case. The best-laid plans ...

Another tale, preserved in the Ethiopian book of legends known as the *Kebra Negast*, relates that the daughter of the Egyptian pharaoh seduced King Solomon using locusts and a scarlet thread.[19] The pharaoh's daughter in question was, of course, the Queen of Sheba. And once again, the scarlet thread represented the sacred bloodline that passed through the Egyptian queens. This particular queen happened to be the daughter of the pharaoh Seqenenre, whose death Solomon (that is to say Apophis) had himself arranged after the argument over the hippopotamus pool.

Rahab's use of the scarlet cord would be somewhat different, though the symbolism was the same.

Her interaction with the spies reveals her as a harlot just like Tamar and in the tradition of the wise harlot extolled in the proverbs of Solomon. She is the prostitute crying out from the city gates and the street corners, caring little with whom she shares her wisdom — or her bed. The bloodline is, in any event, passed through *her* womb; the identity of the man who lies with her is "hidden" and therefore of little consequence. He might be king or general, prince or pauper. What matters is not his mortal station, but the fact that he is the god personified.

It is this very sort of indifference that seems to characterize Rahab's attitude toward the spies. She is a harlot for hire, a sexual mercenary if you will. The fact that she lives in Jericho makes little difference to her, for she holds no particular allegiance to the city and is just as content to share her resource with the foreign spies under Joshua's command. These men she provides with a measure of her wisdom (traditionally conveyed through sexual intercourse), providing them with the information they need to make their escape.

But this is not the only significant fact about this enigmatic woman. Indeed, it turns out that her name originally belonged to a mythical sea serpent or dragon, thus identifying Rahab as yet another personification of the dragon lady. According to Hebrew tradition, Yahweh smote the sea serpent named Rahab in much the same way that Gilgamesh's heroic companion Enkidu slew Hawawa. Addressing his patron god, the psalmist declares his sovereignty as conqueror of the serpent: "You rule over the surging sea; when its waves mount up, you still them. You crushed Rahab like one of the slain." [20]

So was Rahab a sea serpent or a harlot?

The answer is not a simple one, for the Hebrew scribes themselves seem at a loss to distinguish between dragon and dragon lady. This is, in hindsight, somewhat understandable. Indeed, the similarity between the names for Eve and the serpent — *hawwa* and Hawawa — would seem to indicate that the first woman was, in some way, a serpent herself.

Even Isis, whose Greek name so closely resembles the title *issa* worn by Eve, seems to have originated as a serpent goddess. Her name in Egyptian was Au Set, which appears to be derived from an epithet worn by a more ancient figure known as Ua Zit. This was the neolithic cobra goddess of Lower Egypt, whose name literally meant "great serpent." [21] Her imagery survived in the royal crown worn by the pharaohs in the image of the uraeus, the fearsome cobra depicted in a menacing pose, its head reared and its hood flaring.

This animal symbolism links the prehistoric goddess even more closely with Isis, who was portrayed as having created the serpent by mixing the saliva of Ra with the dirt upon which it had fallen.

It is further worth noting that the second half of the name Au Set is identical to that worn by Horus' nemesis, Set or Seth, who was likewise depicted as a fearsome serpent. Some versions of the myth even depict Isis as the lover of Seth, thus creating a union of two serpent figures — all of which makes perfect sense in light of the symbolism of the sacred grove. The priestess of the garden was, after all, the consort of the *kher heb* priest or wizard, whose totem animal was the wise serpent. It was therefore only natural that she, as his mate, should also have been depicted as a serpent.

In fact, it seems probable that the feminine partner was the first to be depicted in this manner.

If prehistoric cultures indeed failed to recognize the male role in procreation, the infant's emergence from the womb would have seemed miraculous. It would have appeared as though the mother had given birth spontaneously, without any external catalyst. And it would have been natural to equate such an event with the serpent's shedding of its skin — the mother being the "old skin" that was discarded by the pure being, which emerged rejuvenated in the form of the infant.

Only later, when the male role in conception was recognized, would the need for a consort become apparent. It would have been at this point that the natural phallic symbolism took hold, allowing the male partner to become more closely linked to the serpent than his female consort. Despite this, however, the ancient identification of the woman and the serpent remained strong, even though it was suppressed and obscured to the point where it was no longer always recognizable.

Indeed, the motif of the serpent couple appears to have been pervasive throughout the ancient world. The Chinese, for example, attributed the founding of their civilization to divine king and queen Fu Xi and Nu Wa, whom they imagined to have been amphibians of sorts. Popular depictions show each with the torso of a human but the tail of a fish or serpent, their tails intertwined in a manner reminiscent of the two serpents wrapped around the caduceus pole of Hermes. The same pole later wielded by Moses.

It survives today as a symbol of medicine, an emblem that signifies life and healing. And thus it was also to the ancients. To them, the two serpents would have represented the *kher heb* priest and priestess, whose union perpetuates the sacred bloodline and thus sustains the tree of life — or in modern parlance, the family tree. Though death may claim one member of the line, the wound is "healed" through the coupling of the two great serpents. By their joining, they conceive a new earthen vessel for the divine spirit, paving the way for its magical rebirth and thus perpetuating the eternal cycle.

Hence, Rahab was both harlot and serpent. She was in fact the archetypal mermaid, a fair damsel endowed with the tail of a fish (or sea serpent) who seduced unwitting mariners and lured them to their deaths. She was the Meri-maid, or maid of the sea queen Isis. And she was the priestess of the grove, reveling in her dual role as passionate lover and bringer of death — a bloodletting vampire in the mold of Circe and Lilith. The name Rahab itself is borrowed from a word that denotes pride or loud boasting, attributes ascribed in the proverbs of Solomon to just such a treacherous harlot. Warning his reader to beware of such dragon ladies, the author calls forth the image of a naïve young man fallen in with the wrong woman. He comes across her as he travels along the street near twilight, a woman "dressed as a prostitute with crafty intent ... loud and defiant." [22]

He submits to her, and it costs him his life.

The same crafty intent attributed to the proverbial harlot may also be found in the serpent of Eden, described as the craftiest of all living creatures. But the serpentine imagery does not end there. Indeed, the harlot's "loud and defiant" manner recalls another story involving our old friend Orion, whose star-crossed love for Diana was not, it turns out, his only romantic entanglement.

Whose Side Are You On?

In addition to Diana, the stellar giant was also linked to a certain woman named Side, who is described in myth as his wife. Like the archetypal dragon lady, she was an arrogant and boastful woman — an attitude that got her in hot water when she dared to compare her beauty to that of the goddess queen Hera. The divine matriarch, who plays a role analogous to that of the wicked stepmother in the tale of

Snow White, is mightily offended by Side's hubris and punishes her severely by driving her to commit suicide on her mother's grave. Her blood seeps into the ground, causing it to bring forth the pomegranate.[23]

Literally, the "apple of many seeds."

Again, the parallel to Snow White (whom we shall meet again shortly) is apparent, as she supposedly entered a coma after eating a poisoned apple. This motif was almost certainly drawn from the Eden account, wherein the forbidden fruit has long been associated with an apple. And there are other parallels with the *Genesis* narrative worth noting, too. Side, like the primordial humans of Eden, is punished for presuming to think she could be like one of the gods. Moreover, the blood that seeps into the earth in her tale recalls the blood of Abel, the slain son of Eve, that is said to have cried out from the earth after his murder.

But perhaps the most interesting aspect of the Orion story is the name of its heroine.

Side.

It seems almost comical at first, until one remembers a key passage in the *Genesis* text that describes the origin of Eve. She was taken, the passage states, out of Adam's rib or *side*. Either translation here is possible. The word appears to be related to quite a number of similar-sounding terms in various languages, many of which serve to illuminate its significance. It seems to have been, above all else, cognate of magical power wielded by a master wizard. In India, for example, master yogis were said to possess a gift known as *siddhu*, which enabled them (among other things) to walk on water.[24]

The most celebrated wizards of Ireland were known as the Aes Sidhe, a title that appears to stem from the same root, with the word *sidhe* (pronounced shee) referring to a round barrow fortress.[25] Here is the archetypal mountain that rose out of the primordial sea, the burial mound that became the model for ziggurat and pyramid.

The feast of the Jewish Passover, known as the Seder, may stem from the same root. Red wine occupies a prominent place in this feast, symbolizing the blood of the lamb that was spread on the doorposts of Hebrew dwellings in Egypt — a sign to protect them from a terrible plague sent to kill every firstborn creature, man or animal, in the land. The wine, and the blood which it represented, were known to contain a very potent sort of magic, capable of forestalling the angel of death as it "passed over" the Egyptian countryside. This was because, as the Hebrew scriptures revealed, the life of a creature was in its blood.[26] And life was the only antidote for death.

The intoxication brought on by wine and other fermented beverages must have seemed to the ancients as a heightened form of life, a gateway to the land of the gods. The Babylonian goddess of wine and eternal life appeared in the tale of Gilgamesh and warned him that the jealous gods would never allow mere mortals to taste her wine, for they did not want men to share in their immortality.[27] This goddess' name, Siduri Sabitu, would seem to connect her with Orion's consort Side. And the nature of her warning correlates well to the prohibition decreed by equally jealous gods of Eden, the Elohim, who would not allow man to eat from the tree of life for fear that he might become immortal.

Quite naturally, this wine came to be associated with the apple tree and thus came in some traditions to be identified with an apple-based fermented drink.

Cider.

Again, the common etymology is apparent. When the storytellers said that Eve had been taken out of Adam's side, they were invoking a sly play on words. The "side" referred to much more than an anatomical position — indeed, it connoted Adam's *siddhu* or magical power. This was what was taken out of him to form the woman. He lost, indeed, much more than a rib. The legend in fact speaks to the loss of man's ability to invoke the ultimate form of magic by creating new life — this *siddhu* was now transferred to the woman, who alone was empowered to bring forth new life from the womb. This was the real reason the first man needed a "helper." The power to engender new creation was locked inside him in his rib (a metaphor for his penis) and had to be released in order to bear fruit.

In light of this, it is illuminating to read that Jesus was pierced in the side as he hung on the cross. Like Adam, his magical power was being taken from him. And the author of one text, *The Gospel of Peter*, may have recognized that fact all too well. Its author provides a unique account of Jesus' dying words, quoting him as acknowledging the lifeblood pouring out of him in quite magical terms: "My power, my power, thou hast forsaken me." [28]

Two Serpents

That power had taken up residence in the dragon lady.
In Tamar.
In Eve.
In Rahab, whose loud and defiant nature conjures up images of the fire-breathing dragon and, furthermore, recalls the proud roaring of the fearsome beast Hawawa in the Gilgamesh legend.

It is no accident that the theme of that ancient tale appears to center on the pride of the dragon. As the plot unfolds, the hero is confronted by this impressive creature and warned that he is no match for its great strength. He is, nonetheless, determined to challenge it and eventually succeeds against all odds in vanquishing it, yoking it with a nose ring and binding it fast with thick cords. Where once Hawawa "raised himself up on clawed feet" and "threw himself this way and that," the beast is now reduced to groveling in the dirt for mercy at the hero's feet. [29]

Having conquered his enemy, Gilgamesh takes pity on the creature and is about to release it, but Enkidu suspects that the serpent is not entirely sincere in its humility and therefore counsels against such action. The serpent, he knows, is a deceiver. If Gilgamesh releases Hawawa, Enkidu warns in blunt language, the hero will not live to see his home again. This advice is sufficient to get a rise out of the captive dragon, who — just as Enkidu suspected

— has been humbled but not completely cowed. Infuriated that Enkidu is trying to undermine its imminent release, Hawawa is unable to contain its fury. "Hired man, hungry, thirsty and obsequious!" the dragon spits at Enkidu "Why did you speak ill of me to him?" [30]

Enkidu, known for his propensity to rash and violent acts, is not about to take this sort of verbal abuse from the creature, so he draws his blade and cuts off the monster's head.

The parallels with the Eden tale are numerous.

The serpent in the Hebrew myth is reduced to crawling on his belly in the dust, much in the manner of the groveling Hawawa. Moreover, it is consigned to a future of enmity with Adam's descendants, who are destined to strike or crush its head — just as Enkidu slices off the head of the unfortunate dragon. Even Hawawa's rebuke of Enkidu sounds familiar, describing the stalwart companion of Gilgamesh as a hired hand destined for a life of hunger, thirst and pitiful enslavement. A better description of Adam's state could not have been found.

Consider the following descriptions:

- Adam is a hired hand or slave: "God took the man and put him in the Garden of Eden to work it and take care of it." [31]
- Adam is destined for hunger and thirst: "Cursed is the ground because of you. Through painful toil you will eat of it all the days of your life." [32]

In Eden, as in the tale of Hawawa, the serpent is subdued. Yet it is not entirely clear *which* serpent has been conquered.

Is it the wizard priest?

Or is it his consort priestess?

The tanist ritual obviously revolved around a fight to the death between the dragon wizard and his would-be successor, so the answer would appear obvious on the face of it. But there is more to the ritual than meets the eye, for Rahab and Hawawa are both names applied to feminine characters — the dragon ladies Rahab and Eve (*hawwa*). From this evidence, it would appear that the serpent under attack isn't the Seth wizard at all but his consort. This is, to say the least, a rather surprising turn of events — one that requires some added investigation.

A good first step in such an inquiry would involve another look at the tale of Gilgamesh and Hawawa. Here, too, the narrator appears to hint that the serpent in question — which, after all, gave its name to Eve — may have been a female. At one point in the tale, Gilgamesh is described as slapping the cheek of Hawawa "as if he were pressing a kiss on him." [33] It is almost as though the hero is engaged in forcing himself on the creature sexually, rather than engaging it in battle. Once the beast is subdued, Gilgamesh's faithful companion Enkidu proceeds to cut off its head.

As it turns out, this particular act is a crucial point in the narrative. In addition to providing an clear parallel to the Eden myth, in which the serpent's head is fated to be "crushed" or "struck," it also recalls another myth involving another dragon lady — perhaps the most famous serpent woman in ancient lore. Her name was Medusa, and she was one of three sisters (it is worth noting the parallel to Morgan, who was likewise one in a trio of three sister goddesses) born to a pair of ocean divinities. And, not surprisingly, her story bears several obvious hallmarks of both the ark and tanist rituals.

The tale begins with the imprisonment of yet another feminine figure whose name links her to such figures as Diana and Dinah. This is the beautiful Danae, a woman who is visited by the god Zeus and conceives a son by him. By now, this story should be extremely familiar. It is, of course, just one more instance of a god taking on the aspect of mortal man, in effect hiding his true identity so that he might lie with the sacred priestess and conceive a child. This was an actual ceremony enacted time and again, based on the model of the "hidden one" Amen in the temple at Luxor. And such a ceremony was natural this context, for the Greeks regarded Amen as the

Egyptian manifestation of Zeus.

As the story continues, the fruit of this sacred tryst becomes manifest, and the great hero Perseus is born. As it turns out, however, not everyone believes him to be the product of a sacred union. Indeed, Danae's father brands him a bastard based on his suspicion that Danae has managed to find a way to rendezvous with a former suitor for whom he has little regard. In a rage, the father therefore encases mother and child in a wooden ark, which he casts into the sea. But they manage to survive a perilous crossing and wash ashore on a small island called Seriphos, where they are pulled in by a fishermen named Dictys.

The ark and the island are two obvious recurring themes. And the fisherman, whose name means "net," is yet another manifestation of the Fisher King.

Even the name of the island itself is illuminating, as it appears to be based on the same root used to form the Hebrew word *seraph*. This was used to describe a fabled creature with six wings and more than one face that "flew with a live coal in its hand." [34] Could this coal have been the meteoric benben stone?

And could the *seraph* have been the phoenix?

The answer becomes apparent when one considers that the word seraph means, literally, "fiery serpent." And the phoenix was just such a winged firebird or flying cobra. Perseus, as the son of the god-king Zeus, was its human manifestation — as the hero destined to be king, he was (in Egyptian terms) the new Horus. Even his very name may connote this role, for it appears closely related to the Egyptian *per Isis*, meaning "brought forth by Isis." And his birth would have therefore been attended by the sign of the phoenix. This was the significance of his arrival on Seriphos, otherwise known as the island of the serpent.

After landing on the island, Perseus grows up to become his mother's defender, assuming the role of the tanist wizard by warding off a long line of suitors who seek her hand in marriage. Among these is a persistent king who, repeatedly confounded in his attempts to force marriage upon her, devises a ruse to trick Perseus into releasing her. The king tells Perseus that he has lost hope of marrying Danae and plans instead to wed another woman, news that cheers Perseus to such an extent that he agrees to help the king achieve his goal. On an impulse, he even proclaims that he will win for the king whatever object he seeks to achieve his goal.

Such impulsiveness never seems to turn out well.

A similar proclamation would come back to haunt the tetrarch Herod Antipas, who would offer half his kingdom to a dancing girl — only to commit himself unwittingly to provide the head of John the Baptist.

Interestingly, Perseus' boasting binds him to perform a similar grisly task: He is charged to go forth and find the hideously ugly Medusa, who has snakes for hair, and cut off her head. It is considered an impossible feat, because the creature's appearance is so revolting that any man who looks upon her becomes petrified with fear. Even the greatest hero's courage will fail him when confronted by the sight of her, and he will become a coward. It is fascinating to find that this is the exact same reaction the normally fearless Enkidu has to the dragon Hawawa. In counseling Gilgamesh to refrain from attacking the creature, he warns him: "My master, you who have not seen that 'fellow' are not terror-stricken. I who have seen that 'fellow' am terror stricken." [35]

Despite his fear, Enkidu eventually cuts off Hawawa's head, imposing upon the poor creature the very same fate Perseus has been asked to inflict upon Medusa. (He eventually succeeds in his task with the help of a mirror). So it would appear that, despite the Sumerian narrator's references to Hawawa as a "fellow," the beast in the original myth was actually a female. Just as Eve, or *hawwa*, was a female; just as Rahab the sea monster was also the very feminine harlot. It would therefore appear that the tanist ritual involved not only slaying the serpent king and supplanting him as guardian of the sacred tree, but also cutting off the head of the serpent queen.

But this doesn't make any sense. The young prince who slays the old king or wizard does so, according to the tanist custom, in order to claim the priestess as his bride. If, in the process, he manages to cut off her head, this would only seem to defeat the purpose — unless, of course, this rather gruesome act is somehow symbolic. What if this apparent decapitation did not result in death at all, but served another purpose altogether?

Given the circumstances, one might expect it to somehow prepare the dragon lady for her impending sexual union with the prince.

But how?

The answer may be found in another name for Rahab, the great sea serpent who has proved to be so pivotal to this inquiry.

That name is Leviathan.

That these two creatures are closely related is made plain enough by the few, yet similar, references each receives in the Hebrew texts. The psalmist declares that Yahweh has stilled the waves of the sea by conquering the monster Rahab. In the same way, the prophet Isaiah proclaims:

> *Yahweh will punish with his sword*
> *His fierce and powerful sword*
> *Leviathan the gliding serpent*
> *Leviathan, the coiling serpent*
> *He will slay the monster of the sea* [36]

A psalmist relates that Yahweh "crushed the heads of Leviathan and gave him as food to the creatures of the desert." [37] The plural reference to heads is intriguing, for it indicates that Leviathan has more than one of them, putting it in the same category as the *seraphs* and Medusa with her myriad snake heads. But it is Leviathan's name itself that is of the greatest interest. It is actually a translation of the word *lwtyn*, with the "v" sound being substituted for the more accurate "w" in the same manner that Yahweh is often construed as Jehovah.[38] In addition, the "t" is exchanged for a "th" sound, as it often was in the ancient Near East.

The more natural reading of the name would produce something like *lowtin* or *lowtan*. So it is with some interest that one finds a myth in which Baal, the Phoenician storm god considered the rough equivalent of Yahweh, actually slays a sea dragon by the name of Lotan.

The name Lotan actually appears in the Hebrew texts in a passing reference as the name of an individual.[39] It means "covering," a definition that opens the door a crack for what is to follow with the variant name Leviathan. This has a more specific meaning, referring to a wreathed animal, specifically a serpent. Now we are getting somewhere. But what does the reference to a wreath indicate? A wreath is generally something round that encircles one's head — such as perhaps the skin flaps on either side of the cobra's fanged maw.

Before going further, it is worth noting that the name appears to have a close relationship to the name Levi, the name of Israel's priestly tribe and its patriarch. This name has a meaning of its own: "attached." Additionally, it recalls the name Lot, worn by the brother of Abraham and meaning "veil" or "covering" — the same definition applied to the name Lotan.

All these names and definitions together form a revealing picture: a veiled covering that encircles the head of a serpent. The imagery is unmistakably that of the foreskin, which likewise covers and encircles the head of the penis before it is removed during the ritual of circumcision. When the male is circumcised, this covering is cut away from the head of the penis. In symbolic terms, the head of the fearsome serpent has been cut off.

This explains everything quite nicely — except for the fact that the serpents Rahab, Hawawa and Medusa appear to have been *female* and therefore would not have had a penis. But that did not prevent them from being circumcised.

Indeed, female circumcision is still practiced to this day in several countries, including Egypt. Only a few years ago, that nation's courts and legislature took part in a heated debate over the merits (or lack thereof) pertaining to this ancient and horrific custom. The operation itself is similar to male circumcision in that the covering or *lotan* of the clitoris is cut away. The clitoris is the most sensitive region of the female genitalia, analogous to the head of the penis in a man. The idea of female circumcision probably was to dull the sensitivity of this region, rendering a woman less likely to become sexually aroused and therefore engage in promiscuous activity. This would have been especially important for temple priestesses, who were expected to be virgins and give themselves to an "incarnate" god such as Zeus or Amen. At the temple of Inanna, for example, women were required to give themselves as prostitutes to the first man who propositioned them. Thereafter, however, they were forbidden from lying with another man no matter how much money he might offer.

The circumcision of the clitoris would have, in the ancient mind, helped guarantee that such a vow was kept. Just as the circumcision of Shechem immediately preceded his imminent marriage to Dinah, so the circumcision of the woman would have been undertaken in conjunction with her marriage.

The resulting blood, in addition to the blood generated by her ruptured hymen during intercourse, would mingle with the man's blood produced by his circumcision and ensure the continuance of the bloodline.

The head of the serpent cut off by such heroes as Perseus and Enkidu wasn't the creature's literal head. It was the head of the priestess' clitoris.

This is why Enkidu cautioned Gilgamesh against releasing Hawawa after vanquishing the creature with a slap and a kiss. The fact of the matter is that Gilgamesh was claiming Hawawa (or Eve) as his wife, enabling him to perpetuate his lineage in the Land of Life. But this was not enough to complete the binding. Enkidu believed, as did the ancients, that unless a woman underwent this operation, she was likely to become sexually aroused and deceive her husband, lying with other men. He therefore took his blade and cut off her "head" — actually the head or covering of her clitoris — to prevent this from occurring.

Gilgamesh's forceful conquest of Hawawa recalls the so-called rape of Dinah, who likewise appears to have been taken in a somewhat forceful manner. In the story of Shechem, the young prince seizes her to be his bride and afterward behaves tenderly to her; Gilgamesh acts in precisely this manner toward Hawawa, seizing her forcefully to kiss her, then acting with compassion and intending to release her before Enkidu cuts off her "head."

This was a painful exercise, and one can imagine that a woman chosen to undergo such an ordeal would have naturally resisted.

Even if she truly loved the man.

Here, perhaps, is the true nature of the so-called rape. It is not necessarily out of enmity toward her sexual partner that the woman resists, but for fear of the painful reality of female circumcision that she is forced to endure. When she is at last subdued and faces the prospect of losing her clitoral head, Hawawa vents her wrath not against her intended husband, Gilgamesh, but against Enkidu. Why? Because it is Enkidu who has been assigned the task of performing the operation. He is acting in the capacity of the priest in the narrative, serving as a Levite — a devotee of Leviathan, whence this title doubtless originally stems. Though Gilgamesh himself, who plainly cares for her, has second thoughts about putting her through the agony of this operation, his objections carry no weight with the pious priestly figure. Before the hero can change his mind, Enkidu has brought forth his blade and performed the deed.

The fact that circumcision was originally required for both men and women who intended to enter the marriage bed sheds some light on two facets of the many related stories concerning this ancient custom. For one thing, it further explains the confusion or ambiguity surrounding serpent figures. Sometimes they appear to be male; at other times, female. Even the same character in a given narrative will be referred to at one time in the masculine sense, only to be recast in a feminine role later on. This applies to both Rahab and Hawawa, and it is probably because circumcision was required of both serpent partners in advance of their joining.

This realization also explains the indignation of Jacob's brothers at the treatment of Dinah, who apparently was subjected to this operation even though Shechem himself had not been circumcised. This was an outrage in their eyes, and they defended their slaughter of Shechem and his countrymen with the simple question: "Should he have treated our sister like a prostitute?" [40]

Apparently, she was not the only one to receive such treatment.

It is here that the second woman named Tamar enters the picture. Her story is even more tragic than that of Dinah, who at least seemed to have been genuinely loved by Shechem. The same could not be said for this Tamar, whose suitor likewise forced her to his bed — but unlike Shechem, later spurned her as repulsive in his sight.

The suitor in question was a prince, like Shechem, but with an even more noble pedigree. He was a son of no less a man than King David himself, and Tamar was his sister. His name, Amnon, marked him as a manifestation of the hidden god Amen seeking the bed of his sister-wife and divine priestess. This he did by feigning sickness and withdrawing to his chamber, then entreating David to send Tamar in to him, that she might nourish him with some homemade cakes.

Once he got her alone, however, his true intentions became clear. Turning aside the cakes, he instead laid hold of his sister and, despite her protestations, forced her into his bed. His motivation was anything but love, for he brusquely dismissed her upon completing the vile act and "hated her with an intense hatred." [41] Doubtless his real reason for raping his sister was to ensure that the royal bloodline passed through him and not his brother, Absalom. His efforts turned out to be in vain, however, for Absalom later had the last laugh by arranging for his murder.

The bloodline would not pass through this Tamar, after all, but her story would endure as yet another example of the ritual joining of the young prince with the dragon lady — a term I use here in recognition of this archetypal figure's power. It is a story that had already been told for generations by the time Antiochus took the throne of Seleucia and the righteous priest Onias was slain during his attempts to denounce the usurper Menelaus.

In light of the flood myths, it is extremely fitting that the high priest in the temple of Yahweh at Jerusalem should have been named Onias after the fish-man Oannes who served as the flood hero's protector. And it is equally appropriate that the brother who replaced this man in the priestly office should have born the name of the *Argo*'s captain, Jason. Each name signified a guardian of the ark, and this had been the high priest's role from the beginning. The temple itself had been built to house the sacred Ark of the Covenant, and the high priest was the only one deemed worthy to enter the holy inner chamber designed to contain it. He tended it, preserved it, watched over it as the chosen agent of the temple's patron deity.

In Onias' day, the ark had long since disappeared and the sanctuary stood empty. Yet it remained the place where the divine presence dwelt, the inviolable "belly of the ship" where no wave of turmoil could intrude and no storm of intrigue could encroach. It was, in the truest sense of the word, a sanctuary. And so it had been for as long as anyone could remember.

Until, that is, Antiochus decided to change all that.

II

Abomination

The humiliating defeat by the Romans at the Battle of Magnesia was still being felt two decades later. Despite the hefty indemnity imposed on the Seleucids, Antiochus had managed to rebuild his army into a formidable military machine. There was only one problem: He couldn't use it — at least not in the manner he would have preferred. The treaty with Apamea expressly forbade him from attacking any state allied with Rome, and that seemed to rule out an assault on the territory he coveted most.

Ptolemaic Egypt.

But certain extenuating circumstances convinced the Seleucid emperor that the time was right for just such an assault. For one thing, he had received intelligence that the Egyptians were planning a strike of their own against *his* territory in the hope of bringing a portion of Palestine under their control. Antiochus could hardly be faulted under the treaty for protecting his own interests in the face of imminent attack. Moreover, Rome was otherwise engaged in yet another war with Macedonia, and Antiochus reasoned that he might be able to take advantage of this rather convenient distraction. He therefore launched an attack against the Ptolemaic armies, meeting them as they came up out of Egypt on their campaign. He engaged them in the western Sinai and so thoroughly routed them that the way was suddenly clear for his armies to march forward into Egypt itself. Not about to let such an opportunity pass him by, Antiochus led his forces all the way to Memphis, where he imposed conditions on the young boy king (who also happened to be his own nephew) that effectively made Egypt a vassal state to the Seleucid Empire.

This situation hardly went over well with the Egyptians, especially residents of Alexandria who resented the young king's quick capitulation to the invading armies. Accordingly, they renounced any allegiance to the boy, elevating his younger brother to the throne in his stead. Antiochus responded by mustering his troops for a strike against the city, but found to his surprise that the Egyptians were ready for him. The defenders succeeded in holding the city against the Seleucid armies, forcing them to withdraw for the time being and regroup.

Antiochus' plan was to invade Egypt again when the time was right. But the unexpected setback at Alexandria left him in something of a predicament.

When he had marched out to meet the Egyptians the first time, Antiochus had been defending his borders against a foreign aggressor as permitted under the terms of Apamea. But things would change if he launched any new assault on Egypt. Then there would be no doubt that *he* was the aggressor — and the Romans were bound to take notice an act such as this, which would fly in the face of the treaty. Antiochus, however, was counting on the Romans' continued preoccupation with their war against Macedonia and hoped that he could dispense with any Egyptian resistance before that issue was decided. With any luck, the Macedonians would inflict enough damage to make the Romans think twice about marching back into battle so soon.

But luck, so firmly in Antiochus' corner the year before, seemed to have deserted him in this instance. For one thing, the young princes who had divided the country between them were now reconciled, having agreed to rule jointly under an arrangement that weakened Antiochus' position considerably. The Seleucid monarch could no longer play one faction against the other, feigning support of the "rightful" sovereign against a usurper for the good of Egypt.

Henceforth, Egypt would decide what was in its own best interests — it would not be bullied about by Antiochus.

This situation, understandably, did not sit well with the Seleucid emperor, who marched his armies back to Memphis and prepared to besiege Alexandria with renewed vigor, confident that he would succeed in taking the city where he had failed the year before. And he might very well have done so, except for one rather significant complication. Just before he set out on his campaign, the Romans concluded their war with Macedonia with another decisive victory, putting them in a position to set their sights on previously neglected matters — matters that now required their attention. Having taken note of Antiochus' aggressions in Egypt, they immediately dispatched an envoy to deliver a warning to the Seleucid emperor.

The man chosen for the mission happened to be an old friend of Antiochus' from his days as a "house guest" in Rome. So when the two men renewed their acquaintance in Alexandria, the emperor naturally extended his hand in a gesture for friendly greeting.

His old friend did not accept it.

Instead he handed Antiochus a scroll bearing the seal of the Roman senate, the contents of which must have driven the smile from the emperor's face and the color from his cheeks. It was an official decree demanding that he withdraw his troops from Egypt at once, adding by way of a not-so-veiled threat that the war with Macedonia had ended and the Romans were now in a position to enforce the treaty of Apamea. To the letter.

Antiochus squirmed. One can picture him clearing his throat, glancing about nervously as he tried to stall for time. Nonplussed by this turn of events, he told his old friend that he would need time to consider the document and seek the counsel of his advisors. One can picture the envoy slowly shaking his head as he took a stick or baton and pressed it against the earth, then began walking, drawing a proverbial "line in the sand" as he encircled the bewildered emperor. It was a dare. A threat. A promise. Before he stepped across, Rome would have an answer — and it had better be the right one.

With nowhere to turn and no prospect for delay, Antiochus knew he had no choice but to relent.

Reluctantly, he agreed to withdraw his forces.

Only then did his old acquaintance accept his hand in friendship.

Desolation

As one might imagine, Antiochus was in no mood for any further bad news after this humiliating incident. Yet bad news is exactly what he received as he pulled his troops out of Egypt. Pious Jews had been enraged at his decision to plunder the temple in preparation for his campaign, and there was at least one man ready to exploit this seething anger.

That man was Jason.

After being ousted from the high priesthood by Menelaus, the former high priest had gone into exile beyond the Jordan River. Unlike his brother Onias, he had not raised an objection to Menelaus' unscrupulous actions — and therefore, also unlike Onias, he had managed to stay alive. But Jason still had ambitions of recapturing his former position, and with his brother dead he was left as the eldest surviving member of the favored Zadokite clan.

Pious Jews might have objected to Jason's use of bribery to seize the high priesthood from his brother, and they might have chafed at his promotion of Greek culture. When set against the despicable Menelaus, however, he was still a less onerous of two evils. And moreover, he was of the proper bloodline. He therefore had little trouble recruiting a thousand followers to join him in an assault on Jerusalem that succeeded in retaking the temple mount and forcing Menelaus to take refuge in the citadel.

The operation came off with barely a hitch, as Antiochus was still occupied in Egypt at the time and had left a minimal contingent behind to safeguard the city. A rumor had even circulated that he was dead, giving Jason the excuse he needed to organize his expedition against Jerusalem. But when the rumor turned out to be false, what had appeared to be a promising venture turned all at once into a catastrophe. Before he could consolidate control over the city, Jason's revolt collapsed as he started killing his own countrymen. He eventually fled back across the Jordan and ultimately perished as an exile in the Greek city of Sparta.

The failure of the uprising, however, did not stop Antiochus from responding. Already irate over Rome's intervention in his Egyptian campaign, he turned his fury against Jerusalem in an act of brute savagery. What followed was a three-day onslaught one writer described as "a massacre of young and old, a killing of women and children, a slaughter of virgins and infants." In the end, forty thousand people were dead and the same number had been sold into slavery.[42]

Such genocidal behavior, however, was not enough to sooth Antiochus' rage. His mood was made all the worse by the fact that he had spent a rather large sum of money financing the Egyptian campaign — a campaign for which he now had nothing to show. Consequently, he was forced to seek new sources of revenue if he hoped to rebuild his treasury. And as it happened, the most convenient source available to him was not new at all — it was one that had been utilized by his predecessor under similar circumstances a few years earlier.

The Jerusalem temple.

The puppet high priest Menelaus, restored to his position after Jason's departure, was only too happy to smooth the way for Antiochus, accompanying him personally into the sanctuary and helping his men empty the temple treasury of its fine ornaments and holy devices.[43] Not only did the emperor rob the temple, he provoked the situation further by personally defiling it — his very presence violating the holy prohibition on laymen entering the inner courts. Orthodox Jews considered this the most brazen affront to their piety, yet they had little choice but to sit by allow the emperor to commit his sacrilege. They may have gritted their teeth, clenched their fists and uttered the foulest of curses under their breath, but it was all to no avail. There would be no horseman to ride forth out of nowhere and preserve the temple's riches. Not this time. Onias, the righteous high priest who had summoned him forth, was dead, his position usurped unjustly by the apostate Menelaus.

But the worst was yet to come.

No doubt blaming the pious Jews for Jason's rebellion, Antiochus determined to cut off any further resistance to his rule at the root. The Persians had manipulated the idea of monotheism to serve their purpose in isolating the Jews, but in doing so they had created a monster of fierce nationalist fervor. And Antiochus was determined to slay that monster. Jewish nationalism might have served the Persian emperors very well, but it was at odds with Antiochus' vision of an empire based on Greek culture and Greek ideals. He had pursued this vision with some degree of subtlety early in his tenure, rewarding Hellenists such as Jason and Menelaus with positions of influence in exchange for their help in promoting Greek culture (and in exchange for their bribes, of course). But such subtlety had failed to have the desired effect, and the attempted rebellion by one of his former cronies — Jason — must have convinced Antiochus that the time had come for harsher measures.

He therefore instituted a strict policy outlawing the monotheistic cult of Yahweh, prohibiting the sacred rites associated with it and ordering them replaced with so-called pagan rituals. Henceforth, parents would be forbidden from circumcising their sons on penalty of death. One writer recalled the brutal and humiliating punishment meted out to a pair of women who defied this decree: They were paraded through the streets with their babies at their breasts, then summarily hurled to their deaths from the city walls.[44]

And this was not all.

Traditional feast days could no longer be celebrated, having been replaced with festivals honoring the Greek wine god Dionysus and the king's birthday. And worst of all, the temple and its sacrifices were defiled in the most demeaning ways. Pious Jews were forced to sacrifice unclean swine on pagan altars, and the temple itself was converted into a sanctuary of Olympian Zeus. This became known as the so-called "abomination of desolation," an altar (some say a statue of the god) placed atop the traditional altar to Yahweh.

In itself, none of this might have seemed like such a grave offense in the eyes of Antiochus, a cosmopolitan Greek who understood well enough that one god went by many names. The storm god might have been named Zeus by the Greeks, but was he not also Baal to the Syrians?

Enki to the Mesopotamians?

Seth to the Egyptians?

Yahweh to the Jews?

Antiochus may or may not have realized that the flood hero who passed through Enki's deluge in his ark had served as a model for the story of Noah as it appeared in the Hebrew scriptures. The names of the hero and his patron god might have changed, but the story itself was nearly identical.

Antiochus knew this principle well enough. It didn't much matter what you might call the god in question, he reasoned; what mattered was that they were all names for the same divine protector. A rose by any other name. ...

But pious Jews, so thoroughly indoctrinated into the cult of monotheism under the Persians, no longer saw things this way. To them, Antiochus' attempts at cultural synthesis constituted nothing less than a genocidal attempt to eradicate their heritage. And there is little doubt that they were right: The emperor hoped to accomplish exactly this. Antiochus, like so many before and since, considered cultural distinctions a threat to his personal power. So long as the Jews retained their own unique culture, there remained a profound threat to that power, one that might someday express itself as a unifying element in political revolution. This was Antiochus' fear. And to his way of thinking, it had very nearly come to fruition in the form of Jason's aborted rebellion. In light of this event, he could no longer afford to be complacent, content to engage in subtle attempts at persuasion.

Force must be met with force.

And so it was.

Yet Antiochus had not counted on the prospect that superior force might not necessarily produce capitulation — especially where religious fervor was involved. Instead of cowing the Jews into submission, his brutal campaign of repression only succeeded in creating a backlash that spawned one of the most celebrated guerrilla wars in recorded history.

The Maccabees

It is an uprising still recalled today at the feast of Hanukkah, which marks the rededication of the temple after its desecration by Antiochus. This was accomplished only after more than three years of sporadic and intense fighting that succeeded in wearing down Antiochus' forces. The leader of this guerrilla war was a man named Judas, a member of the Hasmonean clan whose nickname Maccabeus meant "the hammer." His father Mattathias had begun the rebellion by refusing to offer a sacrifice on one of Antiochus' pagan altars — and then killing the first man who stepped forward to do so. He and his sons had then fled into the hills, whence they conducted a hit-and-run campaign of ambushes and strategic attacks on Antiochus' forces.

The rebellion began with Mattathias' famous rallying cry to revolution: "Let everyone who is zealous after the law and who stands by the covenant follow me!" [45] It was a call that appealed to the piety of Jews chafing under the restrictions imposed by a pagan emperor. Yet while piety may have fueled this newborn revolution, there can be no doubt that the movement was founded as much on political ambition as it was on religious devotion. This became clear soon enough when the practicality of waging war ran headlong into the sacred law of Moses.

A group of a thousand rebels who heeded the call to revolution followed Judas' father out into the desert, where they found refuge in the myriad caves that dotted the desolate hillsides. But only temporarily. It was not long before they were confronted by a contingent of Antiochus' men sent out to crush the rebellion in its infancy. Still hoping to defuse the situation, the general in command of these forces issued an offer of limited amnesty to the rebels: "Come out and obey the king's command, and your lives will be spared." [46]

It was no use.

The rebels remained holed up in their caves and refused to come out. A major battle might very well have ensued, but the Seleucid troops had a secret weapon on their side. It was a Sabbath, and Jewish law expressly prohibited any exertion on a Sabbath. In the minds of the pious rebels, this included fighting in defense of one's lives. So what might have been a fiercely fought battle instead became a wholesale massacre, with the Seleucid troops slaughtering a thousand men, women and children who stood their ground but refused to so much as pick up a stone to defend themselves.

The grisly episode made it clear enough to Mattathias that political expediency outweighed the need to adhere to Mosaic law: "If we all do as our kinsmen have done and do not fight against the Gentiles for our lives and our traditions, they will soon destroy us from the earth," he lamented.[47] Ironically, the reality of war had forced him to abandon one of the very traditions he was taking up arms to protect. Political freedom had its price, and it could be steep.

No one understood this better than a man named Onias.

He was the namesake and son of the former high priest, who grew older as the revolution progressed — old enough to expect that, if it were to succeed, his clan would be restored to the high priesthood it had held for so long. These expectations, however, were not to be realized, and Onias had the political pragmatism (not to mention the ambition) of the Hasmoneans to thank for it.

Eventually, Judas and his brothers managed to capture the temple and remove the "abomination of desolation" from the altar in a triumph celebrated to this day at the Jewish feast of Hanukkah. It is characterized by some as the culmination of a great war of independence. But independence had yet to be won. The Seleucids still claimed sovereignty over Palestine, and despite his successes on the battlefield, Judas was not in a position to argue the point. Success in a series of guerrilla skirmishes was one thing; decisive victory in a war was quite another.

Still, Judas continued to look for an opportunity to step things up a notch.

That opportunity presented itself unexpectedly in the form of news that Antiochus had died suddenly while campaigning in the east. This turn of events left the empire in a state of disarray, with two rival factions emerging in a struggle to succeed the emperor. Before his death, Antiochus had named his 9-year-old son as heir apparent and had designated a court official named Philip to act as regent. But this did not sit well with a general named Lysias, who had been placed in command of the imperial forces in the west. And, as generals were prone to do, Lysias determined to defy Antiochus' dying wishes and seize power for himself.

This Lysias was no stranger to Judas, who had engaged his forces twice in the past few years. On both occasions, Judas had emerged victorious. And now, Lysias appeared to be quitting the field altogether by marching his forces north to Antioch for the purpose of claiming power there. This appeared to leave the way clear for Judas to consolidate power in southern Palestine, perhaps even founding an independent breakaway state under his own leadership.

Upon Lysias' departure, Judas immediately laid siege to the fortress adjacent to the temple in Jerusalem where the few remaining Seleucid troops were garrisoned. He had not bargained for a quick response from Lysias, assuming he would be preoccupied with securing his place as regent. But this is exactly what he got. Lysias' rival Philip had not yet returned from the east, and the western general was therefore able to consolidate power in Antioch much more quickly than Judas had expected. As a result, he was free to lead his armies south again when he received word of Judas' siege from the deceitful high priest Menelaus.

This time, Judas' forces were defeated and he found himself in a weaker position than before. But Philip's arrival in Antioch again distracted Lysias, who recognized the prudence of concluding a quick armistice with Judas so he could turn his attention once more to the capital. Each side found itself in a poor position to bargain: Lysias was in a hurry to withdraw his forces and march them north to Antioch, while Judas had just suffered a severe setback on the battlefield and was in no position to dictate terms. The result was a compromise. Lysias agreed to ratify the Jews' right to worship in the temple as they saw fit and to remove the widely despised pretender Menelaus from the high priesthood. He even agreed to accept a descendant of Aaron as high priest, but he would not go so far as to support a member of the house of Onias. Instead, he appointed a man named Alcimus, and Judas accepted him as a compromise candidate — effectively denying the younger Onias the position to which he had been born. Once again, pragmatism had won out over idealism in the minds of Judas and his brothers. It is entirely possible that they coveted the high priesthood for themselves, and in fact they would eventually claim the position by taking advantage of further intrigues involving the Seleucid throne.

The young Onias must have recognized that he was not about to be restored to the position he felt was his birthright, for he soon quit the country altogether and withdrew to a location from which he could plot his eventual return at a time when circumstances were more propitious.

That location was Egypt.

Politically, it was the obvious choice. The Ptolemaic rulers of Egypt had long been rivals of the Seleucids and were still smarting from Antiochus' attempt to divide the country and bring it under his control. They might easily be persuaded to sponsor an alternative high priest (one who actually held a strong claim to legitimacy) in preparation for the day when they might strike back and bring Palestine under their sway. In the meantime, Onias persuaded the sixth Ptolemy, who went by the throne name Philometer, to grant him the right to build an alternative temple to Yahweh in Egypt. The site chosen for this grand endeavor was Leontopolis, the "city of the lions" that stood within the nome or precinct of a much more ancient and famous city. Heliopolis.

Such a choice could hardly have been accidental. According to the legend preserved by Manetho, Moses himself had been a priest of Heliopolis. This was the city of the sun, where the ancient celestial priesthood studied the stars for signs and portents. One day, these astronomers were sure, they would see a sign indicating the arrival of a new phoenix on the benben stone — a messiah who would deliver Jerusalem from the clutches of the infidels who had seized control of the temple on the pretext of cleansing it from Antiochus' "abomination." Judas and his family talked a good game, but when it came right down to it, they were not defenders of the faith at all. First they had violated the Sabbath to fight off the Seleucids, then they had agreed to a compromise high priest in order to maintain their own position.

So Onias built his temple in Heliopolis and watched the skies with the great astronomers or magi.

But as it turned out, he would have a long wait.

Indeed, the moment for reclaiming the family heritage would not come in Onias' lifetime, nor in that of the next generation. Judas, too, would die in battle. But his brother would succeed him as leader in Jerusalem, and another brother after that. The first brother, Jonathan, used his political acumen to secure the high priesthood for himself, a title that would be worn by his successors for approximately the next century. The Seleucid Empire would finally collapse in the wreckage of its own internecine struggles, and the Ptolemies of Egypt would suffer the same fate.

There was a new power on the horizon, one that had already flexed its muscles in defeating the Seleucid forces in Asia Minor and forcing Antiochus to forsake his campaign against Egypt.

But that had been just the beginning.

The Roman Republic had always been balanced against some other great power — Carthage, Alexandria, Macedonia or Antioch. But as these various rivals failed one by one, the Romans soon found themselves in a unique position on the world stage, the lone superpower between the Atlantic and China. It would be up to them to cow the Hasmoneans, and in so doing to provide Onias' family with the opportunity to reclaim the high priesthood.

To usher in what came to be known as the kingdom of God.

III

Rainmaker

In the century since Onias had fled to Egypt, the political landscape had changed dramatically. The Seleucid Empire was no more. It had crumbled beneath the ever increasing weight of dynastic squabbles, leaving any number of petty kings to fight over its remnants like so many vultures at a rotting corpse. Their objective? To divide the spoils before the great eagle arrived and forced them to scatter — the eagle that was the symbol of Rome.

Those who fight among themselves inevitably leave themselves vulnerable to an assault from without. This had been the fate of the last Seleucid king, whose weakened empire was ripe for the taking when he was slain during a conflict with a certain Aretas, ruler of an Arabian kingdom called Nabataea. In the aftermath of this defeat, the vultures descended to carve up the former Seleucid lands among them: Aretas took the south, including the capital of Damascus, while the armies of Armenia advanced to overrun the north. Palestine had already been independent for some time under the Hasmonean dynasty.

The scions of Judas and his brothers had declared themselves, by this time, not only high priests but also kings. Yet now they, too, had fallen victim to the same sort of internal strife that had been the downfall of their former overlords, the Seleucids. The priest-king Alexander Jannaeus had held the throne for nearly three decades, leaving it upon his death to his wife, who ruled for another nine years afterward.

At her death, all hell broke loose.

Her two sons each staked a claim to the throne, with rival political factions supporting each of the brothers. The younger, Aristobulus, garnered the support of the ascendant party known as the Pharisees, a populist movement led at the time by a rabbi named Simeon ben Shetah. But these were not the only two potential claimants to the high priesthood and the throne that now went with it. About the time of the queen's death, another appeared on the scene with a claim of his own and a following to back it up.

His name?

Onias.

For nearly a century, the Jewish temple at Heliopolis had been operating under the auspices of the true high priestly family — the family cast first aside by Antiochus, then ignored by the Hasmoneans in the aftermath of their restoration. This family may well have attained a degree of prominence in Egypt under the Ptolemies. At some point after the refugee priest Onias fled to Heliopolis, a certain Jewish man by the same name rose to command the entire Egyptian army.[48] Whether this man was the original Onias, one of his descendants or simply someone who shared his name is uncertain. But the temple at Heliopolis was still functioning at that point, and it seems at least plausible that such a noble family would have produced a personage of this rank.

Whatever the identity of this Onias, it is certain that yet another man bearing this name appeared in Palestine around the time of the conflict between the rival Hasmonean brothers. Though nothing is written of him before this time, his reputation appears to have preceded him: Onias (better known by the Hebrew form of his name, Honi) was already well known and highly respected at the time of his arrival on the scene. This would have been only natural if he served as high priest in Heliopolis, a position lofty enough to earn him admiration or notoriety — depending on what one thought of the rival temple.

He seems to have made a grand entrance in Palestine, where his first recorded act was quite a show-stopper. The land was plagued by drought, and the people sent word petitioning to him pray for rain. In response, he boasted: "Go out and bring in the ovens (in which you roast) the paschal lambs, so that they do not disintegrate." [49] Clearly, he meant to put on a demonstration.

As he prayed at first, no rain fell, but this only made him more determined. He drew a circle, stationed himself inside it and declared that he would not move until it started to rain. The significance of this action was not lost on his chroniclers. It was common practice for magicians to draw figures in the sand as they prepared to recite some divine incantation. Yet Honi might well have been sending a political message as well. A century earlier, a Roman delegate had gone to Egypt and drawn a circle in the sand around Antiochus — a circle that signified Rome's power to enforce its will upon the Seleucid emperor. As long as he remained within the circle, Antiochus was protected. But he would place himself in great peril if he stepped outside the circle before agreeing to withdraw his forces.

Now, Honi was drawing a similar circle.

He was, in effect, protecting himself. The question is, from what?

The story continued: Honi again besought Yahweh to send rain upon the earth, and at last a few drops began to fall. His disciples complained that this was not enough to alleviate the drought, at which point he petitioned for a rain of such intensity that it would fill all the cisterns, caves and ditches. Just such a downpour began immediately. It must have seemed to his disciples that a deluge worthy of Noah had begun, for they feared that the world might be destroyed if it continued. Honi therefore prayed yet again, and the rains moderated, though the water they provided rose to such heights that everyone sought refuge on the high ground of the Temple Mount.

Finally, his followers besought Honi to seek an end to the rain. The rabbi did so, only commanding that a bullock be brought forth as an offering of thanks. This was no simple act of humility; on the contrary, it was a demonstration of power. Only a priest could offer a sacrifice, and in laying his hands upon the bull to offer such a sacrifice, he was claiming the authority of the priesthood. Yet he was also claiming something much more: He was claiming to be the new Noah, the man the Samaritans claimed as a model for their messiah. Indeed, a close inspection of the narrative reveals that the story of Honi's appeal to heaven is modeled point by point on the legend of Noah.

➤ Both stories involved a flood of such proportions that, it was feared, it signified the end of the world.
➤ Noah and Honi were both granted protection from the deluge, Noah within his ark and Honi inside his circle.
➤ In each story, the hero and his associates find refuge on a mountain — Noah on the "mountains of Ararat" and Honi on the Temple Mount.
➤ Both stories conclude with the offering of a sacrifice.

The fact that a bull was chosen as the sacrificial animal is significant, for it was the very animal slaughtered by the *kher heb* priest in conjunction with the Egyptian opening of the mouth ceremony. It was then that the dead king's mummy or *djed* column was raised into an upright position, signifying his resurrection and readiness to ascend to heaven as Osiris. This ascent, of course, would be accomplished in the celestial ark casket.

In this light, the true magnitude of Honi's demonstration is revealed. By drawing a circle around himself, he was creating a symbolic arc or *ark* protecting him from the deluge to come. Drawing a protective circle around oneself was common practice for wizards and magicians. Interestingly, at least one Assyrian incantation invoked by a circle-drawing mage called upon the name of Ea — the counterpart to the Sumerian god Enki, who warned the flood hero of the impending deluge.[50] And Ea/Enki was another name for the fish-god Oannes, whose name is related to that of Honi. In following this example of circle drawing, Honi was in effect declaring himself a master of the waters, a king in the mold of the ark priest-kings Noah and Osiris. The circle was the universal symbol of the sun, and Honi was designating himself as the sun king. The new Horus. The rightful heir to the throne of the great king Solomon who himself supposedly built a ship. This identification is confirmed by rabbinical tradition, which declares that the hall of the temple lit up brightly whenever he entered.[51]

It was as though the sun had risen.

Honi's actions in proclaiming himself a messianic figure served as a direct challenge to the claims of the rival Hasmonean brothers, both of whom sought the dual roles of high priest and king for themselves. The magic circle was meant to protect Honi not only from the rains, but also from the political consequences of his action. Such a brazen demonstration was certain to make him a marked man, a threat to Aristobulus and Hyrcanus alike — both of whom had sought Roman support for their respective claims.

The circle had protected Antiochus from the Romans; perhaps it would protect Honi as well.

Or so he may have hoped.

But as events unfolded, no circle in the sand could withstand the storm of conflict that was to come. The fallout from Honi's actions in declaring himself the messiah came quickly. Simeon ben Shetah, the leader of the Jewish council or Sanhedrin, was far from pleased. As a Pharisee, he supported the cause of Aristobulus, who seemed to be gaining the upper hand in his dynastic struggle with Hyrcanus. But now Honi had injected himself into the mix, and his provocative rainmaking was just the sort of distraction that could upset the apple cart. Already Honi was being credited with alleviating the drought, an act that enabled him to draw populist support away from Aristobulus and cast himself as a viable contender for the throne. Simeon had to be careful. He could not simply have Honi arrested, given his popularity and his viable claim to be of high priestly descent. This was likely to cause a riot. So instead he issued a rebuke:

"If you were not Honi, I would pronounce a ban against you," he declared. "For were these years like those concerning which Elijah said no rain should fall — for the keys to rainfall were in his hands — would not the result of your action have been the desecration of God's name? But what can I do with you, since you offend God but he does your will, like a son who sins against the father, who then fulfills his son's desire?" [52]

This is a revealing statement on several levels. For one thing, it reflects Simeon's desire to punish Honi for his impudence, along with his unwillingness to do so for fear of the repercussions. Certainly he would have liked nothing better than to dispense with Honi in some fashion, yet he dared not act against a man widely regarded as the legitimate high priest. Even so, he could not accept the claims Honi was making about himself. One of these claims, though not stated directly, is implicit in Simeon's response to the circle-drawer: Honi was claiming to be endowed with the spirit of the prophet Elijah (or Elias, Helios). Perhaps he was even claiming to *be* Elijah returned to earth. This may well have been why Simeon sought to draw such a clear contrast between the days of Honi and those of Elijah, seeking to undercut any similarity between the two figures themselves.

Honi appears also to have declared himself the son of god, a title reserved for the messianic sun king, for Simeon sought to counter this notion as well. If Honi was the son of god, he was a prodigal son at best. Yahweh did not honor him because of any righteousness on his part, but on the contrary chose to do so in spite of Honi's grievous offenses against his name. Simeon's message was clear: Yahweh's will was inscrutable, but Honi was not about to get any of the credit.

This confrontation between Honi and Simeon was an ominous sign of things to come for the circle-drawer. Despite his significant following, it was clear he would not gain the support of the Pharisees. Nor did he command a fighting force, a fact that put him at a serious disadvantage compared with the two Hasmonean brothers, each of whom had an army at his disposal.

As their dispute escalated, Hyrcanus and Aristobulus lost no time in putting their forces in the field. And when Hyrcanus' supporters besieged the temple, where Aristobulus and his forces had taken refuge, it put Honi the Circle-Drawer in a difficult position. As a claimant of the high priesthood, he was naturally in the temple precincts at the time, but had been careful to hide himself lest he be discovered by one of the armies and taken into custody.

Not, however, careful enough.

Hyrcanus' troops discovered Honi's hiding place and dragged him out to their encampment. Recalling his success at calling forth rain from the heavens, they demanded that he place a curse on their adversaries. This, of course, was more than a mere superstitious request. It was a political maneuver designed to put the circle-drawer in his place. If he gave in to their demands and cursed Aristobulus, he would be abandoning any personal ambitions by publicly endorsing Hyrcanus. The alternative, however, was worse. He was in enemy hands now, and his refusal to do so would bring certain death.

But Honi, unlike the Hasmoneans, was not a political pragmatist. He was an idealist, who had been raised to believe that he was of pure priestly blood and destined to serve as priest-king of the Jews. He therefore stood his ground, refusing to curse either one side or the other and trusting in his god to honor his faithfulness. It was a noble act — for which he was stoned to death.

Rip Van Honi

That was the end of Honi.

Or so it must have seemed.

But a tradition survives that seems to indicate that Honi didn't die in the civil war at all. According to this clearly fanciful version of his legend, he was traveling down the road one day when he happened upon a man planting a carob tree. Stopping for a moment, he questioned the man: "Look here," he said. "It takes seventy years before a carob tree bears fruit. Are you sure you will live another seventy years to eat from this tree?" 53

The man answered that, when he arrived in the world, he was greeted by the sight of carob trees that had been planted by his ancestors. Now he, too, was planting a carob tree for his descendants to enjoy.

The narrative does not reveal whether Honi was satisfied with this answer, but goes on to report that he grew drowsy and began to sleep. And sleep. And sleep. At length, a grotto grew up around him to conceal him, and by the time he finally awoke, he had been asleep a grand total of seventy years. Seventy is, of course, the same number of days that the star of Isis dipped below the horizon before being resurrected at the time of the inundation — the flood of waters that cascaded down the Nile from the highlands far to the south.

The first sight to greet him upon rousing from his slumber was that of a man eating from a carob tree. Who had planted that tree, he wanted to know. The man responded that it had been his grandfather — the man Honi had been talking to before he fell asleep. Honi also noticed that several generations appeared to have been born of his donkey.

As one might imagine, this was all extremely disconcerting. Honi therefore hurried home, looking for his son — only to be told that the boy had passed away, though his son survived to carry on the family name.

This continuity from one generation to the next is the obvious theme of the fable, which bears a resemblance to the latter portion of Jonah's tale. This makes a certain amount of sense: Jonah was a flood hero, and Honi's own rainmaking demonstration had drawn heavily on the legend of another flood hero, Noah. In Jonah's tale, the prophet likewise falls asleep in the shade of a plant that grows up around him — in this case, a vine. The vine was a symbol of Osiris, who had taught the people *"the culture of the vine, as well as the way to harvest the grape and to store the wine."* The new shoot that grew out of his bones was his successor, the new Horus. And it was probably for this reason that Jesus would refer to himself as the vine.[54]

In the tale of Jonah, the vine grows up around him after his ark passage through the storm amidst the deluge. He has therefore crossed the waters of death and ascended to heaven, whereupon a new vine sprouts over his sleeping (mummified) body. This vine is his progeny, who shield him from the sun and thus preserve his name and legacy upon the earth.

This vine, however, does not endure: "At dawn the next day, the Elohim provided a worm, which chewed the vine so that it withered. When the sun rose, the Elohim provided a scorching east wind, and the sun blazed on Jonah's head so that he grew faint. He wanted to die."[55]

Jonah didn't merely want to die.

He *was dead.*

The worm, which dwelt in the soil where the dead were placed, was a universal symbol of mortality. The image of it eating away at the vine represented the end of Jonah's bloodline. He was already dead. Now the vine that had sprung forth from him — his family line — was dying out, as well. As in the case of Osiris, the vine had grown out of his bones. Now it was being eaten away by the worm. Meanwhile, a new king form a different line had arisen like the solar orb to replace his bloodline on the throne of the sun king Horus. This new sun king was joined by his consort the east wind. This could well have been a reference to Isis, who was associated with the hieroglyph of a sail that signified the breath (or wind) of life. Among the goddess' many titles was *"Jewel of the Wind."*[56]

This story, like the fable of Honi, was intended to convey the miracle of life passing from generation to generation through the bloodline.

The *royal* bloodline.

But even though the hero had "survived" his perilous journey in the ark/fish and reached the land of immortality, the line of kings who had succeeded him was dying out.

This theme is, by now, extremely familiar. Yet despite the

similarities between the two tales, one glaring difference is at once apparent. In the legend of Jonah, it is a vine that grows up to shade the sleeping prophet, which is to be expected given the vine symbolism associated with Osiris. In the story of Honi, however, the vine is replaced with another sort of plant that appears out of place in such a narrative — a carob tree. The storyteller must have had some purpose in making this substitution. But what could it have been?

As the carob is an evergreen tree, its use as a symbol of continuing life is appropriate. But there is something more in play. One might be well served to ask whether the name is older than the tree itself, and if so, how the tree came to acquire this designation. Its name, it so happens, stems from the Arabic word for the plant, *kharrub*. And at this stage we begin to get at the root of the tale — and its significance in the story of Honi.

The words carob and *kharrub* are virtual homonyms for the name of the figure who guarded the tree of life with the flaming sword.

The cherub or *kher heb*.

It was he who served as priest-king of the sacred grove until a warrior greater than he should arise to slay him and take his place. This was the nature of the tanist ceremony. Yet the bloodline would continue, for the new king would take the vanquished monarch's wife, daughter, sister or even mother to bed and thus preserve the royal house generation upon generation. This was the very theme of Honi's legend, in which his sleep (or death) did not prevent the carob tree from bearing its fruit and his own family line from continuing.

The fact that his line continued identified him as one greater than Jonah, whose line apparently withered and died.

One more fact about the carob tree is worth noting. This particular tree is repeatedly associated with no less a figure than John the Baptist.[57] John's name was, of course, yet another member of the linguistic family stemming back to Oannes and including such familiar variants as Onias, Jonah, Yohanan, Joannes, Jonathan and Honi. The important point to note is that John was, like Honi, looked upon as a new manifestation of the prophet Elijah. And like

Honi, he commanded the waters that symbolized the passage from this world to the next — Honi baptized the nation of Israel with waters from heaven, and John did so in the River Jordan.

Perhaps most important, John and Honi were both closely associated with the carob tree that symbolized the priestly succession. John therefore must have been part of that succession. The author of *Luke* offers confirmation of this when he states that not only was his father a priest, but his mother was a descendant of Aaron — a prototypical ark figure and founder of the priestly dynasty. This dynasty had stretched down through a succession of Onias priests, one of whom had established the temple at Heliopolis a century and a half before John's birth. It is reasonable to conclude that John was likewise a member of this dynasty, and that he therefore had some connection with the Heliopolitan temple.

Probably he, like his namesake Onias, was its high priest or *kher heb*.

The messiah guarding the tree of life.

By the time he arrived on the scene, it would have been nearly seventy years since Honi's death — the precise length of time the rainmaker is said to have slept. Can it be that John was seen as Honi reborn? Or reawakened? The answer, it scarcely need be asserted, is an unqualified yes.

IV
The Man Who Would Not Die

The rainmaker was nothing if not resilient.

Onias the Just would be reborn as Honi, who in turn would be manifest once more as John the Baptist — all through the sacred mystery of the bloodline. Each was heir to the tradition of the *kher heb* priests in ancient Egypt, the wise astronomers of Heliopolis who gazed intently at the evening sky and wore star-studded cloaks in emulation of the heavens. It was a cloak that would re-emerge centuries later as the garb of one Ambrosius Merlinus.

Merlin for short.

He has become the prototypical wizard, renowned as the most learned man on earth, practitioner of the lost arts and infallible prophet of destiny. And he is, in many ways, the key to understanding the Arthurian saga. His cloak marked him as another in the line of *kher heb* priests that included Onias, Honi and John the Baptist. And more than this, his character appears almost to have been drawn whole-cloth from the legend of the Baptist.

The similarities between the two were so apparent that Merlin and John are even referred to as identical in an old Celtic verse attributed to the famed Irish bard Taliesin — who claimed to be the keeper of their legacy.

> *Johannes I was called*
> *And Merddin the diviner*
> *At length every king*
> *Will call me Taliesin* [58]

Here again one has the picture of the *arit-hur* principle, by which the spirit passes from one "chariot" of flesh and blood to the next, migrating at death to another human vessel. The essence of some great ancestor is thus passed on to a successor, preserving the greatness that has come before and building upon it with each passing generation. In this context, Jesus' enigmatic statement is easily understood:

"I and the father are one." [59]

As were John and Merlin. Both were prophets, renowned for their accuracy in predicting things to come. And both were savage men of the wilderness, marking them as avatars of Seth. John the Baptist went out into the desert and lived as a rustic, wearing clothes of camel's hair bound by a leather belt. Such attire was hardly accidental. The camel-skin coat made him appear to be extremely hairy, and thus identified him with such wild men as Enkidu and Esau. Most specifically, he was seen as a new Elijah, a figure with whom Jesus specifically identified him. In fact, the gospel writers' description of John appears to mimic that of the legendary prophet, who was said to be "a man with a garment of hair, and with a leather belt around his waist." [60]

Then there was the later, equally hairy figure of Merlin, whose hide was described by one author as "rough as a swine." [61] The pig, of course, being another animal closely linked to Seth.

The sorcerer was said to have been so hairy at his birth that he repulsed his mother. Like the Baptist, he was said to have withdrawn to the wilderness in his waning years, where he went "mad" and eventually disappeared altogether. But this so-called madness was not insanity — on the contrary. Madness was a word often used to describe a state of euphoria achieved by prophets as they delivered their oracles. Such prophetic frenzies must have been sights to behold, and it is no wonder that men who entered into them were described as wild men. Frequently, they were associated with bouts of uncontrolled laughter.

This may be why another Seth avatar, the patriarch Isaac, was given a name that meant "laughter." According to Hebrew lore, Abraham laughed aloud at the prospect of bearing a son at his advanced age (he was supposedly a hundred years old at the time).[62] But the Hebrew scribes seem to have misunderstood. Abraham's laughter was not a measure of his incredulity, but an indication that he was about to prophesy. He *would* have a child in his dotage, though such an utterance might seem like the word of a madman. Or prophet.

Another figure from Hebrew legend also laughed in conjunction with an oracle. This was a certain demonic fellow named Asmodeus, a nemesis of Solomon's who is said to have laughed at two people — a magician putting his knowledge on public display and a man who asked a cobbler to craft him shoes that would last for seven years. As it turned out, there was a certain degree of ironic humor in both events. The magician who claimed to be so wise did not realize that a treasure lay buried beneath his very feet. And the man who ordered the durable shoes would not keep them for seven days.[63] Asmodeus knew this because he was a prophet, and his laughter was an indication of his prophecy.

Stunning correlations to these two events are found in an account of Merlin's life known as the *Vita Merlini*. In this work, Merlin makes sport of a poor fellow who has the soles of his shoes patched.

Why?

Because the wizard knows the man is destined to die. He also has fun at the expense of a beggar seeking alms in front of a church, for this particular beggar happens to be sitting on a treasure.[64]

If Asmodeus was a demonic character, so was Merlin, who was said to have been born from the union of a nun and a daemon spirit. And Merlin was likewise known to laugh before he prophesied.

The famed sorcerer had another kindred spirit in an ancient Celtic prophet known as the Gruagach, whose name meant literally "the hairy one."

This prophet, it was said, was actually incapable of delivering an oracle unless he first entered into a fit of laughter.[65] Such mad laughter could be heard in the braying of the ass, totem animal of Seth, which itself takes center stage for one of the more amazing stories in the Hebrew canon. It is a story immersed in prophesy, for it concerns a prophet named Balaam and involves a prophetic utterance by the ass itself.

The figure of Balaam is yet another Seth avatar. His name seems related to the storm god Baal, the Syrian lord of the mountain who was regarded in Egypt as the counterpart of Seth. Hebrew lore depicts him as something of a double-crossing trickster in the mold of Asmodeus and Merlin. And like Merlin, he is also a magician of some renown. In the legend of Moses' campaign to take Ethiopia, for example, he is depicted as conjuring up poisonous serpents or dragons to help him fortify the capital against the hero's impending assault.

But Balaam's most famous story involves his employment by the kingdom of Moab as a sort of prophet-for-hire. As the story begins, the Moabite army is encamped opposite the forces of Israel, which have invaded their territory and appear ready to overrun it. Indeed, the Moabites' prospects for success on the battlefield are so poor that their leaders deliver this rather colorful report:

"This horde is going to lick up everything around us, as an ox licks up grass from a field." [66]

As in so many of the Arthurian tales, only one resource is deemed potent enough to stop an armed contingent in its tracks.

A wizard.

And so Balaam's services are enlisted. If he were to prophesy the defeat of Israel, and do so in a very public manner, the superior forces that threatened to assail Moab might think twice about carrying through with their intentions. Balaam, being a wizard (or wise man) recognized Israel's superiority and was not about to put his reputation on the line with such a faulty prophecy. His answer was no. But the Moabites were desperate — this was their only hope of victory, and they were willing to sweeten the pot. Their leader therefore sent another group of high-ranking emissaries to the prophet and implored him: "Do not let anything keep you from coming to me, because I will reward you handsomely and do whatever you say." Offers of gold and silver were apparently made, yet Balaam stood by his original answer.[67]

For the moment, that is.

But after sleeping on things, he must have reconsidered, for the next morning he set off toward the Moabite encampment, presumably to deliver the requested prophecy. The story is somewhat confusing in this regard, for it portrays Yahweh as instructing Balaam to set off and visit the Moabites; yet in the very next verse, it declares that the deity is livid with him for doing so. This is a rather fickle picture of Yahweh, to say the least, and it adds a bit of confusion to the story. But if these exchanges between god and prophet seem odd, what follows is far more fantastic.

Yahweh shows his displeasure at Balaam's visit to the Moabite camp by setting an angel armed with a drawn sword in the roadway to block his path. Balaam himself seems to have been oblivious to this apparition, but the donkey upon which he was riding saw the angel quite clearly. Fearing for its life, the animal turned aside into a field — only to have its master beat it for straying from the road.

As they moved closer to the sword-wielding angel, the donkey again tried to turn aside. But by this time, they were hemmed in on both sides by a walled vineyard, and Balaam's foot was crushed against the stone when the donkey pressed against it in another attempt to avoid the angelic warrior. Balaam's answer was the same: He beat the unfortunate animal.

At last, when there was nowhere to go, the donkey resorted to lying down in the roadway.

Again, the animal was beaten.

But this time it spoke up in its own defense, beginning a fabulous and somewhat comical give-and-take between the prophet and his animal. The donkey was, in fact, prophesying. And after a short argument, Balaam finally became aware of the armed angel standing right in front of him and relented.

The story has become a favorite of Sunday school teachers, who use it to entertain children and comment on topics ranging from bribery, loyalty and obedience to animal cruelty. But the original imagery had little to do with any of these themes. This story, like so many others, depicted the ritual confrontation between the old *kher heb* priest and his challenger. Balaam, as an obvious Seth figure, is the old king of the sacred grove whose time has passed. As he passes along the road, he is confronted by the valiant young hero in the guise of a warrior angel.

When the donkey sinks to the ground, it is a sign that the Seth character cannot go on any further and must relinquish his role as *kher heb* to his young successor in the tanist ritual. The fact that this successor is depicted as a sword-wielding angel, or a cherub (*kher heb*) confirms the purpose of the tale. So does its setting between two vineyards, symbolic of the eternal bloodline. The message was clear: It was time to pass the mantle to the next generation, with the nameless successor taking on the role occupied by Balaam to this point.

Just as John the Baptist would pass his mantle to Jesus, declaring, "He must increase, but I must decrease." [68]

And so it passed also from Merlin to King Arthur.

St. Pendragon

Though there is no explicit reference to a tanist challenge made by Arthur to Merlin, echoes of such a story can be found in, of all places, the traditions surrounding the life of a famed saint. The man in question is one of the more famous figures in western history, and his day is more widely celebrated than most, with parades, shamrocks and green attire being its hallmarks. According to tradition, it was he who brought a new religion of Ireland — the religion of Jesus. And he had little tolerance for pagan beliefs, overpowering the druid masters with his wisdom and the power of his holy mandate.

It comes as some surprise, therefore, to find that his life reads like a page out of a tanist instruction manual.

His name provides the first clue as to his true identity.

It is, of course, Patrick, a name that in the original Irish is rendered as Padraig. The suffix of this name, *draig*, is the Welsh word for dragon; and indeed the entire name has something of a familiar ring to it. In fact, the similarity of the name to Arthur's reputed surname, Pendragon, seems unlikely to be coincidence. The two men lived, according to the most widely accepted timelines, during precisely the same period. And, according to legend, Patrick played a role in Ireland that paralleled that of Arthur in Britain — a man who inaugurated a golden age of civilization and set an example of reverence for the holy truth.

Patrick's name identified him, like Arthur, as "son of the dragon." Like Arthur, he might therefore be expected to fit the pattern of a Horus character — the tanist heir to the throne occupied by the dragon himself, the old Seth king or wizard. Under the tanist code, he would be expected to do away with this dragon and claim the throne for himself. And this is exactly what transpires.

Perhaps the most famous tale connected with St. Patrick is a bit of folklore that supposedly explains the absence of serpents (or dragons) from Ireland. This account tells of Patrick's confrontation with these serpents on a certain mountain overlooking the ocean, known as Cruach Padraig. Patrick's mountain.

This conflict was reportedly decided when Patrick lifted something called the "staffe or wand of Jesus" against them, thereby driving the vile creatures over the precipice and into the sea.[69]

The staff or wand here mentioned is unquestionably the wizard's caduceus or serpentine rod used by Moses, Merlin and the rest of their ilk. It is also an obvious phallic device, symbolizing Patrick's mastery of the most important "magic" in the tanist arsenal — the ability to reproduce and thus perpetuate the bloodline. It is this ability, as manifest in the tanist prince's superior strength in his struggle with the aging Seth king, that enables him to expel this king (or serpent) and replace him.

Patrick reportedly fasted for forty days before undertaking to do battle with the serpents, thus submitting to the ancient wilderness ritual traditionally linked to the conflict with Seth.[70]

Any doubt that Patrick saw himself in the role of Horus in the eternal struggle with Seth is erased upon referring to his own writings, where he relates an affinity with the sun god Helios: "It was suggested to me in the spirit that I should invoke Helia, and meanwhile I saw the sun rising in heaven. And while I was calling out for Helia with all my might, behold the splendor of the sun fell upon me and immediately struck from me the oppressive weight." [71]

This would seem to demonstrate clearly enough that Patrick regarded the sun, or Helia, as his special ally in the fight against his enemies. He was able to control the sun by entreating or commanding it to do his bidding, just as Joshua — the first Jesus — had done.

It is apparent from all this that Patrick must have considered himself the latest incarnation of the sun god, just as Jesus had been. The spirit of Jesus indwelled his body, which itself was a mere vessel.

Or chariot.

The chariot of Horus, or *arit hur*.

The Seth figure in his story is not named, his status having been reduced to that of the totem animal itself. The serpent. But one might conjecture that his name was Merlin, and that Patrick's legend was imported part and parcel to the island directly east of Ireland, with the hero becoming known as Arthur Pendragon (a.k.a. Padraig or Patrick) in the process.

Elements of his story, in turn were dependent upon the legends surrounding one of the original serpent kings, Balaam, whose name probably was originally the plural Baalim to signify a council or gathering of *baals* — literally "lords." These *baals*, when taken together, made up a group of serpents the likes of which Patrick expelled from the shores of Ireland. And indeed, the wizard Balaam is said to have created any number of poisonous serpents or dragons to keep Moses at bay during the Ethiopian campaign.

In like manner, Merlin was also known for his connection with dragons. One of his most famous prophecies involved a prediction that two such dragons — one red and one white — would wage war against one another for the sovereignty of Britain. This dragon war is reminiscent of the epic battle for the two lands in Egypt between Seth and Horus. The colors assigned to the two dragons fit nicely into this scheme: Seth's traditional hue was red, the color of the sun as it rode close to the horizon during late autumn and early winter. This was the season of Seth. During the season of Horus, on the other hand, the sun burned white-hot in the summer sky, blazing down on the earth in all its glory.

But though dragons could symbolize the sun in its various seasons, they were even more closely linked to the storm. One such example is the ancient sky serpent Apophis, supplanted to some extent in later myth by Seth. Dragons were natural creatures of the storm, their mighty roar being heard in the peals of thunder and their flaming breath bursting forth in flashes of lightning. And storms were in turn linked to rainmaker priests such as Honi and his successor John the Baptist.

Could Merlin have played a similar role?

Indeed. The wizard played a decisive part in what may be classed as the most pivotal campaign in young King Arthur's career, the battle of Carmelide. Though Arthur and a number of vassal knights and princes do the dirty work, steadfastly warding off the enemy assault, it is Merlin who seems to be orchestrating the entire battle as it unfolds. It is he who carries the standard into battle, a pennant bearing with the likeness of the red dragon — an appropriate symbol for a Seth avatar. (This symbol survives to this day as the centerpiece of the Welsh flag.)

Yet Merlin is much more than a mere standard-bearer. He is a master wizard who controls the ebb and flow of the battle in a manner reminiscent of Moses' role against the Amalekites. During that famous scene, Moses took his magical staff to the top of a mountain whence he surveyed the battlefield with his cohorts, Aaron and Hur. Whenever he held his staff over his head, "the Israelites were winning, but whenever he lowered his hands, the Amalekites were winning." [72] But after a time, he grew weary of standing and sat down on a rock. Aaron and Hur then held up his fatigued arms to ensure his army's triumph.

This scene served as a premonition of Moses' imminent death. He was old and tired, unable to stand for any length of time or even hold his arms above his head. Like Merlin, he was a Seth figure in the twilight of his life. On one side stood Hur or Horus, the young prince destined to would supplant him; on the other stood Aaron or Orion, the Osiris figure who had come before.

Each of these three figures was present at the battle of Carmelide, as well. If Merlin was the Seth figure, Arthur (whose very name contained the suffix *hur*) was the new Horus. The third prominent role was that of Aaron or Orion, a role that fell to the enemy king — who just happened to be Urien, the same king identified elsewhere as the husband of Arthur's half-sister, Morgan.

But despite the presence of these other formidable figures, this was Merlin's day. It was, perhaps, his finest hour. Just as Moses had stood at the forefront during the campaign against the Amalekites, so now Merlin took center stage during the battle of Carmelide. Raising his dragon banner high like Merlin's staff (which, if may be recalled, had the ability to transform itself into a serpent or *dragon*), he called forth a fierce wind to drive back the enemy and cornered them against a sudden flood that he summoned to surround the combatants.[73]

He was Honi, the rainmaker, reborn. And like Honi, he was a circle drawer, for it was Merlin who directed the construction of a famous table at which the bravest knights in the kingdom might sit.

A *round* table.

Merlin was Oannes the fish king — or Fisher King — in his latest incarnation. And though his name deviated from the standard form adopted by the Onias priests of the sacred bloodline, it was revealing nonetheless.

Merlin was the name given to a certain kind of ocean fish, and it also (amazingly enough) denoted a breed of falcon.[74] These were, of course, the two manifestations of Horus, who flew as a sun falcon across the sky in daytime yet descended beneath the waters in the form of a fish each eventide. Merlin was, like Horus, a king.

And he was, like Oannes or Enki, the fish-man and keeper of all wisdom.

His link to water was well established. Not only was he a rainmaker in the mold of Honi, but he also presided over a fountain renowned for its curative properties. It is worth recalling once again that the word for fountain in French was *aquae*, which gave rise to the legend of lady del aquae, subsequently garbled to become the "lady of the lake." And this particular lady was none other than Nimue, Merlin's lover and eternal consort.

These two figures, the priest and the lady of the fountain, seem to have been linked in ancient lore — inextricably so. For one thing, the shrine at Delphi in ancient Greece was guarded by a priestess known for her foretellings. Visitors to this particular shrine noticed the sound of running water, symbolic of eternal life, wisdom and the oracle's gift. But the shrine housed something else as well, the meteoric benben stone from heaven that was sacred to the sun god Apollo. This same Apollo was the brother of Diana, mistress of the sacred grove guarded by the tanist *kher heb* priest.

Here is where the connection rests.

These four figures appear to be at the core of the tanist ritual that determined the course of monarchies across the ancient world. God was paired with goddess; priest with priestess. Merlin was the latest in the line of *kher heb* priests, and Nimue was the prophetic lady of the fountain, so their pairing made impeccable sense.

But according to the ancient creed, everything on earth was but a reflection of some heavenly reality — and this was no exception. The tanist ritual was not some human invention but a gift from the gods, who themselves had inaugurated the practice and continued to follow it in the heavens.

Apollo and Diana were, therefore, deified counterparts of the *kher heb* priest and fountain priestess.

This, too, made perfect sense. Diana and Apollo were brother and sister, and both were renowned as hunters. The hero of one Greek legend even went so far as to dedicate a temple to them jointly as god and goddess of the hunt.[75] This might seem a bit peculiar, for another figure has already been identified as a hunter god — Orion. Legend had it that Diana was in love with Orion but slew him with an arrow, having mistaken him for a pirate crossing the ocean with the intent to rape her. (Just as her counterpart Dinah was raped in the Hebrew legend).

But Diana was not culpable in the murder. She had drawn her bowstring at the behest of her brother Apollo, whose protective nature had caused him to seek Orion's death.

The symbolism of the myth comes through loud and clear.

➢ Orion = Osiris, or dead king.
➢ Apollo = Horus, the sun king: his successor.

Apollo was engaging Orion in a celestial tanist battle with Diana as the prize, just as Arthur would take on Urien on the battlefield in a later epoch. On earth as it was in heaven. Arthur and his knights were merely renewing the sacred ritual of the tanist succession handed down from the gods uncounted generations before. Hence the similarity of the names Urien and Orion. And hence also the apparent origin of Arthur's name in the Egyptian phrase "chariot of

Horus" — doubtless the same solar chariot that Apollo drove across the sky.

The sexual component of these legends is not to be missed. The prize was always a maiden, and the weapon was either sword or arrow. The phallic nature of such devices is plain enough. Excalibur, the magical sword of King Arthur, was the equivalent of the flaming sword wielded by the *kher heb* priest in front of the sacred tree, a sword obtained from the prophetic fountain priestess known as the "lady of the lake." Not only does the hero use a sword to slay his rival, he also uses a sword (in the figurative sense) to father the child destined to succeed him. The fountain priestess is both his lover and his undoing.

Such is the irony of the Arthurian myth.

➢ Arthur loves Guinevere, yet she eventually betrays him with the young knight Lancelot du Lac — whose very name identifies him with the lady of the lake.

➢ Arthur lies with Morgan le Fay, and the result of their union is the child Mordred who is to slay him.

➢ Merlin is smitten by the lady of the lake Nimue, who winds up stealing his knowledge and imprisoning him in a tree.

The fountain survives even today as the baptismal, which just so happens to be called a font. Here again is a link between John the Baptist and his successor, the wizard Merlin.

The baptismal was the site of ritual death and resurrection, through which one crossed the waters of death and entered paradise. In Arthurian lore, this paradise was Avalon, the famed "isle of apples" veiled in the western mists. The apple was the fruit of Apollo, whose name resembles that of the fruit itself, indicating that the two may be derived from a common root.[76] And it was also the fruit sought by the hero Hercules in one of his famed twelve labors, which conveniently also involved a land on the western horizon.

The Viking Lord

Hercules is the more familiar name for the Greek demigod Heracles, whose name supposedly meant "glory of Hera." This proposed derivation, however, makes little sense given his family history. Hera was the consort of Zeus, the king of the gods who also just happened to be Hercules' father. In light of this, it would be natural to assume that the goddess in question must have been his mother. But she wasn't. Hercules was, in fact, the product of a dalliance by Zeus with a mortal woman — a fact that the jealous Hera never allowed the legendary strongman to forget. So wroth was she at her husband's infidelity that she bore a grudge against the unfortunate hero from the moment of his birth, making repeated attempts against his life.

Hercules, it would seem, was anything but the glory of Hera. Bane of Hera would have been a more appropriate title.

But whence, then, his name?

A clue may to its origins may be found in the assertion by one ancient writer that Hercules was not originally a Greek hero at all, but rather an Egyptian who had lived a full ten thousand years earlier.[77] This would have placed him well back in the mists of time, during the era when (the Egyptians believed) the gods still walked the earth — gods such as Horus. The falcon god whose name was synonymous with the royal house was known as Heru among the Egyptians. And this would appear to be the true source of the name Hercules.

It doesn't mean "glory of Hera" at all, but "glory of Horus."

This is borne out by his connection with Apollo, the Greek sun god and counterpart of the Egyptian Horus. It was this god's priestess oracle at Delphi who bestowed his name upon him, and it was likewise she who set before him the task of performing several feats in the service of a certain king.[78] His reward for accomplishing these labors would be immortality, so they had to be sufficiently difficult to thwart any mere mortal who undertook them.

For the next-to-last of these twelve labors, he was charged with retrieving a crop of golden apples from a garden planted in a distant land to the west. The exact location of this land is never stated explicitly, an omission that puts Hercules at a distinct disadvantage before he even begins his journey. He is, in this sense, much like the questing knight of Arthur's court who goes forth seeking the elusive castle where the grail is kept without knowing its whereabouts. This uncertainty offers a clue to the nature of the land in question — it is in the otherworld, beyond the realm of mortal man. Perched on the edge of the western horizon, it is the place where the solar chariot comes to rest each night; it is the land of the setting sun, the Egyptian realm of the dead.

Hercules eventually finds his way to this place, which is ruled by the titan Atlas. This is the familiar figure who has been fated to stand forever upright as he supports the weight of the world on his shoulders. As king of the western land, he serves as a clear counterpart to Osiris, who likewise ruled the land of the dead and stood forever upright in the form of the *djed* column or pillar. In some versions of the Atlas myth, the titan is even said to support the world by means of a column set upon his head and shoulders. He is also, like Osiris, associated with a mountain range — the Atlas Mountains in northwest Africa that rise up far to the west of the mighty Nile, the place identified in Egypt as the land of the dead.

Hercules arrives in this land to find the tree that bears the golden apples is guarded by a ferocious dragon named Ladon, a beast he must slay in order to claim his prize. The dragon's name is clearly derived from that of the familiar Lotan or *lwtyn*, a.k.a. Leviathan, the seven-headed serpent slain by Baal in Phoenician lore (the seven heads once again representing the seven spirits guarding the mansions of the underworld, through which Sirius passed during its time below the horizon).

As a serpent, Lotan or Ladon was obviously either a wizard or a dragon lady. The question is, which one?

His name provides a valuable clue.

By subtracting the first letter from Ladon, one obtains the name

Adon, which means "lord" and is a shortened version of Adonai — a title often used by the Hebrews to refer to Yahweh himself. Another variation is perhaps even more enlightening. By removing the same letter from the original *lwtyn*, one arrives at a name that sounds nearly identical to that of Wotan or Woden, the head of the Germanic pantheon who is known in Scandinavian lore as Odin.

And this raises yet another question: Is it just possible that the traditions of these northern gods are in fact derived from those contained in the Phoenician myth?

Not only is it possible, it seems highly likely.

The Phoenicians were famous for two things — their mastery of written language and their sailing skills. In their day, they were the world's foremost navigators, sailing far and wide as they expanded their trading network across the Mediterranean and beyond. But how far beyond? Evidently, as far as the snowy lands that are known to us as Germany and Scandinavia, where their traditions are found embedded in a culture that one might expect to be entirely foreign to them.

Foremost among these traditions is a love of the sea, perhaps inherited by the Vikings from their Phoenician forebears. Like the Egyptians, who buried ships next to their great pyramids, the men of the north believed they would be taken to the next world in an ark. They therefore were known to inter their dead in such vessels, as they did with two female corpses found in a buried ship at Oseberg, southern Norway. The Viking ships that sailed forth in the land of the living were captained by men with names like Erik, bestowed perhaps in some vague remembrance of the city of Erech whence their traditions may have been born. An ark of the Norsemen was fearsome to behold, its ornately carved bow jutting forth into the misty waters like a dragon's maw challenging the open sea.

Perhaps this dragon was Lotan. Or Odin.

This god stood, after all, at the head of a vast pantheon that rivaled the Greek or Roman deities. Specifically, he served as patriarch of a divine group known as the Aesir, a name that recalls the Egyptian name for Osiris, Asir. As the wisest of the gods, he was a wizard par excellence, a heavenly scribe in the mold of Enoch who is lauded as the creator of written language. Like Merlin, he could determine the outcome of a battle by raising his magical spear — a counterpart to the serpentine staff of Moses.[79] Like Merlin, he was a master of disguise, able to transform his appearance at will to become the hidden one. During the course of one myth, he was charged with retrieving a potion of blood and honey created by a race of dwarves. This potion, a peculiar variation on the sweet-tasting alcoholic beverage known as mead, was said to impart an unusual degree of inspiration to any who might partake of it. It had been stolen by an unfriendly giant who had hidden it in a mountain, and it was up to Odin to find it and restore it to the hall of the gods at Asgard.

This he did by transforming himself into a serpent, taking upon himself the ancient aspect of the dragon wizard and becoming the image of *lwtyn*. In this form, he slithered into the mountain and found the missing potion, which he obtained by tricking the giant's daughter into giving him a drink. He did not swallow the potion, though. Instead, he transformed himself into an eagle — taking on a form similar to that of the Horus falcon — and flew back to Asgard with the treasured concoction safely in his care.

The message of the myth is to be found in its symbols.[80]

Foremost among them is the potion. Its ingredients make it seem somewhat less than appetizing, but they were never meant to be taken literally. The blood doubtless represents the bloodline, which is passed from one generation to the next through the magic of sexual intercourse. This is where the honey comes in, for honey was widely considered an aphrodisiac by the ancients, who also viewed it as helpful in ensuring fertility.[81]

The theft of this potion by the giant must have symbolized a war in which a foreign usurper had claimed the crown and thus interrupted the sacred bloodline, carrying the seat of power off to his own land. This recalls the language of Sumerian myth, which signals repeated shifts in power among the city states in the region by using formulaic statements such as these:

- "Erech was defeated; its kingship was carried off to Ur."
- "Kish was defeated; its kingship was carried off to Erech."
- "Erech was defeated; its kingship was carried off to the Gutium hordes." [82]

In much the same way, the kingship seems to have been carried off by the giant in the legend of Odin. Because this particular god was known as the all-father and progenitor of kings, it was his duty to retrieve the stolen drink of inspiration that could restore the kingship to his own land. All this sounds suspiciously like the story of Inanna, Enki and the *me* tablets, which recalled a similar transfer of power from Enki's cult center to the city of Inanna — Erech or Uruk. The parallels between this story and the myth of Odin are too numerous to be dismissed.

Odin, like Enki, is a wise god and keeper of the written word. In the Sumerian tale, Enki falls prey to the wiles of Inanna, who gets him drunk and persuades him to part with his precious *me* tablets that contain the fruits of his divine inspiration. Odin finds himself faced with a similar problem when he discovers that the magic mead has been stolen from his kingdom. Like the tablets, this potion is closely linked to the concept of heavenly inspiration. (Is it mere coincidence that the words *me* and mead sound so similar?) And the character of mead as an alcoholic beverage connects it to the episode of Enki's drunkenness in the Sumerian tale. It also recalls the invitation of Asherah to partake of the "blood of the vine from the golden cup" — the wine or blood mingling with the golden honey that gives mead its distinctive taste, appearance and consistency.

The fact that this font of inspiration is then carried off to a mountain in Odin's tale ties the two stories even more closely together. In the Sumerian version, after all, the *me* tablets were removed to the mountain-shaped ziggurat temple of Inanna in Erech.

The only significant difference between the two myths involves Enki's inability to recover his tablets despite attempts to do so, which contrasts with Odin's triumphant return to his homeland with the mead.

Odin's great effort to recover the blood-and-honey potion is understandable, given the sacrifice he had to make in securing his status as the wisest of the gods. Legend had it that he had obtained his inspiration from a well or fountain called Mimir at the base of the world tree, Yggdrasil. The name of the fountain may have some connection to the mummer's dance around the maypole, which represented both the *djed* column/Asherah pole and world tree. It also may be derived from the same root as the word memory, a necessary precursor to knowledge. To the ancients, memory was particularly important, for knowledge was passed from one generation to the next in the form of ritual and story. In order to maintain this knowledge, one had to memorize the proper order of things — how the ritual was to be enacted; how an epic tale proceeded from start to finish. This was the foundation of wisdom.

It was Odin who mastered this act of memorization and used it to create a written language of mystical runes, much as Enki had inscribed the secrets of the universe on his *me* tablets. But he had paid a price for doing so: In exchange for being allowed to drink from this enchanted fountain, Odin had cast his eye into it, leaving him with but a single eye.[83]

The story of the fountain makes the it obvious how the Norsemen came to identify the *me* tablets of ancient Sumer with the honeyed elixir known as mead. They must have assumed that the name *me* actually referred to the water that poured forth from this enchanted spring. Because this was no ordinary water, but a revitalizing force that imparted the gift of wisdom, they came to associate it with the rich and potent drink they subsequently called mead.

Though no priestess or goddess attends the well in the myth of Odin, such a presence is common in various related myths. This "lady of the waters" was also a prophetess who imparted wisdom, mirroring the power of the fountain itself. In later times, she came to be known as a Sibyl, a name that recalls that of Cybele, the great mother goddess of Asia Minor. But throughout history she was renowned for her ability to speak words of insight and foresight.

It is no wonder, therefore, that the word *me* can be found as an element the names of mythical goddesses and serpent ladies. Foremost among them, perhaps, are the figures of Medusa and Medea — whose names both appear to mean "goddess of the *me*." This title, of course, would have been most appropriate to Inanna, who became the keeper of the *me* tablets after tricking Enki into relinquishing them. It is fascinating to find that Medea was associated with the ark hero Jason as his consort — and was also the niece of none other than Circe. In the course of the *Argo* narrative, Medea even plays a role later assigned to Mary Magdalene, presiding over a resurrection that enables the subject of her spell to assume his place as rightful king.[84] This is exactly what was said to have happened to Jesus.

Odin, likewise, became king of the Norse pantheon by virtue of his adventure at the well, during which he sacrificed an eye to acquired his fabled wisdom.

The sexual imagery of this episode is apparent.

Odin the dragon king has now become a "one-eyed serpent," an epithet used even today in reference to the male sex organ. In fact, he has not actually deprived of his sex organ but merely of its *lotan* or foreskin, in preparation for casting his penis into the well — a symbol for the female sex organ. One version of the myth even associates this well of inspiration with a disembodied head, recalling the rite of female circumcision implied in the legend of Gilgamesh and Hawawa. In related traditions, the head itself rises out of the well to impart its wisdom, imitating the rising of the clitoris out of the depths of the vaginal well upon arousal.[85]

This is the disembodied head Baphomet, also known as Sophia or wisdom.

The wisdom imparted during sexual intercourse.

This connection is confirmed by the famous legend of Eden, which has long been recognized as a tale of sexual seduction. In this tale, as in so many others, the heroine succeeds in stealing wisdom (referred to here as the knowledge of good and evil), in this case by partaking of the sacred tree's fruit. She is convinced to do so upon observing that the fruit in question is "pleasing to the eye, and also desirable for gaining wisdom."[86] Here we have the motifs of the eye and wisdom that occur in the legend of Odin's well. But something more lurks beneath the surface of the proverbial waters in this case: The Hebrew word for eye in this passage is *ayin*, a word that can just as easily denote a spring or fountain. Or a well.

And as if this is not enough, the link between sexual intercourse and wisdom is further cemented by the cult of Freya, a fertility goddess viewed as the Norse counterpart to Isis. This goddess was particularly linked to a soothsaying priestess known as the *volva*. This title bears no small resemblance to the word vulva, which denotes the external genital organs of the female — the surface of the well from which wisdom was said to arise. And this connection would seem to be clinched by the fact that Freya was specifically associated with the falcon, the bird of Horus and Circe.[87]

The circumsiser.

Like Circe, who was connected with the weeping willow, Freya was known for her tears. In this case, they were tears of gold, shed for a lost consort after the manner of Isis weeping for Osiris.[88] These tears were the color of the grain that sprang up from the ground and produced such great abundance upon the god-king's death. The color of corn. The color of wheat. As Jesus would put it, "Unless a kernel of wheat falls to the ground and dies, it remains a single seed. But if it dies, it produces many seeds." [89]

This golden grain might have been wheat or corn, but it might also have been a flowering plant known as flax. The Germanic tribes who worshipped Woden called it *lin*, and it was the source of such varied products as oil cakes and linseed oil.

Because it dried quickly and held its form on paper, this oil was used in creating printer's ink and oil paints. It was therefore associated with writing, the magical means by which knowledge was captured and transferred from one *wisard* to another. But perhaps its most prominent use resulted not from its oil but from the strands of fine thread it produced, which were suitable for spinning and weaving into a material called linen.

This is the very material the Egyptians used to mummify their dead. Most likely, the Phoenicians brought it to Europe along with their written alphabet when they traveled north on their trading missions.

Hence the popular fairy-tale image of the long-haired maiden weeping as she works at her spinning wheel, perhaps the most famous version of which occurs in the tale of Rumplestiltskin.

The Wheel and the Mill

This famous yarn concerns a poor miller's daughter who is brought to the king and asked to spin straw into gold. Of course, she has no idea how to do this, so she is distressed to find that her penalty for failing to perform the task assigned her will be death. At this point, a little man named Rumplestiltskin arrives on the scene and offers to fulfill her obligation if she can give him something of value. She therefore offers him her necklace, which he accepts, and he immediately proceeds to spin the straw, miraculously transforming it into gold.

The poor maiden appears to be off the hook. But to her chagrin, the king only becomes more greedy and returns the following evening with even more straw for her to spin — threatening her with death once again should she fail to comply. Again, the little man comes to her rescue, spinning the straw for her in exchange this time for her beautiful ring.

The cycle then repeats itself yet again, with the king offering this time to make the poor maiden his wife if she succeeds in spinning a still greater quantity of straw into gold. Unfortunately, the young woman has run out of valuables to offer the little man, so she must promise him her first-born child if she in fact becomes queen. Seeing little alternative, the maiden assents and the little man once again does his part. In due course, the king and the maiden are married and give birth to a daughter, which the little man demands as his payment for services rendered. But the new mother, being understandably protective of her child, balks at the idea of fulfilling her part of the bargain. The little man therefore presents her with a loophole: If she can guess his name within the span of three days, he will cancel her debt to him.

It turns out to be a nearly impossible task, considering the little man wears the unique moniker Rumplestiltskin. But as luck would have it, a servant of the new queen happens to overhear the little man reveal his name while gloating over his impending triumph. The servant reports this bit of information to the queen, who uses it to get out of her deal with Rumplestiltskin.

This story is filled with interesting scenes. The image of the maiden weeping as she toils at her spinning wheel is that of Isis weeping as she spins the linen wrappings in which the dead Osiris is to be mummified. The fact that she is a miller's daughter is also significant, for the mill was seen in ancient myth as a symbol of heaven. And Zeus, the king of heaven, was considered the great miller.[90]

In light of this, it would seem that the miller's daughter is no poor and simple maiden after all. Quite to the contrary, she is in fact the queen of heaven, through whom the sacred bloodline must pass. And this makes perfect sense, for "queen of heaven" was one of Isis' most famous titles.

Not only does this piece of information identify the heroine of the tale more clearly, it also serves to clarify the little man's purpose in seeking custody of her newborn daughter. He recognizes that as a female child, this infant is the keeper of the royal bloodline. If, therefore, he can gain custody of her and — when she has come of age — father her child, he will have succeeded in establishing himself as the patriarch of kings.

The first two payments he obtains in exchange for his services are equally symbolic. Both the necklace and the ring are circular adornments, identifying them as acts of circumcision. One is performed on the male; the other on the female. Immediately upon offering these two gifts to the little man (who plays the role of circumcising Levitical priest), the maiden receives an offer of marriage from the king. And immediately after this, she conceives a child by him.

This is the very sequence of events called for under the ancient tradition — circumcision of the male and female, marriage, and finally conception of the divine child.

The Grim Reaper

Though the maiden in the tale of Rumplestiltskin spun straw into gold, most variations on this theme speak of a maiden spinning flax. She spins it to form the burial garment of her lord, the linen shroud to be used in mummification. And this is why she weeps. Flax was called *lin* by the Germans, but it had another name among the Nordic nations — *horr*. And if this sounds something like the name Horus, perhaps it helps explain why maidens such as Freya and Circe were so closely associated with the falcon, the bird of Horus.

The symbolism embedded in the tale of Rumplestiltskin seems to confirm that circumcision was the ritual employed to prepare both husband and wife for this sacred rite. This seems to have been a more widespread practice than Herodotus realized when he declared that the Egyptians, Cholchians and Ethiopians were the only races to take part in such a ritual. In fact, aboriginal people as far away as Australia also practiced this particular rite — at least for males, who had their foreskins removed at puberty, doubtless to make them ready for the marriage bed. This is the same purpose for which the ritual was first employed in the ancient Near East. But there is an even more striking parallel between the two cultures: When a young male was preparing to undergo this ritual, he was told by the elders of his clan that the great father snake smelled his foreskin and was calling for it.[91]

The involvement of such a serpent or dragon figure — and one specifically referred to as a "great father" — seems nothing short of astounding. It would seem that a figure analogous to that of Seth, the wise and fatherly dragon king, or wizard, was known to the Australian aboriginal tribes as well. What makes this so incredible is the prolonged isolation of these tribes from any outside human contact. After all, they lived in the desert interior of the island continent called the outback, where they are known to have maintained their primitive culture virtually intact and unmolested for a period spanning several millennia. The question therefore arises: How could they possibly have known of the Seth myth and its accompanying ritual?

Or is it simply that two disparate cultures concocted similar myths to fit similar circumstances?

These are questions that, alas, must be left unanswered.

All that is certain is that somehow, some way, myth and ritual seem to have permeated a variety of human cultures — even the most isolated — from the nether regions of the southern hemisphere to near the Arctic circle in the north. It was there that the serpent figure known as Odin held sway and served as a model for the very same ritual of sexual initiation. In his case, this ritual was expressed symbolically as the god losing one of his eyes. This was hardly an original concept. Horus likewise lost his eye in a dual with the serpent king Seth, and his father Osiris was deprived of his phallus in a more literal form of the myth. In the latter instance, the organ was swallowed by a fish, most likely a female fish or mermaid who guarded the waters as yet another lady of the fountain.

There is even a parallel to be found in the myth of Cronus, the Greek titan who succeeded to the throne of the gods by castrating his predecessor. The events that led up to this power grab are worth relating in brief. They involve the divine sky father Uranus — whose name recalls that of another sky figure, Orion. Both names may perhaps be related to the German *ur-ahn*, meaning "primitive ancestor." [92] Such a connection would make sense given Osiris' identity as the father god of Egypt and Uranus' similar position in Mediterranean lore.

According to the storytellers, it seems that Uranus had been challenged to a tanist battle by his rebellious sons. This encounter had ended badly for the younger generation, who had failed to unseat the old king and had been cast into the underworld for their troubles. It was an outcome that did not sit well with Uranus' wife Gaia, the earth goddess, who did not take kindly to seeing her sons put to death. (Incidentally, the sons involved were known as Cyclopes, giants who had only a *single eye*).

Gaia therefore hatched a plot to ensure that the next challenge posed to Uranus would be his last. She armed her youngest son, Cronus, with a stone sickle and arranged to seduce Uranus; at the point of their intercourse, the young prince was to produce the sickle and castrate his father.

Or perhaps circumcise him.

Cronus' sickle identifies him as the infamous father time, the grim reaper who ushers out the old year in winter. Indeed, Cronus' very name means "time" — it serves as the root for such words as chronicle and chronology. It is also the root of the word crone, used to describe an aged woman. The menacing hooded figure of father time, also known as the grim reaper, appears at the close of each annual cycle to usher out the old year and make way for the new. And it is no accident that this changing of the guard takes place in the dead of winter, during the season of Seth.

This makes perfect sense, for the Romans identified the Greek god Cronus by a different name.

Saturn.

The relationship of this name to Seth (or Set) is clear enough — as is the connection between the tale of Cronus and the legend of

Seth. Recall that it was Seth who cut Osiris into several pieces and scattered them across the land of Egypt. Recall, too, that Isis eventually recovered all the pieces save one: the phallus. The severed phallus of Osiris therefore emerges as a perfect parallel to the severed genitalia of Uranus, whose constellation Orion was the heavenly symbol of the dead Egyptian god-king.

In the Greek myth, Uranus' severed genitals fell into the sea and were transformed into white foam. Thence was born the sea goddess of love, Aphrodite, yet another mermaid or lady of the waters. This particular deity had much in common with the Sumerian love goddess Inanna and doubtless provided the inspiration for the beautiful Queen Guinevere, whose name means "white wave" and who is involved in King Arthur's struggle with the wounded thigh or *morddwyd tyllion*.

The thigh was nothing more than a euphemism for the male genitalia.

Knowing this, we are finally in a position to explain the mysterious issue of Arthur's son Mordred. The lingering question is this: If the king had been rendered impotent by a wound to the genitals, how then could he have conceived a child? Indeed, the child's name is all the more puzzling because it appears to indicate that he was born not despite, but *as a result of* this wound. The mystery is solved, once again, by the ritual of circumcision. Such an operation was originally performed as a prelude to intercourse and left the patient bedridden for a period of time. This explains why the Fisher King was incapacitated.

The relationship of the wounded thigh to circumcision is confirmed by rabbinical texts that amplify on the story of *Genesis*. The passage in question concerns Jacob's last request, that he be buried not in Egypt but in his ancestral homeland. To ensure that his instructions are carried out, he asks his son Joseph to swear an oath in the following manner: "Put your hand under my thigh and promise that you will show me kindness and faithfulness." [93]

According to the rabbis, Joseph at first shrank from swearing such an oath, protesting that "it is unseemly for a son to touch his father's circumcision." [94]

There it is. The region under the thigh is specifically equated with the rite of circumcision.

This connection enables the reader to bring a peculiar episode from Sumerian myth into sharp focus. The incident in question is Enkidu's angry response to Inanna after slaying the bull of heaven: Having done so, he tore loose the dead animal's thigh and flung it disdainfully in the goddess' face. "If I could only get at you," he shouted in a fury, "I would do the same to you as I have done to him."

What had he done in tearing off the creature's so-called thigh? He had circumcised it. In fact, Enkidu was merely performing his function as a Levitical priest (priest of the Leviathan) in charge of carrying out this ritual act. He had done so with Hawawa. And now he had done so with the bull of heaven by cutting off its thigh, or foreskin. This is what he hurled at the love goddess Inanna in the midst of uttering his boastful threat. It was a threat to circumcise her as well.

The Challenge

The act of circumcision that preceded the marriage ceremony appears to have acted as a sort of trigger for the tanist ritual. It served as the cue for a young rival to challenge the king — before he could lie with his queen and produce an heir. It was certainly a propitious time to do so, for the monarch would be sore from his recent operation and at his most vulnerable. Dinah's lover Shechem and his brothers certainly learned this when they were assaulted three days after undergoing this very ritual, meeting their fate at the hands of Jacob's sons.[95]

The third day after the ceremony appears to have been significant, for it was then that the bedridden patient suffered the most pain as the result of his wound.[96] Thereafter, the discomfort gradually lessened until the bridegroom was able to rise again from his bed.

If the imagery recalls that of the resurrection, it is no accident.

The ritual of circumcision was closely linked with death, and its aftermath with rising again. This is why the enchantress Circe, whose very name bespeaks the procedure, served as a cemetery goddess and gatekeeper to the afterworld. It is why bloodletting symbolized death for no less a hero than Robin Hood. And it is why Osiris was portrayed as a mummy lying prone with an erect phallus, which was said to have been cut off after death in a rather extreme example of circumcision. All these tales are signs that the act of circumcision was more than a mere physical operation. On the contrary, it was an initiation of sorts into the realm of immortality, paving the way for the prince to perpetuate the bloodline by sharing the bed of his goddess wife — if, that is, he survived the tanist challenge.

A distant echo of this challenge may survive today in the traditional wedding ceremony, during which the priest or minister is bound to ask that fateful question: "If any man knows just cause why these two should not be joined in holy matrimony, let him speak now or forever hold his peace." This scene has been played out time and again in films and television dramas, where it can be counted on each time to produce an objection from some ill-fated suitor in the pews. That suitor is none other than the tanist jack, who would supplant the reigning king.

In the tale of Hercules, the hero played the part of the jack while the dragon Ladon took the role of the wise old serpent. In challenging this creature, the hero would be taking on a task that has since become deeply ingrained in popular legend. Indeed, the epic battle between knight and dragon is so familiar to modern readers that it has become little more than a caricature, a stock feature in the repertoire of storytellers for uncounted generations. It is the story of good versus evil, light versus darkness.

St. George slays the dragon.

Apollo vanquishes Python.

Horus conquers Seth.

All these are retellings of the same basic story, the tanist ritual in which the youthful king challenged the wise but aging monarch — the wizard. The wizard literally *was* the male dragon, consort of the dragon lady and ferocious stormbringer who rode forth on the clouds to meet his nemesis, the sun. This is why Merlin bore the red dragon banner and Moses carried the serpentine staff. It is also why the pharaohs of Egypt wore a headdress guarded by the uraeus, a cobra with fangs bared that stood poised to strike the enemies of the royal house.

In Hebrew tradition, sages — i.e. wise men or wizards — were known as *tannaim*, a word that originally referred to serpents. It was derived from the root *tny*, which likewise formed the basis of the name Tany, worn by the Queen of Sheba. Her name marked her as the serpent queen of dragon lady in the mold of Eve, and it is perhaps for this reason that she was depicted in legend as a maiden trapped in the branches of a tree by a fierce dragon and saved by the seven valiant heroes. This image would linger in medieval lore as that of the damsel in distress, imprisoned in the high tower and molested by an evil dragon. The tree and the tower (or *migdol*, whence Mary's title Magdalene) were one and the same, as were wizard and serpent.

Each of these elements was crucial to the tanist ritual, literally the ceremony of the serpent.

It is first seen in the Hebrew scriptures during the famous myth of Eden, which has its own queen, tree and serpent. All that seems to be missing is the hero. But there can be little doubt that Adam fills this role.

In the original tale of Eden, the wise serpent who guarded the tree of knowledge must have been slain by the upstart princeling Adam. The scribes themselves hinted at such an outcome in a declaration that inaugurated the perpetual nature of the tanist ritual from generation to generation: "I will put enmity between you and the woman, between your seed and hers. He will crush your head, and you will strike his heel."[97]

Eventually, Adam would wind up on the losing end of one such battle and be cast out of the garden — sentenced to die and blocked from reaching the tree of life by a cherub wielding a fiery sword. The imagery makes clear that the aged Adam has been replaced as *kher heb* priest and guardian of the tree by this more youthful "cherub," just as he himself had supplanted his predecessor, the wise "serpent" or wizard. And so the cycle continued. The aging king would strike at the upstart's heel, and the young warrior would deliver a death blow to his rival's head. The young prince, with his superior strength and agility, had the obvious advantage in such confrontations, but victory was by no means assured. The aging king was a formidable foe well capable of defending what was his. The hero Achilles, for example, was considered invulnerable in every part of his body save for one — the heel. It was there that his enemy's arrow found him, whereupon he perished.

It was an arrow, too, that Hercules used to slay the dragon guarding the sacred apple tree. As such, he was an archer or arker, and it was therefore fitting to find him among the crew of the *Argo* for Jason's legendary voyage. The goal of that voyage was, of course, to recover the fabled golden fleece that had been stripped from the magical ram. But what does this have to do with Hercules' quest to recover the apples? Quite a bit, it turns out.

The word for apple in Greek was *melon*, a term that gave rise to our more inclusive label for a variety of fruits. But this particular word had another meaning to the Greeks, as well.

Melon meant "sheep."[98]

This means that the golden apples and the golden fleece (which, like the apples, was guarded by a fierce dragon) were, for all intents and purposes, the very same thing. It would also seem to indicate that Hercules was a shepherd king who conquered death by becoming immortal, just as the Hyksos pharaohs of Egypt had done before him and just as "good shepherd" Jesus would do years later. He did so by partaking of the golden apples that grew on the tree of life, the very same tree that had been set in the midst of Eden and the same tree that grew on the enchanted isle of Avalon.

And just as Odin must have done in the Nordic version of the tale.

The Garden of Iduna

Like the serpent of Eden, the Norse god ascends the branches of the tree at the center of the world to guard it. This helps identify the father of the Norse pantheon as yet another Seth figure in the tradition of Merlin; in fact, he probably served as a model for the famous wizard. Like Merlin and other Seth characters, Odin was a great master of disguises. Like these others, he was considered the oldest and wisest of his generation. And like them, he was hairy. One chronicler depicted him as "an old man of great height, lacking one eye and clad in a hairy mantle." [99]

And Odin also appears to have been an ark figure. He often was depicted as riding an eight-legged steed into the underworld, an image that seems peculiar at first glance and seems to have little connection to the ark legend.

One explanation, however, serves to provide that connection. According to this interpretation, the horse in question was no horse at all, but a burial casket borne by four pallbearers. Thus, it had eight legs, two for each man carrying it.[100]

Another possibility is that the legs were not legs at all, but oars on one of the Norsemen's famed ships.

In either case, the horse in question was not really a horse, but an ark.

Odin must therefore have been dead. And if anything, the manner of his death is even more interesting than his subsequent journey to the underworld. According to legend, he died by sacrificing himself to himself, his body hanged upon the great tree and side pierced by his own divine spear.

This would seem to be the very same ceremonial death in which Jesus took part at his crucifixion, wherein he, too, was depicted as god incarnate being sacrificed to himself. Wherein he, too, hung on a tree. And wherein he, too, was pierced by a spear. The poem *Havamal* portrays Odin as describing his own death in very Christ-like terms:

I know I hung
On the windswept tree
Through nine days and nights

I was stuck with a spear
And given to Odin
Myself given to myself…

They helped me neither
With meat nor drink
I peered downward

I took up the runes
Screaming, I took them
Then fell back [101]

Odin's goal was to gain mastery over the runes, the mystical secrets of the universe. There can be little doubt that these were the very same secrets contained on the *me* tablets of ancient Sumer, the sacred emerald tablets of Thoth, the ancient tablets of Seth and the tablets Moses is said to have received upon the mountain. But if Odin sacrificed himself to gain mastery over the runes, is it not possible that Jesus had a similar motive in undergoing the crucifixion? Indeed, he appears to have hinted at a just such a purpose with one particularly enigmatic statement: "Just as Moses lifted up the snake in the desert, so the son of man must be lifted up." [102] This is an amazing disclosure. Jesus was, in no uncertain terms, identifying himself as a snake or serpent — the keeper of wisdom and the avatar of Seth.

The serpent and the tablets themselves were both symbols of

wisdom.

And both were identified closely with the figure of Moses.

Jesus must therefore have believed that, by allowing himself to be crucified, he would gain access to this wisdom and would thus be able to impart it to those who had stood by him during his quest. This was the purpose of his crusade: "The son of man must be lifted up," he is said to have declared, "that everyone who believes in him may have eternal life." [103] Once Jesus had obtained this wisdom, he believed, he would be able to impart it to his followers mystically in the form of a holy ghost. They would then be able to use it in their quest to vanquish the Roman legions, restore independence for Yahweh's chosen nation and inaugurate a heavenly kingdom on earth.

Jesus' movement was, first and foremost, a revolutionary movement dedicated to shaking off imperial Rome. This much shall become clear enough in due course. And if Jesus hoped to obtain the wisdom of heaven for military purposes, it only made sense that he should have partaken in a ritual sacrifice to a god known as the "lord of hosts."

It was, in a sense, the ultimate irony. By allowing the Roman imperialists to arrest and crucify him, Jesus was manipulating his enemies into offering a sacrifice to the god of Israel. He would become a martyr, inspiring a new generation of men to fight for his cause. But more than this, his sacrifice would rouse Yahweh to action, and the lord of hosts would hasten to avenge his death.

The hosts in question were armed warriors, whose first allegiance was to the battle god Yahweh. They were earthly soldiers sworn to his service, and they were heavenly hosts of angelic warriors called to fight the forces of evil.

This same duality existed in Norse myth, where Odin was the battle god to whom the heroes swore fealty. When these faithful warriors died, the god would call them to Valhalla, where they would be conscripted into his divine army and commissioned to defend the realm of Asgard. This great city of the gods had its counterpart in

Hebrew speculation, which envisioned a heavenly Jerusalem.

Odin, like Jesus, was the serpent lifted up in the desert — the realm of Seth.

He would gain mastery over the sacred runes, retrieve the mead (*me*) from the wicked giant and return the sacred bloodline to its proper place. The legendary portrait would be truly complete if the tree upon which he hung turned out to have been apple tree. In fact, however, it was not. The tree in question did not bear apples, or any other fruit for that matter; it was an ash tree — perhaps linked by its name to the Osirian name Asher. Be that as it may, there is a related myth in the Nordic cycle that does involve a garden, an apple tree, a giant and a guardian goddess who is deceived into parting with the apples.

The goddess' name is rendered variously as Iduna or Idun, a simple sort of maiden whose name once again recalls the archetypal goddess of the grove, Diana. It also shares a certain resonance with Eden, the name of the more famous garden from Hebrew tradition. In the Norse myth, this apple garden would most likely have been known by a similar name, as the garden of Iduna.

Iduna herself tends an apple tree in this garden, the fruit of which is so fine that it imparts eternal youth to those who partake of it. The gods make it a habit of sustaining their vigor by paying regular visits to Iduna's garden and partaking of the fruit of this "tree of life." But all this changes when a mischievous character named Loki gets involved.

Loki is yet another Seth figure whose colorful offspring include a fierce wolf, a hellish damsel and a son who takes the form of a serpent. He is also associated with a magical sword he is said to have fashioned, known as the "wounding wand" and called by the proper name *laevateinn*. The similarity between the name of the legendary serpent *lwtyn* or Leviathan and that of the mystical blade is too close to be easily dismissed. (And the sort of wound the sword inflicted can be guessed easily enough — a wound in the thigh perhaps?)

It seems just possible that the sword and Loki's serpent son were in fact one and the same.

This would have made Loki the father of Leviathan.

Also known as Lotan. Or Odin.

This conclusion may come as something of a shock considering that, in Norse mythology, Odin himself was the great patriarch of Asgard and progenitor of the gods. Yet Loki was only half god. His father was a said to have been a wind giant, and many believed that the giants belonged to a race even older than the gods. In Greek mythology, the titans who had preceded the gods of Olympians were depicted as a race of giants — the most famous of whom was the mighty old Atlas. And Zeus himself, while he was hailed as the father of the gods, was not a self-created deity. On the contrary, he was the son of the Titan Cronus, whom we have met before.

Could Loki have filled a similar role for Odin?

Certainly this would explain the close connection between these two figures, who travel together on many of their adventures. It would also solve the difficulty of Loki's place in the legends of the north, which is unique to say the least. Indeed, this strange figure has managed to defy most attempts at classification. On occasion, he acts as a benefactor; at other times, he plays the role of a mischief-making fiend.

Perhaps the most likely conclusion is that, like Cronus, he is the product a more ancient mythic cycle whose legends were incorporated into those of the new gods at Asgard. Probably his character was so popular that it could not simply be shunted aside when the new pantheon was introduced.

All of which leads to the question: Where did he come from?

His name may contain the answer. It is related to the name Lucifer, the fiery morning star who was cast down from heaven for opposing the highest god. The name literally means "light bearer." Other echoes may be heard in the name Luke and in Lug, an ancient Celtic god or hero whose name similarly meant "bright one." [104] This Lug was a leader of the Tuatha de Danaan, the legendary race that colonized Ireland from Carthage or Phoenicia. He was considered one of the three greatest figures in Irish lore, and he gave his name to the premier city in all of Britain — London, originally called Lugdunum or "stronghold of Lug." [105]

Loki bears more than a superficial resemblance to Lucifer, whose name in Hebrew was *Heylel*.

If this sounds a lot like "hell," it should.

The Book of Revelation had decreed that Lucifer or Satan would be cast down into this fiery abyss and bound with strong chords. Identifying him as "the dragon, that ancient serpent," the writer declared that an angel would seize this miscreant and place him in chains, locking him away beneath an unbreakable seal. There he was destined to stay for a millennium, at the end of which time he would have to be set free for a brief period.[106]

Amazingly, the same sort of fate awaited Loki, who would be punished for causing the death of the beloved savior-god Balder. His destiny was to be chained to three rocks until the end of time, at which point he would break free to lead an army of giants against the gods and their minions in apocalyptic battle.[107] The common thread running through the two myths is apparent, especially when one considers that Loki was the father of a goddess named Hel. And Lucifer, like the Norse god, was supposedly punished for engineering the death of a beloved savior.

In this case, Jesus.

It is also worth noting that these light bearers who fell from the sky, Lucifer and Loki, had something in common with yet another mythic figure — Prometheus. This was the legendary titan who had stolen fire from heaven and bestowed it upon mankind. He had done so, however, in defiance of Zeus, who was understandably irate to learn that his authority had been flouted so openly. In retribution, he sentenced Prometheus to be chained (like Loki) to a rock and subject to repeated torment for a millennium before he could finally be released.[108]

This tale mirrors that of Lucifer almost exactly.

- Lucifer and Prometheus both come down from heaven.
- Both are associated with brightness or fire.
- Each opposes the most high god — Yahweh in one myth, Zeus in the other.
- Both wind up in chains.
- But both are destined to be freed after a thousand years.

In fact, the only significant difference between the two tales lies in the conclusions drawn about the protagonist's character. Whereas Prometheus was celebrated as mankind's benefactor, Lucifer was cursed as a rebel against God. Perhaps these conflicting verdicts merely represented conflicting values on the part of the myth's two audiences. In Greece, the birthplace of democracy, a thief who challenged the tyranny of Zeus to deliver some great gift to the masses would have naturally been viewed as a hero. In Palestine, an ancient stronghold of theocracy, the same act would have been seen as the height of insolence against the lord of the universe.

From all this, it is quite apparent that Loki was a Seth figure. And it is therefore quite understandable that the second syllable of his name should match that of yet another Seth figure, the Sumerian god Enki. This is a tantalizing possibility, and one that appears to grow stronger as the name is dissected. The suffix *-ki* in Sumerian meant "earth," leading to the meaning of Enki's name as "master of the earth."

But what of the prefix?

Consider the possibility that, in its original form, the name in question was Luki. The prefix *lu-* means "man," so the resulting title in the Sumerian tongue would have been "man of the earth." And Lucifer was therefore Lu-ki-fer, a word that might be seen to contain the root word for the Latin *ferrum*, meaning iron. This would hardly be unexpected, considering Lucifer's association with a meteorite that fell to earth — most likely an iron meteorite. The name could therefore be construed as meaning "man of earth and iron." It is appropriate to mention here that iron, when it grows old and rusts, turns a reddish color that would seem to identify it with Seth. Hence, Lucifer's association with Seth's alter-ego, Satan.

As for the name in its abbreviated form, Loki or "man of earth" is hauntingly reminiscent of the Eden myth. There, the gods mold a man out of earthen clay and name him Adam in a supposed play on the Hebrew word for earth, *adamah*. The first man is therefore, literally, a man of the earth.

But not just any earth. Red earth.

The word *adam* in Hebrew means rosy or ruddy, a reference to the color of Seth. Adam became a Seth figure when he was exiled from the garden, just as Loki took on the role of this particular deity and likewise became exiled from the garden of the sacred apples. He found himself in this position thanks to a trick played on him by a giant, who had imprisoned him on an iceberg and refused to release him — unless he managed to lure Iduna and her apples beyond the safety of Asgard.

Faced with little alternative but to comply, Loki agreed to the giant's terms and lured the goddess to his mountain, tricking Iduna into leaving the protective confines of Asgard by challenging her to prove that her apples were truly the finest.

Her pride wounded by any suggestion to the contrary, the naïve goddess took the bait and departed for the world of men with her apples. The minute she set foot outside of Asgard, however, the giant appeared in the form of an eagle to seize her. Thereupon he flew away with her safely in his clutches, imprisoning her in a cavern at the root of a great mountain.

Once he had taken Iduna, the giant wrenched the basket of apples from her hands. But he found that when he took hold of them, they withered at his touch. It therefore dawned on him that he would never be able to enjoy their benefits until she gave them to him willingly. So he warned her that he would keep her imprisoned in his mountain until such time as she consented to offer him her apples.

Iduna steadfastly refused.

In the meantime, the gods suddenly found themselves without the means to retain their eternal youth. Deprived of Iduna's magic apples, they began to age as mortals do, with wrinkles forming on their formerly smooth faces and gray hair growing on their heads. The apples, of course, had to be retrieved. So Loki borrowed Freya's falcon suit and flew off to retrieve them (along with Iduna) from the giant's clutches. This he succeeded in doing, transforming the goddess into a sparrow and escorting her back to Asgard just ahead of the pursuing giant, who had once again taken the form of a great eagle.[109]

This tale appears to follow the theme as the tale of the mead. Once again, a giant succeeds in stealing a precious commodity with certain magical properties and hiding it in his mountain — or ziggurat/high temple. As in the mead tale, the "commodity" in question is the sacred bloodline. This is made clear enough by several clues. It is interesting, for instance, that the giant not only takes the apples but also abducts the goddess herself. Indeed, the apples appear to be worthless by themselves, their efficacy depending upon the presence of Iduna to bestow them upon the partaker.

Why should this be?

Apples have long been associated with sex and fertility. They are associated with the love goddess Aphrodite in one Greek myth, and in cross-section, they take on an appearance similar to that of the female genitalia, or vulva.[110] Iduna, as the keeper of the apples, would therefore appear to have been a sex priestess of some sort. And in fact this theory is confirmed by a passage from one of the Norse myths, in which Loki describes her as a whore for lying with her brother's killer.[111]

Here again is a portrait of the ancient harlot, the priestess of wisdom who gives her treasure to any man who will have her. It was through her that the bloodline passed, and it was therefore of little consequence with whom she mated. In Darwinian terms, it was a matter of natural selection — the fittest consort or dominant male would have her. If this meant a fight to the death between her brother (who according to Egyptian custom might also have been her husband) and a rival suitor, so be it. If it meant a giant had to kidnap her and hold her prisoner in a "mountain" until she consented to give him her apples, that was fine as well. It was all part of the game.

But the losers of this game would be the gods at Asgard, who lost their link to immortality when the sacred keeper of the bloodline was taken from them. For this reason, they began to grow old and gray, their eternal character having been stripped away from them with the taking of Iduna and her apples. Loki succeeded in restoring both the goddess and her treasure to Asgard by taking on the likeness of a falcon, the bird of Horus, indicating that a new king has arisen to take back what belongs to the gods. Iduna was returned, the bloodline was restored and the gods resumed their youthful appearance as they once again partook of the sacred apples.

Despite a few variations, the parallels between the tales of Iduna and Eden are obvious. As in the *Genesis* account, the Norse myth involves the fruit of a magical tree. And this fruit, in both tales, is said to have been imparted by a woman. Just as the "man of the earth" Adam is exiled from the garden in the Hebrew tale, so the "man of the earth" Loki is removed from Asgard (where Iduna's garden was located) against his will in the Norse myth. Iduna and her counterpart Eve are also both removed from the garden as a result of deception or trickery.

The absence of a giant in the Eden account is rectified a short time later in the Hebrew narrative, which proclaims that "the sons of the gods saw that the daughters of men were beautiful, and they married any of them they chose." The rather shocking admission of intermarriage is followed by the enigmatic statement: "The *nephilim* were on the earth in those days, and also afterward, when the sons of the gods went to the daughters of men and had children by them. These were the heroes of old, men of renown." [112]

The Hebrew word *nephilim* appears in some translations as "giants," a description confirmed by another writer who describes this race in comparison with the children of Israel. Clearly, they were men of great stature. "We saw the *nephilim* there," the writer declared. "We seemed like grasshoppers in our own eyes, and we looked the same to them." [113]

These giant heroes of old seem to be the equivalent of the titans, the older race of gods who lay with the daughters of men — just as the giant in the Norse myth seeks to lie with Iduna. These illicit relations help the Elohim make their decision to flood the earth and start from scratch with a single righteous man. Why? Because just as the giant's actions posed a direct threat to the gods in the Norse tale, so the *nephilim* placed the gods at risk in the Hebrew myth.

The mountain inhabited by the giant is merely another name for the artificial mountain or ziggurat built on the plains of Mesopotamia. Just as the giant took the mead, the apples and Iduna to his mountain, so the *me* tablets, the priestess and her sexual rituals were transferred from the mythical garden to the ziggurat temple of Inanna in Erech. This became the new Eden, a role that would later be filled in similar fashion by the temple in Jerusalem.

In the Norse myth, Iduna and her apples were taken from the realm of the gods known as Asgard and transferred to Midgard, the realm of men. The same thing appears to have occurred with the transfer of the priestess and the tablets to the ziggurat at Erech, which appears in the Hebrew texts as the famed tower of Babel. This intention of the ziggurat builders to challenge the gods is plainly stated in the text, wherein they declare their intent to "build ourselves a city, with a tower that reaches to the heavens, that we may make a name for ourselves." [114]

The clichéd nature of this phrase only serves to obscure its original meaning, which is quite important to the sense of the story. In vowing to make a name for themselves, the builders were pledging to become gods by obtaining a secret name of power by which they could rule the world. A name such as Yahweh, or the secret name of Ra, or even Rumplestiltskin. Such names were signatures of power, the strongest sort of magic.

Yahweh and the rest of the Elohim knew this all too well, and the prospect that these builders might succeed in making a name for themselves clearly alarmed them. They believed, and rightly so, that their position as lords of heaven was threatened directly by these would-be intruders: "If as one people speaking the same language, they have begun to do this, then nothing they plan will be impossible to them." [115] Including, it would seem, overthrowing the gods and setting themselves up as the masters of heaven. Yahweh therefore proposes to his fellow gods on the heavenly council: "Come, let us go down and confuse their language so they will not understand each other." [116]

Whatever the source of this myth, it is fascinating to find remnants of common language and tradition in cultures as diverse as the Sumerians, Celts, Norsemen, Germans, Greeks, Egyptians and Persians. In mythic terms, this common thread has defied the efforts of the gods themselves to sever it, for it still ties together stories that span mountains, seas and even continents. Hence the tree of life and its magic apples may be found not only in the tales of Eden and Iduna, but also in a the parallel Greek myth of Hercules and the apples of the Hesperides.

Hercules too was confronted with a giant — in this case the titan Atlas — from whom he claimed the apples for which he had come questing. Having arrived safely on the magical island and slain the dragon Ladon, the hero offered to take the world on his own shoulders (thus relieving Altas of his perpetual burden) while the giant went off to pick the sacred apples. The titan, finding himself free of his load for the first time in ages, enjoyed the feeling of freedom and wasn't about to give it up. He therefore attempted to trick Hercules by offering to take the apples personally to Greece if the hero would consent to continue supporting the world.

Hercules, however, was not fooled. He agreed, but only with the provision that Atlas take the burden back for only a moment — long enough to put a pad on his head that would ease the weight of the world. Atlas consented, only to watch helpless as the hero departed with the apples and left him standing there without any hope for a further reprieve.

Hercules went on to complete his twelfth and final labor, descending to the underworld known as Tartarus in a journey that paralleled Jesus' descent into hell. Having accomplished all he had set out to do, he returned home triumphant and married a woman named Deianeira, whose name would seem to link her with Diana.

She is not the only woman in the tale, though. The golden apples Hercules sought were not only guarded by a dragon, they were also tended by the daughters of Atlas — three nymphs known as the Hesperides or "daughters of the night." [117] This epithet identifies them clearly as priestesses of death in the mold of Circe and Lilith. And it also links them to Hesperus, the evening star that was the first to appear in the sky after sunset. Though often identified as the planet Venus, it could also have been Sirius, the brightest true star in the sky and the symbol of great goddesses ranging from Isis to Inanna.

The daughters of Atlas fit the equation pretty much as expected. But their numbers raise a question: Why were there three of them?

The land of apples was obviously the equivalent of Avalon, which was ruled by a single woman, Morgan Le Fay. The identity of Arthur's half-sister as a daughter of the night is undisputed, for she often appeared in the form of a black carrion crow — another harbinger of death. It would seem certain that she was one of the three nymphs, but if so, who were the other two?

This is not such a difficult question as it might first appear.

In early Celtic myth, Morgan was in fact the most prominent of three sisters who served as goddesses of war and death.[118] In some versions of the Arthurian myth, her name is given simply as Morgue.[119] And it seems more than plausible that name is related to the term morgue (a body's initial resting place after death) via the Latin root *mort*, meaning death. Avalon was such a place, an island ruled by Morgue or Morgan, one of the three sisters who tended the sacred apple tree of life.

This was the tree of regeneration, beneath which the priestess would lie with her royal consort and conceive the king who would succeed him. Merlin himself engaged in such a ritual with an apple queen, of which he would later exult:

> *Sweet apple tree of luxuriant growth*
> *I used to find food at its foot*
> *When, because of a maid,*
> *I slept alone in the woods of Celydonn,*
> *Shield on shoulder, sword on thigh...*
>
> *Sweet apple tree, growing by the river*
> *Who will thrive on its wondrous fruit?*
> *When my reason was intact*
> *I used to lie at its foot*
> *With a fair wanton maid of slender form* [120]

In these verses, Merlin is seen performing his function as *kher heb* priest, guarding the tree and partaking of its fruit. The river that flows nearby is the equivalent of a fountain or baptismal font, and the wanton maid is the priestess of Diana. The reference to the sword on Merlin's thigh is interesting, for it seems to confirm the phallic imagery associated with the weapon. The reference also evoking images of the pierced thigh or *morddwyd tyllion* that supposedly afflicted King Arthur as well as the young Horus. The same condition also seems to have plagued Hercules, who was wounded in the thigh during one encounter with an enemy and thereafter was known as Hercules of the Wounded Thigh.[121]

One bit of information in the passage seems at first innocuous, but upon closer inspection yields another important nugget. Merlin refers to the shield on his shoulder, a natural counterpart to the sword upon his thigh. But if the sword carries a clear symbolic meaning, might not the shield be expected to do the same?

Indeed.

The shield's position on his shoulder is crucial to interpreting the passage, which carried a hidden message. Its meaning could be deciphered if one recalled an ancient tale in the Hebrew scriptures — a tale in which this particular part of the anatomy played a crucial role. The world for "shoulder" in Hebrew was *shikmah*, from which the name Shechem was derived. This was, of course, the name given by storytellers to the besotted prince who deflowered the virgin Dinah. At the center of that story was the rite of circumcision, which Dinah's brothers demanded of Shechem in exchange for their consent to marry his beloved. Such a demand makes it clear that Shechem was, in fact, not circumcised. In other words, his male organ was still shielded by the foreskin. Once this shield was stripped away, Shechem and his countrymen were helpless against the sword-wielding brothers of Dinah. This was the allegorical point of the story.

So the shield on Shechem — the shield on the *shikmah* or shoulder — was therefore Merlin's foreskin. This fits perfectly with the archetype of the harlot priestess who in so many tales subjects the hero to a ritual bloodletting, a process that is meant to signify the act of circumcision.

One might hypothesize that this ritual was originally meant to be performed just before the priest engaged in intercourse with the menstruating virgin priestess, allowing their blood to mingle and thus ensuring the continuance of the bloodline. This was, however, supremely impractical. The severe pain that afflicted Shechem and his countrymen after they were circumcised is evidence of the difficulty with adhering to such a sequence of events. And indeed, the story of Shechem may have been intended to illustrate why it was acceptable (and eventually mandated) that a male be circumcised in infancy; the act thereby retained its symbolic efficacy while its painful side effects were alleviated.

This explains the anger of Dinah's brothers when they found she had been deflowered by an uncircumcised prince. The problem was not that they were opposed to a dynastic alliance with Shechem; in fact, this is exactly what they *wanted*. But in their eyes, such an alliance was impossible unless the blood of the two nations was allowed to mingle in the marriage bed of Dinah and Shechem — and this could only happen if the prince were circumcised.

Merlin the *kher heb* priest had to undergo the very same ritual before his blood could be mingled with the sacred priestess of the apple grove. She was doubtless a priestess of Diana, the great huntress whose name echoes hauntingly in that of the Hebrew princess Dinah.

Call her Nimue or Niniane or Vivian. Or perhaps Circe, the priestess of the circumcision. Her name might change from one tale to the next, but always the ritual was the same.

It demanded the presence of these principle elements:

- The *kher heb* priest or dragon.
- His rival, the young prince.
- The fountain.
- The maid or priestess.

This ritual formula accounts for the presence of Mary Magdalene, in the mystical form of the dove, at Jesus' baptism. Her advent completes the picture, in which John the Baptist plays the part of the wise old serpent priest (Seth) and Jesus takes the role of his young successor (Horus). The river acts as the baptismal font, and the dove is the priestess of wisdom or sophia who initiates Jesus into his new position. But this is not the end of the enactment. After his baptism, Jesus immediately withdraws into the wilderness for a contest of wills with "Satan." In point of fact, however, he is continuing the tanist process by taking part in the ancient forty-day wilderness ritual, during which the new king was tested by Seth.

The wilderness was Seth's domain.

But it was something else, as well.

It was also the domain of John the Baptist, whose numerous attributes identify him without question as a Seth figure. His coat of camel's hair. His reputation for wisdom. His prophetic voice. In light of all this, it seems likely that Jesus' opponent during this time of testing was not some incorporeal "Satan" but the decidedly flesh-and-flood figure of John the Baptist, who personified the wise old king doing battle with his young successor. It was a contest that followed the pattern of Elijah's tanist struggle with his protégé Elisha in the wilderness — a struggle that ended with Elijah departing in a fiery chariot and Elisha donning his mantle of authority, having received a double portion of his master's spirit.

John the Baptist, it will be recalled, was considered the reincarnation of Elijah. And Merlin, in turn, was the reincarnation of John.

So it was that Merlin was said to live forever, appearing in a variety of aspects over the span of time and serving as counselor to several generations of kings. In fact, Merlin must have been several different men, each of whom laid claim to the same heritage as a member of the ancient *kher heb* priesthood. In earlier times, these men appear to have been called or johns (priests who lay with temple prostitutes; today, the same term is used to describe men who solicit streetwalkers); now, they were called merlins. They were masters of disguise, changing form with each new generation but always maintaining the sacred bloodline or spirit — which they passed on to their successors.

The merlin who advised King Arthur perished like everyone else. One legend says his sister built for him an observatory equipped with seventy windows and a like number of doors, through which he might observe the stars and planets.[122]

The significance of the reference to seventy should not be missed, for this was the same number of days required for mummification — the time during which Sirius remained below the horizon. Such references make it clear that Merlin did in fact die, though his spirit was said to have lived on.

Like Jesus and Arthur, his return was inevitable — as certain as the ascension of Sirius each summer after its seventy days in the underworld. So the ancients believed. Just as the star returned from its "grave" to light the evening sky anew, Merlin too was destined to emerge once more, reborn and resurrected. With a new face, to be sure, but endowed with the same spirit of prophecy and magic that had imbued his immediate predecessor and the rest who had come before. It was said that Merlin merely retired to his *esplumoir* for a period of time, the word in question referring to a molting cage. During this interval, new feathers would replace the old, and in due time the wizard would emerge with a bright new plumage. This imagery was certainly appropriate, given his name's connection to the falcon, the bird of Horus so often associated with the dying and rising phoenix.

It would seem that Merlin was merely following the phoenix principle.

According to this legend, Merlin told his dearest friends that God had decreed he "would not be able to die before the end of the world." [123] This is an extraordinary statement, and not merely because of the fantastic nature of the claim being made. In fact, it is remarkable for another reason as well, for it identifies Merlin quite closely with one of Jesus' disciples. According to legend, Jesus spoke similar words about one of his followers in particular, based upon which "the rumor spread among the brothers that this disciple would not die." [124]

The passage leaves this disciple nameless, but tradition has long identified him as one of Jesus' closes associates. Like Merlin, he appears to have been a rainmaker, for he was nicknamed a "son of thunder."

His actual name however, is much more familiar.

It was, hardly surprisingly, John.

V

Eclipse

Jesus' mournful cry from the cross echoed from Golgotha toward Jerusalem and down through the centuries. *Eli, Eli lama sabachtani?* The fiery chariot of Elijah had abandoned him, and the sky had grown suddenly dark in the midst of the day. It was as if the sun itself had been extinguished, consumed at last by the mythical serpent Apophis that had pursued it relentlessly across the sky.

Of course, the sun would emerge from this veil of darkness — as it always did — three hours later, mirroring the three days Jesus himself would spend in the lightless realm of the tomb. And it is fairly clear to modern eyes what must have occurred at the moment of Jesus' anguished question: The sun had indeed been "swallowed up," not by the Egyptian sky serpent but by the moon.

The Egyptians were not the only ones to depict the sun being consumed by an evil serpent. The idea can also be found in South America.[125] And dragons were identified as similarly devouring the sun's nocturnal counterpart, the moon, in cultures scattered from Finland to China.[126] In these cases, of course, the phenomenon being described is a lunar eclipse, during which the earth passes between the sun and moon, casting its shadow briefly across the surface of the latter. (If one were to view such an event from the moon, one would clearly see a *solar* eclipse.)

The loss of a heavenly luminary, whether in daytime or at night, was a fearsome calamity.

What if the serpent chose not to relinquish its prey this time?

What if the world were plunged into a state of perpetual darkness?

What then?

The ancients knew they would be better off if they never discovered the answers to such questions. They therefore launched an all-out assault on the horrible creature that sought to rob them of their divine light. One tribe in Peru shot flaming arrows toward the sun in the hope of striking down the serpent that so threatened it.[127] Another widespread practice involved banging on pots and pans during a lunar eclipse, shouting and making such a commotion that the beast or spirit assailing the moon would retreat to the realm whence it came. The ancient Sumerians ritualized such practices by directing the people to raise a clamor in the event of a lunar eclipse. "A dirge for the fields you shall intone; a dirge for the streams that water shall not devastate, you shall intone," they were instructed. "Until the eclipse is past, you shall shout."[128]

In Egypt, the pharaoh was charged with warding off any threat of a solar eclipse. As the sun god Horus personified, this task fell naturally to him. And he may have had a vested interest in fulfilling it — if the sun itself were eclipsed by a dark entity, it could well have served as an omen that the pharaoh's power, likewise, was about to be eclipsed. The pharaoh, understandably, would not have been too keen on this idea. So he sought to guard against it by partaking in a ritual wherein he walked around the walls of the temple.[129]

This ceremony brings to mind Joshua's march around the walls of Jericho before they miraculously fell to the ground. Joshua was, in fact, Amenhotep Djeserkare, the son of Ahmose, who further consolidated his father's holdings in Palestine. As a pharaoh, he was simply performing the pharaonic function of manipulating the sun to his own ends by performing the expected ritual. His ability to command the sun is confirmed a short time later in the Hebrew texts, wherein he is depicted as stopping the sun in its tracks by means of a prayer.

As a result, his armies were granted sufficient time to defeat the enemy Gibeonites.

In point of fact, the sun actually *does* stand still in the sky for roughly three consecutive days each year. It reaches its nadir closest to the horizon at the winter solstice and appears in the same position for three days in a row. Likewise at the summer solstice, it reaches its apex in the heavens and stands majestic over the earth for three straight days — the longest days of the year. This was probably the point in time when Joshua defeated the Gibeonites. The long days during which the sun occupied the same position in the sky allowed him the maximum amount of sunlight by which to defeat his enemies. As the sun god manifest on earth, this "miracle" was naturally attributed to his divine power. Later chroniclers, however, took the story a bit too literally and declared that the sun had remained in the sky for a full cycle of twenty-four hours, making for a day the likes of which had not been seen before or since.

The truth of the matter was, however, that three such days occurred every year at the summer solstice. It was at this point that the sun — and therefore its royal counterpart on earth, the king — reached the height of its power.

Woman in the Moon

If the sun was seen the king's majesty, the moon was similarly equated with the glory of the queen. This was only natural, for ancients realized at an early stage that the moon's cycle of waxing and waning corresponds roughly to a woman's monthly fertility cycle. They also noted the influence of the moon upon the tides and currents of the sea, the realm so closely equated with matronly deities such as Isis.

The most famous of the moon goddesses was, not surprisingly, Diana. She was particularly associated with the harvest moon, which marked the time when the earth brought forth its plenty.[130] The connection with fertility is apparent. And whether the moon was full or in its crescent guise, this connection was maintained. Cronus, for example, used a sickle to castrate his father, whose testicles fell into the ocean and conceived the love goddess Aphrodite. What could this sickle have been but the crescent moon, its sharp arc mimicking the curve of the sickle used at harvest time? Men may harvest crops in the field and Father Time might harvest souls — both actions symbolized the cycle of death and rebirth.

And it was the moon who presided over this never-ending cycle. She was the queen of heaven whose image was reflected in the clear waters of a silver lake known as the mirror of Diana.[131] Probably, in the original version of the story, the body of water in question was Lake Tana in the highlands of Ethiopia, the mountainous reservoir through which passed the waters of the Nile.

It was this mirror into which the beloved goddess or lady of the lake must have gazed and asked that eternal question, committed to the memory of all young children long before they are sent off to kindergarten: "Mirror, mirror on the wall, who is fairest of them all?" The answer was always the same. The goddess herself was the fairest — until, that is, someone was born to replace her. Someone with skin as white as snow, lips of ruby red and hair as black as a raven's feathers.

This description, of course, is that of the beautiful maiden named Snow White, immortalized by the Brothers Grimm in their collection of faerie tales and later adapted by Walt Disney to the silver screen — a mirror of sorts in its own right. The story itself is much more than a faerie tale, however. It is, in fact, the ancient myth of Diana's counterpart and Sumerian predecessor Inanna, carefully preserved in the language of childhood.

Inanna's identity as a moon goddess is confirmed by her role as a goddess of love and fertility. Though more closely associated with the star Sirius, Inanna's name also links her with the lunar orb, for the Sumerian moon god wore the nearly identical name Nanna. And while Nanna was in this instance a male, the name surfaces in Norse mythology as that of a decidedly feminine figure. It belonged in this case to the wife of Balder, a son of Odin who had the misfortune of being pierced by a dart of mistletoe.

The wound was fatal, and his death so affected his beloved wife that she died from grief in mourning him. Indeed the entire world wept at his passing, and in doing so sought to free him from the bowels of the underworld. The keeper of the nether regions had demanded such a universal display of grief in exchange for releasing the fallen god-prince from captivity.

The effort very nearly succeeded.

But Loki, the trickster who had arranged for Balder's death in the first place (by instructing the blind god Hoder to throw the mistletoe in his direction) was not about to let Balder escape. He therefore disguised himself as a giantess and steadfastly refused to mourn his passing. This refusal was enough to consign poor Balder to the underworld in perpetuity.

One can find several parallels with the legend of Jesus' death in this tale, though the Christian hero succeeded in escaping the underworld where Balder failed.

- Jesus is pierced by a spear, Balder by a dart of mistletoe.
- Mistletoe is found hanging on trees, just as Jesus was crucified on a "tree."
- Jesus, like Balder, is the son of the most high god.
- Both figures descend to the underworld.

The story of Balder includes a scene in which his body is placed on a funeral pyre aboard his personal ship. This scene identifies him as yet another ark hero, set adrift toward the otherworld on a floating casket. It is also worth noting that Balder's name bears some resemblance to that of Baal, whose name meant simply "lord" and who — like Jesus — died and rose again. Baal was the most popular god of the Phoenicians, a whose seafaring prowess was unmatched in the ancient world, and this would certainly explain Balder's funeral aboard a ship.

But perhaps most noteworthy is the emphasis on grief and weeping in the story, specifically on the part of Balder's widow, Nanna. Her sorrow parallels once again the grief of Mary Magdalene at the death of Jesus and also recalls the presence of the weeping willow in the grove of Circe or Lilith. Most importantly, it once again reflects the grief of Isis at the death of Osiris, identifying the Egyptian goddess clearly with the figure of Nanna — and Inanna, with whom Isis has already been linked as "queen of heaven."

The echoes of this legend have proved to be enduring, with the grief-stricken widow's name having passed into the modern lexicon as a term of endearment bestowed upon older female relatives. To this day, many children call their grandmothers "Nana," thus equating them in some sense with the wise and kindly old moon.

Snow White's pale complexion identifies her likewise with the silvery moon. And her story parallels that of Inanna almost exactly.

According to legend, Inanna once attempted to conquer the underworld, which was ruled by her dark older sister Ereshkigal — just as Isis' sister Nephthys ruled the nether regions in Egyptian lore. Inanna hoped to supplant her sister on the throne of the underworld realm, and in doing so perhaps gain the power to raise the dead. Seeking to make an impression, she decked herself out in her finest clothes and jewelry, then left word with her vizier to seek help if she had not returned within three days.

This turned out to be a prudent precaution.

Upon arriving in the netherworld, the goddess was immediately put on the defensive. Instead of making an impression with her fine raiment, she was told by the gatekeeper that she would have to discard her fine apparel piece by piece as she advanced toward the throne room. Powerless to escape this humiliation, she was stripped of some article of clothing each time she passed through one of the seven gates of the netherworld, until at last she stood naked before her sister's throne. Thus humbled and completely vulnerable, she was affixed with the stare of death and hanged from a stake — crucified — inside the great hall.

Also playing a key role in this drama are the seven judges of the dead, known as the Anunnaki. They correspond in number to the seven gates of the underworld, and their name is revealing. It appears to share the same root as the Latin *annunciatus*, meaning "to announce." Their function was therefore to deliver specific proclamations, to serve as official messengers, if you will. This function reveals that they were in fact angels, a word that likewise means "messenger." They delivered the judgments of the gods and goddesses (in this case, Ereshkigal), and their word was final.

Things did not look good for Inanna, to say the least.

All was not lost, however, for her loyal vizier remembered her instructions to him and, after three days, set forth to petition the gods in her behalf. He went first to Enlil, king of the gods; but upon hearing the vizier's plea, he refused to offer any assistance. Then the vizier entreated the moon god Nanna, who likewise dismissed him empty-handed. Finally, he approached the wise Enki, who concocted a scheme whereby Inanna's evil sister would be tricked into restoring the goddess to life.

The plan worked to perfection, and Inanna's life was renewed. But she was not out of the woods yet. Unfortunately, the law decreed that she could not be freed from the realm of the netherworld unless a substitute could be found to take her place. She could only be allowed to rejoin the living temporarily — chaperoned by a group of daemonic creatures — for the purpose of seeking out such a substitute. The search led her to her husband, known variously as Dumuzi or Tammuz, the shepherd king of Uruk. As a ruler of Uruk, he was an arker. And as one destined to set forth inside the ark (or casket), it was natural that he should have been chosen as the substitute.

According to the legend, Inanna found him gazing down

haughtily from his throne, reveling in her misfortune. Understandably livid to find him behaving in such a manner, she instructed her daemonic companions to seize him as her substitute. He was able to escape temporarily by appealing to the sun god, who enabled him to slip free of his shackles by changing his body into that of a serpent. In the end, however, he was captured again and it was decreed that he should spend half of each year in the netherworld.

Because Dumuzi was a fertility figure, his fate reflected the passing of the seasons. During the fertile spring and summer, he was allowed to remain in the realm of men; but during the harsh and bitter fall and winter, he was fated to remain below the earth.

The parallels with the story of Jesus are apparent enough.

- Like Dumuzi, Jesus is "the good shepherd."
- Each is considered a king.
- Jesus is crucified, while Inanna is hanged from a stake.
- Jesus serves as a substitute for mankind; Dumuzi is a substitute for Inanna.
- Inanna and Jesus both rise again after three days in the realm of the dead.

Jesus even had a disciple named Thomas, whose name is said to have meant "twin." According to some very early traditions, he was Jesus' identical twin brother. And who better to serve as a substitute than an identical twin? Several early strands of tradition state that Jesus himself was not actually crucified, but that someone who looked exactly like him hung on the cross in his place. That someone could well have been Thomas, whose name sounds suspiciously like that of Tammuz, who served as a substitute for his consort Inanna. According to legend, Jesus likewise served as a substitute for his consort — the church (Circe), who is called the "bride of Christ."

All these overlapping traditions seem to have been used, in a somewhat confusing manner, by those telling the story of Jesus' death.

But what of Inanna?

What role did she play?

As the star Sirius, she dipped beneath the horizon and into the underworld for seven ten-day weeks each year. During this time, she was stripped of her brilliant raiment, just as the sky itself was robbed of her star's bright presence. Though the legend of Inanna is compressed into three days, her passage through the seven successive gates of the underworld indicates the passage of Sirius through the seven heavenly gates beneath the earth during its annual trek.

The seven guardians of these gates reappear in the Snow White tale as seven dwarfs. The dwarfs, like the sentinels in Inanna's tale, are creatures of the underworld. They spend their days mining for gold beneath the surface of the mountains — a vocation that identifies them as the minions of death, who work beneath the burial mounds to rob and tarnish the treasures often interred with the deceased. As in the story of Inanna, the heroine must pass through each of their stations in succession. Consider the dwarfs' reaction upon finding that she has been in their cottage:

- ➤ The first dwarf asks who has been sitting in his chair.
- ➤ The second realizes someone has been eating from his plate.
- ➤ The third comments that a portion of his loaf is missing.
- ➤ The fourth notices someone has been tasting his porridge.
- ➤ The fifth complains that his fork has been used.
- ➤ The sixth asks who has been using his knife.
- ➤ And the seventh wants to know who has been drinking from his cup.

The scene climaxes with the dwarfs revealing that someone has been sleeping, in turn, in each of their beds.[132] Like Inanna, Snow White has passed through each "gate" of the dwarfs' realm — the underworld — en route to the throne room of the temple. Like the goddess, Snow White is fated to die during her trip to this realm. And like Inanna, she is destined to be resurrected with the help of her royal consort.

Even the nature of the conflict that underlies the two stories is the same. Inanna is pitted against her dark and bitter older sister in a sibling rivalry for the throne, while Snow White finds herself targeted by a similarly dark and bitter stepmother unable to cope with her jealousy of the young girl's beauty. Her beauty, in this case, is more than skin deep. As the daughter of the true queen (who died giving birth to her), it is Snow White who is the keeper of the royal bloodline under the matrilinear system; her stepmother is an interloper of impure blood who has no hope of giving birth to the rightful heir.

Unless, that is, Snow White is out of the picture.

The proper bloodline produces unsurpassed beauty. And because Snow White's stepmother is indeed quite beautiful, she believes her position as matriarch of the royal line is secure. Just to make certain of this, she strokes her ego time and again by asking a magic mirror "who is fairest of them all?" The mirror, of course, corresponds to the glassy surface of the lake that reflects the moon for Diana, the lady of the lake and fairest goddess of them all. Each time, in the tale of Snow White, the mirror confirms the queen's unmatched beauty — until the day that Snow White passes out of childhood and becomes a young woman. On this occasion, for the first time, the response is different: "Queen, thou art of beauty rare, but Snow White living in the glen with the seven little men is a thousand times more fair." [133]

The queen, enraged at this response, determines to do away with her budding rival. She instructs a huntsman to take her out into the woods, dispose of her and cut out her heart as evidence. He is about to do so when, at the last minute, he takes pity on the young maiden and instead dispatches a wild boar that happens to be passing by. Figuring the queen will not know the difference, he cuts out the animal's heart and presents it to his mistress, who promptly cooks it up and eats it.

This vignette mirrors the ancient battle between Osiris and Seth, though this time it is the former who emerges victorious. The constellation of Orion served as the heavenly manifestation of Osiris and was universally known as the hunter; the boar, meanwhile, was a well-known symbol of Seth. By killing the boar, the huntsman takes on the role of Osiris in slaying his evil brother.

Snow White is safe for the moment.

But the evil queen is far from finished. Upon consulting her magic mirror a second time, she discovers that Snow White remains "the fairest of them all" and must therefore still be alive. No longer content to trust another with her dirty work, she disguises herself as an old merchant lady and sets out to visit the dwarfs' domicile herself. In her bag she bears a selection of silken garments, one of which she offers to Snow White. The maiden, taken by its beauty, allows the old woman to help her try it on. But the queen, maliciously, laces it up so tight that it takes her breath away and she falls down as if dead.

The picture of a corpse being wrapped tightly in linen during mummification springs to mind at once. And because Snow White is in the dwarfs' cottage — the realm of the underworld — it makes perfect sense. The dwarfs are able to revive her from her death-like state by freeing her from the wraps that bind her. But this is far from the end of the matter, for the queen is persistent and tries again: This time, she gives Snow White a poisoned comb that once again renders her as good as dead; and once again the dwarfs manage to revive her. The comb, it may be recalled, is closely associated with such figures as Guinevere and other long-haired sirens, not the least of whom is Mary Magdalene. It identifies Snow White as a lady of the lake in their mold, a mermaid or moon princess.

But again, the heroine is safe only for the moment.

The stepmother consults her mirror yet again and finds out that, once more, her plans have been thwarted. She therefore concocts her most underhanded scheme yet, creating a poisoned apple potent enough to kill whoever takes a bite from it. As before, Snow White falls prey to the woman's machinations and partakes of the apple, falling into a sleep of death from which even the dwarfs cannot rouse her. They therefore seal her in a crystal casket and carry her up a mountain, where they leave her on display for all to see.

In one version of the tale, three birds come to visit and mourn for her: the owl, the raven and the dove. Eventually, of course, a handsome prince comes along to break the spell. They wed, the evil stepmother is thwarted, and everyone (except the wicked queen) lives happily ever after.

The mountain upon which Snow White is lain to rest is the ziggurat temple of Inanna. The handsome prince who comes to visit her is the sun king. And the apple is the same fruit of which Eve partook in the garden, consigning her to the realm of mortality. The only element that seems to be missing from the story is the serpent, who is seen only in the shadowy person of Snow White's remarrying father — the old king. Snow White's identity as Lilith, the wise temple priestess of the sacred willow tree, is even confirmed by the presence of the own upon her casket.

The owl is, of course, closely associated with the moon as a creature of the night. Its wide, round eyes mimic the shape of the full moon, and its nocturnal flights are often associated with the glowing white satellite. The other two birds, likewise, may be seen as aspects of the moon.

Each of the dove's outstretched wings mirrors one-half of the moon midway through its luminary cycle, while the raven's presence signifies the darkness of a new moon.[134]

The dove is familiar as a symbol of the divine spirit and the goddess Astarte — the Phoenician counterpart of the Mesopotamian goddess Ishtar or Inanna.

Inanna, like Jesus, spent three days in the underworld. But unlike Jesus' descent, which corresponded to the three days of the sun's "death" at the winter solstice, Inanna's sojourn seems to have symbolized the nearly three days each month that the moon is dark. Recall that she arrays herself in a brilliant attire, only to cast it off piece by piece as she passes each of the seven underworld portals. In the end, she is naked, stripped of her adornments just as the full moon is stripped of its radiance gradually as it wanes each month. After three days, however, she ascends from the underworld, once again gathering her garments as she passes through each sacred gateway — in exactly the same way the waxing moon reclaims its luminescence.

But even in its fullness, the moon is not completely white. Part of its terrain appears bright and clear, whereas other portions seem muted with splotches of gray. These areas are the shadowy craters that give the moon's surface its distinct appearance of having been strewn with ashes.

Like a celestial Cinderella.

Legend of the Glass Slipper

Indeed, the Cinderella story appears to be another tale of the moon goddess reduced to the status of a children's faerie tale.

The story, like that of Snow White, begins with the death of the heroine's mother and with the father's remarriage to a wicked stepmother. This time, however, the woman arrives with two daughters to further torment the poor young maiden: "His new wife brought with her two daughters, whose features were beautiful and white but whose hearts were foul and black." [135] This description, with its blatant reference to the sisters as half-white and half-black sisters, identifies them as clearly enough as halves of the full moon.

Cinderella soon finds herself stripped of her beautiful clothes. First, her malicious sisters force her to exchange her glorious raiment for an old gray smock; then, they toss handfuls of lentils and peas into the ashes and compel her to sit there picking them out. Throughout all this, it is amazing that her father never intervenes. No explanation for this is given, but it seems unfathomable that any father worth his salt would tolerate his daughter being treated so shamefully. Perhaps the father is simply as cruel as his new wife and stepdaughters, yet the story itself — which clearly condemns the three women for their behavior — never indicts the apparently complicit father.

Why?

Perhaps because he, too, has died.

During one of his few appearances in the story, he announces that he is going into town for a fair and asks each of his three daughters what they would like him to bring back. His two stepdaughters lose no time in asking for jewels and dresses (hoping to improve their status from half-moons to full moons). But Cinderella limits herself to a single request: She wishes to have the first branch that brushes against her father's hat on the way home.

Her reasoning is simple. Even though she has been adorned in rags and relegated to picking through the ashes for peas and lentils, Cinderella remains the true full moon. Her face, like the moon, may be strewn with ashes, but — unlike her stepsisters — she has no need of grand adornment to prove her true nature. What she does need is her father's blessing, and this he provides by granting her request. When a hazel twig brushes against his cap on the way home from the fair, he breaks it off and brings it to her. She then takes it to her mother's grave and plants it there, setting the stage for it to grow into a beautiful tree.

Does this sound familiar?

Recall the shoot that arose from the stump of Jesse and the vine that grew from the bones of Osiris, whose body became encased in a tree of life. This is exactly what is happening here. It explains why the father never intervenes to rescue Cinderella from her wicked stepsisters. He cannot — until Cinderella invokes the magic of the hazel wood to resurrect him in the form of a sacred tree, united with his consort at her gravesite. It is no accident that her father brings her a twig specifically from a hazel tree, which was closely linked by the ancients with such concepts as fertility and wisdom. Wizards wielded a hazel wand, and it was from the wood of a hazel tree that Hermes (Thoth) fashioned his famous rod.[136]

The caduceus with its two serpents.

The central pole of the caduceus symbolized the tree of life, guarded by the serpent wizard and his dragon-lady consort Hawawa. In the same way, Cinderella uses the hazel twig to reunite her dead parents by planting a new tree of life. Like the willow priestesses, she waters the tree with her tears until it grows tall and strong. She visits the tree three times a day, each time being met by a little white bird — the spirit of her mother, the goddess Astarte or Inanna. And whatever she wishes for at these moments, she receives.

This ability comes in handy before long, when the king announces he is planning a great three-day festival to choose a bride for his son. He invites all the fair maidens of the kingdom to appear, dressed in their finest clothes. And of course the two stepsisters are thrilled at the prospect of winning the prince's heart. They comb their hair, put on their finest clothing and make ready to attend the festival while Cinderella bemoans the fact that she will not be allowed to go. She pleads with her stepmother to grant her permission, and the woman finally agrees to let her attend — if she can manage to pick all the peas and lentils out of the ashes in two hours' time.

This seems an impossible task, and indeed the stepmother intends it as such. But she has not counted on Cinderella's wishing tree and its guardian bird spirit, to which she appeals for help. She calls upon the birds of the sky to help her pick through the ashes, and immediately two doves appear at the windowsill. These are followed by a group of turtledoves, which in turn are followed by all the birds of the air.

The arrival of the doves is significant, for these are birds of the half-moon. As such, they symbolize the two wicked half-moon stepsisters who are subject to Cinderella as the full moon. Indeed, all the birds are subject to her. This reveals Cinderella as the future queen, to whom all the women of the kingdom will be subject when she comes into her own. With the help of these servant birds, she succeeds in meeting the deadline for completing her stepmother's "impossible" task.

Needless to say, the stepmother is flabbergasted. But despite

Cinderella's success with the task assigned her, the older woman has no intention of keeping her part of the bargain. She instead forces her to repeat the chore, this time allowing her only an hour to complete it. The scene then repeats, with the birds once more enabling Cinderella to succeed. But once again the stepmother demurs, saying that Cinderella has no clothes fit to wear to the festival. Once again, the tree of life comes to her rescue, responding to Cinderella's invocation:

> *Shake your branches*
> *Little tree*
> *Toss gold and silver*
> *Down on me* [137]

She is thereupon adorned with garments of gold and silver, along with slippers embroidered in silk. (This version of the story, told by the Brothers Grimm, does not include the famed glass slipper that is in other renderings, nor does it have the coach that turns into a pumpkin at midnight.) Cinderella then heads off for the festival, where she captivates the prince — who steadfastly refuses to dance with anyone else, declaring simply: "She is my partner." Despite his devotion to her, however, she refuses to allow him to escort her home on each of the festival's three evenings. Instead, she flees from him, finding refuge on the first night of a pigeon coop and on the second night in the boughs of a tree. On the third night, however, he coats the steps to the palace in pitch so that one of her shoes sticks and falls off. The familiar search for the shoe's owner then ensues.

Cinderella is finally found, the two are married and live happily ever after.

It is no surprise that Cinderella should come into her own during a great three-day festival, for she is the full moon — and the moon is full for roughly three days each month. Its shining raiment and the dazzling clothes Cinderella receives from the tree of life are one and the same.

Even the pumpkin in other versions of the story can be seen as the full, orange harvest moon on the horizon. But perhaps the most intriguing lunar element of the tale is the lost slipper, which identifies Cinderella as the true princess and serves as a symbol of her conjugal union with the prince. One might not immediately think of the foot or shoe as a lunar symbol, much less an emblem of fertility, but several ancient strands of tradition identify it as such. Perhaps the most common version of the tarot deck includes a trump card depicting a figure known as the high priestess standing between two pillars engraved with the letters "B" and "J." The reference to the twin pillars of Solomon's temple known as Boaz and Jachin is unmistakable. Yet perhaps even more interesting is the crescent moon symbol that appears to cover her left foot.

Even more tantalizing is a reference in *The Book of Revelation*, which describes a woman "with the moon under her feet." According to this passage, the woman is clothed with the sun and crowned with a diadem of twelve stars, imagery that identifies her clearly as the queen of heaven, a title shared by such luminaries as Mary, Isis and Inanna. She is further identified as a dragon lady, for she is associated with an "enormous red dragon with seven heads and ten horns and seven crowns" who sweeps a third of the stars from the sky with a single stroke of his tail. The woman is in labor, and the dragon stands ready to devour her child, but the son she bears is instead caught up to the throne of God.[138]

It is worth a short digression to dissect this passage. The numbers seven and ten identify the dragon as an agent of the underworld, hearkening back to the ancient tradition of Sirius' descent below the horizon. The seven heads and their crowns stand for the seven weeks, while the ten horns signify the days in the long Egyptian week. When multiplied together, the result is seventy — the exact number of days Sirius spent in the underworld each year.

By sweeping a third of the stars from the sky, the dragon was condemning them to the underworld. This represented the season of the fallow ground in Egypt, where the year was split up into three seasons instead of our customary four. The Egyptians called this season *schemu*, literally signifying deficiency.[139] It was the season of death, during which the seeds were planted and lay seemingly dormant beneath the soil (in the underworld) before sprouting to life again. The stars falling from the sky are analogous to the seed that falls to the earth, laying the foundation for a new harvest. It is probably no accident that some dying gods and goddesses were consigned to the underworld for one-third of the year. These included the god Adonis, whose name approximates the Hebrew *adonai*, meaning "lord." This title was notably applied to Jesus, who told his followers that a kernel of grain could not bear fruit unless first consigned to the earth. This saying was widely interpreted as referring to his own death.

It is no coincidence that Jesus, like the child in the vision from Revelation, was said to have been caught up to heaven. But this did not occur until he had faced down the great dragon known as Satan, or Seth. As in all tanist symbolism, the dragon in Revelation represents the old king who must do battle with the young heir apparent — in this case the son of the unnamed celestial Madonna, the woman with the moon beneath her feet.

This brings us back to the symbolism of the foot itself.

When viewed from the side, the foot appears to be a crescent shape. And its lunar connection may go even further, for the appendage comes equipped with five digits, the toes, each of which corresponds to a phase of the moon. The little toe is the new moon, which is adjacent to a slightly larger toe that represents the first quarter. This in turn is followed by a still larger "half-moon" toe and an even larger toe corresponding to the third quarter. The rounded big toe is, of course, equivalent to the full moon. The importance of the five toes to the moon priestess' identity is revealed in one version of the Cinderella tale, wherein the heroine's eldest stepsister resorts to cutting off one of her toes in an attempt to fit into the slipper.[140] This act, however, only serves to confirm her true nature — she is not the true moon princess but a pale imitation.

The five toes may also correspond to the five epagomenal, or extra, days of the year added to the Egyptian calendar. One may recall that these five days were fashioned from a portion of the moon's light, which it ceded to the god Thoth after losing a wager on a game of draughts. If the toes were in fact identified with this myth, the link would provide another connection between the foot and the moon — with which Thoth himself was often associated. And this link is strengthened by the fact that Thoth was identified in Greek myth with the messenger god Hermes, who was known for the winged sandals he wore upon his feet.

These wings were essential to Hermes' occupation as divine messenger, enabling him to traverse vast distances in the twinkling of an eye and deliver the decrees of the gods to mortal men. They made him the patron of runners, who credited him with the invention of the footrace and erected a statue in his honor at the entrance to the stadium at Olympia, site of the original Olympic games. It was here that another deity was held in high regard. She was the goddess Nike, whose name meant "victory" and who was equipped — like the sandals of Hermes — with wings. Perhaps because of this association, a successful modern shoe company took the goddess' name as its own and adopted a variation on the winged sandals of Hermes as its trademark.

Be that as it may, it is clear that the foot or shoe was a lunar symbol.

And it was apparently also a symbol of fertility.

One peculiar superstition, once observed among peasant maidens in parts of England, serves to illuminate the connection. When girls in these parts saw the first new moon of the new year, they would remove the stocking from one foot and run forward until they arrived at a stile. They would then check the space between their big toe and its neighbor with the expectation of finding a newly grown hair, which, it was said, would be the color of their fated lover's tresses.[141] This odd ritual brought together two key elements of the Cinderella story — a pervasive lunar influence and the removal of a foot covering.

The latter motif is a common one in myth and religious practice. Moses, when he was confronted with the divine presence in the form of a burning bush, was instructed in no uncertain terms: "Take off your sandals, for the place you are standing is holy ground." [142] And even today, it is customary in many cultures to remove one's shoes when entering a sacred precinct.

But why?

One possible explanation rests in the ancient belief that the earth itself was the divine mother. In touching the ground with his bare flesh, the devotee symbolically unites himself with the earth mother in an act of intimacy. This might seem simple enough, for many people make it a habit to travel barefoot over the naked earth. But in order for the act to be efficacious, it must be performed at a specific location. Not just any ground will do — it must be *holy* ground. In Moses' case, the act was accomplished at the holy mountain; in other traditions, it is undertaken in a temple sanctuary. In reality, however, there is little distinction, for the artificial mountain ziggurat was in fact the temple of the mother goddess Inanna.

As time passed, the mountain design was abandoned. But the temple itself — whether in Jerusalem, Thebes or Avaris — was still considered holy ground, site of the sacred bridal chamber. It was in such a chamber at Luxor that the god Amen, incarnate as the pharaoh, lay with the queen-priestess or "wife of god" to produce an heir. And it seems reasonable to assume that both partners removed their shoes or sandals before undertaking such a task.

Indeed, the Egyptians appear to have been well aware of the link between the shoe and fertility: One ancient ritual practiced by the Nile involved the insertion of a phallic object into a woman's shoe.[143] Apparently, the shoe was taken as a metaphor for the vagina, while the foot itself represented the penis.

This would explain an otherwise obscure precept of the Hebrew law code set forth in the book of *Deuteronomy*. The topic is the practice of levirate marriage, under which the brother-in-law of a widow was required to take her as his wife and raise up children to his deceased brother. The subject is familiar from the story of the widow Tamar, whose first husband died without leaving her offspring. His brother was then ordered to take her to wife, but he balked at the prospect of fathering children in his dead brother's behalf and spilled his semen on the ground.

The punishment for such insolence, in his case, was death. But the prescribed penalty according to *Deuteronomy* was somewhat less severe. If a man refused to take his dead brother's widow to wife, he was to appear before the village elders. They most likely would admonish him to follow the sacred code, but if he still refused, his obstinate behavior would trigger an odd ritual. The widow herself would step forward and remove one of the man's sandals, spit in his face and declare, "This is what is done to the man who will not build up his brother's family line."

From that point forward, the obstinate brother and his offspring would be branded as the "family of the unsandaled." [144]

In some respects, the ritual is straightforward. When the widow responds to her brother-in-law's stubbornness by spitting in his face, she is obviously demonstrating her contempt for his behavior. The law has been breached, and punishment must be meted out. But what about the removal of the sandal? Without the knowledge that the sandal represented the vagina, the meaning behind such an action would be obscure indeed. But once this symbolism is understood, the purpose of widow's response is readily apparent: In removing his sandal, she is in effect cursing him by removing the feminine reproductive principle from his life. Even if he does succeed in overcoming the curse and fathering children with another woman, they will be branded for life as the "family of the unsandaled" — the equivalent of illegitimate children or bastards. His bloodline will no longer be pure. The presence of the sandal signified fertility, while its absence connoted barrenness.

This has fascinating implications for a well-known statement made by John the Baptist concerning Jesus: "He is the one who comes after me, the thongs of whose sandals I am not worthy to untie." [145] In plain terms, John lacked the power to invalidate the bloodline of Jesus by removing his sandal — effectively thwarting his marriage by denying him access to the bridal chamber. On the contrary, he would confirm Jesus as the bridegroom at his baptism, an event during which the messiah was symbolically joined with the goddess spirit that descended upon him in the form of a dove. By declining to unfasten Jesus' sandal, the Baptist was blessing the fertility of this union. The sandal or shoe was the key.

And so it was in other traditions, as well.

A familiar nursery rhyme refers to an old woman who lived in a shoe, who had so many children she didn't know what to do. Her residence in a shoe seems comical until one realizes the symbolic nature of the verse, which links her unorthodox domicile to her abundance of offspring. In a related tradition, Irish clans made it their practice to toss a woman's shoe over the head of their new leader in celebration of his symbolic union with the earth goddess.[146]

Here is yet another manifestation of Cinderella's glass slipper, a pervasive element in several versions of the faerie tale. It seems an oddity at first, but the smooth, clear glass serves as an effective contrast to the foggy, sooty ashes to which Cinderella had been consigned. One explanation is that the slippers were originally fur slippers, but through a mistranslation, they were transformed into glass. This is based on the idea that the Old French word for fur, *vair*, sounds almost identical to the word for glass, *verre*.[147] This fails to explain the presence of glass slippers in other, non-French versions of the story, but it does raise intriguing connections to a pair of other, much older stories.

One involves the legend of Veronica, whose veil Jesus supposedly used to wipe his face as he went forth to be crucified. Though the story is not contained in any canonical text, it was so popular that it became an accepted element in the story of Jesus' crucifixion.

The name Veronica is an interesting one. The prefix sounds an awful lot like both *verre* and *vair*, which is interesting in itself. But its ultimate origin is the Greek prefix *phero* — a word pronounced exactly like the title of the Egyptian king. The suffix has been linked with the Greek word *ikon*, meaning "image," probably because of the legend that the woman's veil came to bear Jesus' likeness after he wiped his face with it. This explanation, however, probably owes more to the cult of sacred relics than it does to the study of linguistics, which reveals that the suffix actually stems from the Greek word *nike*, meaning "victory."

This is, of course, the same name worn by the Greek goddess whose wings seem to have adorned the shoes of Hermes. And it leads to the intriguing possibility that the woman's name meant "victory of the pharaoh." If so, it was likely a nickname meant to illustrate Jesus' impending victory on the cross as the true messiah of Israel, the keeper of a tradition that stemmed back to the pharaohs of ancient Egypt — pharaohs such as Solomon Apophis, who plays a key role in the second legend related to the tale of the glass slipper.

This is the Hebrew legend that tells of King Solomon's first meeting with the Queen of Sheba.

According to this legend, the king received word of her from a bird known as the hoopoe, which had embarked on a journey all over the world to "see whether there is a domain anywhere which is not subject to the lord my king." [148] This trip brought him to the Queen of Sheba's domain, which indeed was not subject to Solomon. It is interesting to note that, in this tale, the queen's realm lies to the east rather than to the south as one might expect. She was, after all, the Queen of the South and appears to have ruled from Ethiopia.

As noted previously, however, the Ethiopians were said to have also ruled over the lands to the east. And indeed, several Mesopotamian legends that refer to a certain Queen of the East, a title that doubled as the woman's name in Sumerian: Ninshubur. The prefix *nin* refers to a queen or lady, while the suffix *shubur* was a proper name indicating a land to the east. It would therefore have been natural to translate the prefix, but leave the suffix intact, forming the title Queen of Shubur.

The resemblance to the familiar title Queen of Sheba needs no elucidation.

This queen is introduced into the Sumerian texts as the servant girl or priestess of Inanna. The eastern realm over which she ruled seems to have been India, which was in fact to the east of ancient Sumer. The pantheon of this faraway land was headed by a peculiar deity named Shiva, a name that once again bears a close resemblance to that of the famous queen. According to tradition, Shiva was an androgynous deity known as the "great black one" — recalling the symbolism of the black queen from Ethiopia who became the lover of King Solomon.[149] The native populations of both India and Ethiopia are known for their black skins, and it is perhaps for this reason that the ancients seemed to believe the two were in fact different regions of *the same kingdom*. The Roman poet Virgil had boldly (and erroneously) stated that the Nile's headwaters could be found in India.[150] And the confusion over the extent of the Indian realm persisted for quite some time after that, culminating in the absurd decision to name a group of islands in the Caribbean the West Indies and label the inhabitants of the entire Western Hemisphere as Indians.

In light of all this, it seems entirely possible that the Queen of Sheba might have been credited with ruling "India" from Saba — the capital of the land now known as Ethiopia. This would explain quite nicely how she could have worn the dual titles Queen of the South and Queen of the East.

It is no wonder her realm was said to have rivaled that of King Solomon. And quite a fabulous realm it was, according to the legend of their meeting. Solomon's messenger bird reported that its people worshipped the great solar orb, and that they wore garlands that had been picked in paradise. Indeed, the trees of the land had been planted at the beginning of time, their roots still drinking in water that flowed from the garden of Eden. Upon presenting this news to Solomon, the hoopoe proposed to take a contingent of birds on a second journey to this mysterious land, bearing a message that would summon the Queen of Sheba to appear before the king.

Solomon approved of this plan, and the birds took flight. Before long, they had arrived at their destination, their wings darkening the sun at the very time the queen went forth to worship its golden rays. When the hoopoe landed nearby, she noticed that a message was attached to its wing. She therefore opened it and read the summons Solomon had written. It was clear that she had little choice but to obey: Solomon was a mighty king with huge armies at his disposal, but the queen's people were peace-loving and had no knowledge of weapons.

She therefore set forth in a great caravan, arriving to find the king holding court in a house of glass. This peculiar sight confused the queen, who assumed that Solomon was sitting in water. She therefore raised her robe in an attempt to keep it from getting wet — revealing a coating of hair on her bare foot and eliciting this comment from the startled king:

"Thy beauty is the beauty of a woman, but thy hair is masculine; hair is an ornament for a man, but it disfigures a woman." [151]

This statement once again links the queen with the androgynous Indian deity known as Shiva, for it identifies Sheba as part man and part woman. But the most incredible aspect of the imagery is its similarity to that employed in the tale of Cinderella. Here, incredibly, are both the fur and the glass associated with the heroine of our faerie tale. (The fur also recalls the hair expected to grow between the English peasant girls' toes at the year's first new moon.)

The references to Eden further link the tale of Solomon with the faerie tale, which contains such clear paradisiacal symbolism. And that is not to mention the massive flock of birds that descends upon the Queen of Sheba in much the same way that all the birds of creation descend to help Cinderella. In the Hebrew legend, the birds come to summon the queen to a meeting with the great King Solomon; in the faerie tale, they prepare Cinderella for a meeting with the king and his son, the prince.

Why was the queen's realm the only one not subject to the king?

Perhaps because Solomon was the sun king, the Egyptian incarnation of the sun falcon Horus. Yet the sun does not rule over the night — that is the domain of the moon goddess. The Queen of Sheba, in this story, is just such a figure. Yet though she rules the night, she is aware that her brilliance is no match for that of the sun. This is why she and her people are depicted as worshipping the sun; it is also why she so readily assents to Solomon's summons. As the sun king, he is the rightful representative of the golden disk on earth. And she is therefore subject to him.

Still another connection between Cinderella and the fabled queen can be found in the story of the dragon and the seven heroes — in which the queen is trapped in a tree by the terrible beast and subsequently freed by the noble knights. When the heroes kill the dragon, however, its blood spatters on her foot and transforms it into a donkey's hoof. This is all quite fascinating when one considers that Cinderella, too, hid in a tree during her tale. And that, whereas the Queen of Sheba lost a foot, Cinderella lost one of her magic slippers.

This odd hoof further identifies the queen as a moon figure. Anyone who has ever looked at the underside of a horse's or donkey's hoof will attest that its appearance is something like two half-moons with a cleft in the center. The hoof, actually a huge, thick toenail of sorts, serves a convenient purpose for animals so equipped: It protects them quite effectively from poisonous ground snakes. Any serpent that strikes a hooved animal in that part of its body will succeed only in blunting its teeth against the hard surface.

One woman was immune to the bite of the serpent, the only creature that she herself had created.

Isis.

The original "black virgin" and counterpart of Inanna.

She was black because she was mourning for her dead husband Osiris, weeping for him just as Cinderella wept at the grave of her mother to water the magic hazel tree. And it was traditional in many places across the Near East and elsewhere to heap ashes on one's head while in mourning.[152] The Hebrew custom of showing sorrow or penitence by donning "sackcloth and ashes" is well known and documented at several points in Hebrew scripture. This is where Cinderella comes in. Since she had access to the magic wishing tree, she could have certainly wished for a fine array of clothing immediately. Yet she did not. She waited. In part, this is because she was waiting for her season — the three days of the full moon at the festival. But in part it was also because she was still in mourning for her mother (and, it seems, her father, who appears only briefly later in the story).

She therefore remained covered in ashes.

In this state, Cinderella is therefore a black virgin in the tradition of Isis and the Ethiopian Queen of Sheba.

She is the moon goddess betrothed to the sun god incarnate — the handsome prince — following in the footsteps of the moon queen of Sheba and the sun king Solomon. This marriage of the two mortals on earth reflected an even greater union in heaven, that of the sun and the moon themselves in a celestial ceremony. And what could that ceremony have been but a solar eclipse?

During such an event, the moon passes gradually in front of the sun. Because the moon's orbit is elliptical rather than circular, its distance from the earth at any given point can vary by slightly more than thirty-one thousand miles.[153] During some solar eclipses, when the moon is relatively close to the earth, the sun can be completely obscured. When the moon is farther away, however, it can leave a ring of the sun's outer edge visible behind it (though looking directly at such an event can cause blindness). Even when the moon is closer to the earth, a golden glow is visible surrounding it, giving the impression of a golden ring.

Such as the golden ring given during a marriage ceremony. It seems just possible that the solar eclipse is the heavenly model for the earthly tradition of slipping a ring on the new bride's finger.

Even more intriguing, though, is the so-called "diamond ring effect" that occurs at the very last moment before the moon completely covers the sun in a total eclipse. This effect is a flash of brilliance caused by the last bit of the sun's light as it escapes through a lowland valley on the moon's horizon.[154] In the same way, a diamond ring is traditionally given upon engagement — the last step before marriage. The diamond ring is therefore an obvious symbol of the eclipse.

And so is the ceremony of circumcision, which in ancient times was performed just prior to marriage. The ring was the circle cut around the sex organs of both the male and female partners, the ritual cutting off of the serpent's head. This connection is preserved in a Celtic faerie tale called "The Sea-Maiden," in which a hero identified as a fisher's son — and therefore heir to the throne of a Fisher King — went forth to do battle with a three-headed sea serpent. His objective was to save a dairymaid fated to be sacrificed to the creature, a job that had been assigned to a certain famous general who was too scared to complete the task.

Each time the fisher's son cut off one head of the beast, the dairymaid would reward him with a ring — first a golden band, then on the next two occasions, one of her earrings. The general, who tried to take credit for these feats, was exposed as a fraud, and the fisher's son eventually married the former damsel in distress.[155]

This tale contains several key elements of the circumcision and eclipse lore: the golden rings, the serpent, the rescue of a lady from dire straits and her sacred marriage to the hero. The hero cuts off the serpent's three heads just as Enkidu severed the head of Hawawa (a.k.a. Eve) in the Sumerian tale. The connection between this act and the maiden is made apparent when she rewards the fisher's son with her rings. Instead of the single head of Hawawa, though, this particular serpent has three heads. Why should this be?

Again, the answer can be found in the three days of the full moon, which is an important symbol in the Cinderella tale as well. This symbol is confirmed by the damsel's vocation as a dairymaid, a woman who milks cows. Perhaps no animal is so closely associated with the moon as the cow, which is even depicted as jumping over it in one popular nursery rhyme. The cow's horns can be observed mirrored in the crescent moon, and its milk is the color of the pale white orb.

It was widely believed that weddings should take place during a full moon because the lunar body's "pregnant" state was considered a positive omen of motherhood. And the cow's udders, perpetually full of milk, further marked it as a totemic symbol of this condition. The Greeks were among those who performed wedding ceremonies during the full moon, while maidens in Scotland refused to schedule such events at any other time.[156] The harvest moon, which seems to have given rise to the image of Cinderella's carriage turning into a pumpkin, was particularly seen as a time of fertility associated with marriage.[157]

The circle, as manifest in both the solar and lunar bodies, was a symbol of perfection and eternity to the ancients that remains unmatched to this day. It was the ancient serpent swallowing its own tail in perpetuity, ringing the oceans of the world in Norse myth with its body and thus defining the limits of existence. It seems possible, considering her name, that Circe herself was originally such a serpent lady, a cosmic circle like the great self-devouring snake. Certainly the primordial Babylonian water goddess Tiamat qualifies as such, having originated as a divine sea serpent and mother of the gods. Eventually, she would find herself at the center of a conflict between the old gods and the younger generation — a conflict that would result in her death. When she was slain, her body was divided in two, half of it used to create the earth and the other half becoming the vault of heaven.[158] The dividing line was the horizon.

The ancients viewed the heavens as a half-circle and judged that the earth beneath their feet must somehow mirror this geometry. The division of Tiamat therefore formed a line (the horizon) cutting midway across this massive circle of heaven and earth, with half of the great serpent's body above this line and the other half relegated to the nether regions. All of this was quite fanciful, but it didn't stop the goddess' name from being immortalized by those down-to-earth scholars known as mathematicians. From the name Tiamat they constructed the concept of the diameter, a line of separation between the two halves of the serpent goddess' circular body.

Despite her death, however, Tiamat would be resurrected, after a fashion, in the form of the Greek goddess Demeter. The similarities between the two figures do not stop with their names, for Demeter's titles included "mistress of the sea" and her symbolism includes a circle bisected by a single horizontal line.[159] Without beginning or end, this sacred circle stood as a symbol of the eternal cycle of birth, death and rebirth that has continued without interruption since the beginning of time. It was the unbroken bloodline, continuing infinitely like the magical number pi — the ration of the figure's circumference to its diameter.

Protection.

Eternal life.

Renewal.

A worthy symbol for the fabled phoenix itself, which like Cinderella, succeeded in rising from the ashes.

VI

The Idumean

    The man who would become known to history as Herod the Great rose to power through a combination of military prowess, shrewd political maneuvering and sheer blind luck.

    The process that culminated in his appointment by the Romans as their client king in Judea began with the ambitions of his father, Antipater.

    A nobleman from Idumea — the Greek name for the ancient kingdom of Edom — Antipater thrust himself onto the political stage in time-honored fashion, marrying a woman of royal (or at the very least noble) blood. The woman in question was an Arabian lady from the kingdom of Nabataea to the south, and Antipater's marriage to her seems to have helped cement an alliance of sorts between the two nations. Unfortunately for Antipater, it was an alliance that put him in the rather unenviable position of being at odds with Rome.

    In order to determine how this came about, we must return to the period immediately following the death of Honi the Circle-Drawer.

    When civil war had broken out between Hyrcanus and Aristobulus, the two brothers of the ruling Hasmonean clan who vied with one another for the throne, each had appealed to Rome for support. They both seem to have realized that the backing of such a formidable power could prove decisive, but neither appears to have grasped the implications of allowing the Romans to mediate their dispute. The king is ever subservient on the kingmaker, and by offering the latter role to the Romans, the two rival claimants were in effect acknowledging their dependence on Roman arms. It was a risky game to play, but each of the two brothers was more intent on defeating the other than on preserving the nation's hard-won independence.

Each had assembled constituencies of supporters for his cause. Aristobulus had gained the backing of the populist Pharisaic party, while Hyrcanus had forged an alliance with the Nabataeans. This is where Antipater came in. As an Idumean aristocrat with ties to the Nabataean nobility, he may well have been instrumental in that country's decision to side with Hyrcanus ... and this would have been all well and good — if the Romans had made the same decision.

As it happened, however, they did not.

The Roman general Pompey had embarked on a campaign that would lead to a series of decisive victories at the eastern edge of the empire. He was now in the process of consolidating power for himself in the region, and this involved, among other things, subduing the upstart kingdom of Armenia. While he was thus engaged, Pompey appointed a certain Scaurus as governor of Syria. And Scaurus made it his first order of business to visit Jerusalem and assess the unstable situation there.

This was just what Hyrcanus and Aristobulus had both been waiting for. Upon the Syrian governor's arrival, they both sought and received audiences with him.

The two brothers each came well prepared to make their respective cases, which in Roman terms meant they were amply endowed with riches to offer as bribes in exchange for imperial favor. Their gifts were in fact roughly equal at about four hundred talents apiece, but for some reason Scaurus favored Aristobulus. The first century Jewish historian Josephus explains that this was because Aristobulus "was rich and had a great soul, and desired to obtain nothing but what was moderate; whereas the other (Hyrcanus) was poor and tenacious, and made incredible promises in hope of greater advantages." [160]

Whatever Scaurus' reasons for favoring Aristobulus, the implications of his decision were immediate and far-reaching. He ordered Aretas, the Nabataean king who had supported Hyrcanus, to leave the city or be declared an enemy of Rome. He then returned to Damascus, leaving Aristobulus in command of a great army that he used to rout the forces of Hyrcanus. According to Josephus, some six thousand men loyal to the elder Hasmonean claimant were slain in battle — a high price to pay for Hyrcanus' failure as a diplomat.

Antipater paid the price as well: his brother Phalion was among the dead.

The Idumean, normally a shrewd politician, had made a major miscalculation in backing Hyrcanus. But as so often seemed to happen with the Herodian clan, he was able to right himself on the strength of uncommonly good fortune. In this case, that good fortune involved an even greater misstep on the part of Aristobulus, who let his ego get the better of him at the very moment he seemed on the verge of gaining the prize he had so coveted.

Pompey's return to Damascus following his successful campaign in Armenia presented Aristobulus with the chance to cement his claim to the throne and Hyrcanus with one last opportunity to reverse the tide.

Upon learning of the general's return, the two brothers wasted no time in organizing formal delegations and traveling at their head to meet him. Pompey, however, was in no hurry to render judgment. He was, in fact, quite content to bide his time, perhaps reasoning that a delay might help him determine something more about the character of these two rivals. In the meantime, he would launch a campaign against the Nabataean king Aretas, the ally of Hyrcanus and Antipater.

Such a campaign would certainly have put Hyrcanus' loyalty to the test. If he truly honored Rome, the elder Hasmonean would refrain from intervening on behalf of his longtime Arabian ally. Yet surprisingly, it was not Hyrcanus but Aristobulus who failed the test. The reason for his failure is by no means clear, but there is room for conjecture. Certainly the postponement gave Aristobulus time to do some thinking, and during that time he may well have begun to grasp the ramifications of his appeal to Pompey. Perhaps it dawned on him that, by putting the decision in the general's hands, he was very likely conceding the royal authority he so greatly coveted. Ultimately, Pompey would be the only winner in this bitter conflict between brothers, neither of whom could now hope for anything better than to serve as a vassal to Rome.

But Aristobulus did hope for better. And it was based upon these hopes that he withdrew from Damascus abruptly — before Pompey had given him leave to do so — taking his men with him and finding refuge in a mountain fortress known as the Alexandrion in the Jordan valley.

Needless to say, this did not go over well with the general, who put his Nabataean campaign on hold and diverted his troops to deal with Aristobulus. The latter subsequently withdrew to Jerusalem — where he began whipping up nationalist sentiment against the Romans — with Pompey in hot pursuit. This, Hyrcanus realized, was the opportunity he had been waiting for. He knew that even if Aristobulus succeeded in gaining substantial support inside Jerusalem, the city could only withstand a Roman siege for so long. Its defeat was already inevitable, but if Hyrcanus could be seen helping to expedite that defeat, he would gain favor with Pompey and thus assure himself of the succession. He therefore had his men throw open the gates of Jerusalem to the Romans, who took the city after a three-month siege.

Pompey himself entered the inner chamber of the temple, an act of sacrilege that he sought to remedy the following day by having the sanctuary ritually purified.

In the end, Pompey had Aristobulus carted off to Rome and rewarded Hyrcanus by confirming him as high priest. Notably, however, the general refused to recognize him as successor to the throne, for all intents and purposes leaving the position vacant until such time as someone more suitable should step forward to claim it. That someone, it just so happened, would be named Herod.

The Rise of Herod

Hyrcanus' failure would be Antipater's opportunity. Despite his earlier miscalculation, the Idumean now found himself on the winning side of the Hasmonean family quarrel and in a position to enhance his status as a result. It soon became clear that he was the power behind the relatively weak Hyrcanus, and it was not long before the Romans were dealing with him directly. At one point, he assembled an army to march alongside the Syrian governor on a Roman expedition into Egypt. During this campaign, incidentally, the company stopped at the Jewish temple at Leontopolis where Antipater persuaded the garrison to let the invading force pass unmolested into the Egyptian heartland.

Eventually, Antipater was appointed procurator of Judea, becoming the first man to hold that position under Roman imperial influence. And he used his power to appoint two of his sons to important posts as well. The elder, Phasael, was placed in charge of Jerusalem and the region surrounding it, while Herod was given charge of the fertile lands to the north known as Galilee.

Over the next few years, Herod would use his political skill to expand his base, currying favor with a series of Roman generals who appeared intent upon assassinating one another. Often he found himself on the wrong side of these power struggles, but each time he somehow managed to persuade the victor that he was more valuable as an ally than as a corpse. It was this uncanny ability to ingratiate himself with whoever happened to be in power that won him the favor, in succession, of Julius Caesar, Mark Antony and finally

Octavian — the man who would establish imperial rule under the title Augustus. Yet this ability somehow never translated to the people at large, many of whom still supported the deposed Hasmonean dynasty and looked with suspicion on the new king's Idumean background. He was not, they whispered, a real Jew. He was a foreigner. And the law of Moses specifically forbade a foreigner to rule over them. The task before Herod was, therefore, a formidable one: Somehow, he had to convince his subjects that he was not only a loyal supporter of Yahweh's cult, but also that he was worthy of being counted as an ethnic Jew.

Both these objectives would be difficult — and ultimately, impossible — to reach, though for vastly different reasons. On the surface, it was simple enough for Herod to bolster the cult of Yahweh. He was, after all, a rich man and could afford to give extravagantly to promote the mode of worship that had been accepted practice since the days of the Persian Empire. Most visibly, he did so by embarking on one of the most extensive (and expensive) building projects ever undertaken, vowing to rebuild the magnificent Temple of Solomon on a far grander scale than its original builders could have ever envisioned. The project was of such immense proportion that it was not finally completed until decades after Herod's death, and only a few short years before its ultimate destruction.

Such an act of piety and devotion should have earned Herod great popularity among the masses, and perhaps it would have — if it had been the only great temple project Herod undertook. But the Hebrew religion was an exclusive one, inextricably tied to a warlike and "jealous" deity who was a symbol of Jewish national pride and integrity. He demanded exclusive devotion, and that was one thing Herod could not offer. He had other considerations to address, such as his political patrons and the need to honor them — and their gods — with similarly magnificent gifts.

In Rhodes, he financed the construction of a temple to the Greek sun god Apollo entirely out of his personal funds.[161] He built the city of Sebaste in Samaria and dedicated it to the emperor, then celebrated with lavish games during which contestants competed naked in Greek fashion. Such behavior was eerily reminiscent of the programs sponsored by the third Antiochus, a Greek who had ruled Judea before the days of the Hasmoneans, and who had compelled his Jewish subjects to take part in such activities as part of his attempt to integrate them into his Seleucid Empire. While no one was compelling anybody to participate this time around, Herod's sponsorship of such "pagan" events reopened old wounds that had never been allowed to fully heal. His were hardly the actions of a strict monotheist, but Herod knew that such compromises were necessary to curry favor with those he needed as his allies. He was the classic middle manager, squeezed between his patrons on the one hand and his subjects on the other.

Herod shared at least one trait with Antiochus — an appreciation for what a well-placed bribe or "gift" could accomplish. Whereas the Seleucid emperor had most often been on the receiving end of such exchanges, Herod was more frequently the bestower of gifts. But this hardly made him any more popular, as it was constantly necessary that he replenish the treasury he used to so generously endow his friends and supporters. This meant taxation.

And taxes are seldom popular.

Not only did Herod alienate the pious by offering gifts to foreign gods, he incurred even greater resentment by taxing his subjects to pay for them. In light of this, even his ambitious temple project was not enough to tip the scales of public opinion in his favor. Not nearly enough. While Herod was making friends and gaining influence among the imperial nobility, he was fast accumulating enemies among the people at large.

And, predictably, those enemies were gathering around that once-powerful family of deposed rulers.

The Hasmoneans.

Crushing the Opposition

Herod was quick to recognize that his greatest threat lay in the remnants of the "legitimate" Jewish government he had supplanted. These were the Hasmoneans, descendants of the family that had risen up to fight for — and gain — Israel's independence a century before. Hyrcanus, who had effectively surrendered that independence by appealing to Rome in his civil war with his brother Aristobulus, had been the last of these to claim the throne.

But though the Hasmoneans were no longer kings, they continued to hold one advantage that would vex Herod through much of his reign: As members of Israel's priestly caste, they could assume the office of high priest, a position to which Herod himself could not aspire because of his Idumean blood. And for this reason, they continued to wield significant clout — especially with the masses.

For centuries, the priesthood had occupied a pre-eminent role in Jewish life. The high priest, who alone was permitted to enter the innermost sanctuary in the temple, held a position of honor rivaling (and at times surpassing) that of the king. It was an arrangement that dated back at least a thousand years to the reign of David, who had shared power with a priest named Zadok. This legendary figure, whose name literally translates as "The Just," would become in many ways a prototype for his successors, the high priests.

In the generations that followed, the arrangement between David and Zadok would develop into a dual system of authority. The royal line would govern the nation's secular affairs, while the priestly line would oversee religious matters — at least in theory. This was in keeping with the ancient model of the sacred grove, in which the *kher heb* guardian of the tree served as high priest and senior ruler, while his heir apparent and tanist rival served as prince.

The system had been thrown into considerable disarray when first the Babylonians and then the Assyrians had conquered and occupied Palestine, cutting off the royal line of princes but leaving the high priesthood intact — stripping it of its political significance and redefining it, insofar as was possible, in strictly religious terms. Prophets spoke of a day when the kingdom would be restored under a member of the traditional royal line — a new "shoot" born from the long-dead "stump" of David's father Jesse [162] — but the fulfillment was a long time coming. And in the meantime, the priesthood was left as the only native bastion of power in all of Israel.

It was through the priesthood that the Hasmoneans had risen to power, their leaders winning independence for Israel and eventually assuming the office of high priest. In the decades to follow, they had consolidated power by naming themselves as kings as well, thereby restoring the power inherent in the position under the ancient model while at the same time placing the nation's two most powerful titles in the hands of a single family.

Herod, however, did not have the same option — as an Idumean, he could never hope to hold the office of high priest himself. Yet he could take action to ensure that his deposed rivals would not. And it was to this end that he embarked on a long-term strategy to neutralize them once and for all by usurping their position in the most fundamental way possible.

Herod himself would become the titular head of the Hasmonean clan.

He began laying the groundwork for this strategy a full three years before he was even named king. Even then, as governor of Galilee, there can be little doubt that the ambitious young man had his eye on the prize — and that he knew what it would take to obtain it. For one thing, he seems to have recognized the ancient principle of matrilinear succession. He must have known that, according to tradition, the bloodline was passed on through a sacred princess. If, therefore, he could marry a such a woman from the Hasmonean clan, he would be able to secure for himself the role of clan patriarch — and for his children indisputable royal status should he succeed in ascending the throne. A trifling obstacle stood in his way in the form of his first marriage, to a woman named Doris, but this was handled in expeditious fashion with a divorce that paved the way for his betrothal to the Hasmonean maiden. She was a granddaughter of the high priest Hyrcanus, who had retained that position for more than two decades since being confirmed by the now-deceased general Pompey. Her name, interestingly enough, was Mariamne, a Hebraized form of the revered title of the ancient Egyptian "wives of god" Mery-Amen. Indeed, though this may have been her actual name, it might just as easily have been a title adopted to signify her status in relation to Herod as mother of his divine children.

Once he had arranged this strategic marital alliance with the Hasmoneans, the only person standing in the way of Herod claiming the coveted status of family patriarch was Hyrcanus. And he was conveniently removed from the picture with help from an unlikely quarter. This came in the person of Antigonus, the son of Hyrcanus' disgraced brother Aristobulus. He, like Herod, had an appetite for power, but he sought it from a different source. Whereas Herod had courted the Romans as his patrons, Antigonus turned to their emerging rivals in the east, the Parthians, who had arisen from the ashes of the old Persian Empire.

For a time, it seemed to be a shrewd decision.

The ambitious Roman general Marc Antony, who had planned an expedition against the Parthians, was momentarily distracted from the task at hand by the seductive Egyptian queen Cleopatra, who had brought him to Alexandria. At the time, this might have seemed like only a temporary postponement for the libidinous general, who must have thought he had sufficient time to deal with the Parthians. Indeed, he might have gone ahead with his planned eastern campaign had he not received word from Italy that his forces there had been expelled by his rival Octavian (later to reign as Rome's first emperor under the title Augustus).

Under these circumstances, it was clear that Parthia would have to wait. Antony abruptly quit the east and headed for Rome, where he hoped to — and eventually did — make peace with Octavian. His absence, however, created a vacuum that the Parthians were all too eager to fill. Their troops rushed in to plunder Jerusalem and the surrounding region, barely allowing Herod enough time to flee for his life. Hyrcanus, however, was not so fortunate. He was taken prisoner by the Parthians and handed over to his nephew Antigonus, who "welcomed" his uncle by slicing off both of the poor man's ears. This had the effect of rendering Hyrcanus physically imperfect and therefore ineligible to continue his duties as high priest. Having thereby eliminated the competition, Antigonus seized the post for himself and had the Parthians crown him king for good measure.

The Romans were not about to recognize him as such, but they were in no position to contest the matter until Antony and Octavian could resolve their differences and turn their attention once again to the eastern frontier.

It was only a matter of time before they would do so.

And when they did in fact reaffirm their alliance, Herod was the natural beneficiary. The disfigured Hyrcanus was no longer an option, and Antigonus had aligned himself with the enemy — all of which left Herod as the most obvious candidate to look after Rome's interests in the region.

Having fled Jerusalem in the face of the Parthian onslaught, the Idumean eventually made his way to the capital, where Octavian and Antony together offered him the throne. He of course accepted, though it was by no means as simple as that. With Antigonus and the Parthians firmly in possession of Jerusalem, Herod would be king in name only unless and until he could recapture the seat of his power. Though a formidable task, he now had the full support of a Roman force no longer distracted by internal squabbles. And this made all the difference. Within three years, he and his armies had defeated the Parthian forces and Antigonus had been turned over to Antony to be executed.

On the eve of his victory, Herod finally wed the princess Mariamne, to whom he had been engaged for several years. Mariamne's tender age had kept them from finalizing their compact before this, for she had not yet entered puberty at the time of their betrothal. Now, however, the time seemed perfect for the couple to be celebrate their union. Indeed, it was a time of celebration all around. In a matter of months, Herod had recaptured Jerusalem. And the following year, Hyrcanus was released from his captivity in Parthia and returned to the city.

The situation had changed drastically during the old man's absence.

Hyrcanus' mutilation had disqualified him from serving as high priest, creating a vacancy in the position that had to be filled. And creating an opportunity for Herod. This, he believed, was his chance to seize the last vestiges of power from the Hasmoneans and cement his status as undisputed ruler of Judea. He therefore submitted his own candidate for the post, choosing a Babylonian priest in a stroke of symbolism that was not to be missed. He no doubt meant to send a message that a foreign-born Jew was suitable to serve as high priest, thereby implying that he himself was suitable to reign as king despite his own foreign birth. He also hoped to marginalize the Hasmoneans, for whom he had even less affection in the wake of Antigonus' treacherous behavior.

Those hopes, however, were quickly dashed.

The Hasmoneans still had the support of the people and a good deal of political clout in Rome. The Romans, for their part, had no desire to fuel any further discontent in the region by antagonizing its inhabitants. And as a result, Herod and Rome suddenly found themselves working at cross purposes. While Herod scrambled to dispose of his rivals, his sponsors were seeking to appease them. So when Hyrcanus' daughter Alexandra lobbied Antony to bypass Herod's choice for high priest and install her son instead, the Roman general acquiesced. It didn't matter that the boy, who was only seventeen years old at the time, seems to have been too young to serve in that capacity — at least based on any traditional criteria.[163] What mattered was that his appointment would placate the masses and increase the prospects for peace in a region that had been beset by conflict for decades.

Herod, for his part, had little choice but to go along with Antony's decision. For one thing, the boy priest was Mariamne's own brother and it would have been unseemly for him to openly resist such an appointment. But more importantly, Herod did not dare challenge his own patron, the man who more than anyone else was responsible for placing him on the throne in the first place. So he gritted his teeth and acquiesced, despite his fears that the boy priest might serve as a rallying point for those who opposed the king — fears that turned out to be well-founded. Indeed the boy, upon assuming the office, elicited such an enthusiastic response from the populace that "the multitude, in great crowds, fell into tears." [164]

Herod, understandably, was concerned.

The Romans might not want to risk popular discontent, but they had the wherewithal to deal with it if necessary. Now that the Parthians had been expelled, Rome's grip on Palestine was secure. But Herod's own hold on power was much more tenuous. A popular uprising touched off by this boy priest might not succeed in dislodging the Roman legions, but it could easily destroy Herod if he failed to act. He knew full well that if he became a liability to the Romans, they would not hesitate to replace him. Unless, that is, he acted first. He therefore took the extraordinary step of "arranging" for the young priest to drown while bathing, the first in a series of political assassinations that would mar his reign.

It was a bold step, and not without considerable risk. Indeed Antony, who had ordered the boy's appointment in the first place, was so disturbed that he called Herod to Egypt to answer for his crime. And Herod, though he feared for his life, had no choice but to go.

Trouble in Paradise

Having watched her husband's antipathy toward her family blossom into a murderous plot, Mariamne the Hasmonean princess was understandably wary and bitter. Unfortunately for her, Herod's possessiveness — some might say paranoia — when it came to his kingdom did not stop at the foot of the throne. It extended into the bedroom, as well. Although he had clearly married Mariamne first and foremost for political reasons, Herod was also quite enamored of her. She was, to all accounts, a beautiful woman, who had attracted the attention (some say intentionally) of several admirers. Among them, notably, was Antony himself, whom Herod believed had fallen in love with her.

It was not the first time Antony's romantic entanglements had posed a threat to Herod. A few years earlier, the Roman general's infatuation with the Egyptian queen Cleopatra had caused similar problems. The queen, whose ambition had earlier led her to poison her brother and arrange for her sister's death, wanted Herod's kingdom for herself. When Antony refused to grant it, she attempted to seduce Herod himself, a strategy that ultimately failed. The king now faced the prospect of defending his murderous actions against Mariamne's family on the very soil ruled by this woman. And he would have to do so before Antony — a man he believed now had designs on his wife. The prospect was hardly pleasant, to say the least. In fact, Herod became increasingly convinced that he would not return from Egypt alive. Antony, he feared, would have him put to death either to please Cleopatra or as a means of having Mariamne for himself.

The realization that he might not only lose his life and his kingdom, but also his wife, sent him into a jealous rage. He therefore called upon his brother-in-law Joseph to manage his affairs (and his wife) during his absence. Joseph had taken over the duties formerly assigned to Herod's father under Hyrcanus and was serving as procurator of Judea. Not only did Herod charge him with administering the kingdom, but he also left secret instructions that Joseph was to kill Mariamne should the king fail to return from his meeting with Antony. If he could not have her, nobody would. And perhaps, if Antony got wind of these "secret" instructions, he might have second thoughts about killing him.

Whether Herod actually used his hostage wife as a bargaining chip is not known, but he did manage to smooth things over with Antony with the help of some well-timed bribes.[165]

Meanwhile, in Jerusalem, Herod's "secret" instructions to his uncle did not remain a secret for long. Once the king had departed, Joseph confided in Mariamne what Herod had told him. And not long afterward, rumors began to circulate in the city that Antony had, in fact, slain the king. This, not surprisingly, threw the palace into an uproar. Joseph, who had already betrayed Herod by telling Mariamne of the king's order, defied him further by refusing to kill Mariamne. On the contrary, he began to consider arguments from her family that he should flee the palace and seek sanctuary with the Roman forces that surrounded the city. Before any such action could be taken, however, letters arrived from Herod himself to discredit the rumors. Joseph, counting on Mariamne to keep his words to her in strictest confidence, sat tight as Herod returned from Egypt and hoped that nothing more would come of it.

It was an error in judgment that would cost him his life.

Herod's sister Salome (who also happened to be Joseph's wife) and his mother at once accused Joseph of conspiring with the Hasmoneans during his absence and holding a "criminal conversation" with Mariamne.[166] The king, in response, confronted his wife with the accusations until she confessed that Joseph had revealed his "secret" instructions. Herod, ever jealous, took this as evidence not merely of his brother-in-law's betrayal, but of an adulterous affair between the two of them. In a rage, the king ordered Joseph executed. It was but another example of his obsession for protecting what was his — an obsession that would keep him on the throne for more than three decades.

And it was an obsession that would grow to consume him as he passed first into his middle years and on into old age.

Who could really blame him?

Even a master politician such as Herod, a born survivor skilled at walking the tightrope of political intrigue, could find such an occupation taxing. One might easily accuse him of paranoia, of imagining that enemies were lurking everywhere in the shadows, just waiting for an opportunity to get the better of him. But to do so would be to overlook the fact that, often, such enemies were not imagined in the least. Indeed, they were all too real.

If Herod behaved ruthlessly toward the Hasmoneans, it was in no small measure because certain members of the once-royal family had behaved in like manner toward him. There had been Antigonus' attempt to seize the throne with the help of Parthia. And there had been the ploy by Hyrcanus' daughter to undermine Herod's position by nominating her teenage son to preside over the temple cult over and against his choice for high priest.

Who was to say that Mariamne herself was not capable of acting against him? And what of her two sons by him? On the one hand, they cemented Herod's connection to the popular family; on the other, their Hasmonean blood made them a natural focal point for anyone wishing to overthrow Herod and reinstate the old regime. Could Herod really trust any of them?

Ultimately, his answer to this question was "no." The old priest Hyrcanus was the first to die, having foolishly taken his daughter's suggestion to seek asylum from the king of Nabataea. He sent a missive to the Nabataean monarch containing such a request, but it fell into the hands of Herod courtesy of a duplicitous messenger. Since the Arabian monarch happened to be at odds with Herod at that particular time, the request looked suspiciously like an act of treason to Herod's suspicious eye. He therefore ordered Hyrcanus taken into custody and, presenting the letter as evidence of an intended alliance with the Arabs, ordered the aged priest executed.

The next to feel the king's wrath was Mariamne, who roused her husband's suspicions by spurning his advances. They engaged one another in a series of arguments over the course of a year, but their quarrels were interrupted by even more serious developments abroad — developments that forced Herod to leave Mariamne in the care of his trusted advisors while departed for the island of Rhodes and a meeting with Octavian, Antony's partner in the delicate alliance that sustained Roman rule.

Or former partner.

This was a crucial meeting for Herod, as it came in the aftermath of perhaps the most pivotal event in Roman history to that point. Octavian and Antony had experienced another falling out, but this time matters were more serious. There would be no patching up the fragile partnership on this occasion, and the rift came to a head with the two rivals declaring all-out war upon each other. Herod, who had been more closely aligned with Antony than with Octavian, had hoped to fight at his patron's side in the climactic battle. The general, however, had other ideas. Fortunately for Herod, Antony instructed him to focus his attention instead on the Nabataeans, who he believed were acting treacherously toward him.

In truth, if anyone was guilty of treachery, it was Cleopatra.

The Egyptian queen, with whom Antony was still desperately in love, hoped to enhance her position by pitting Herod and the Nabataean king against one another. Her reasoning was simple: If they managed to weaken each other sufficiently, or perhaps even do away with one another on the battlefield, she would be in a better position to expand her territory at their expense. Yet by persuading Antony to redirect Herod's energies toward the Nabataeans, Cleopatra robbed her lover of help he desperately needed against Octavian. Whether Herod's forces would have been sufficient to tip the scales is doubtful, but there can be little question that Antony needed all the help he could get.

In the end, he was crushed by Octavian in the battle of Actium and would eventually commit suicide along with Cleopatra.

Herod, meanwhile, got the best of the Nabataeans.

It was a satisfying victory. But in its aftermath, he found himself more vulnerable than ever. He had made a rare tactical error, backing a losing horse in Antony. And as a result, he suddenly found himself in the unenviable position of having to face his patron's conqueror — with the full knowledge that this rare mistake could be his last.

Had Antony accepted Herod's offer to stand beside him at Actium, it probably would have been. But his absence from the decisive battle distanced him just enough from the fallen general to spare him from Octavian's wrath.

Herod managed to work his diplomatic magic and strike an agreement with the new emperor, who not only confirmed him in the monarchy but even added to his territories. (Antony had taken some of these lands from Herod previously and given them as presents to Cleopatra.) In the end, Herod emerged with more than he could ever have dared to hope for. Yet when he returned home from his triumphant meeting with Octavian, he found that things were not as he had left them.

Understandably, Herod had been quite concerned for his own well-being before his departure. Would Octavian condemn him for his loyalty to Antony? Would his own enemies seek to defame him before the emperor-to-be? Would he be stripped of his kingdom? Imprisoned? Would he even return home alive? Such questions must have raced through Herod's mind as he set out to meet Octavian, spawning a potent mixture of fear and distrust — directed first and foremost toward those he felt were most likely to betray him: the Hasmoneans.

Antigonus was dead. So were Hyrcanus and the boy priest who had been chosen to replace him. That left Mariamne, whose disdain for Herod's affections had already served to arouse his suspicion and provoke his enmity. In light of this, he had once again taken the precaution of instructing his deputies to kill her if he failed to return from his meeting with Octavian alive. But once again, his deputies betrayed him, informing Mariamne of his instructions in a disclosure that was sure to further tax their already strained relationship — or destroy it altogether.

And indeed, it had this effect. Mariamne's continued disaffection from him apparently convinced him to launch an inquiry that he both feared and suspected would reveal an affair. What it did reveal was something different, but close enough in Herod's book to confirm his misgivings. In torturing a court eunuch, he learned that that one of the men he had left in charge of Mariamne (a certain Sohemus) had disclosed his instructions to her — his directive that she be slain if he should fail to return. What made this all the more damning was the fact that Mariamne had asked Herod to bestow a large chunk of prime real estate on this very same Sohemus. Taken together, this information was enough to convict Mariamne and Sohemus of adultery — at least in Herod's mind, which was all that mattered.

In a rage that he should have been so betrayed, he ordered them both to be executed.

It was an order he would quickly regret.

Herod had loved Mariamne deeply, and he was so deeply affected by her death that he slipped into a stage of severe depression. Her ghost seemed to haunt him, refusing to let him rest. And his love for her grew beyond even the passion he had known for her during life. Indeed, so great was his remorse over what he had wrought that he refused even to accept that she was dead and "would order his servants to call for Mariamne, as if she were still alive and could still hear them." [167] In time, his despair began to affect his administration of the kingdom, which he neglected in order to punish himself by withdrawing into the desert to mourn her. Ironically, it seemed that the most ambitious man of his time had lost the will to live.

It would take a severe crisis, one that would nearly cost him his throne, to restore it.

… VII

A Child is Born

Herod had to snap out of it.

His old nemesis was on the prowl again, and now was hardly the time for complacency. Hyrcanus' daughter Alexandra, who had successfully opposed Herod in having her son named high priest, saw the king's distraction as her chance to finally wrest control from him. She managed to occupy certain key fortresses and urged Herod's commanders to join her against their master. Her plan was simple: She would claim the kingdom on behalf of Herod's two young sons by Mariamne — her grandsons, neither of whom had reached puberty yet — and act as regent until they reached maturity. In this way, she could restore the Hasmonean clan to its rightful place on the throne of Jerusalem.

But though the plan was straightforward, the execution was deeply flawed. Despite Herod's mental condition, his commanders were not about to desert him for Alexandra. Instead, they reported her scheme to Herod, who was finally roused to action by the imminent crisis. The attempted coup against him seems to have transformed Herod's state from one of depression into white-hot fury, and that fury was directed squarely against Alexandra, yet another scion of the Hasmonean dynasty who had plotted to be rid of him. Upon hearing of her machinations, he ordered his loyal commanders to arrest her and have her executed, thus eliminating yet another member of the Hasmonean house.

In fact, Herod had now succeeded in nearly wiping out the Hasmoneans altogether. The older generations had all perished, leaving only Mariamne's two sons by Herod as a link to the past.

The time had come to move forward.

With the Hasmoneans deprived of the high priesthood on a permanent basis, Herod set about establishing a new line of priests — the line of Boethus. This man was a well-regarded "priest of great note." And, more importantly, he came from well beyond the Hasmonean circle of influence, in the Egyptian capital of Alexandria. Of course, it didn't hurt that he had a beautiful granddaughter who happened to strike Herod's fancy, a woman he ended up making his latest in a string of wives that would eventually number no fewer than nine.

Actually, it seems that Herod's fondness for this woman was the main impetus behind his decision to make a change in the high priesthood. There was, if Josephus is to be believed, good reason for the king's desire. The historian describes the object of Herod's affection as beyond compare, "esteemed the most beautiful woman of that time." And, he says, Herod was determined to have her: "When the people of Jerusalem began to speak much in her commendation, it happened that Herod was much affected with what was said of her. And when he saw the damsel, he was smitten with her beauty." [168]

But there was a problem. Though Herod might have taken her as a concubine, he rejected this option on political grounds. To do so, he realized, would create a backlash against him and reinforce the popular notion that he was a tyrant who simply took what he desired when he desired it. He simply could not afford to so trample on accepted notions of propriety without further alienating his subjects.

That left him with only one viable option — marriage. But this, too, presented certain difficulties, for although she was the daughter of a priestly family, the maiden was not of sufficiently noble birth to qualify her as a suitable mate. Fortunately for Herod, there was a relatively simple way to resolve this matter: By appointing the woman's father as high priest, he could elevate her to sufficient status that his proposed marriage would be legitimized.

This was, therefore, the avenue he took.

The current high priest was deposed, and the woman's father Simon, son of Boethus, was elevated to the position — the first of three priests in the line of Boethus to hold the honor. After this, Herod and his beloved were married, and the king was so pleased with his bride that he erected a tower and named it in her honor. It would be called the Mariamne, for this second great love of Herod's life shared her name with the first. This may have been pure coincidence, or it may have been that Herod was seeking to revive the passion he had felt for the first Mariamne. It also may have been that he wished to participate in the ancient Egyptian ritual whereby the king joined himself with the beautiful Mery-Amen, the "wife of god." The fact that this particular Mariamne hailed from Egypt would appear to lend at least some credence to this idea, though it is impossible to know for sure.

What is intriguing is the fact that, in naming a tower for this woman, Herod was in effect creating a Tower of Mary. When one realizes that the Hebrew word for "tower" is *migdol*, one arrives at a rather revealing title.

Mary Migdol.

The Road to Ruin

Who was this Mary who had such a profound effect on Herod's life? Little is actually written about her, but it is perhaps revealing that her marriage to Herod coincided with one of the most turbulent periods of his life. It was a period during which Herod became increasingly determined to prove himself a worthy king for his people — and when he failed to do so, became increasingly bitter and willing to lash out at anyone he considered a threat.

It was during this period that he embarked upon an ambitious building program designed to modernize and secularize Israel. Where it was possible, he would downplay the ancient traditions that had helped put the Hasmoneans in power. Where it was not, he would outdo his rivals them by implementing them on a grander scale.

Many of his projects were dedicated to his Roman benefactors. Among them was a city he named Caesarea on the west coast, which he established as a seaport complete with an elaborate breakwater that formed a manmade harbor suitable for merchant ships. The city, which took twelve years to build, included a stone theater, an amphitheater, a Roman temple and housing for mariners. When it was finally completed, he inaugurated an Olympic-style festival featuring horse races, animal and human combat, and other events common to the Roman games.

He also built several other cities, typically naming them for some imperial figure or a member of his own family. Such projects served to Romanize the nation considerably, but at the same time enraged traditionalists who viewed the worship of any other deity but Yahweh as sacrilege. And it was these traditionalists whom Herod sought to appease with his most ambitious project, rebuilding of the new Jerusalem temple to Yahweh. According to legend, two temples had been built in Israel: the first attributed to King Solomon and the second a less ambitious endeavor following the end of the great resettlement project under the Babylonians.

Herod's temple, he promised, would surpass them both in its magnificence. In a public speech announcing his plans, the king sounded thoroughly like the politician he was. He played all the angles, recounting his own successes as he promised the traditionalists a new era of piety, while at the same time lauding his Roman sponsors for making such an endeavor possible. It was a masterful balancing act. But it did not sway the traditionalists, who were not so much interested in ostentatious tributes to Yahweh as they were in loyalty.

Exclusive loyalty.

And that was one thing Herod could never give them.

The traditionalists firmly believed that Yahweh was the only deity, and they would not stand for any recognition of (let alone deference to) competing religious agendas. Herod, on the other hand, could not afford to withhold such recognition without jeopardizing his political patronage. Herod was learning the truth of the adage that you can't please all of the people all of the time, and it would be an expensive lesson. As long as the masses remained dissatisfied with him, they would continue to search for someone to take his place.

As this became more apparent, Herod grew more suspicious of those he believed might challenge him for the throne. Foremost among them were his two eldest sons by the first Mariamne, whose link to the Hasmonean line made them attractive candidates for Herod's opponents. When rumors began to circulate that they were plotting against him, he decided to distance them from the throne by welcoming his eldest son, Antipater, back to the royal household. This made sense in two respects. By naming Antipater as his new favorite, Herod was able put some distance between his two scheming sons and the throne. And at the same time, he was able to move the remaining Hasmonean influence further toward the margins.

It seemed like a sound approach, but it ultimately failed to produce the desired effect. Indeed, it seems that under the circumstances, any action Herod took was likely to fall short of the mark. In point of fact, he was getting old. And no matter what steps he took to protect himself, he could no longer avoid the political maneuverings that inevitably surface during a fight for succession. The vultures were circling, and it was only a matter of time before they began to descend. Yet Herod was determined to keep them at bay as long as possible. In the final ten years of his life, he changed his last will and testament no fewer than six times in an attempt to stay one step ahead of whomever he considered the most serious threat at the moment. And the identity of that pre-eminent threat was constantly changing. At first, it was the Hasmonean princes, so he stripped them of their privileged position at court and brought in Antipater to take their places.

Antipater was the son of Doris, the woman Herod had divorced to marry the first Mariamne some three decades earlier. As Herod's eldest son, he was in a way the natural choice to succeed the king, but his position as the child of a divorced wife had hurt his standing. Now that he had been reinstated by Herod himself, he suddenly found himself in the catbird's seat. But instead of resolving matters, Herod's decision to elevate Anipater only complicated the situation. Rather than clarifying the succession and heading off any attempts to bring about Herod's premature demise, it polarized the situation by creating two camps of rival claimants. Almost immediately, factions formed around the Hasmoneans on the one hand and Antipater on the other.

Before long, their plots against one another led to serious accusations of treachery from both sides. As a result, Herod's suspicious nature led him to believe he was now being targeted by not one but two groups of aspirants to the throne. In his mind, he had little choice but to end the threat once and for all. If changing his will didn't work, he would change his heirs in a more concrete fashion — by eliminating them. First Alexander and Aristobulus were charged with treason and executed. Later, Antipater met the same fate as the result of a rather comical series of events.

Herod imprisoned him for another alleged plot against him but held off executing him and had failed to remove him from his will. The king, almost on his deathbed, was in such excruciating pain (perhaps from syphilis) that he tried to commit suicide with a paring knife. He botched the operation, but the resulting scream of agony reverberated throughout the palace and reached the cell where Antipater was imprisoned. Thinking Herod had breathed his last, he assumed that he would soon be elevated to the throne and attempted to bribe the guard to release him.

His impatience would cost him his life.

Herod would indeed die within days. But in the meantime, the overeager prince had sealed his own fate. Instead of accepting the proffered bribe, the jailer reported the matter directly to Herod, who no longer had any excuse to hold off on his plans to execute his ambitious eldest son. The act was carried out post haste, and five days later, Herod himself was dead. One of his final acts before his demise was to order that a large group of esteemed Jewish nobles be locked inside a structure known as the Hippodrome and slain en masse on the news of Herod's death. This order demonstrates how far Herod's paranoia had evolved, spurred by his advancing age and deteriorating health. He had become so convinced that no one would grieve his passing that he developed a twisted idea to ensure that he would be mourned: If the nobles locked in the Hippodrome were executed at the moment of his death, the city would be engulfed in a wave of sorrow. Even if that sorrow wasn't actually expressed for Herod, at the very least it would coincide with his departure. Fortunately for the captive nobles, Herod's sister — whom he had charged with carrying out the grisly deed — declined to go through with it and instead released the hostages upon hearing of the king's death.

So ended the final, tragic chapter of Herod's life. It was a period marked by the growing realization that, no matter how he tried, Herod would never be a popular monarch. As the end of his life approached, he grew increasingly bitter and paranoid, clinging tenaciously to the throne he had held for more than three decades. If he had no love, at least he had power, and he would preserve it at any cost. Even if it meant killing his own sons.

Ewes, Lambs and Shepherd Kings

Another vile deed attributed to Herod, but recorded only by the author of the Christian gospel known as *Matthew*, is the so-called slaughter of the innocents. According to this account, Herod feared that a new messiah had been born and therefore ordered his men to round up all male children two years of age and younger in the village of Bethlehem, where prophecy said the messiah was to be born.

The story, however, seems odd.

The author of *Matthew* states that it took place in fulfillment of an oracle recorded by the prophet Jeremiah:

> *A voice is heard in Ramah*
> *Weeping and great mourning*
> *Rachel weeping for her children*
> *And refusing to be comforted*
> *Because they are no more* [169]

This particular oracle seems to have its origins in the ancient Sumerian myth of Inanna's descent into the netherworld. In this tale, the queen of heaven is slain by her sister Ereshkigal and brought back to life by the wise god Enki. When he descends to rescue the goddess, however, he is confronted by a strange sight: Ereshkigal is in agony, groaning like a woman in labor as she laments all the children who have died prematurely and been sent to her underworld abode.[170] The scene appears to foreshadow the arrival of Dumuzi, the youthful king so integral to the tale's climax: As a condition for releasing Inanna from the netherworld, Ereshkigal demands that she find someone to take her place. And that someone turns out to be the unfortunate Dumuzi, whose identity as the shepherd king links the tale more certainly to the prophecy concerning Rachel. In a bit of irony, Dumuzi the good shepherd was transformed into Dumuzi the sheep — the lamb of God sacrificed upon the altar of Ereshkigal as a surrogate to ransom Inanna from the land of the dead.

Centuries later, Jesus would also assume this dual role as shepherd of the flock and sacrificial lamb of God. And in doing so, in an odd twist, he would become the male counterpart of the matriarch Rachel — a woman whose name meant "ewe" or female sheep, but who is also identified explicitly in the Hebrew texts as a shepherdess.[171] As such, she was the *migdal-eder* or watchtower of the flock; the Magdalene who was the consort of Jesus and who would reappear centuries later as the shepherdess Marian, beloved of Robin Hood.

Indeed, the importance of Rachel in the mythic imagination is not to be underestimated. She is yet another lady of the waters, first encountering husband-to-be Jacob at a vaginal well, where he immediately kisses her and begins to weep.[172] The dual motifs of sexuality and mourning so commonly found in such situations are obvious in this context. And the significance of Rachel's name bears closer examination, as well.

The word "ewe" itself is quite similar to the name Eve, with the middle letter in the two words being interchangeable in many cultures. And just as Eve was the mother of mankind, so Rachel, as Jacob's consort, was the mother of the nation of Israel.

The word also sounds exactly like the name of the yew tree, a symbol for immortality and the source for the kind of wood used in making a bow — the weapon of choice for the archer.

Interestingly, the only other time the subject of ewes is raised in the Hebrew texts also involves a well. And not just any well, but one that is in fact associated with Rachel's husband Jacob. The incident in question does not, in fact, involve Jacob but his grandfather Abraham. It involves a dispute between the great patriarch and a rival ruler named Abimelech over a well of water that had been seized by the latter man's servants.[173] Abraham complained about the apparent theft, but Abimelech pleaded ignorance. The patriarch responded by setting aside seven ewes from his flock and offering them to his rival in exchange for the well: "Accept these seven lambs from my hand as a witness that I dug this well." [174]

In the aftermath of this treaty, the Hebrew scribes declared, the place became known as Beersheba. And to mark the treaty, Abraham planted a tree there — but not just any tree. A tamarisk tree.

The symbolism contained in this short story is so thickly layered it is hard to know where to begin deciphering it. Clearly, a tanist ceremony of some sort is involved. By claiming the well, Abimelech was challenging Abraham's sovereignty over the region; but Abraham was having nothing of it. He met his rival's challenge by calling on seven ewes as witnesses that the well was his.

These ewes represented the seven spirits of the underworld, guardians of the seven gates through which the shepherd king must pass in order to achieve his immortality. Only he knew the proper magic words to utter in order to traverse this underworld gantlet. Only he, the rightful king, could hope to survive such an ordeal. Jesus himself would describe it: "The man who enters by the gate is the shepherd of his sheep. The watchman opens the gate for him, and the sheep listen to his voice." [175] The spirits of the netherworld were sheep, obligated to obey the word of their shepherd king.

Jesus was such a shepherd king.

So was Abraham.

And the depiction of these seven underworld spirits as sheep or ewes makes perfect sense — they are the same seven spirits said to have possessed the woman known as the watchtower of the flock. Mary Magdalene. Only Jesus could free the shepherdess of these seven spirits, and he did so, thus releasing her from the bonds of the netherworld and restoring her to life.

The imagery in the story of Abraham is similar. It is he, not Abimelech, who commands the seven sheep. And it is therefore he who retains possession of the well. The only thing missing from the story is the lady of the waters, the guardian of the vaginal well to which both rulers laid claim. Her apparent absence from the story seems to leave a gaping hole. One would have expected the confrontation to involve a female figure such as Abraham's wife Sarah, but she is nowhere mentioned in this passage.

She is, however, mentioned previously in *another* tale involving Abimelech. And this tale provides the very information that might have been expected in the account of the well: Abimelech takes a fancy to Sarah and claims her as his own, only to find out that she is

Abraham's wife and relinquish her to the patriarch. The parallel between Sarah and the well — the lady of the waters and the waters themselves — cannot have been clearer. In each tale, Abraham and Abimelech spar over possession of one or the other. Originally, these two scenes must have been a single episode, which was subsequently divided by scribes either wary or ignorant of its mythic symbolism.

The final point worth noting is the name of the well, Beersheba.

The suffix, *sheba* (meaning "seven") referred to the seven ewes but also recalls the name of the legendary queen. The prefix, *beer*, meant "well" and may even have served as the origin for the identically named alcoholic beverage. It is yet another fermented drink associated with the well, adding to a growing list that already includes wine (especially the red variety), honeyed mead and hard apple cider. The intoxicating effect of such beverages, it seems, was always closely related to sexual ecstasy and the impartation of divine inspiration or wisdom.

Going to the Well

A short digression is in order at this point to look more closely at the "well" theme in the story of Abraham and his progeny. It is a theme that recurs with almost annoying frequency in the annals of his legend; in addition to the incident at Beersheba, mentioned above, several other events are associated with a sacred well in *Genesis*. A few of them:

- Hagar and Ishmael come upon a well after being exiled.
- Abraham's servant meets Rebekah at a well.
- Isaac digs a well and enters into a dispute over it with some herdsmen.
- Isaac digs a second well, which gives rise to a similar dispute.
- Isaac digs another well, then moves on to Beersheba (yet another well).

> Jacob meets Rachel at a well.

The first well of significance is the well or spring of Hagar, Abraham's concubine who was sent into exile with her son Ishmael at the request of his favored wife Sarah. They set off into the desert realm of Seth, where they discover a well or spring called Beer Lahai Roi, or "well of the living one who sees." The word *roi* is familiar to students of the French language as the word for a king. In the Hebrew lexicon, it denoted the ability to see — both in a physical realm and in the spiritual or prophetic sense. The ability to prophesy, as we have seen, was often associated with wells and their living water with its intoxicating quality. Such intoxication could be induced by fermented drink such as (beer, cider, mead or wine) as well as by a state of sexual ecstasy; often, ancient mystery rituals involved both. Moreover, the concept of sight in a physical sense was closely connected to the presence of light, which was associated first and foremost by the all-seeing eye of heaven, the sun.

In Egypt, this heavenly eye was associated with the solar deities Horus or Ra, both of whom were likewise styled as kings. The name Ra itself sounds remarkably like the Hebrew word *roi* used in connection with Hagar's well, and it also appears to have given rise to several related words, such as the Spanish *rey* (again denoting a king) and the English term "ray," referring to emanations from the sun disk. The name of Hagar's well, therefore, carries any number of connotations. It was the well of life and prophecy; the well of the king's life; the well of the living one, whose name was Ra.

The location of this particular well is also important. The author of *Genesis* places it on the road to someplace called Shur or *sur*. In its original tongue, the word would not have included vowels and would have been rendered as s'r, making it remarkably similar to the place-name Seir or Asir. This was Yahweh's land of origin, the desert wastes of the Arabian Peninsula where the storm god was originally worshipped. It was here that Cheops had established a presence for the Egyptian kingdom in the middle of the third millennium B.C.E., a presence that most likely continued there in some form or another from that point forward. Indeed, the land of Shur is specifically identified as being "to the east of Egypt," near the border.[176] And this can only be a description of the Arabian Peninsula, the geography of which is even today riddled with place-names that refer to Egyptian gods, thus preserving the memory of its days as a colonial possession under Cheops and his successors.[177]

One of those successors was Abraham or Abram, founder of the Hyksos dynasty, whose name in Egyptian was Ma'abra. This name was reworked at some point by a scribe (or scribes) who transposed the syllables to create the name Abram, which meant "exalted father." This was only fitting when one considers that every pharaoh ascended to the heavens at his death, taking on the form of Osiris and thereby becoming in a very real sense an exalted father.

But the name Abraham also survived on the Arabian Peninsula in yet another form, Abu Ruhm. This Arabic name was based on the roots *ab*, denoting a father, and *rhm*, indicating a gentle rain.[178] This appears to identify Abraham personally with the storm god worshipped by the Hyksos (under the name Seth) and by the Hebrews (as Yahweh). As Abraham was both the first Hyksos king and the patriarch or founder of the Hebrew nation, this fits nicely. As the king, he was the earthly manifestation of the heavenly father, just as Jesus would claim to be nearly two millennia later.

Abraham was associated with any number of wells, markers that served to establish his kingship over the land. They symbolized his own fertility as royal consort to the divine mother who served as guardian for the bloodline. According to the author of *Genesis*, the Philistines at some point stopped up all the wells that Abraham's servants had dug for him, thus not only depriving him of crucial water but also signifying their confiscation of his lands. No longer would his bloodline rule this territory, for the womb of the earth had been stopped up so that no more kings in the line of Abraham could be born. This, at any rate, was the message the Philistines were sending. As always, the king and the land were one.

Wells were reservoirs where the water of the rain god who fertilized the earth were collected. They were, symbolically, vaginal gateways to the otherworld, collecting the fertilizing semen of the heavenly father in the womb of Mother Earth. The product of this union was an overflowing abundance of good things such as those produced by the legendary grail or cornucopia. It is therefore natural that the product of Abraham's union with Sarah was a son by the name of Isaac — a name that translates into Arabic as a word denoting overflow or abundance.[179]

Isaac was the living water that sprang forth from the well of his mother Sarah, and it was therefore natural that he dug several wells of his own.

His grandson, Joseph, would be thrown into a dry or empty well. This is literally a cistern, a shaft in the rocks that collects water. Afterward, he naturally becomes a great interpreter of dreams, having likely gained this ability from the time he spent in the well. Prophets and wells, after all, very often went together. His confinement bears a certain similarity to that of Jesus in a rock tomb and to that of another prophet, Jonah, in "the roots of the mountains" (a ziggurat tomb?) and the earth that barred him in.[180] Jonah was buried beneath the waters in an act of baptism before being born again; similarly, Joseph was sent into a cistern designed for holding water before he re-emerged. Though the well was dry, the imagery of ritual baptism and rebirth remained. And it was repeated in Jesus' legend on two fronts — first at his actual baptism, then later at his burial.

Massacre in Bethlehem

This, then, is the background behind the legendary slaughter of the innocents (albeit with a few detours along the way).

Herod supposedly took this action after being warned by three visiting dignitaries, astrologers known as magi, that a child destined to be king had been born. At first glance, such a tale might seem quite plausible in light of Herod's reputation for brutality. But upon closer inspection, something seems amiss. Why should Herod have embarked on such a campaign of terror, based on nothing more than the word of three foreign astrologers? This seems rather flimsy evidence upon which to launch a massacre of innocent children, even given the ancients' affinity for signs and portents, and the heightened level of Herod's paranoia at the end of his life. It hardly seems that a peasant child born in a backwater village — even one connected with a prophecy — would have commanded so much attention. The key to the throne was royal blood, and without it one could scarcely hope to attract much of a following. Herod knew this all too well, and for this reason he consistently focused his suspicions on two groups who possessed it: the Hasmoneans and his own children. During his reign, he ordered the execution of nearly all surviving members of the Hasmonean clan, while also condemning three of his own sons.

If the child reportedly born in Bethlehem was a mere peasant, Herod had no reason to fear him. But if the infant were somehow connected to royal house, a campaign to find and kill him would have been entirely in character for the paranoid king.

The infant in question was, of course, a boy named Jesus. The date of his birth has been much disputed, having been erroneously set on our calendars at 1 C.E., four years *after* Herod's. Such a date, of course, would have been quite impossible if Herod in fact launched a deadly purge in an effort to eliminate the child. He could hardly have undertaken such an enterprise from the grave.

Jesus, therefore, must have been born sometime before or during the early part of the year we now know as 4 B.C.E. This was a turbulent time in the court of Herod. Alexander and Aristobulus had been executed more than two years earlier, relieving him of one burden. But even so, the king remained beset by intrigue. The latest scandal to rear its head began with the death of Herod's brother Pheroras and would eventually result in the downfall of several notable members of his court. Not long after Pheroras' funeral, two of the man's servants came forward and declared that he had been poisoned. As was his custom, Herod resorted to torture and extracted evidence implicating Antipater and his mother Doris in the alleged plot.

This obviously put Antipater, who was at this point heir to the throne, on uncomfortably thin ice. The tenuous nature of his position was made all too clear when Herod decided to divorce his mother for the second time. All that would be needed to strip Antipater of his status and put him in chains was the slightest nudge, the smallest suspicion that he might be involved in some other shady dealings.

That nudge was provided soon enough when yet another murder conspiracy was uncovered at court. This time, however, the target was Herod himself. Antipater's name surfaced in connection with this scheme as well, but he was not the only notable personage to be implicated. More damaging still were the words of Pheroras' widow, who confessed to a role in the plot and jumped from the palace roof in an attempt to take her own life.

She failed.

And that failure had profound implications for another member of Herod's retinue, the Egyptian woman he had married eighteen years earlier. This was the second Mariamne, who had so beguiled Herod that he had elevated her father to the high priesthood and named a tower in her honor. But something was about to happen that would change Herod's feelings for her dramatically. Having failed in her suicide attempt, Pheroras' wife was suddenly willing to implicate someone else in the plot to murder Herod — and that someone turned out to be Mariamne. On the strength of this revelation, Herod divorced his Egyptian wife and removed her son (also named Herod) from his will. Even her father, who had been high priest since their wedding, was not immune to the purge. Herod summarily dismissed him from the position, replacing him with someone not from the house of Boethus.

The historian Josephus, who records the story of Mariamne's fall from grace, has nothing more to say about her, leaving her subsequent fate an apparent mystery. But he does go on to mention that other members of her family, notably two of her uncles, somehow managed to get back into Herod's good graces. Within a year, the king's ire toward the family seems to have cooled, for he appointed one of these uncles, a man named Joazar, as high priest. But his tenure was only a few short months before he was replaced by another uncle, Eleazar.

The question is, why?

And the answer may lie with the author of *Matthew*.

At first blush, his story might appear unrelated to the intrigue surrounding Herod's final years. Yet the author himself brings Herod into the picture by accusing him of ordering a mass slaughter of infant boys in a bizarre attempt to thwart a possible coup. He also identifies Jesus' parents, intriguingly, by the names Mary and Joseph. The former is but a shortened version of Mariamne, the name worn by the Egyptian woman Herod divorced right around the time of Jesus' birth. And the latter is somewhat similar to the name of the high priest Joazar.

Apocryphal literature has much to say about Mary, who was supposedly placed in the care of priests and raised in the temple itself. This would make sense if she belonged to a priestly family, as Mariamne the Egyptian did.

According to tradition, Mary was transferred to the care of Joseph when she reached puberty, Joseph having been chosen as her new husband in an odd ceremony staged by the priests themselves. Events unfolded as follows. The priests summoned the men of the land to the temple, instructing each to come bearing a wooden rod or staff. None of these rods was particularly noteworthy — except for Joseph's, out of which emerged a dove that ascended to alight on his head.[181]

This is the same imagery seen at Jesus' baptism, where a dove likewise alights on *his* head. The dove, it may be recalled, was an emblem of the love goddess, signifying sexual bliss and childbirth. In the legend of Mary's betrothal to Joseph, it was a natural sign of their impending union.

But the symbolism of the rod is perhaps even more noteworthy. In another form of the legend, the rod actually buds forth like a flower, again indicating that Joseph has been chosen to care for Mary.[182] This imagery, too, seems highly sexual, for it recalls the "budding" of the male sexual organ during intercourse and the emission of semen (the white dove?).

More important, however, it hearkens back to an incident related in the Hebrew texts, in which another man's rod or staff budded forth in a similar fashion. The rod in question belonged to Aaron, and the narrative involved his confirmation as the nation's first high priest.[183]

The Joseph Connection

All this would seem to indicate, by implication, that Joseph likewise held the position of high priest — the very position held by Joazar, who was named to the post immediately following the tenure of an obscure figure who held the post for only a single day.

His name?

Joseph.

The names Joazar and Joseph are sufficiently similar that it would have been a simple matter to mistake one for the other. And despite Joazar's considerable prestige and popularity, there was ample reason to pass along a tradition that listed someone named Joseph as father of the messiah. In point of fact, such a tradition already existed — according to which the messiah is identified clearly by the name Ephraim, the tribal patriarch who was the *son of Joseph*.[184] And the name Ephraim had another application as well: It was the name given by the Hebrews to the star Sirius, the very same star that hailed the coming of the messiah and even referred to in several Middle Eastern cultures by the name Messaeil.[185]

Indeed, many of those who lived in the region Jesus would call home did not identify the messiah as the son of David, but as the son of Joseph.

This was the steadfast belief of the Samaritans, a people who dwelt in Galilee and just to the south — a people who held to their own specific beliefs and traditions regarding faith and ritual. They also had their own set of prophecies about the messiah, whom they specifically named as Ephraim. According to his legend, which is contained in a medieval manuscript but is obviously much older, God would announce his messiah to the heavenly host. "His name is Ephraim, my true messiah, who will elevate his own stature and the stature of his generation. He will light up the eyes of Israel and deliver his people. All his enemies and adversaries shall be in awe and flee from him. And even rivers will yield to the power of his right hand and stop flowing." [186]

Jesus is closely associated with the Samaritans at several points in the gospels, most notably when he lauds a fictional good Samaritan for stopping to help the victim of a robbery. His favorable attitude toward such a person, who belonged to a group despised by mainstream Jews, is worth noting. Yet even more remarkable is another incident, during which he stops to speak with a Samaritan woman at a well. The presence of the well, which is specifically located on a plot of ground given by Jacob to his son Joseph, identifies the woman as a lady of the lake — a prophetess guarding the sacred waters of wisdom. If there is any doubt about this, it is erased by her admission that she has taken five husbands and is currently involved with a man to whom she is not even married. Such scandalous behavior would have been expected of a temple priestess, whose role it was to lie with men in acts of ritual copulation.

Jesus asks her for a drink. And, once he has partaken of her waters of wisdom, he is granted the gift of prophecy and a knowledge of the woman's situation. She recognizes this and declares him to be a prophet.

The suspicion is that Jesus himself has lain with her — a suspicion heightened by the name of the place where they meet. It is identified by the author of *John* as Sychar, a name that would have been expressed in Hebrew as *skr* or *sqr*.[187] If this root sounds familiar, it should, for it also provides the basis for the place-name Saqqara, site of the first Egyptian pyramid, along with the term ziggurat applied to the temple of Inanna. It was at the ziggurat where the sacred harlots plied their trade, lying with men and imparting wisdom to them.

Whatever transpired at the well, the woman was certainly excited about it. She ran off to tell her countrymen about Jesus, and he gained a large measure of respect among the Samaritans, who welcomed him to their country and urge him to stay with them.[188] This close association with the Samaritans may well indicate that they accepted him as the messianic son of Joseph. Indeed, the mutual admiration expressed between Jesus and these people was such that indignant Jews sought to slander him by scoffing: "Aren't we right that you are a Samaritan and demon-possessed?" [189] Notably, Jesus denied the second charge but remained silent on the first. Clearly, he was comfortable with being associated with the Samaritans and declared the son of Joseph. It was a label that would remain with him for the rest of his life and well beyond.

Out of Egypt

All these tidbits of information would seem to link Joazar and Mariamne quite closely with Joseph and Mary. And there is another intriguing connection, as well. Upon learning of Herod's plan to massacre the infants, the parents of the destined messiah are said to have taken refuge in Egypt, supposedly at the behest of an angel who appeared to Joseph in a dream. In reality, however, there is a much more plausible explanation for their decision to head south — if one considers the possibility that Joseph and Mary were in fact Joazar and Mariamne. In that case, Egypt would have been a perfectly natural destination. It was, after all, their homeland, where they might have taken refuge with family members or old associates. As members of a priestly family from Egypt, they would have been safe there. Indeed, if Herod wanted to hunt them down, they could have found no safer haven than the land of the pharaohs.

And it is quite possible that Herod wanted to do just that.

The king had divorced Mariamne and stricken her son Herod from his will. But what if she were pregnant with another child? She had been married to Herod for eighteen years, but she was quite probably still of childbearing age when he divorced her. The king had a penchant for young beauties: He had become engaged to the first Mariamne when she was not yet even a teenager, and if he had done the same with Mariamne of Egypt, she would have been in her thirties when the marriage was dissolved — still young enough to bear children. If Herod had divorced her and later found she was pregnant, he would have been livid. Mariamne's family in Egypt was influential and would not take such an insult lightly. They might be expected to provide strong political backing for Mariamne's unborn son and promote him as an alternative to Herod.

This would have provided the king with all the incentive he needed to launch a search for the child and even order the murder of innocent newborns in his quest to eliminate a perceived rival to the throne. But it is unlikely that he did so immediately. Indeed, Herod's actions in the period after his divorce of Mariamne appear to be those of someone willing to bide his time, waiting for the other shoe to drop. That proverbial shoe, in this case, was Mariamne's unborn child. Herod, however, must not have known that. Had he realized Mariamne was pregnant at the time of their divorce, he would have almost certainly sought to terminate the pregnancy — either by forcing a miscarriage or by ordering his wife's execution. If he had commanded that the first Mariamne be put to death for plotting against him, he certainly would not have hesitated to issue a similar order in this case.

Unless he believed he could learn more by allowing her to stay alive.

If Herod was suspicious, this would explain his decision to elevate Joazar to the high priesthood in the year following his divorce of Mariamne. He may have suspected that Mariamne was pregnant, or that her family had been part of a larger conspiracy to assassinate him. If so, what better way to confirm his suspicions than by keeping Joazar close at hand?

Events unfolded quickly from there. Herod's health was deteriorating quickly, and he had a scant few weeks left to live. During this time, Herod probably became aware that Mariamne was pregnant and issued an order that the child be killed. When Joazar became aware of this edict, he decided to flee with Mariamne for Egypt before it could be carried out. Despite his high-profile position as high priest, it might not have been too difficult to slip away without alerting the king. Herod's final days were spent in agony, and he left Jerusalem in a desperate attempt to find relief for his ailments at the hot springs of Callirrhoe on the eastern shore of the Dead Sea. When he attempted to end his suffering with a botched suicide attempt, he only succeeded in roiling the political waters further by raising Antipater's hopes and spurring his ill-conceived bribe of the prison guard. Amid all this torment and confusion, it would have been quite a simple matter for Joazar and Mary to escape — as it appears they did.

Joazar's treachery came to light shortly after Herod's death, when the greatest part of his kingdom passed to his son Archelaus (the product of yet another marriage). Upon being confirmed as Herod's primary heir, Archelaus made it his first order of business to accuse Joazar of "assisting the seditious" and quickly removed him from the high priesthood.[190] This amounted to a charge of treason, the sort of charge that should have carried a death sentence under the circumstances. Herod's passing had brought with it a mass of uprisings across the country aimed at wresting the province from Roman control and restoring its independence. Certainly Archelaus, who faced the prospect of quelling these disturbances, would have exhibited little patience for seditious actions on Joazar's part.

Yet Joazar was not executed.

This is apparent because he reappears in Josephus' history a decade later in 6 C.E., when he is said to have briefly reclaimed the office of high priest. Interestingly, this is the same year that a man named Quirinius was appointed as Roman governor of Syria. The author of *Luke* would refer to this Quirinius by name, asserting that the Roman government ordered a worldwide census during his tenure. According to *Luke*'s account, it was this census that brought Mary with Joseph to Bethlehem, where the prophecy said she would give birth to the messiah. Strangely, however, the author also contends that Jesus was born during the reign of Herod.

These two statements present the reader with a dilemma, for both cannot be true. Herod's reign and the tenure of Quirinius simply do not overlap — indeed, Herod died a full decade *before* Quirinius took office. But Joazar's return to the office of high priest at that later date makes it possible to understand such a discrepancy. If the author's sources linked the birth of Jesus with the priestly tenure of Joazar (a.k.a. Joseph), the author might have simply assumed that it occurred during his *second* stint in office rather than his first. Under this timeline, Jesus would have been born in the same year that Quirinius began his governorship.

Whatever the author of *Luke* was thinking, it is clear that Joazar was indeed still alive ten years after being stripped of the high priesthood. The question is, why?

Given the opportunity, Archelaus would certainly have ordered his execution. The most likely reason he failed to do so was that no such opportunity presented itself. The most plausible explanation is that Joazar had gone into hiding. In all probability, Archelaus relieved Joazar of his office in absentia, for the simple reason that the high priest had become a refugee — he had already fled the country and was therefore beyond reach of the authorities. In Egypt.

Child of the Nile

The story of Jesus' birth and the events surrounding it leave little doubt that the traditions of Egypt had a profound effect on his story.

One of the most memorable aspects of this story involves a

brilliant star that appeared in the sky at the time of his birth. According to the author of *Matthew*, this star guided a group of astrologers known as magi to the site of his advent, where they presented him with gifts of gold, frankincense and myrrh. One tradition — not mentioned in *Matthew* but so often repeated that it has become an ingrained element of the story — states that these magi were three in number, and that they were in fact kings of foreign lands.

Just who were these magi?

According to the author of *Matthew*, they were foreign dignitaries known for their wisdom who had been drawn to Jerusalem by a star in the sky. This star, they reported, heralded the arrival of the messiah, who was destined to claim the throne of Israel. Upon arriving, they declared succinctly, "We saw his star in the east and have come to do him homage." [191]

The author seems to have concluded from this pronouncement that the magi themselves came from the east. But could this have been a misunderstanding? The statement of the magi is, in fact, rather ambiguous. "We saw his star in the east" could mean, on the one hand, that the magi themselves were in the east when they first caught sight of this celestial phenomenon. This is how the author of *Matthew* appears to have understood it. Yet it is equally possible that was *the star*, not the magi who observed it, was "in the east."

Where, then, were they?

The obvious answer is Egypt — more specifically, the city of Heliopolis. It was there that the science of astronomy had been developed to its fullest, under the auspices of the priests in service to the sun god. So sophisticated were these men that they were considered without peer in the ancient world. The historian Strabo stated simply: "The Egyptian priests are supreme in the science of the sky." [192]

Not only did the priests of Heliopolis have the credentials to qualify as magi, they also had the motive to establish contact with the baby Jesus. To discover the nature of this motive, one has merely to recall that Mariamne and Joazar belonged to important priestly family from Egypt. And as members of the priestly aristocracy, they no doubt had connections with the Jewish temple in the land of Egypt — the only place outside Jerusalem where priests could actually carry out the ritual sacrifices mandated in the law of Moses. This was the temple of Yahweh at Leontopolis, established by the exiled high priest Onias within walking distance of Heliopolis.

It was to Heliopolis that the mystical phoenix was fated to return in the proper course of days, again fulfilling the destiny of death and rebirth that fueled the ever-turning wheel of eternity. It was there that it would alight on the fiery benben stone, to be consumed in the merciless flames of heaven and rise again from the ashes three days later.

Who would be the next phoenix?

And when would he arrive?

It was the task of the astronomer priests at Heliopolis to answer these questions. And to fulfill this charge they watched the skies, immersing themselves in the laws of probability and mathematics as they diligently tracked the movement of the heavenly bodies — the planets and the stars.

One star in particular.

"We saw his star in the east," the magi would proclaim. But to which star were they referring? Only one answer is truly possible, for only one star was associated with the birth of Horus, the god embodied by the mythical firebird. This was the star Sirius, which disappeared below the horizon for seventy days each summer only to be reborn with the Nile flood or inundation. Sirius was the star of Isis, also known as the sea goddess Meri, whose tears for her fallen husband fed the river and cascaded down across the desert to the sea. It was she who would give birth to the new king, the one known as "Horus who is in Sirius." [193]

The appearance of the star marked the birth of such a king, the sun god whose power was greatest at this very season.

The summer solstice.

If a prince of royal blood happened to be born on the exact day that Sirius crept back above the horizon, it would have been an indisputable sign that the phoenix had returned. And this is apparently just what happened. Even the author of *Luke* places Jesus' birth during a period when "there were shepherds living out in the fields nearby, keeping watch over their flocks at night." [194] This would seem to indicate that he was born during the spring or summertime, when sheep could be found in plentiful numbers grazing the pastures and the hillsides, rather than during the harsher seasons of autumn or winter.

Jesus' birth to a woman named Mary therefore corresponded perfectly with Horus' birth to a goddess known as Meri, further confirmation that the phoenix had arrived.

And so the magi went forth to greet him.

The legend that they were actually three kings further strengthens the link with Egypt and the myth of Horus. In this regard, it is worth recalling the three stars in the "belt" of Orion, the constellation equated with Horus' father Osiris. The three great pyramids on the Giza plateau were apparently designed to reflect these three stars, the celestial phallus from which the god's seed issued forth to conceive his son and heir Horus. It is no accident that these pyramids were built to serve as the resting place to three pharaohs — or *three kings*. Even today, the memory of this connection is preserved in the tradition that refers to the three stars of Orion's belt as the "three kings."

Though this aspect of the story is clearly legendary, it appears likely that a delegation of astronomer priests from Heliopolis did in fact venture out across the desert in search of the phoenix.

The question was, where would they find him?

The authors of *Matthew* and *Luke* take great pains to place his advent in the town of Bethlehem, in accordance with a prophecy that the messiah would be born there. Yet nowhere in the accounts of his adult life is Jesus connected with Bethlehem in even the most indirect way. Indeed the author of *Mark*, whose narrative does not include any information about Jesus' early life, seems to exclude the possibility that he was born in Bethlehem by indicating that his hometown was somewhere in Galilee.[195] This is the region where Jesus would spend most of his adult life and with which he would be most closely associated.

The author of *John* even goes so far as to indicate that Jesus *wasn't* born in Bethlehem. In fact, his critics were well aware that he had been born somewhere else and used this information to discredit him. "How can the messiah come from Galilee?" they asked. "Does not the scripture say that the messiah will come from David's seed and from Bethlehem, the town where David lived?" [196] The obvious implication is that Jesus couldn't be the messiah because he had failed to fulfill the scripture and had not been born in Bethlehem.

This fact presented an embarrassing difficulty that the authors of *Matthew* and *Luke* sought to cover up.

This is how *Luke* arrived at his farfetched story of the worldwide Roman census under Quirinius, which supposedly led Joseph and Mary to leave their native village in Galilee. The idea was that Joseph had to register in the village of his forefathers — Bethlehem, naturally — in order to comply with the census edict. When he arrived in Bethlehem, his wife gave birth to Jesus in a happy coincidence that enabled him to fulfill the words of the prophet Micah: "But you, Bethlehem Ephrathah, though you are small among the clans of Judah, out of you will come for me one who will be ruler over Israel, whose origins are of old — from days of eternity." [197]

It was a fine story, but it never happened. In his attempt to place Jesus' birth in the little town of Bethlehem, the author of *Luke* appealed to the famous census that supposedly took place "in the time of Herod" [198] — a worldwide census "when Quirinius was governor of Syria" [199] — under which everyone went to his ancestral home to register. Unfortunately for the author, such a solution was untenable on several counts.

For one thing, as already noted, Herod had died a decade *before* Quirinius was installed as governor. For another, the Roman government never conducted a worldwide census under Quirinius, Herod or anyone else. There was, in fact, a regional census taken in under the Syrian governor — a census that sparked a significant anti-tax rebellion during Jesus' childhood. But whenever a regional census was taken, it only applied to those lands under direct Roman rule. In Judea, such a census was natural: By the time Quirinius was installed as governor of Syria, Herod's son Archelaus had been expelled from office and supplanted by a Roman procurator, who wanted to set up a new (and no doubt harsher) tax system. Galilee, however, was still under the jurisdiction of the tetrarch Antipas, another of Herod's sons. As a result, no census could have been imposed there.

The reason was simple: Galilee, unlike Judea to the south, was *not* under direct Roman rule.

It is therefore apparent that no resident of Galilee would have been forced to take part in such a census. If Joseph and Mary had been living there at the time, they would simply not have been affected. Nor would they have been required to travel seventy miles in order to register at Joseph's ancestral home. Such a requirement would have made no sense. The purpose of such a census was to take inventory of a family's possessions so that the owner might be taxed. Yet how could such an inventory be obtained if the family was forced to leave its belongings behind?

It couldn't.

It is hard to imagine every adult male in Palestine pulling up stakes and traveling across the country to register at his ancestral home. The result would have been mass confusion, full-scale disruption of trade and economic disaster — none of which would have been in the empire's best interests. In seeking to cover up the reality that Jesus had not been born in Bethlehem, the author of *Luke* only made matters worse by concocting a story that could never have happened.

But if Jesus was not born in Bethlehem, where *was* he born?

If Mariamne was pregnant with Herod's child, she would have certainly gone into hiding for fear of her life. Even the rabbis, in their

Talmudic collection, recalled that Jesus belonged to "the wicked kingdom of Edom" — the ancient name for Idumean, whence Herod and his father came. They also styled him as "near to the kingdom" in terms of succession to the throne. Such references can only mean that he was, or claimed to be, Herod's son.[200]

In light of this, it was only natural that Mariamne should go into hiding. Upon hearing that she was pregnant, Mary "got ready and hurried to a town in the hill country of Judea."[201] The reference to her hurried departure is worth considering. An abrupt departure would have certainly been in order if she feared the consequences of being discovered pregnant. And her chosen destination, the hill country of Judea, was a desolate land renowned for its caves, crevices and other hiding places. It was to this region that David had reportedly retreated with his band of guerrillas during his civil war with Saul, and it was here that Judas Maccabeus and his brothers had found refuge during their conflict with the Seleucids.

It was, in short, a haven for outlaws and revolutionaries.

Once he learned the truth of her condition, Herod would certainly have regarded his former wife as both.

According to the Quran, Mary eventually gave birth not in a manger at Bethlehem but out in the open — apparently in the middle of nowhere. This version of Jesus' advent states that she was driven to the trunk of a palm tree by the pains of childbirth. There she bemoaned her lot and declared: "Ah, would that I had died before this. Would that I had been a thing forgotten and out of sight." Even this lament, the desire to be "forgotten and out of sight" would seem to indicate that she was a hunted woman. But her place of refuge, under a palm tree, indicated that she was about to give birth to the phoenix with whom that particular tree was so closely linked.

In answer to her travails, a voice spoke to her from beneath the tree admonishing her, "Grieve not, for the lord has provided a rivulet beneath you. And shake the trunk of the palm tree, for it will let fall fresh ripe dates upon you."[202] This brief account contains all the elements familiar from the sacred grove:

- The maiden, in her role as wife of the god.
- The healing spring or rivulet, source of wisdom and prophecy.
- The tree of life, with its nourishing fruit.

Even the serpent's presence is implied in the voice that issues forth from beneath the tree, advising her to partake of the fruit just as Eve was prompted to do in the garden. The fact that the voice comes from the ground beneath the tree further identifies it as that of the serpent, which is fated to crawl in the dirt.

The Quran is not the only source that records the palm tree incident. A similar account occurs in a in a document called *The Gospel of Pseudo-Matthew*, a narrative unrelated to the canonical *Matthew* that deals extensively with legends concerning Jesus' childhood. This version, too, records an incident in which the holy family stops by a palm tree and enjoys refreshment from a fountain that springs forth from its roots — and places the incident in the midst of their journey to Egypt. This would seem to indicate that Jesus was born not in Bethlehem, but at some point during the flight to Egypt.

This seems like a reasonable conclusion.

If Mariamne had given birth in Jerusalem, Herod would certainly have found out and had the baby killed. It was imperative to leave before the child was born and find refuge somewhere beyond the dying king's reach. That somewhere was Egypt. But before they could arrive at their destination, Mariamne gave birth to a baby boy. The question remains: Where were Joazar and Mariamne headed? What was their ultimate destination?

The Egyptian Coptic Church preserves a memory of their journey, which reportedly included a stop at the town of Mattariya. Among the prized possessions of the church there is a stone trough, covered with hieroglyphs, that Mary supposedly used to wash her newborn's clothes. This legend is corroborated by the account of a medieval merchant, who reported the existence of a garden that contained a marble well in which the infant's clothes had supposedly been washed.[203] The existence of the well seems to connect this account with the legends of the palm tree, from the base of which flowed a miraculous spring. The picture is one of a desert oasis, a new Eden with a tree of life surrounded by the harsh and barren wilderness of Seth.

This particular site, at Mattariya, is a scant three miles north of modern Cairo — which in turn occupies much the same ground claimed by the ancient solar city of the phoenix, Heliopolis. If the magi were indeed astrologer priests from this ancient city seeking the newborn king, they wouldn't have had far to travel in their quest. And they would have been able to determine, much more readily, whether his birth had indeed coincided with the reappearance of Sirius above the horizon.

There remains, however, one difficulty to work out.

According to the author of *Luke*, Jesus was presented at the temple eight days after his birth to undergo the ritual of circumcision. There is no reason to doubt that Jesus did, in fact, participate in this ancient custom. Yet if he were born near Heliopolis, how could he possibly have returned to the Jerusalem temple in the allotted time? The answer is, he couldn't have. Even had it been possible, Joazar certainly would never have risked such a trip under the circumstances. To do so would have been to condemn himself and the child to death at the hands of Herod's executioner.

Fortunately for Joazar, the only other Jewish temple on the face of the earth lay only a few miles away at Leontopolis.

The temple founded by the exiled high priest Onias.

It was doubtless here that the infant Jesus was dedicated to Yahweh and circumcised as he began his second week of life. And the temple precincts where this ritual was conducted must have seemed quite familiar to Mariamne and Joazar. They were, after all, natives of Egypt and members of an elite family of priests. And as this was the only temple of Yahweh in all of Egypt, it seems highly probable that Joazar served as a priest here before attaining (however briefly) the high priesthood in Jerusalem. Likewise, the legend that Mariamne had been raised in the temple courts makes sense only if the temple in question were this one. She, like her uncle, was a native of Egypt and therefore could not possibly have enjoyed access to the temple in Jerusalem.

Her family's priestly status makes it quite likely that she was, in fact, raised in close proximity to this temple. But although this aspect of her legend seems entirely plausible, another facet of her story is riddled with difficulties. This, of course, is the patently ludicrous assertion that Mary was a virgin when she conceived (and gave birth to!) Jesus. Such a contention is quite clearly outlandish for biological reasons, but there are other difficulties to be considered as well. First of all, Mariamne had already given birth to an older child of Herod's, who shared his father's name. It was therefore quite impossible for her to be considered a virgin in any sense of the word.

But it is precisely the sense of the word that is the cause of the problem.

The concept of the virgin birth rests, quite precariously, on a single word contained in the prophecies of Isaiah. This is the Hebrew word *almah*, which is to be found in the following declaration attributed to the prophet: "The virgin will be with child and will give birth to a son, and they will call him Immanuel, which means 'God with us.' " [204] This is how the author of *Matthew* remembered this particular prophecy, which he did not hesitate to quote in connection with Jesus — even though there is no record of Jesus ever being called Immanuel. And even though the prophecy in question was uttered in connection with events long passed by the time Mariamne brought Jesus into the world.

The original prophecy was directed specifically at a man named King Ahaz, who lived several centuries before Jesus' birth. And it did not end with the proclamation concerning the "virgin" — it continued: "Before the boy knows enough to reject the wrong and choose the right, the land of the two kings you dread will be laid waste. Yahweh will bring on you and your people, and on the house of your father a time unlike any since Ephraim broke away from Judah. He will bring the king of Assyria." [205]

This declaration could not possibly have come to fruition during Jesus' lifetime, for the simple reason that the kingdom of Assyria no longer existed.

It hadn't for more than six centuries.

But despite these problems, perhaps the most obvious error made by the author of *Matthew* was the mistranslation of the word *almah*. Writing in Greek, he rendered the word as *parthenos*, a word that indeed meant "virgin" and was closely associated with the virgin goddess Athena. This was all well and good — except that the word *almah* meant something else entirely. It referred, quite simply, to a young woman, and it carried no specific sexual connotation whatsoever. The woman might well have been a virgin, but she could just as easily have found her way around the proverbial block a few times. Indeed, the latter possibility is actually far more likely given the origins of the word *almah*, which comes from the name of an ancient Persian goddess.

This particular deity, named Al-mah, was a moon goddess. As such, she served as a prototype for Cinderella, Snow White and similar faerie-tale heroines associated with the lunar disc. The term alma mater, commonly applied to a high school or university from which one has graduated, actually means "young mother" and was applied in ancient times to a Roman priestess — probably to the moon goddess Diana — whose role it was to offer instruction in the sexual mysteries.[206] Such a commission implies a certain level of experience in such mysteries and pretty much disqualifies any virgins at the very outset.

The title alma mater appears to have been abbreviated at some point to *amata*, meaning "beloved." [207] This is, of course, the exact meaning of the Egyptian word *meri*, which serves as the prefix for the name Mariamne, which literally means "beloved of Amen." It was this very title that was worn by the wife of the god, who took upon herself the role of the goddess in sacred union with the god-king

Amen. Can it be mere coincidence that Mary herself is said to have experienced just such a mystical union with the divine male principle?

Hardly likely. Nor can it be mere chance that the original *amata* were involved in the same sort of sexual ritual in the Roman temple. As such, they formed a sisterhood of sorts known as the vestal virgins, which served as a model for the later institution of the convent or nunnery. In fact, the nuns of a later era would even appropriate the name *amata* for themselves, retaining their chastity on the grounds that they were now somehow married to God. Their role model in this virgin exercise? None other than Mary, whose example as bride of God they sought to emulate. And their decision to call themselves nuns? This, too, makes perfect sense.

The warrior king Joshua, who had led the wandering Hebrew army into the promised land, had been known as the "son of Nun." Now Jesus — whose name was the Greek equivalent of the Hebrew Joshua — was the son of Mary.

The first nun.

It may be recalled that Merlin, too, was said to have been the son of a nun who had sexual intercourse with a daemon or spirit. Such references ultimately may be traced back to the ancient concept of Nun, the Egyptian name for the watery chaos out of which all things were formed. This was a decidedly feminine concept, recalling the waters of the womb as well as the primordial reservoir that produced sea monsters such as Tiamat and Hawawa — or Eve.

These female sea serpents or mermaids were the mothers of all creation, having produced the world in an act of sexual union with the divine male principle that, according to *Genesis*, "was hovering over the waters." [208] And this is precisely what Mary supposedly did in conceiving Jesus, a savior who himself was destined to usher in a new world by proclaiming the kingdom of God.

The word nun also appears closely related to the Sumerian term *nin*, which most often simply referred to a lady. For example, just as the god Enlil's name translated to mean "lord of the air," so his consort Ninlil was "lady of the air." It is altogether likely that

Inanna's name was originally rendered as Ninanna, which would have meant "lady of heaven." [209] And of course this is reminiscent of the title shared by Isis and Mary — queen of heaven.

The suffix *anna* signified something pertaining to the heavens, the Sumerian realm of the great god An. This makes it especially relevant to note that not one but two women associated with Jesus bore the name Anna. One is Mary's own mother, who is mentioned in apocryphal literature and whose name identifies Mary explicitly as the daughter of heaven, priestess-avatar of the great celestial goddess Inanna.[210]

The other figure is mentioned in the text of *Luke* as an aged prophetess who predicted great things for Jesus (though the exact content of her prophecy is, for some reason, not included in the account).

According to the narrative, this Anna never left the temple.[211] She was the daughter of a man named Phanuel, a name that means "face of El" and pays homage to the ancient Canaanite father god. The face of god was a common metaphor for the sun, which no man may look upon without risking damage to the eyes. This was the consequence of the ineffable god attempting to enter the realm of sight, making himself visible yet at the same time bestowing blindness on any who dared to gaze upon him. The sun was the image of the invisible god.

As was the son, the heir to the throne of Egypt.

Horus the son was also Horus the sun, image of the invisible god Osiris or Asir. Just as the king was the god incarnate. The same claim, of course, would be made about Jesus. And in light of all this, it is hardly surprising to find that Anna the prophetess is a scion of the tribe of Asher, the name of which virtually mirrors that of the Egyptian father god Asir. Her role as a prophetess who lives in the temple clearly marks her as a serpent priestess in the mold of the python oracle at Delphi, a temple sacred to Horus' Greek counterpart Apollo.

None of this can be accidental.

Indeed, it is quite clear from all these connections that those who wove together the myths and prophecies surrounding the promised messiah knew exactly what they were talking about. They knew precisely the imagery to use in setting the stage for their hero's advent, drawing upon several streams of tradition to create an intricate tapestry of sacred tradition — one that is indeed so intricate that following each strand to its point of origin can be a difficult and task. Yet because each strand fits together with its fellows so neatly, those who undertake the task are in for a dazzling experience.

To the magi who went in search of Jesus, it must have seemed as though everything were coming together perfectly. Here was a child born on the very day when Sirius emerged above the horizon. He was a child of royal blood, the son of no less a personage than King Herod. And through his adopted father, his uncle Joazar, he was heir to the high priesthood as well. Because of this, the infant Jesus had it within his heritage to achieve the task of uniting the royal and priestly offices in a single person. Indeed, he must have seemed almost destined to do so.

And this is why Herod would have been desperate to stop him.

The reference in *Matthew* to a "slaughter of the innocents" reflects this desperation, though such a massacre probably never occurred. The story itself appears to have been borrowed from the life of Moses, whose birth likewise sparked a campaign (this one by the pharaoh) to murder all the newborn children in the region.[212] Indeed, the theme was so popular that it was even incorporated into the life of Arthur, who supposedly employed a similar strategy in trying to rid himself of his would-be successor Mordred. In this case, he assembled all the infants who had been born on May Day and cast them adrift on the open sea in a ship.[213] Most were killed, but Mordred survived.

In Herod's case, however, there appears to have been at least some truth to the tale. Despite the author's reliance upon the traditional "slaughter of the innocents" theme, there can be little doubt that the king did in fact want Jesus dead and that his heir

Archelaus had a similar intentions toward the would-be usurper.

The author of *Matthew* reports that, shortly after beginning his sojourn in Egypt, Joseph received word from an "angel" — probably from an informant loyal to his family — that Herod had passed away. But this message came with a warning: Archelaus had succeeded to the throne and was no more likely to provide a hospitable welcome than his father had been.[214] Joseph was therefore afraid to return. And when he did, he avoided Jerusalem altogether and settled instead in Galilee, the region that subsequently became known as Jesus' homeland. This district was now being governed by another of Herod's sons, Antipas, to whom it had been bequeathed in a complicated three-way partitioning of the kingdom. Archelaus had received the title of ethnarch and the most prestigious endowment — Jerusalem and the surrounding environs of Judea. Galilee had been assigned to Antipas, while a third region to the northeast had gone to a son named Philip. Evidently, Antipas must have been viewed as a lesser threat to Jesus than Archelaus, considering Joazar's decision to settle in his territories. The two brothers were rivals more than allies, and Antipas aspired to rule the land assigned to Archelaus. He was therefore not likely to cooperate in handing over a political refugee who had sought asylum in his territories.

This was what Joazar was counting on.

And apparently, his hunch paid off, for he lived at peace under Antipas' jurisdiction and eventually returned to reclaim the high priesthood when Archelaus was stripped of his position. In the meantime, with Joazar safely out of reach, Archelaus was left to sit and stew. Unable to rid himself of the young messiah-in-waiting, he was forced to look for other alternatives. And the most obvious of these was a campaign to discredit Jesus as a legitimate heir to the throne. There is no direct evidence that Archelaus actually undertook such an enterprise, but this should come as no surprise. The architect of a rumor seldom reveals himself, for fear of undermining the rumor's credibility. Archelaus had an axe to grind against Jesus, and if anyone had become aware that he was the source of the slander that began to circulate, the story itself would have immediately been dismissed as propaganda.

The slander itself, whatever its source, survived in the form of a persistent accusation that Jesus was not a legitimate heir to the throne of Jerusalem but was in fact a bastard.

Two centuries after Jesus' death, the rumors persisted. The so-called *Acts of Pilate*, a document from that period purporting to contain a record of Jesus' trial before the Roman prefect, puts the charge of his illegitimate birth on the lips of his accusers at the time of his trial. They bluntly charged that he was "born of fornication" and that his parents had fled to Egypt "because they counted for nothing among the people." [215] Both these charges were absolutely false. Jesus was the product of Herod's marriage to Mariamne, who had fled with Joazar to Egypt for fear of the king — not because the general public held them in disdain. In fact, the opposite was true. Joazar appears to have been quite a popular high priest, and he would be welcomed back to that lofty position ten years later to broad general acclaim.

The charges contained against Jesus in the Acts of Pilate are precisely the sort of slander one would have expected to emanate from Herod or Archelaus. These men, more than anyone else, stood to benefit from discrediting Jesus' claim to the throne. And it is for this reason that they can be identified as a likely source for the rumors of his illegitimacy. One such rumor went even further and identified him as the son of a Roman soldier named Pandera or Pantera. Interestingly, a tombstone still marks the gravesite of a soldier by that name who was killed about the time of Jesus' birth. The soldier in question, whose full name was Tiberius Julius Abdes Pantera, was born in the city of Tyre and died on the German frontier.[216] This is the same Tyre that served as the ancient capital for the Phoenicians.

It may be only coincidence that this Pandera's role in the army was that of an archer. But then again, perhaps the choice was quite deliberate. Perhaps those who started the rumor that identified an archer (or arker) as Jesus' father meant to convey a certain sense of irony. Jesus, in time, would clearly identify himself with the ark hero Jonah. Moreover, his name was but a variant of Jason's, linking him at least vaguely with the captain of the *Argo*. And the star that marked his advent, Sirius, was known to the Sumerians simply as the archer's weapon of choice, "the arrow." [217] In this sense, Jesus really was the son of the archer.

According to one version of the tale, this Pandera was the father of a Jewish prostitute known as Miriam of Magdala.[218]

Or Mary Magdalene.

Though this might seem to be a case of confusion, it actually serves as helpful confirmation of Jesus' parentage: It identifies the woman in question as none other than Herod's second Mariamne, for whom he named the tower or *migdol*. The same title was also later worn by Jesus' consort, who was viewed as her successor in the role of "god's wife."

But what about the name Pandera?

A mere cursory look reveals it is in fact just one letter removed from Pandora, the name given by the Greeks to the first woman ever created. Pandora was a key player in the legend of Prometheus, whose audacious act of stealing fire from the gods so enraged Zeus that the king of the gods set about plotting his revenge. That revenge was to take a decidedly feminine form, as he instructed the blacksmith god to forge a woman out of the soil and decreed that she be adorned in the finest garments. He then offered her as a gift to Prometheus' brother, who accepted this seemingly gracious boon despite his sibling's warning that it might be a trap.

And a trap is exactly what it was. For before he sent Pandora on her way, Zeus bestowed upon her a vessel containing all the world's evils. Zeus knew that curiosity would eventually get the better of her and she would unseal the vessel, unleashing all the pent-up plagues and woes upon mankind. The popular version of this myth refers to the vessel in question as a box, but the original tale makes clear that it was something else entirely. In fact, it seems to have been a jar of some sort, a honey vase known as a *pithos*.[219]

The description sounds suspiciously like the chalice or grail, and the name *pithos* strikes yet another chord. It draws upon the same root as the word python — the kind of serpent found in the temple at Delphi. All of a sudden, it seems, we have another dragon lady on our hands. Pandora is yet one more manifestation of the serpent priestess, whose name has been adapted to explain Jesus' origins as the son of such a person. If this is the case, Pandera was not a slur on the name of Jesus' father, but his *mother* — Pandora being a decidedly feminine figure.

Whatever we are to make of this, it seems quite likely that Archelaus began a smear campaign to counter any claims being made about Jesus with a barrage of innuendo and slander. Faced with such an officially sanctioned onslaught of propaganda, Joazar decided to keep a low profile in Galilee for the time being, counting on Archelaus to dig his own political grave. He knew the ethnarch from his time at court with Herod, and he must have realized that Archelaus had failed to inherit his father's knack for diplomacy and compromise. Eventually, he knew, the ethnarch would slip up and lose his tenuous grasp on power.

It was only a matter of time.

VIII

The Galilean

Joazar was, in many ways, the least of Archelaus' worries. As long as the former high priest kept a low profile, he could be of little threat to the new ethnarch. In the meantime, there were other enemies who far less willing to bide their time.

Many nationalists saw Herod's death as a great opportunity. After nearly four decades, they were finally free of his iron-fisted rule, and there was cause to hope that the despotic behavior they had endured under the old king might finally be at an end. His kingdom was in a state of complete disarray, sectioned off into three parts among three sons — none of whom was Herod's equal when it came to suppressing rebellion. And rebellion was exactly what these folks had in mind.

The seeds of revolution had been planted before Herod's death.

Religious purists and nationalists had always chafed under his regime, but the last straw came when Herod insisted on placing a golden eagle — the symbol of Rome — over the entrance to the temple.

The presence of such a likeness was viewed by the pious as a major breach of the law handed down by Moses, who had prohibited the display of "graven images."[220] It was also a humiliating reminder of the nation's status as a vassal state to the Roman Empire. Even in the face of vigorous protests, Herod refused to remove it. So a pair of popular teachers named Judas and Matthias — the names that had been born by Judas Maccabeus and his father — took it upon themselves to do the job for him.

These men had developed quite a reputation in Jerusalem. They were considered "the most eloquent men among the Jews, and the most celebrated interpreters of the Jewish laws." Judas was somehow associated with Sepphoris, the main city in Galilee, and both men had attracted a considerable following among the younger crowd of the city.[221]

When they heard that Herod had fallen gravely ill, they seized upon the opportunity to do something about the profane eagle he had placed over the temple, inciting their followers to tear the it down and hack it to pieces with axes.

They were, for their trouble, promptly arrested.

Herod, it turned out, was not quite on his deathbed yet. Wishing to make an example of these rabble-rousers, he laid out the charges against them. Matthias and several of his companions were summarily condemned to death and burned alive, but Judas of Sepphoris apparently escaped to his home district of Galilee and began preparing to stir up more trouble.[222] Matthias' execution, meanwhile, only deepened public resentment of Herod.

Unfortunately for Archelaus, he inherited this resentment at his father's death. The public directed its outrage over the "eagle incident" toward the new ethnarch, and large groups of protesters had begun to gather, demanding an apology. Archelaus knew full well that he risked an all-out uprising unless he acted, so he sent representatives out to address the crowds — only to have them shouted down when they tried to speak. The volatile situation quickly degenerated into a melee pitting the protesters against a group of soldiers sent out by Archelaus to keep the peace.

In the meantime, Archelaus faced another obstacle closer to home: His brother Antipas had challenged his claim to the throne and had sent papers to the emperor seeking Roman support. The situation was complex. Archelaus had been named as successor in Herod's latest will, but Antipas had been named in a previous document and had recruited a number of supporters eager to discredit his brother. The situation was so muddled that both men were summoned to Rome for a personal audience with the emperor to straighten the things out.

While they were gone, any remaining semblance of order collapsed.

With Herod's two prospective heirs both absent, a number of pretenders to the throne rose up around the country. "At this time," it was later noted in a bit of hyperbole, "there were ten thousand disorders in Judea." [223]

Foremost among these was a man named Judas, apparently the same person who had helped orchestrate the eagle incident at the temple. Josephus mentions three men named Judas in conjunction with disturbances around the time of Herod's death. And although he never says so explicitly, similarities among them indicate they were probably the same man:

➢ Judas of Sepphoris, instigator of the eagle incident, was connected with Sepphoris in Galilee and disappeared mysteriously when Herod killed had his partner, Matthias, executed.

➢ Judas son of Ezekias looted the temple in Sepphoris, raised a large number of followers and started a rebellion against Rome. He was never captured.

➢ Judas the Galilean, also associated with the region around Sepphoris called Galilee, drew a large following and started an uprising against Rome. He, too, was never captured.

With his partner Matthias facing execution for his treachery against Herod, Judas had fled to Galilee. It was here that, a generation earlier, his father Ezekias had assembled a substantial rebel force and conquered portions of Syria. Herod himself — then just fifteen years of age — had put an end to the conquest, defeating Ezekias and putting him to death along with a number of his followers.[224]

It was not the end of his movement, however. Judas had seen to that. With Matthias, he had attracted a considerable following in Jerusalem. And now, he proceeded to follow in his father's footsteps. Assembling a fighting force of his own, he made an assault upon the palace at Sepphoris, making off with all the money and weapons stored therein.

This done, he set his sights on obtaining the throne. In fact, Judas was not the only Jewish revolutionary with royal aspirations to emerge with the death of Herod. Another man set himself up as king and burned the royal palace at Jericho, while still another proclaimed himself king and began an uprising with four of his brothers. But Judas was, unquestionably, the dominant figure — and the man behind an assault on Jerusalem that nearly succeeded in expelling the Romans, at least temporarily.

In the Jewish capital, the Roman procurator Sabinus had aggravated already tense relations with the masses by seizing Herod's assets and imposing harsh new restrictions. In response, "a great many ten thousands of men" from areas as diverse as Galilee, Jericho and Idumea rose up to oppose him.[225] The situation escalated rapidly out of control, and it soon became apparent that Sabinus would not be able to handle matters on his own. He therefore sent out an urgent appeal to Varus, the governor of Syria and his immediate superior in the Roman chain of command. Varus had left Sabinus at the head of a Roman legion — one of three under Varus' command in Syria. But now he received word that these soldiers were on the defensive and Sabinus feared they would be routed if help did not arrive soon.

The Jewish rebels had split into three main groups. The first seized the Hippodrome, the second made an assault on the temple, and the third targeted the king's palace. Sabinus' soldiers tried to slow them down by setting fire to portions of the temple itself, then dug in and waited for help to arrive from Varus.

The Syrian governor wasn't taking any chances. He assembled his remaining two legions and recruited auxiliary units from various rulers in the area who were either enemies of the Herodians or allied with Rome. But, tellingly, he did not march directly to Jerusalem. Instead, he made for Sepphoris, where Judas had raided the palace and set up his headquarters. There was likely a simple reason for this decision: Varus knew that Judas was behind the Jerusalem uprising and hoped to deal the Galilean a crushing blow on his own turf.

Sepphoris was, at the time, a major metropolis of some thirty thousand people. An important crossroads, it marked the midpoint of the main east-west thoroughfare linking the Sea of Galilee and the Mediterranean coast. It was also the terminus of a major north-south road winding up through Samaria from Jerusalem. As a city of commercial importance, it had all the amenities: a theater, a palace, two marketplaces, courts, a fortress and archives, all enclosed within two city walls.

When Varus' troops marched into the area, they took no chances. After routing the resistance they encountered in the city, they "made its inhabitants their slaves and burnt the city." [226]

They did not, however, capture Judas.

His first objective achieved, Varus proceeded through Samaria, where he pitched camp but encountered no resistance, on his way to reinforce Sabinus in Jerusalem. Several other villages were plundered and burned along the way in a show of force that eventually paid handsome dividends for the Syrian governor. The Jews who had instigated the uprising not only faced a huge army of Roman soldiers and auxiliary forces, they also had no doubt heard reports of what had happened at Sepphoris and the other rebel strongholds in Varus' path. So it was not surprising that, by the time the army itself reached Jerusalem, the resistance itself had basically evaporated.

The situation resolved, Varus eventually returned to Syria and

Archelaus, having been confirmed in his claim to the throne by Augustus, returned to govern Judea for the next decade.

It was not, however, the end of trouble in Palestine. It was, on the contrary, just the beginning.

The Judas Revolt

Although Archelaus won his father's throne in Jerusalem, his brother Antipas did not go unrewarded in his petition to the emperor. He was ultimately granted the territories to the north and east — Galilee and Perea — and the title of tetrarch (literally, ruler of one-fourth of the kingdom). His half-brother Philip received the same title in lands to the northeast.

As it turned out, the latter two brothers both fared better than Archelaus, who was so widely disliked by his subjects that the emperor removed him from the throne after ten years in power. He was subsequently stripped of his wealth and banished to Vienna, to be replaced by a procurator named Coponius — the first in a series of such Roman appointees who would govern Jerusalem and the lands surrounding it directly for the next three decades.

Coponius brought with him a man named Quirinius, a Roman senator sent by the emperor "to be a judge of that nation and take account of their substance." [227] His job would be to take a census in Judea that would serve as the basis for taxing the people. This was the census that the author of *Luke* used (erroneously) as a reference point in dating the birth of Jesus. Needless to say, such a project did not go over well with the Jews. They had already endured decades of severe taxation to pay for Herod's extravagances, and the idea of paying still more taxes — this time directly to Rome — was intolerable.

The issue became a focal point for the already seething discontent among Jewish nationalists, led once again by Judas of Galilee — this time in conjunction with a new partner called Sadduc. For them, such a tax plan was nothing less than an affront to Jewish sovereignty. At least under Herod, the Romans had provided Jerusalem and her people with a semblance of independence. Now, the Romans were taking even this from them.

Judas and Sadduc protested that "this taxation was no better than an introduction to slavery, and exhorted the nation to assert their liberty." [228] The tax protest would become a rallying cry for their movement. And their movement, in turn, would become the foundation of organized opposition to Roman rule in Palestine for the next several decades. Its scope would broaden to include several factions, among them the militant Zealots responsible for planning the revolution and a group of assassins known as the *sicarii*. The question, "Is it right to pay taxes to Caesar or not?" [229] would become the defining question for the followers of Judas, Sadduc and their successors. It was the issue over which they had vowed a fight to the death. Judas and Sadduc felt that the empire had robbed the Jews of all that was rightfully theirs. The Romans had installed their own king, and then — even worse — had taken direct control with their own governor. They had made the high priesthood subject to the whims of Herod and now Archelaus. And now, for their trouble, they were demanding direct payment to their already bulging coffers.

The burden of imperial taxes caused a continual drain on the nation's resource and left many in a state of perpetual destitution. Perhaps as a result of this, the members of the resistance movement born under Judas would eventually designate themselves simply as Ebionites — a word that means "the poor." They were those who had nothing, quite simply because the Romans had stripped them of everything. Unable to claim the seats of power in Jerusalem that had belonged to their ancestors, they set up a sort of government in exile to the north, in Galilee, modeled after the ancient Davidic kingdom, ruled by a king and a high priest. Judas occupied the former role, while his partner claimed the rank of opposition high priest. He was called Sadduc, probably not his true name but a title that identified him as the "Just" or "Righteous" one. It was the same title borne by David's high priest, Zadok, a thousand years earlier, and it would continue to be borne by his successors.

Who was this mysterious Sadduc?

It is perhaps impossible to answer this question, as he emerges as little more than a shadowy character in Josephus' narrative. The writer himself probably didn't even know his true identity — if he had, he would have certainly revealed it. But perhaps the most likely candidate was none other than Joazar, who had been deprived of the high priesthood once before and still enjoyed a considerable degree of popularity. He was, at this point, living in Judas' home region of Galilee. And he was also a former high priest who had been forced from office on charges of treason by the ruling family. As a result of these charges traitor, he had already been branded as a rebel; as a former high priest, he was eminently qualified to serve in that capacity once again.

Even though Joazar had been living in exile from Jerusalem for a full decade, he had not been forgotten. Far from it. Indeed, his popularity remained so great that, at the time of the tax revolt, a groundswell was beginning to build in favor of restoring him to the high priesthood.

Legitimately.

According to Josephus, this groundswell eventually reached a crescendo, and Joazar was swept back into office by popular acclamation. The historian reports that Joazar was elevated to the high priesthood for a second time when the office was "conferred upon him by the multitude." [230] This is, on the face of it, an amazing statement. High priests were not usually chosen based on their popularity, but rather in deference to family connections or political considerations. Or favoritism. Or bribes. The fact that Joazar was selected in such an unorthodox manner reflected the unorthodox times in which he was living. And it indicated the intense level of popular support he enjoyed. Indeed, this support seems to have been so strong that the Roman establishment thought it unwise to oppose him — at least for the moment.

Joazar, however, knew the politics of the situation all too well.

He realized that his hold on power was tenuous at best, for he was now caught squarely between two rival constituencies. On the one side stood Judas and the rebels; on the other, the Roman establishment. Having risen to power on a wave of discontent over the tax issue, Joazar could be sure that the Romans would remove him from office as soon as they felt it was safe to do so — unless, that is, he made some sort of conciliatory move to end the crisis. At this moment in time, his influence was unrivaled. With the nation teetering on the edge of all-out war, he had the power to nudge it over the precipice or pull it back from the brink.

His choice?

Despite his possible association with Judas and his personal opposition to the census, he chose the latter course. According to Josephus, it was Joazar who issued a formal plea to "leave off any further opposition" to Roman taxes, thus averting a rebellion that would have undoubtedly cost thousands of lives and resulted in the imposition of martial law by the Romans. Forced to wear the mantle of rebel or statesman, he took the higher ground. And such was the level of his influence with the masses that, even though they were fiercely opposed to paying Roman taxes, they nonetheless heeded his call for restraint and submitted to the empire without further dispute.

What was Joazar's reward for defusing such a volatile situation? When all was said and done, Quirinius unceremoniously deprived him of the high priesthood and conferred the office on someone else.

Joazar should, perhaps, have expected as much. He had risen to power as an opposition high priest, yet he himself had been instrumental in silencing the opposition. And in doing so, he had effectively cut off his own base of support. Once the furor over Roman taxation died down, Quirinius and the empire no longer had any reason to fear Joazar.

Nor did they have any further use for him.

After this, nothing more is written of Joazar (or about his apparent alter-egos Joseph and Sadduc, for that matter). His political career seems to have come to an end. But the legacy of the tax revolt in which he had played such a pivotal role lived on, as did the adoptive son he and his niece had so faithfully protected for the first ten years of his young life. The Romans might have extracted their tax payments on this occasion, but the opposition movement Judas and Sadduc had begun was not about to go quietly into the night.

Far from it.

Indeed, its story was just beginning.

IX

Voice in the Wilderness

For the better part of two centuries, the temple at Leontopolis had operated independently of its counterpart in Jerusalem. It had its own sacrifices, its own priesthood and its own claim to be the true center of Yahweh's cult. Yet ever since the exiled high priest Onias founded this rival sanctuary, the hope had been kept alive that a descendant of this man would return to claim his rightful place at the altar in Jerusalem.

Now, at last, that time had come.

And the man destined to stake that claim was also named Onias, though he was better known by a variant of that name: John.

The history of the man who would become known as John the Baptist is complex, muddied by myth and inconsistency. According to the author of *Luke*, he was born exactly six months before his "kinsman" Jesus in an event rendered miraculous by the fact that his mother was past the age of child-bearing. Yet this timeline fails to adequately explain an account preserved in the Slavonic version of Josephus' writings, wherein the historian (or someone using his name) indicates that this same John was summoned on one occasion to appear before Archelaus.

Had John been born in the same year as Jesus, he would have been only ten years of age when Archelaus was banished to Vienna.

Yet according to this version of Josephus' history, he was already baptizing people in the Jordan River and living a life of a desert ascetic. Certainly these are not the actions of a ten-year-old. And Archelaus would hardly have summoned a prepubescent boy into his presence for the purpose of answering charges that he was inciting the people to revolt. The charges against him? The Slavonic account indicates that he went forth summoning the Jews to claim their freedom from imperial authority with these words: "God has sent me, that I may show you the way of the law, wherein you may free yourselves from many holders of power. And there will be no mortal ruling over you, only the highest — who has sent me." [231]

This was the talk of a revolutionary.

And more specifically, it was just the sort of language being used by those involved in the tax revolt at about this same period. Judas the Galilean and his compatriots claimed, as did John, that the Jewish people should be free and no mortal should rule over them — only God was their master. According to Josephus, in the primary version of his writings, Judas and his followers held "an inviolable attachment to liberty" and regarded God as "their only ruler and lord." [232]

If John was, in fact, much older than Jesus, it would explain why the author of *Luke* thought his mother was past child-bearing age at the time Jesus was born. The fact is, she was. The legend that John was born six months before Jesus has nothing to do with history and everything to do with symbolism. John's birthday has traditionally been fixed to correspond with the summer solstice, the point at which the sun has reached its apex in the sky. From that time forward, the days grow shorter and the shadows longer as the year begins to age and the dark season of Seth begins to descend .

Jesus' advent, by contrast, has long been celebrated at the winter solstice. This was the time at which the sun itself was said to be born, growing stronger with each sunrise as the days grow longer and usher in the season of Horus. This tension between the figures of Jesus and John is captured perfectly in a statement attributed to the latter: "He must increase, and I must decrease." [233] The new sun must wax, just as the old sun must wane. The new sun was Horus. The old sun was Seth.

It is already clear from his advent at the appearance of Sirius that Jesus fit perfectly into the former role. When Sirius broke above the horizon each year, the event was known as the star's heliacal rising. This meant that it was literally "rising with the sun," the star of Isis bearing the sun disk of Horus across the heavens and symbolically giving birth to it.

John was just as clearly a Seth avatar. Perhaps his most well-known epithet was one he is said to have applied to himself: a voice crying in the wilderness. The wilderness was, of course, the domain of Seth. And John adopted the persona of a wild man so often associated with this particular god. He wore a coat of camel's hair, giving him the hairy appearance that was likewise the hallmark of such figures as Enkidu, Esau and, of course, Merlin. But John bore a still greater resemblance to yet another hairy Seth figure, a heroic judge of Hebrew legend famous for his superhuman strength — and for the source of that strength: his hair.

Lion Man

The story of Samson served as an obvious model for the legend of John the Baptist, from the very moment of the two heroes' conception. The Baptist's mother was said to have been unable to conceive any children, yet she received a visit from an angel proclaiming that she would bear a son. As it turns out, the same exact circumstance had beset the mother of Samson, who likewise received a visitation from an angel declaring womb would be opened. In each, the baby was considered the product of a miracle. And the angel delivered special instructions for both of them, which were nearly identical:

➢ Samson: "Now see to it that you drink no wine or fermented drink and that you do not eat anything unclean, because you will conceive and give birth to a son. No razor may be used on his head, because the boy is to be a Nazirite, set apart to God from his birth. ..."[234]

➢ John: "He is never to take wine or other fermented drink, and he will be filled with the holy spirit, even from his mother's womb."[235]

Both men were to be dedicated from the moment of their conception as members of the elite group known as Nazirites, men who took a vow never to shave their heads or partake of alcohol. The term was based on the Hebrew root *nazir*, which referred to a prince or consecrated person. Clearly, these two men were destined for lives of greatness. But *nazir* had a more fundamental definition: It referred to a vine. The same sort of vine that was said to grow out of the stump of Jesse or the bones of the dead king Osiris. When Jesus proclaimed, "I am the vine and you are the branches," he was in fact declaring himself a *nazir* or a variant form of the same word, *nasi*. A prince.

Yet he did not adhere strictly to the Nazirite restrictions, refusing to abide by the prohibition against alcohol and therefore earning a reputation among his detractors as a drunkard.[236] To these people, he must have seemed a hypocrite and hardly a true Nazirite. Nevertheless, the designation stuck and writers such as the author of *Matthew* — who failed to understand the significance of the term — mistook it as a reference to the Galilean town of Nazareth.[237] Unfortunately, there is no evidence that this town even existed during Jesus' lifetime, and it was probably not founded until after his death. His followers would eventually come to label themselves Nazoreans, though there is nothing to indicate that they had no connection whatsoever to a town called Nazareth. Instead, they were identifying themselves as followers of the *nazir*, the true vine and prince of Israel.

John's identification as a Nazirite indicates that he preceded Jesus in this role, though his life — like that of Samson — would end in tragedy. Each man would be captured through the deceit of a woman, would be imprisoned by his enemies and ultimately die at their hands. The parallels are indeed quite fascinating, and they do not end there.

Samson would grow up to be a man of unparalleled strength. His identity as a Seth figure is confirmed by an incident in which he slew a thousand men with the jawbone of an ass, the totem animal of Seth. And he played out this role in a tanist ritual veiled in the language of symbolism. This ritual stands at the heart of a famous legend involving the mythic strongman, a legend that unfolds with Samson's impending marriage. As Samson journeys to the land of his betrothed to meet her, he is suddenly confronted by a fierce young lion. The beast springs out of a vineyard and comes roaring toward him, but Samson is able to tear the lion apart. Later, when Samson returns by the same path, he notices a swarm of bees has made a hive in the lion's carcass and reaches in to scoop out a handful of honey.

This all sounds very strange unless one recognizes the tanist underpinnings of the tale.

The young lion was in fact a tanist challenger who wished to claim Samson's betrothed for himself. Samson was a Seth figure. And the lion, with its golden face and fiery mane, was a natural symbol for the sun god Horus. In this particular challenge, it was the old king who emerged victorious by slaying the young lion and claiming his reward — the "honey" of his new wife's bed that would have otherwise belonged to his challenger. This imagery was appropriate, for honey had long been associated with the marriage bed, and the honeycomb symbolic of the female genitalia. The intoxicating mead that imparted wisdom contained honey as a defining ingredient, a link that once again attested to the nature of sexual intimacy as a means of obtaining divine insight. And the ritual of the honeymoon seems to have derived its name from a the symbolic joining of the golden sun king with the moon goddess.

What does any of this have to do with John the Baptist?

Perhaps quite a bit, if one considers the likelihood that he served as a high priest at the temple of Yahweh at Leontopolis — the city of the lions.

The association of John with the carob tree identifies him as one who filled the role of an Egyptian *kher heb* or high priest. And his name appears to link him with a line of priests stretching back through the rainmaker Honi (also identified with a carob tree) to the exiled high priest who founded the temple, Onias. It appears to have been somewhat traditional for high priests to wear this name, for it was borne by three of the seven men who served in this capacity before the exile to Leontopolis. It seems quite possible that John's name merely carried on this tradition. In becoming high priest in the city of the lions, he would have succeeded in symbolically subduing his leonine adversary, just as Samson had done.

In the end, Samson's fate was sealed when he submitted to the charms of a woman named Delilah, who persuaded him to share the secret of his great strength with her. This secret was contained in the seven braids of hair on his head — hair that had never been shaved in accordance with his Nazirite vow. Having made a pact with Samson's enemies, Delilah proceeded to put him to sleep in her lap, whereupon she beckoned an accomplice to shave off his long locks and render him as weak as other men. Thus was he subdued by his enemies, who gleefully tormented him by gouging out both of his eyes. In the end, however, Samson would exact his revenge with one last feat of heroic strength: Having been chained between the two great pillars supporting the temple, he pushed with all his might and brought the entire edifice crashing down on a crowd of three thousand men.

This story is entertaining enough, but it can only be truly understood in light of Samson's identity as a Seth figure. The maiden who proves to be his undoing wears a name that literally means "languishing." Samson's association with such a woman reveals that his vitality is waning and he is becoming an old man, a fisher king ready to relinquish his throne. Delilah's name also bears a vague resemblance to that of Lilith, the priestess of Inanna who was responsible for seducing them and then killing them — the precise role Delilah plays in the legend of Samson.

When this treacherous woman lays Samson in her lap, this is not simply a case of colorful description. It is much more.

The lap of Inanna was considered the throne of the king. A Sumerian royal wedding hymn issued forth a plea to Inanna in behalf of the newly crowned monarch: "My queen, queen of the universe, the queen who encompasses the universe, may he enjoy long days in your holy lap." [238] The woman's lap, as the source of her reproductive power, was viewed as the throne to be occupied by those of the royal bloodline. Inanna's Egyptian counterpart Isis was depicted consistently with a throne upon her head and was herself referred to as the Throne. She it was who judged whether a man was worthy to sit in her lap.[239]

Since Jesus' mother was an avatar of Isis, one might expect to find this sort of imagery in connection with her legend as well. And indeed, one does. *The Gospel of Pseudo-Matthew*, which relates the infant Jesus' journey to Egpyt and the legend of the palm tree, depicts the child "sitting with a happy countenance in his mother's lap." [240] At one point in the narrative, he climbs down from her lap to do battle with a group of dragons — the child Horus conquering the serpents of Seth.

The images of ancient mythology likewise pervade the story of Samson. The hero's very name brands him as a sun god, being derived from the Hebrew word denoting brilliance, *shamesh*. This word recalls the name of the sun god from whom Hammurabi supposedly received his famed law code: Shamash. It seems to be likewise related the name of the national god of Moab, a tribal confederacy southeast of Jerusalem. This deity's name was Chemosh, and he is linked in an important inscription with the name Ashtar, a variation on Ishtar — the Babylonian name for Inanna.[241] Apparently, she was his consort. Just as Samson sat in the lap of Delilah, so it appears that Chemosh occupied the lap of Ashtar.

But Samson could not occupy this place forever. He was growing old and weak, as Seth figures and fisher kings are wont to do. His head nodded over easily and he slept, his fatigued mind surrendering to the land of dreams. Age was sapping his strength, though he still took pride in his impressive mane of braided hair. When this too was taken from him, he was shorn of the last vestiges his waning resolve. The gouging of his eyes represented the darkness of deep winter, the season of Seth as his death approached him.

The death of the sun king was a tragic event, mourned by his subjects as a calamity that shook the foundations of existence. So it was fitting that Samson should topple the two main pillars of the Philistine temple, the Boaz and Jachin pillars that represented the stability of the kingdom.

Also worth noting are the seven braids Samson wore in his hair, which must have been undone as his locks were cut away. It is this act that foreshadows Samson's ultimate demise, and it is therefore fitting that it should also parallel the myth of Inanna's descent into the netherworld. Just as Samson was rendered naked of his precious seven locks, so Inanna was deprived of seven garments one by one as she passed through the gates of death. These seven garments found their way into tradition as seven veils, said to have been removed one at a time during a sensual striptease by a woman named Salome. This erotic dance was done before Herod's son Antipas, who in his enthusiasm promised her anything she might desire up to half his kingdom.

Her request, however, was much simpler: She wanted the head of John the Baptist on a plate.

Once again, the stories of Samson and John converge. Samson was robbed of his power by a conniving seductress who cut off his hair, while John was sentenced to die at the word of another seductress who asked that his head be cut off. This incident would be a turning point in the life of Jesus, the man destined to succeed John as leader of the movement he had championed.

Sorcerer's Apprentice

The relationship between John and Jesus was a complex one, characterized by periods of mutual admiration, distrust, uncertainty and even hostility. But such tension was part and parcel of the tanist system. One was the wise old man or wizard, obligated to teach his young apprentice the secrets he would need to succeed him. The former held the throne of Isis; the latter was duty bound to claim it as soon as he was able. It was a relationship where loyalty and treachery were both to be expected. In the final analysis, it was "survival of the fittest" in action, two millennia before Darwin elucidated the concept for mass consumption.

John was the old king, Seth; Jesus the young prince, Horus.

And they first met, according to the author of *Luke*, before Jesus was even born. According to this account, the two men were relatives, though the exact nature of their kinship is never explained. Perhaps they were named as kinsmen as such in imitation of the relationship between Seth and Horus, who were named as uncle and nephew, yet also identified as brothers. Or perhaps they actually were related by blood.

But whatever the true nature of their kinship, they were linked from the very beginning. The narrative describes a curious event during which their mothers met and the unborn John leaped for joy while still in the womb. The account was meant to lend credence to the idea that John, even before he was born, recognized Jesus as his chosen successor.

Whether such an incident ever took place is highly doubtful, especially if one accepts that John was a grown man by the time Jesus was born. It is, however, quite possible that the author retained the memory of an encounter between John and Jesus around the time of the latter's birth. Jesus appears to have been born only a few miles away from the temple at Leontopolis, where the successors of the deposed high priest Onias presented the sacrifices. If John was high priest of this temple at the time of Jesus' birth, an encounter between the two would have been quite possible.

One might have expected the author of *Luke* to preserve some record of such an event if it did occur. His goal was to further the cult of personality that had begun to spring up around Jesus, and the memory of his childhood consecration by John could only have helped his cause. But the author had a problem. He had chosen, erroneously, to literalize the Seth-Horus relationship between the two men by maintaining that they had been born six months apart. He had painted himself into a corner, from which he could extract himself only with considerable ingenuity.

He did so by breaking the story of John's consecration into two parts. The first was the fabulous tale whereby John recognized Jesus from his own mother's womb. The second was an episode whereby John's *father* acknowledged Jesus' position as the new Horus or sun god: "The rising sun will come to us from heaven, to shine on those living in darkness and in the shadow of death." [242] John's father, it should be noted, was in fact a temple priest — just as John would have been if he in fact served at Leontopolis. At the very least, the reference confirms that John was in fact from priestly stock, perhaps from the house of Onias.

The author gave John's father the name Zechariah, and this was no accident. As an adult, John would develop a reputation as a prophet. According to tradition, it had been five centuries since a true prophet had arisen in Israel. Among the last had been a prophet named Zechariah: "When Haggai, Zechariah and Malachi, the latter prophets, were dead, the Holy Spirit departed from Israel." [243] It would return, however, with John, who was said to have been filled with the Holy Spirit from his mother's womb. John was considered the heir to a prophetic tradition not seen since Zechariah. So it was only natural that the author of *Luke* should depict him as the physical heir of a man by the same name — a character whose story was in fact based on the writings of the legendary prophet.

According to these writings, an angel had visited Zechariah and revealed that a high priest named Joshua would arise to rule Israel.

This man, the angel said, would receive a crown and be known as "The Branch" — the same title that had been given to the coming messiah by the prophet Isaiah.[244] The vision was a powerful one. And, it turned out, one of the last received by a prophet in Israel. After Zechariah received this visit, the prophetic spirit supposedly fell silent and remained that way for nearly five hundred years.

Until the time of John.

It was then that the author of *Luke* picked up the story. Or, rather, repeated it. According to his account, another angel visited another Zechariah to announce the birth of a prophet named John — after which Zechariah was struck dumb and remained silent until John was born. The symbolism was unmistakable. According to tradition, the spirit of prophecy had remained silent since the time of the prophet Zechariah, only to be reawakened with the coming of John. The author of *Luke* had symbolically condensed five centuries of history into a fable about the Baptist's birth.

The symbolism behind the name Elizabeth, given as John's mother, is also quite revealing. The Baptist had come from a priestly family, so what better name for his mother? Elisheba, after all, had been the wife of Aaron, the first high priest. It was perhaps a convenient way of acknowledging that John belonged to the legitimate line of high priests — the line of Onias.

Despite the stability of life in the temple at Leontopolis, the members of this line had always sought the opportunity to serve once more at the altar of the original temple in Jerusalem. And the turmoil that followed the death of Herod would have provided a just the sort of golden opportunity for which they had been waiting. It was probably this opportunity that lured John out of Egypt and back to Palestine, where he joined the fledgling resistance movement under Judas the Galilean and began plotting to expel the Roman scourge.

It was there that he would have almost certainly come in contact once again with Joazar, the former high priest who seems to have been a collaborator with Judas. As the general discontent coalesced into a widespread tax revolt, the authorities grew increasingly wary.

Archelaus was sent into exile, and the Romans decided to take control directly. Amid the chaos of this transition, those in the resistance were presented with a narrow but viable window of opportunity. Before the empire could once again consolidate its hold on the region, it might just be possible to elevate a candidate of their own the high priesthood. Though John may have coveted the high priesthood for himself, Joazar was the natural choice to take the post, both because of his immense popularity and because he had held it once before.

And there may have been another factor in play, as well.

There is nothing to indicate that John had an heir. Joazar, on the other hand, had adopted a child named Jesus with a claim not only to the high priesthood but to the throne of Jerusalem as well. (Recall that the high priest mentioned in the writings of Zechariah was named Joshua, the Hebrew form of the Greek name Jesus). Considering this, John may well have been asked to set aside his claim for the moment in favor of Joazar and his young son. But only for the moment. As it turned out, Joazar held the high priesthood for only a short time before being ousted by the Romans. With the tax revolt unraveling and the empire reasserting its supremacy, there was no room for a rebel in the upper echelons of power.

From this point forward, Joazar fades into the mist of history, never to be heard from again except in one or two passing references in connection with his adopted son. These allusions describe Jesus, according to most translations, as a carpenter's son — which would seem on the face of it to imply that Joseph/Joazar was a craftsman or woodworker of some sort. In the Jewish writings of the Talmud, however, the word for carpenter is *naggar*, a word that could just as easily refer to a learned man.[245] And this latter designation would have been perfectly appropriate for a high priest.

Even so, there is another interpretation that fits just as well. It is easy to miss the fact that the passage in question never refers to Joseph by name, although it does refer to Mary: "Isn't this the carpenter's son? Isn't his mother named Mary?"[246] A common method of imparting emphasis in conversation is to repeat something, and such a verbal technique would have fit like a glove in this context. If it were in fact used, it would identify Mary and the carpenter as *the same person*.

The questions are posed in the context of Jesus' appearance at a synagogue in his hometown, where men who have known him all his life are incredulous at his teachings. It would have been altogether natural for them to express their incredulity by repeating themselves for emphasis. But it is just as natural for most readers today to dismiss this idea without even considering it, prejudicially assuming that a woman could not possibly have been a carpenter. Or a learned person.

Yet to do so is to miss what may very well be some highly potent symbolism based on ancient myth. The person at the center of this symbolism is Ninhursag, the ancient Sumerian mountain queen who served as the prototype for the fertility goddess Inanna (and therefore for Meri Isis as well). Ninhursag is described in one ancient passage as "the carpenter of mankind; the carpenter of the heart." [247] She was, therefore, Mary the carpenter. And it is also worth remembering that Inanna was the keeper of the sacred *me* tablets, having tricked Enki into relinquishing them. She was therefore also a *naggar* in the sense that she was a learned one, the keeper of secret wisdom from the beginning.

This reference to the carpenter is generally taken as the last mention of Joseph in the canon. And Joazar, likewise, is not heard from again after his second stint as high priest in Jerusalem.

If Joazar disappears into the background, the same can be said of John. But whereas Joazar never re-emerges from the shadows, John eventually does — albeit some two decades later. Given their rapidly deteriorating political standing in Palestine, it is reasonable to conclude that both men cut their losses in the wake of the tax revolt and made their way back to their homeland, Egypt. Jesus, whose life is similarly a blank slate during this span of twenty years, would have likely gone with them. There, he may have studied with a reclusive group known as the Therapeutae, literally "healers," white-robed men who lived a life of austerity in the desert to the west of Alexandria. The fact that Jesus himself would later earn a reputation as a healer strengthens the possibility that he studied with these men.

The Therapeutae, described by the historian Philo, bore remarkable similarities to the Essene sect that lived in the isolated Dead Sea settlement of Qumran and elsewhere during the same period. And the Essenes, in turn, bore a similarly close resemblance in their lifestyle to a man named John.

The Baptist.

The Prefect and the Poor

The voice in the wilderness was growing louder. The voice of the resistance movement begun more than two decades earlier under Judas the Galilean and reignited under John only became more strident and insistent as time passed.

For the Jewish nationalists, the previous two decades had seen the situation go from bad to worse.

Herod was long dead. His son, Archelaus, chosen to rule from Jerusalem in his stead, was gone as well. After ten long years, the emperor had finally heeded his subjects' demand that he be removed; stripped of his wealth and, banished to Vienna, he had ceased to be a factor. The emperor, however, had replaced him with something even worse — a Roman governor or "procurator" directly responsible to the Augustus.

Herod's other two sons continued to rule the northeastern portion of what had once been Israel — now absorbed into the Roman province of Syria. Antipas and Philip continued their father's policy of modernization, seeking to remake their lands in the image of Rome. Centuries of tradition went by the wayside as they built and rebuilt numerous cities, dedicating each of them to members of the imperial family. Philip rechristened the city of Paneas as "Caesarea" — one of several cities by that name. Antipas rebuilt Sepphoris, so recently destroyed by Varus' army. He also put a wall around the city of Betharanphtha, renaming it "Julius" for the emperor's wife. And, in one of his greatest undertakings, he built an entirely new city on the shores of the inland lake known as the Sea of Galilee. This great new metropolis he named "Tiberias" in honor of the new emperor who had just succeeded Augustus.

It was a grand city. But there was one drawback: No one would live there. The problem was, Antipas had built the city over the site of a graveyard in violation of the Jewish law. Having spared no expense to create this tribute to the new emperor, he was faced with the possibility of a huge embarrassment. He responded by literally bribing people to live in Tiberias, offering them land and houses built at his own expense in exchange for their indulgence. Wherever this approach failed, he resorted to harsher measures. Subjects from other areas under his rule were uprooted "and by force compelled to be its inhabitants." [248]

Such acts hardly endeared Antipas to the Jewish nationalists, but they were mild in comparison to what was imposed upon their fellows to the south.

There, a series of procurators came and went. The first these, Coponius, conducted the census that had spurred Judas' tax rebellion. Coponius lasted three years, as did his successor. Each new Roman appointee served as a reminder that the Jews no longer controlled their own destiny. But it was not until the fourth procurator arrived that the situation reached the breaking point. His name was Pontius Pilate, an Italian general who had used friends in high places to secure the position — specifically, his mentor Sejanus, commander of the elite Praetorian Guard.

The emperor did not put Pilate in charge of the financial affairs of Judea, as Coponius had been — perhaps seeking to avoid a recurrence of the census fiasco. In fact, Pilate's title wasn't "procurator" but "prefect" — a military commander of five hundred to a thousand auxiliary troops. With a reputation as a stern taskmaster, he was just the sort of man the empire needed to keep a tight rein on the potentially explosive situation in Judea.

Or so the Romans thought.

In fact, Pilate's volatile temper and stubborn refusal to compromise with Jewish beliefs only fueled the fire of opposition. His first official act was one of intimidation: In a show of force, he ordered the troops under his command to march from the seaport of Caesarea — the center of Roman administration in Palestine — to Jerusalem. And if that wasn't provocation enough, the army marched into the city under standards bearing the emperor's image. It may have been an act of simple ignorance, but more likely it was a deliberate attempt by Pilate to impose the emperor's will upon the Jews. In either case, it was a provocative move, a clear violation of the Jewish law against "the making of images." None of Pilate's predecessors had dared to bring such images into Jerusalem, and Pilate himself only did so "without the knowledge of the people, because it was done in the nighttime." [249]

The result was predictable. The city was thrown into a furor and the Jews, led by the nationalists, were enraged: "As soon as they knew it, they came in multitudes to Caesarea and interceded with Pilate for many days, that he would remove the images." [250]

Pilate refused.

Removing the images would be an insult to the emperor, and this could not be allowed. Yet the demonstrators refused to give up, continuing their appeals for six days unabated until Pilate's patience finally reached its limit. Wishing to put an end to this fiasco, he granted the protesters a public audience and ordered members of the army to station themselves discreetly throughout the crowd. On his signal, the soldiers surrounded the protesters and drew their weapons, whereupon Pilate warned the crowds to disperse and return to Jerusalem on pain of death.

But the prefect had miscalculated.

These were Zealots, radical nationalists willing to die for their cause, and they were not about to simply "leave off disturbing him and go their way home." Instead, they "threw themselves on the ground and laid their necks bare, saying that they would take their death very willingly, rather than" see the ancient ritual laws broken.[251] In the test of wills, Pilate blinked first, granting their request by removing the images from Jerusalem. He did not want a massacre on his hands. Such an event could trigger a full-scale uprising, and the emperor would find that a lot less palatable than the removal of his image. In any case, the prefect had made his point by sending his troops into Jerusalem: Rome was in charge in Judea.

And the show of force did make a lasting impression. The resistance movement at Qumran certainly never forgot Pilate's audacity. In their writings, the Qumran scribes used the code word *Kittim* to describe the Romans as those who "offer sacrifices to their standards, and the weapons of war are the object of their religion."[252] The reference to Pilate's brazen display of the emperor's standards could not have been clearer.

But the prefect did not stop there. Indeed, he lost no time in further alienating those under his jurisdiction by dipping into the temple funds to pay for a massive irrigation project. The plan involved diverting a stream from its source to Jerusalem. Once again, however, Pilate ran into strong opposition: "The people got together and made a clamor against him," dishing out personal insults and insisting that the project be abandoned.

This time, Pilate had had enough. As he had before, he ordered his soldiers to surround the crowd and arm themselves with daggers they concealed under their garments. Then, they were to wait for his signal. The crowd got no warning. Instead, Pilate gave the signal and watched as his forces "equally punished those that were tumultuous and those that were not. Nor did they spare them in the least. And, since the people were unarmed ... a great number of them were slain in this manner, while others ran away wounded."[253]

Jesus himself certainly knew of this incident. According to the author of *Luke*, "There were some present at that time who told Jesus about the Galileans whose blood Pilate had mixed with their sacrifices." [254] The implication was clear. Sacrifices were offered at the temple, and Pilate had butchered those who had opposed his misuse of temple funds, thus symbolically mixing their blood with their sacrifices. Tellingly, the victims were not Judeans but Galileans.

Why were Galileans instigating an uprising in Jerusalem?

Probably for the same reason Judas the Galilean had done so years earlier. These were his successors. Perhaps they did not even come from the region called Galilee, but they were called "Galileans" because they were members of Judas' group — a group that would remain active at the head of the Jewish resistance until the outbreak of the Jewish-Roman War. Like many opposition movements, however, it was not simply defined. Judas was not the only opposition leader. Even during the height of his activity, several other would-be kings and revolutionaries had set themselves up in opposition to the Romans. The very fact that they were fighting for the opposition made it difficult for them to form any sort of cohesive alliance. To do so would have been to expose their efforts to the authorities — and imperil what they had been working to achieve. It was better to remain underground until they could muster enough popular support for their cause to mount a full-scale revolt.

At some point in time, a loosely defined underground network of opposition communities began to emerge. Because these were resistance groups, they had to take care that the Romans didn't discover them. Hence, such communities were either highly mobile or extremely remote. "They have no certain city," Josephus wrote, "but many of them dwell in every city." [255] They would take nothing with them on their journeys, except their weapons, and would travel to "remote places" such as the Qumran settlement in the Judean desert — doubtless to stay clear of the empire's watchful eye.

Josephus referred to these men as Essenes, a name whose derivation is not clear. They may have actually been known as Jesseans — those who were awaiting a messiah from the proverbial root of Jesse.[256] Josephus himself was a member of this group for a time, spending three years as an acolyte and later serving as a general in the resistance forces. He was, however, subsequently captured by the Romans and wound up defecting to the empire's cause, earning a prominent position in the emperor's service after the war. Having earned such a post, he would hardly have been eager to jeopardize it by flaunting his earlier association with the rebels.

The Essenes/Jesseans.

The resistance, however, went by other names, as well.

Its militant wing included members known as Zealots or *sicarii*. The latter group would see its influence increase as the inevitable war with Rome drew nearer. They were assassins, who employed the same tactics Pilate had used against them: They made use of small crooked swords or daggers that they would hide under their clothing while they lay in wait for their targets. Then there were the Galileans, a group affiliated with Judas of Galilee and later led by his sons James and Simon — two men who were later crucified for their opposition to the empire. Some members of the resistance called themselves Sons of Zadok or Zadokites, named for David's high priest Zadok, whose name meant "righteousness" or "justice." These were the opposition priests who viewed the Sadducees (also named for Zadok) as false priests installed by the Romans and their collaborators. This process had begun under Herod, who had replaced the last of the Hasmonean priests with his own hand-picked supporter, and it continued under the Roman procurators.

In response, the Zadokites had set up their own opposition priesthood, headed initially by Judas the Galilean's partner Sadduc. These priests believed the temple had been defiled by the presence of the "false" Roman-backed priesthood. Not surprisingly, these two groups held each other in mutual contempt. The Zadokites refused to offer sacrifices in the temple and were barred from even entering its common court. "When they send what they have dedicated to God into the temple, they do not offer sacrifices, for they have more pure practices of their own," Josephus wrote. "For this reason, they are excluded from the common court of the temple, but offer sacrifices themselves" elsewhere.[257] The location of these sacrifices is never specified, yet one possibility is the temple at Leontopolis; offerings might also have been prepared in Palestine itself.

Some in the resistance movement referred to themselves as "The Many" — the masses who would rise up and overthrow the empire. Still others called themselves simply Ebionites, or "The Poor." They gloried in their status as men who had nothing. All their possessions had been taken from them. The Romans had stolen their land. Then their tax collectors had swindled them out of their money. The Poor had nothing left. All that was had been theirs now belonged to their adversaries.

The Rich.

The Romans and their collaborators.

The Ebionites looked forward to the day when the tables would be turned. The Jewish kingdom would be restored under God, and the imperial usurpers would be put to flight. "Blessed are the Poor," Jesus would declare, "for yours is the kingdom of God. Blessed are you who hunger now, for you will be satisfied. Blessed are you who weep now, for you will laugh." [258]

When the kingdom of God was restored, he promised, the oppressors would pay. "Woe to you who are rich," he said. "For you have already received your comfort. Woe to you who are well-fed now, for you will go hungry. Woe to you who laugh now, for you will mourn and weep. Woe to you when all men speak well of you, for that is how their fathers treated the false prophets." [259]

Jesus' brother James also warned that the rich were headed for a fall. The rich, he wrote, would wail in misery at what was about to befall them. They would see moths eat holes in their clothing. Their gold and silver coins would grow tarnished and corroded. They were guilty of murdering innocent men and withholding wages from honest workers, likely references to the empire's high taxes and political executions of its opponents. The rich had grown fat, James declared, ready for the day of slaughter — the day the resistance would rise up and overthrow them.[260]

It was a day the resistance eagerly awaited, but not everyone could be part of it. When a young man asked Jesus for advice, Jesus instructed him to join his group. But doing so wasn't a simple matter. The Qumran group required an initiate to turn all his goods over to the community. And Jesus made the same demand on the youth: "Go, sell everything you have and give to the Poor, and you will have treasure in heaven. Then come and follow me." [261]

The young man, however, refused to do so, because he was rich.

The resistance was not generally open to rich people. Most who fell into this category had amassed their wealth by gaining favor with Rome. And Rome was the enemy. Unless one was willing to relinquish any claim the empire might have on him — including the riches it had bestowed upon him — he could not be trusted as a member of the opposition. The conflict of interest would be too great.

"How hard it is for the rich to enter the kingdom of God!" Jesus exclaimed. "It is easier for a camel to go through the eye of a needle than for a rich man to enter the kingdom of God!" [262]

This was not merely a spiritual message, but a political one.

Theocracy

For the resistance, the spiritual always went hand-in-hand with the political. They were, after all, Jewish nationalists. And the Jewish nation had always been a theocracy. Israel's law had come directly from God, its kings and high priests had been ordained by God. In the mind of the pious Jew, there could be no separation between religion and government. The two were inextricably linked. Throughout the Jewish scripture, sages and prophets attributed the nation's political woes to its lack of righteousness — or *zedek*. If a foreign army invaded and conquered Israel, it was a sign that the Jews were not righteous enough.

It is no wonder that the Roman imperial system seemed so

foreign to the opposition. It was not a theocracy at all, but a dictatorship that retained some vestiges of its republican past. The empire, in fact, tolerated a wide variety of faiths ranging from mysticism to monotheism. Worship was not discouraged, but political insurgency was. Pious Jews, however, simply did not make this distinction. To them, the Romans' very presence in Palestine indicated that something was dreadfully wrong: Israel had sinned, and imperial domination was her punishment. So it had been with the Babylonians, the Assyrians and the Greeks; so it must also be with the Romans. To the Jewish mind in the first century, this was the only possible conclusion. The Zadokites (the righteous ones) quite simply believed that the nation had brought the situation upon itself.

In the same way, they also believed the nation could change that situation.

It was, to the outsider, a naïve and even foolhardy belief. The Roman Empire was, quite simply, the preeminent fighting force in the ancient world. During the course of little more than a century, it had expanded its borders to encompass the entire Mediterranean Sea. What was left of Alexander's Greek empire had fallen before the might of Rome, as had the last remnants of the once-powerful Egyptian kingdom. No objective observer would have thought twice about opposing Rome with an loosely organized alliance of poorly armed Jewish rebel groups.

But the Jews were not objective. They did not believe that their numbers or their defenses were important. Ultimately, it was God's favor that mattered. If God was with them, who could be against them? The shepherd boy David had defeated the giant Philistine champion Goliath with nothing more than a slingshot. Gideon had routed an army of thousands with a mere three hundred men because, as an angel had promised, "Yahweh is with you." [263] And Judas Maccabee with his brothers had claimed independence from the Greeks against overwhelming odds because of their righteousness before God. In order to regain that independence, the nation would have to follow the Maccabean example. The Jews would have to purify themselves before God. And once they had done so, God would go to battle for them. Only then could the kingdom of God — the Jewish theocracy — be re-established.

Preparations for this battle were under way in earnest at the Qumran settlement, which seems to have served as the resistance movement's military base. Members of the Qumran community outlined a detailed battle plan. Despite their confidence in God's support, they knew fighting the Romans would be no easy task. Indeed, they were prepared for a war spanning thirty-five years. A command structure was established, and battle formations were drawn up for both infantry and cavalry divisions. The infantry — twenty-eight thousand strong — would go forth armed with formidable weapons. Each soldier would hold shields of bronze bordered with precious metals, inlaid with gems and polished to shine like a mirror. In one hand he would carry a spear, and in the other a sword of purified iron. The hilt would be of pure horn, the work of an artist, shimmering with many colors and encrusted with jewels. Other infantrymen would be equipped with javelins to hurl at the enemy — "bloody darts to bring down the slain by the anger of God." [264] These foot-soldiers would assemble in compact lines of a thousand men and go forth into carrying standards emblazoned with slogans such as:

- Glory of God
- Judgment of God
- Truth of God
- Justice of God

Each line of infantry would be flanked by a hundred cavalry on either side, each horseman wearing a breastplate, a helmet and armored leggings. In one hand he would carry a spear; in the other a round shield. Also among their armaments would be bows and arrows. In all, six thousand Jewish horsemen would ride out into battle against the Romans. Priests from the lineage of Aaron would have their place on the battlefield, as well. Clad in white linen and crowned with tiaras, these holy men would stride back and forth in front of the troops and bestow the blessings of God. Then, when the time for battle approached, they would sound the trumpets as a call to combat — trumpets bearing slogans like "Commandment of God" and "Summoned of God." Trumpets bearing similar slogans would signal an ambush, announce that the battle was joined and proclaim that the enemy was in retreat.

It was a grand plan, complete with instructions for fighting from defensive positions. Catapults and bows would send their deadly ammunition flying from four towers, each named for an archangel of God. Then, the occupants would go on the offensive, and soldiers would pour forth to trample the enemy. With God on their side, defeat was not an option.

The battle instructions closed with a hymn paying tribute to God's greatness: "The battle is yours, and by the might of your hand their bodies are stretched out upon the earth," it declared. "You delivered Goliath of Gath, a valiant giant, into the hand of your servant David, because he set his trust in your majestic name and not the sword or spear....

"The battle is yours.

"The power comes from you.

"Truly, the battle is not ours. It is not won by our might, by the strength of our hands nor our displays of valor. But it is by your might and the strength of your valor, as you have declared in days of old: A star has journeyed from Jacob, a scepter has arisen from Israel...."[265]

That star and scepter were the signs of the promised messiah or anointed one. It was he who would lead them forth into battle, who would embody all was best qualities of Israel, its holiest priest and its most valiant warrior. The sons of light would triumph over the sons of darkness, and the kingdom of God would be restored. Their vision was glorious and their cause noble. But those who pursued it would soon find out that opposing the empire was a difficult task.

Even if they did have God on their side.

XI

Parting the Waters

The scrolls uncovered in caves beside the Dead Sea in the middle years of the past century were nothing short of a revelation. On them were written versions of the Hebrew scriptures far older than anything yet uncovered. *Isaiah. Genesis. Joshua. Ruth. Job.* The list goes on. Yet among these canonical texts were discovered other papers, some of them interpretations of the scriptures and others that were entirely original. These were the law codes and prophecies of the men who had fashioned them, a glimpse into their inner workings, hopes and expectations.

These expectations included, first and foremost, the climactic battle just described, as laid forth on one of the Dead Sea scrolls — an apocalyptic conflict between the so-called sons of light and their archenemies, the sons of darkness. The men of Qumran cast themselves in the former role. And it was their job to usher in this cataclysmic event by pursuing lives of purity and righteousness. In order to do so, they would have to separate themselves from the unrighteous masses and venture forth into the wilderness. Only by purifying themselves in this way could they induce their divine champion, Yahweh, to fight on their behalf. The document known as *The Community Rule* laid forth this requirement explicitly:

"They shall separate from the habitation of unjust men and shall go into the wilderness to prepare the way of him; as it is written, 'Prepare in the wilderness the way ... make straight in the desert a path for our God.' "[266] These were the very words attributed to John the Baptist during his own sojourn in the wilderness, not far from the shores of the Dead Sea and only a few miles from the settlement at Qumran.[267] Like those at Qumran, he believed in an imminent apocalypse and preached that the kingdom of God was at hand.

John had little tolerance for those who remained in the religious mainstream. Indeed, he used caustic language to dismiss them a brood of vipers, bitterly lamenting that someone had warned them to flee from the wrath to come.[268] These words, too, would have been familiar to the Qumran community. *The Damascus Document*, one of the original works discovered among the scrolls, quotes the prophet Isaiah in detailing the blasphemies of the unrighteous, whose "webs are spiders' webs, and their eggs are the eggs of vipers."[269]

And if John's message paralleled that of Qumran, so did his lifestyle. His primary mission involved cleansing through ritual bathing, an activity pursued with great diligence in the Dead Sea community. It was, in fact, considered a necessary exercise for those who wished to practice righteousness. The rule of the community was explicit in this regard, declaring that when the "flesh is sprinkled with purifying water and sanctified by cleansing water, it shall be made clean by the humble submission of his soul to all the precepts of God."[270]

John's baptism was designed to have the same effect.

Like the men of the Dead Sea community, the object of his quest was righteousness, to be attained through strict adherence to law and ritual. To this end, he lived a life of diligent austerity in the wilderness, just as the men of Qumran did, in his case subsisting on a diet of locusts and wild honey.[271] Even in this, his behavior mirrored that of those who dwelt on the shores of the Dead Sea. The rule of the Qumran community even went so far as to offer specific instructions on how to prepare locusts: "Plunge them alive into fire or water, for this is what their nature requires." [272] The description is fascinating, for it would almost seem to be a recipe for baptism. As a matter of fact, John would refer to these same two elements, water and fire, in his own testimony concerning the ritual: He had come baptizing in water, but another would come after him who would baptize men in fire.[273]

Why should locusts have been linked to baptism?

According to the scribes at Qumran, something about their nature required that they be prepared in this specific fashion.

But what was it?

The Hebrew word for locust was *arbeh*, a word used to denote an increase. There was perhaps no more awe-inspiring sight in the rugged land of the ancient Near East than a swarm of locusts approaching from the horizon. The first insects would arrive and cause a nuisance, buzzing about as they descended on wheat fields and occasionally getting tangled in someone's hair. But this was just the beginning. Before long, the buzzing would become a high-pitched wail, and the black dots flying through the air would transform themselves into a wall of frenzied motion that could literally blot out the sun. This is how the locust would increase, or multiply. For this reason, the locust was a symbol of fertility in China.[274] Hence, the term *arbeh* must have seemed entirely appropriate.

This word, in turn, is related to *rabah*, meaning greatness or abundance.

It also was related to the Hebrew word meaning "archer."

One may further recognize the similarity to the word rabbi, meaning "master." In Hebrew, the word is *rhabbi*, only two letters removed from *Rhaab*, the Hebrew spelling for the name Rahab. These linguistic connections may seem somewhat circuitous, yet they all end up fitting together rather neatly. Rahab was, of course, the ancient female sea dragon, whose massive size would have made her the very definition of greatness or abundance. One may recall that

Levites were originally priests of this same sea dragon under another name, Leviathan. And it would therefore appear reasonable to conjecture that the rabbis earned their title in similar fashion, as servants of Rahab. This great sea dragon was often equated with the whale that swallowed Jonah, the ark hero — explaining the linguistic link to the word for "archer." And Jonah's name itself is but a variant on the name John. The name borne by the Baptist.

In light of all this, it seems highly probable that the recipe for locusts in the Qumran scrolls *does*, in fact, have something to do with the activity that defined John's mission — baptism. By submitting to the roiling waters, the initiate was symbolically living the great adventure of Jonah, permitting himself to be swallowed by the sea dragon so that he could emerge reborn from the primal waters. The waters of the earth goddess' womb.

In the words of Jesus, "You must be born again." [275]

Baptism symbolized this new birth or increase, and no one could enter the kingdom unless he was born of water and the spirit.[276] Jesus could offer no other alternative, and neither could the scribes of Qumran, whose *Community Rule* expressed the very same principle in similar words. God, they wrote, would cleanse man "of all wicked deeds with the spirit of holiness. Like purifying waters, he will shed upon him the spirit of truth, to cleanse him of all abomination and injustice. And he will be plunged into the spirit of purification, that he may instruct the upright in the knowledge of the most high and teach the wisdom of the sons of heaven to the perfect of way." [277]

Water and the spirit.

It was always thus.

The Qumran scribes called baptism an act of humble submission, and so it was that Jesus would submit to the authority of John because it was necessary to "fulfill all righteousness." [278] The Dead Sea community would certainly have approved. The one who had undergone this ritual was fit to become a teacher, they said, and it was as a teacher that Jesus would become known first and foremost. It is, furthermore, probably no accident that this teaching would involve something called "the Way," a term used to describe the Qumran path that would come to be applied in similar fashion to Jesus' own movement.

The symbolism of the new birth contained in Jesus' baptism was potent and found expression in the words of the psalmist:

> *You are my son*
> *Today I have begotten you* [279]

This may well have been the original wording used in the gospels, which record a similar declaration uttered by a voice from heaven at Jesus' baptism: "You are my son, whom I love. With you I am well pleased." [280] A fragmentary early document known as *The Gospel of the Ebionites* contains these two phrases but also retains the material about begetting. The psalmist's original language is also retained in some early translations of *Luke*.[281] And, moreover, it is preserved by the author of the canonical epistle to the Hebrews.[282] This material's deletion from the canonical accounts probably reflected a certain discomfort with the rather esoteric idea of a second birth — and its implication that Jesus had somehow became divine at the time of his baptism. Some groups did in fact accept the idea that Jesus had been "adopted" by the heavenly father at this point in his life, but such a notion seemed to clash head-on with the belief that he had been miraculously conceived and had therefore been divine from the beginning. There appeared to be no middle ground between these two positions, creating a dilemma that would be the source of no small controversy in the years to come. The apparent contradiction may well have caused the gospel writers to tone down the adoptionist language of the psalmist in applying it to Jesus, eliminating the phrase "this day I have begotten you." But in doing so, they failed to understand that they had perceived a contradiction where in fact there was none.

This is because the baptism ritual, for Jesus, was more than a ritual cleansing.

Much more.

It was, in fact, a coronation ceremony. Jesus was being proclaimed king in the same manner Solomon had been when he was escorted down to the river and anointed there by the high priest Zadok. In Egyptian lore, this ceremony constituted a new birth. When the pharaoh ascended the throne, he became seated in the lap of the great mother Isis, symbolically emerging from her womb and becoming transformed into the new Horus. He even received a new name, as he had when he was born. Suddenly it is no mystery why Jesus said that, in order to *inherit the kingdom*, one had to be born again. This had been the way of things from the very beginning.

When Jesus told his friend Nicodemus about this process, he was met with incredulity. "How can a man be born when he is old?" Nicodemus asked him. "Surely he cannot enter his mother's womb to be born!" [283]

In fact, however, he could.

By ascending the throne and entering into the lap of Isis, the new king symbolically entered her womb. Not all the way, of course. Nicodemus was right in stating that this would be impossible. But he could penetrate this chamber of eternal life through the act of sexual intercourse with his queen, the earthly manifestation of Isis. In myth, the king assumed the dual role of son and lover of the mother goddess, returning to the source of life to perpetuate it by producing an heir. This was the lot of the king. According to a saying attributed to Jesus in *The Gospel of Thomas*, many might stand at the door, but it was only the solitary who might enter the bridal chamber.[284] In this way the role of the solitary bridegroom stood parallel to that of the high priest, who alone was permitted to enter the sacred inner chamber of the temple.

The holy of holies.

The author of a document known as *The Gospel of Philip* recognized this parallel and referred to the bedchamber explicitly as the holy of holies.[285] This was no accident. Nor is it any coincidence that Jesus is referred to in canonical accounts as both the great high priest and the bridegroom. The roles were one and the same. His baptism was not merely a second birth, it was also a solemn ritual marking his spiritual union with the goddess — she who descended upon him in the form of a dove. This ritual identified him clearly as the bridegroom, the successor and incarnation of the great shepherd king Solomon. It was he who had been the original bridegroom, having been identified as such in the erotic masterpiece known as the Song of Songs. And now, Jesus too would adopt this title.

Even his baptism was closely modeled after the anointing of Solomon beside the great river.

In each instance, the ceremony was overseen by a high priest whose duty it was to anoint the king. In the case of Solomon, this role had been filled by Zadok; for Jesus, it was John who performed the task. As high priest of the temple at Leontopolis, he was eminently qualified to do so. And in accepting this role, he was stepping into the shoes occupied by many Seth figures who had chosen or would choose their successors to the throne:

- Isaac and Jacob
- Moses and Joshua
- Elijah and Elisha
- Samuel and Saul
- Samuel and David
- Merlin and Arthur

The Seth figure typically played the role of high priest, while the Horus figure served as king. This duality probably stretched back to ancient Egypt, where it was not uncommon for the pharaoh to name a successor and rule jointly with his heir for the remainder of his tenure. Under this arrangement, the pharaoh became the old king Seth, while his heir acted as Horus. The original pharaoh remained the senior partner in this arrangement and was generally recognized as holding ultimate power, a fact of life that was brought home quite effectively to the rogue king Saul when Samuel stripped him of his authority and transferred it to his rival.

David.

Samuel's decision to replace Saul was precipitated in part by an incident in which the younger man exceeded his authority. This incident took place during a campaign against an enemy Philistine (Palestinian) army, which appeared to have Saul's men outnumbered. The young prince had agreed to wait for Samuel before initiating any assault, but when the older man failed to arrive at the appointed time, his men took it as an ill omen and began to desert. In a desperate attempt to keep his ranks together, Saul asked that the appropriate animals be brought to him and offered up a sacrifice to Yahweh. Although he succeeded in placating his men, Samuel was furious. "What have you done?" he ranted.

Calling Saul a fool to his face, he vowed that his kingdom would not endure and that another man was destined to be appointed leader of the nation.[286] On the face of it, Saul's offense might have seemed a minor one, and certainly it appears to have been justified, considering the dire straits in which his army found itself. But no emergency could erase the fact that Samuel was the senior authority in this partnership, and as such it was his prerogative to offer up the sacrifice. No one else's. By usurping this fundamental right, Saul was in effect challenging Samuel's authority as high priest. This could not be tolerated.

Saul's brazen act was tantamount to declaring himself the ultimate authority in the kingdom. And while he may well have been concerned with his army's position on the battlefield, he may also have been motivated in large measure by a desire for personal gain. When Samuel was late in arriving, he may well have assumed that the old king was dead and that he was free to claim the throne. Perhaps he had even tried to arrange for Samuel's death and concluded, when the older man failed to keep his appointment, that his plans had met with success.

In the end, however, Samuel had the last laugh.

This tanist confrontation ended with the Seth king still firmly in control. Samuel's identity as such seems to be confirmed by his name, a variant of Sammael — used in some circles as another name for Satan or Seth. Both names, in turn, seem related to the Hebrew *samal*, a reference to the left hand. In light of this, it is fascinating to learn that the residents at Qumran were forbidden to make any gestures whatsoever with their left hands, and those who violated this prohibition were required to do penance for ten days.[287]

The left hand was the hand of the high priest, and no one was permitted to use it. The right hand, by contrast, was the hand of power — the hand of the king. This is the concept behind the repeated declarations that the mystical son of man was seated at the right hand of the heavenly father. In Egyptian terms, this father god was none other than Osiris. At his left hand sat the priestly Seth, while the son/sun king Horus occupied the position to his right. This imagery can be found stated in exactly these terms at the tomb of the pharaoh Unas, where inscriptions described the dead king ascending to heaven on a ladder comprising the bodies of Seth and Horus.

One at the left, the other at the right.

This explains the seemingly arrogant request made by the mother of James and John, two of Jesus' disciples, immediately after his announcement that he expects to be killed. This revelation must have sent shock waves through the entire movement. If he was correct, some provision would have to be made for leaders to succeed him. Otherwise, his movement would be left in chaos. Understandably, the jockeying for power began immediately, with two brothers named James and John reportedly clamoring to the head of the line via their mother's request: "Grant that one of these two sons of mine may sit at your right and the other at your left in your kingdom."[288] What she was asking was simply that Jesus designate her sons as king and high priest, that they might assume the roles of Horus and Seth upon his ascension to heaven as Osiris.

Jesus, however, refused — perhaps because he was not yet fully convinced that he would have to die. As the priestly son of Joazar and royal son of Herod, he was uniquely qualified to fill both messianic roles in the Jewish resistance movement, and he appears to have done so during his final year of life. He had fought hard to achieve this position, and it would have been difficult to even think about relinquishing it. The tradition of two messiahs was deeply embedded in the popular psyche, and it may not have been a simple matter to defy it. The prophets at Qumran explicitly called for two messiahs to emerge and lead them forth into battle, one a priestly messiah of Aaron and the other a royal messiah of Israel. They would not have been expecting these two roles to be consolidated in a single man.

Especially when the role of high priest was already filled — by John the Baptist.

John's status is perhaps confirmed by his designation as a baptizer. In Aramaic, the lingua franca of the region during that period, the word for baptism is *amad*. This in itself is unremarkable, until one notes its resemblance to a Hebrew word with the exact same spelling that carries a different meaning. This word means "to stand" and serves as the root for the quite similar *ammud*, meaning pillar.[289] (Thus the name Muhammad, which originally seems to have meant something like "one of the pillar" or "standing one" — a title we shall encounter again.) This double meaning is illustrative of the fact that, although John was quite clearly a baptizer, he might have just as easily been referred to as John the Pillar. And the pillar in question would undoubtedly have been the priestly pillar of Jachin.

It was in his capacity as high priest that John anointed Jesus as the junior partner in a movement that had begun two decades earlier with the tax revolt but had since lain largely dormant. Now, he was rousing it from its slumber. By publicly designating Jesus as his successor, John was creating the framework for a government in exile, a resistance movement with its own leaders and its own agenda. When the time was right, this nascent army of Yahweh, the sons of light, would move forward to reclaim the holy land that was its inheritance from the lawless sons of darkness who had stolen it. This, too, was part and parcel of the symbolism behind Jesus' baptism.

The author of *John* makes a point of mentioning that the Baptist did his work on the "other side of the Jordan." [290] This was quite intentional. The idea was to set camp on the eastern banks of the river that marked the boundary of the promised land, so that the sons of light could march across and reclaim their birthright — just as Joshua had led the armies of Yahweh into the land more than a millennium before. Only this time, they would do so under the leadership of a new Joshua, a messiah who was better known by the Greek form of his name.

Jesus.

Legend had it that Joshua had parted the waters of the Jordan, enabling his followers to cross on dry land in a miracle reminiscent of Moses' parting of the sea.[291] In the same way, Jesus symbolically parted the waters at his baptism, opening the way to salvation from the empire's legions and inaugurating the new kingdom of God on earth.

When Jesus emerged from the river's flow, he truly became the reborn Joshua son of Nun, a master of the primordial waters capable of calming the raging sea or traversing the surface of a lake without sinking. Nun was also the Hebrew word for "fish," and Jesus' new position as anointed heir to John identified him likewise as son of the Fisher King.

The reference to the land beyond the Jordan is significant for another reason, as well: It was the same land to which Elijah retreated with Elisha before being taken up into heaven by a chariot of fire. The region may therefore have earned the nickname Bethany, the name by which the author of *John* refers to it. The Hebrew prefix *beth* meant "house," while the suffix appears to have some relationship to *an*, the Sumerian name for heaven. An alternate meaning might be "house of dates," referring to the fruit of the date palm or bennu tree — the sacred symbol of the firebird or phoenix. In either case, the name linked the Baptist closely to the imagery of Elijah being taken up to heaven in his fiery chariot.

Speaking of John, Jesus would state the matter plainly: "He is the

Elijah who was to come." [292]

The prophet who had never died was fully expected to reappear, preparing the way for the royal messiah just as Elijah set the stage for Elisha. The sacred texts stated in no uncertain terms that Elisha had received a double portion of his master's spirit.[293] Now, Jesus would in like manner receive a double portion of John's spirit. This was yet another facet of the imagery behind the dove that was said to have descended upon Jesus at his baptism. The Hebrew word for dove was *yownah* or *jonah*, a variant on the name John. The implication is that he had been reborn of the waters just as the original Jonah had been reborn from the belly of the sea dragon or Leviathan — and that John, the Levitical priest of this dragon, had been instrumental in ensuring that he was "born of water and the spirit."

There is evidence to indicate that initiates into the baptism of John became known by the nickname Bar Jonah, or son of John. Jesus himself addressed Simon Peter on more than one occasion as Simon Bar Jonah.[294] And this only made sense, as Simon appears to have been a disciple of John before becoming a member of Jesus' entourage.[295] Early Jewish traditions contained in the Babylonian Talmud even refer to members of the opposition movement by the almost identical name *barjone*, an appellation that appears to reinforce the picture of John and his followers as radical revolutionaries.[296]

Jesus' baptism was, in many ways, the beginning of that revolution. But much more lay ahead. The ancient rites of kingship did not end with the anointing of a new king. On the contrary, tradition demanded that this great ceremony be followed immediately by two equally important events — the wilderness ritual, in which the new Horus confronted his rival Seth, and the divine wedding of the sun god to his goddess consort.

Jesus undertook the first of these steps almost immediately, setting out into the desert to be tempted by Satan (i.e., Seth) for the requisite forty days. John the Baptist, as the avatar of Seth, may well have accompanied Jesus into the wilderness as both mentor and tormentor, instructing him in the art of self-discipline while at the same time putting him to the test in a battle of wits that played out as their enactment of the tanist ritual. One by one, Jesus was presented with three temptations. If he were truly divine, "Satan" taunted him, Jesus would be able to satiate his hunger by transforming the stones at his feet into bread.

Jesus refused. To give in would be to display weakness and a lack of discipline, and thus expose him as unfit to be a king. Jesus was not about to fall for this and countered with the scriptural decree: "Man does not live by bread alone, but by every breath that proceeds from the mouth of God." [297]

He had passed the first test, but the next would be more difficult. From the desert, Jesus was escorted to the pinnacle of the temple and told to prove himself by jumping off. His companion goaded him on by reminding him that angelic spirits were bound to protect heaven's chosen messiah from harm. This, Jesus recognized, was a trap. No angels would come to rescue him, and he would only succeed in killing himself if he chose to jump. The tanist ritual would be over, and John would have won. But Jesus had an answer for this, too: "It is also written, 'Do not put the lord your god to the test.'" [298] This was an ingenious response, for it could be taken two ways — first as an injunction that prevented Jesus from testing the divine word, but also as a rebuke of his companion for testing Jesus, the manifestation of the sun god on earth.

Again, Jesus had prevailed, but the third and final test would be decisive. Jesus' companion took him to the peak of a high mountain so that he might gaze out upon all the kingdoms of the world. These things could be his, he was told, on one condition. He must bow down and worship Satan. Or John. This was the greatest test of all, for it presented Jesus with a seemingly impossible dilemma. John's position as senior partner demanded that Jesus acknowledge him as such, yet tanistry itself demanded that Horus defy the authority of Seth and oppose him in a fight to the death. This was in fact the essence of the wilderness ritual, and Jesus was compelled to see it through to the end. Elisha had followed Elijah out into this very same wilderness, and the old prophet had not returned. Now, Jesus found himself in the very same position, facing a man he viewed as the very incarnation of Elijah. In the end, he had only one choice: "Away from me, Satan," he commanded. "For it is written, 'Worship the lord your god and serve him only.' " [299]

Jesus would not pay homage to John.

The partnership was severed, as it had to be. Jesus had to increase, and John must decrease. This was the way it had always been, and this was the way it had to be. Indeed, there is every indication that the tanist ritual in the desert would play itself out in the events that were to follow. John, like Elijah, was destined to die. Indeed, the very next incident the author of *Matthew* mentions is John's imprisonment by the authorities. As it turned out, he would spend the rest of his life in captivity, and there is reason to believe that Jesus helped put him there.

XII

The Bridegroom

Jesus knew what he had to do.

He had taken the first step toward his goal by persuading John to recognize him as the royal messiah of Israel. The next step would be more difficult: If he wished to add the office of high priest to his resume, he would have to be rid of John — and not just in the symbolic sense conveyed by the desert ritual. In order to truly supplant John, he would have to make transform the ritual into reality.

But there were other matters to attend to first. Most pressing among them was the sacred marriage to the incarnate goddess he had chosen as his queen. The author of *John* places this event shortly after his baptism, reporting that, "on the third day, a wedding took place at Cana in Galilee." [300] This single sentence is packed with symbolism. The place name Cana stems from the Hebrew word *qaneh*, which referred a reed or cane — specifically in relation to its erect stature.

In this, it resembled nothing more than a pillar.

Jesus himself would refer to John enigmatically as "a reed swayed by the wind" — the priestly pillar inspired (or swayed) by the divine spirit, often described in terms of the wind.[301] This reference even has significance in terms of John's identity as a manifestation of Seth, for the reed was considered the scepter of Seth in Egyptian lore.[302] Now, Jesus himself was attending a wedding at a place named for a reed. The sexual symbolism of the erection is not to be missed, as copulation is the ultimate result of any wedding ritual. And the fact that this particular wedding took place "after three days" identifies it as the marriage ritual that typically followed the death and rebirth of the fertility god Dumuzi each year. Inanna had condemned him to spend a portion of each year in the underworld as her surrogate, as punishment for his arrogant behavior during her sojourn there. Even so, she would undertake another journey to the underworld to rescue him.

This annual trip lasted three days and culminated in their wedding.[303]

The wedding at Cana was a re-enactment of this sacred ritual, with Jesus as the dying and resurrected sun god and his bride in the role of Inanna. While the author of *John* never explicitly states that Jesus was the bridegroom at Cana, he does offer some pretty potent clues.

For one thing, Jesus takes responsibility for the festivities, as though he is the host. When the guests run out of wine, it is Jesus who is informed of the matter and expected to resolve the problem. This is exactly the sort of responsibility that might be expected to fall upon the "bridegroom," a title often used by Jesus in reference to himself.

His methods for dealing with the situation turn out to be inventive. He instructs the servants to fill six stone jars, meant for use in ceremonial washing, with water and draw some of the liquid out.

This they are to take to the master of the banquet.

What happens next is quite familiar. The water is miraculously transformed into wine, whereupon the banquet master pronounces it not only fit to drink but actually the best vintage he has tasted all day. He even calls the bridegroom aside and tells him so, complimenting him for avoiding the temptation to serve inferior-quality wine as the celebration wore on, at a time when many of the guests would have been too drunk to know the difference. It is interesting to note that these remarks are made to the unnamed bridegroom, even though Jesus was responsible for producing the wine. The most likely reason is that Jesus *was* the bridegroom, and therefore the natural one to receive such congratulations.

It was equally natural that he should have chosen a wedding celebration as the venue for this startling transformation.

As the messiah, Jesus was the true vine — the source of the fermented grape and therefore the only one capable of performing the miracle. But what did it mean? Why should he perform such a feat at a wedding? Was it somehow symbolic of the bridegroom's impending union with the bride? In fact, it almost certainly was. The water was the water of the sacred well, the female sex organ into which Odin cast his "single eye" (his penis) in exchange for wisdom. Yet sometimes, the clear waters of this well ran red with the blood of the menses, the lifeblood that was passed on to each new generation.

This blood, the ancients believed, was the very source of wisdom. Indeed, women past the age of child bearing were considered wise because of their perceived ability to retain the menstrual fluid inside their bodies. Water from an ordinary well was fine for quenching one's thirst, Jesus said, but it was nothing compared with the stuff he called living water. This could only be the fluid that conveyed the life force from one person to another, from one generation to the next — the red "water" known as blood that issued forth from the sacred well once each month. He who partook of this libation tasted the essence of life itself and partook of eternal life. Otherwise known as the "fountain of youth," the stuff of which young life was made.

The purified water was juxtaposed against the wine, just as the time of menstruation stood in contrast to a woman's normal state. As the water itself was clean, a woman was considered "unclean during her monthly period." [304] Anyone who touched her would also be unclean, and those who suffered the misfortune of touching her bed or clothing would have to wash their clothes and bathe in water. Hence, the purpose of the ceremonial water jars at the wedding, which themselves may have represented the female genitalia in the same manner that Pandora's jar or *pithos* did.

By changing the water into wine, Jesus signaled that he as the bridegroom was ready to drink the red wine from the sacred cup, partaking of the blood that imparted wisdom. This metaphor seems to have developed from a wedding ritual in which the king partook of the priestess-queen's "cup" in a literal sense, during the lovemaking of the wedding night.

The memory of just such an encounter is preserved in a Sumerian text that relates, in erotic terms, the passion of Inanna and Dumuzi for one another. The episode begins with Inanna bathing her loins in water, after which …

> *The king goes with lifted head*
> *To the holy loins*
> *Dumuzi goes with lifted head*
> *To the holy loins of Inanna* [305]

Here, it would seem, is the precedent for the imagery used at Cana. The queen begins by bathing her loins in water, preparing for her encounter with the king. Her consort then lifts his head to partake of the goddess' loins, just as the bridegroom must lift his head to drain a cup of wine at the wedding feast. This imagery follows the process of lovemaking described in the Sumerian texts: The water used by the goddess to purify herself in bathing is thus transformed into the honeyed wine of the sacred cup — the mead of Nordic legend.

Celtic kings attained immortality by imbibing a red mead dispensed by a faerie queen named Mab, a custom that may in turn be derived from the pharaonic practice of drinking a potion called the blood of Isis.[306] As in the case of the red mead, this potion was said to make them divine. It was known as *sa*, a word that should be familiar as the Egyptian word for "son." By ingesting this potion, the pharaoh became the son of the heavenly queen Isis (i.e., Horus) and the keeper of her blood. In this way, he could achieve immortal status.

"Water flows on high from your servant," Dumuzi exclaimed in one Sumerian text. "Pour it out for me, Inanna. I will drink all you offer." [307]

This is again the living water from heaven to which Jesus would refer. Not only did it bring eternal life to the king himself, but it watered the land to ensure a fruitful harvest. Dumuzi is depicted in decidedly agrarian terms when Inanna begs him to plow her vulva, the male sex organ taking on the role of a farmer's tool in preparing the earth for planting. Who would plow her high field? Who would plow her wet ground? The answer is: Dumuzi.

And the imagery is taken to its logical conclusion at the harvest, at which time the goddess' vulva is transformed into a veritable cornucopia of plenty:

Before my lord Dumuzi
I poured out plants from my womb
I placed plants before him
I poured out plants before him
I placed grain before him
I poured out grain before him
I poured out grain from my womb [308]

The womb or cup of Inanna acts in the very same manner as the grail, imparting an endless bounty of wondrous foods to the people. As in the grail legends, the king's virility is thus directly connected to the land's verdure, the sacred living water of her menstrual blood ensuring the continuance of the royal line and the prosperity of the kingdom.

In light of such imagery, it would seem almost certain that the wedding at Cana was in fact Jesus' own. And though the bride is never named in this scene, there can be little doubt as to her identity. She is none other than Mary Magdalene, the woman from whom seven demons were cast out in a representation of the goddess Inanna's seven-stage journey to the underworld as the star we know as Sirius.

Mary Salome

She was Jesus' companion, whom he loved more than all the disciples and often kissed upon the mouth. The name Mary Magdalene was probably an honorific, inherited from Jesus' own mother and worn to denote her elevated status as queen in exile. And it was not the only name by which she was known. Elsewhere, in fact, she is referred to by a different name altogether, one perhaps less recognizable at first but of equal symbolic import.

Salome.

The name meant peace — the very sort of peace that accompanied the prosperity of Inanna's fertile kingdom. This was the land of milk and honey, the milk of the male semen and the honey of the menstrual mead. When mixed together, they created life eternal, abundant crops and a the perfect environment for peace. Salome is also the feminine form of Solomon, the bridegroom from the Song of Songs after whom Jesus sought to pattern his new kingdom. Her name in Greek was Eirene, a name that calls to mind the archetypal Irish queen Eire and her land of peace and verdure to the west, the isle of Avalon where souls found their final peace when they passed from this world, returning once again to the paradise of yore.

Salome was, as might be expected, a lady of the waters who served as a priestess. And her name may be somehow connected with a rock-cut pool on the south side of the main ridge that served as the foundation of Jerusalem. The pool of Siloam. It was to this pool that Jesus sent a man born blind as part of a magical ritual to restore his sight. The healing properties of its waters identify it as yet another healing pool, likely presided over by a pythian priestess. It seems entirely possible that Jesus sent the man to this pool to be cured by such a priestess — all the more so if she was, in fact, his wife.

Salome herself is mentioned directly only twice in the canonical accounts of Jesus' life, both by the author of *Mark*, who names her among the women who helped anoint his body for burial after death. This is, of course, the very same task that was performed by Mary Magdalene. And although the author mentions the Magdalene's name as well, it would seem just possible that he has misunderstood his source. And a closer look at the text is indicated to understand just how this confusion might have arisen.

The references in Mark both appear, at first glance, to indicate not just two, but three women: "Mary Magdalene, Mary who was associated with James, and Salome." [309] Things would appear to be getting quite crowded around the tomb of Jesus. But in fact, the author's intention in placing three figures in this scene may well have been entirely poetic and traditional. In Greek lore, three women guarded the fortunes of men — the spinner, the measurer and the cutter. These were known as the Fates or, more properly, as the Moirai.

The Marys.

It is perhaps for this reason that three Marys are depicted at the tomb of Jesus — Mary Magdalene, Mary the mother of James and (Mary) Salome. In reality, only one woman was present, though she was identified three times. Just as Horus, Seth and Osiris were three aspects of the king, so these women were the three faces of his consort: the lover, the mother and the wise old crone. The only difficulty with this hypothesis lies in the identification of one of women as simply Salome. Yet the hunch that this woman was simply the third aspect of Mary gains support from an early church tradition, preserved by a writer named Papias, that Salome's name was actually Mary Salome.

For all of this, one might expect the name Salome to appear frequently in the gospels, yet it is surprising to learn that the two references in *Mark* are the only ones.

Or are they?

In fact, a woman named Salome *does* make an appearance on two other occasions, both of which shed a great deal of light on her role in Jesus' movement. But on both of these occasions, her involvement has been obscured by translators who have chosen to translate the name Salome as the generic term "peace." (This can be forgiven, considering the fact that, even today, the term *shalom* is used in common parlance as a peace blessing.)

One of these incidents is a peculiar account related by the author of *Luke*, involving a woman with an issue of blood. In this tale, Jesus was walking through a crowd of people one day when this woman, who had been subject to bleeding for twelve years, came up from behind him and touched the hem of his cloak. Upon doing so, the bleeding stopped immediately; Jesus, aware that something had happened, began to search for the person who had touched him. Eventually, he identified the woman, who fell at his feet and explained why she had reached out to him. He responded that her faith had healed her and added: "Go in peace." [310]

This phrase might just as easily be translated as, "Go, Salome."

Indeed, there is much more to the incident than meets the eye. The issue of blood can only refer to the menstrual cycle, which will recur on a monthly basis until one has sexual intercourse and conceives a child. A common indicator that a woman is pregnant is a missed period, in which her bleeding does not come as usual. The implication is that Jesus did in fact stop her bleeding, and that he did so by lying with her to conceive a child.

Supporting this is the framework of the story itself, which appears to have been modeled after the Hebrew story of Ruth and Boaz. This legend begins with the story of a man named Elimelech and his wife Naomi, who pull up stakes and go to live in the country of Moab. The contacts with Jesus' story are apparent from the opening phrases, wherein Elimelech is said to have come from the city of Bethlehem. Even his name is revealing, for it appears to mean "angel of God" — the same angel, perhaps, that announced to Mary that she would conceive a son.

Eventually, Elimelech dies and leaves Naomi as a widow. Unable in this state to support her two daughters, she sends them off to find husbands who will be able to provide for them.

One of these daughters is Ruth.

Her quest for a husband eventually leads her to a man named Boaz, a member of her father's clan who had amassed some considerable degree of wealth as a farmer. Ruth manages to get into his good graces, and with the help of her mother, begins to plot a means of seducing him. Naomi's advice to her daughter leaves no doubt as to their intentions in this regard: "Wash and perfume yourself, then go down to the threshing floor, but don't let him know you are there until he has finished eating and drinking. When he lies down, note the place where he is lying. Then go and uncover his feet and lie down." [311]

As events unfolded, the plan proceeded like clockwork. Ruth waited until Boaz was sated with food and wine, then approached him and uncovered his feet. When the startled farmer discovered her lying there in the middle of the night, she responded with these words: "Spread the corner of your garment, for you are my kinsman-redeemer." [312] All this seems uncannily similar to the incident involving Jesus and the woman with the issue of blood, who likewise pulled back the corner or hem of his garment and fell down at his feet. Though neither story explicitly speaks of sexual intimacy, the language hints strongly that this is what occurred.

Moreover, the prominence of menstrual blood in the Lukan tale connects it to the wedding at Cana, wherein the wine likewise symbolized the blood of the menses. And it is worth suggesting that the story of Ruth may have formed the foundation for the legend of a Celtic faerie queen said to dispense the magic red mead, which like the cup of red wine served as a symbol for the menstrual flow. It is interesting to observe that Ruth was a native of Moab, while the faerie is named as Queen Mab. Though Ruth herself is never referred to directly as a queen, she in fact becomes the matriarch of a royal line — her husband Boaz (who would give his name to one of Solomon's twin pillars in the temple) was said to have been the great-grandfather of King David. And Boaz was the royal or kingly pillar.

The menstrual reference seems to provide a link between Salome and the bride at Cana — Mary Magdalene. But it is not the only connection. There is, in fact, another instance in which Jesus is said to have uttered the very same words he spoke in addressing the woman with an issue of blood: "Go in peace," or "Go, Salome." And the woman to whom he spoke these words was named Mary.

The Sinful Woman

The story of the wedding at Cana is not the only account of Jesus' wedding. In fact, additional details may be found in references to the wedding feast contained in each of the four canonical gospels. These details vary slightly from one narrative to the next, but by placing them side by side, it is possible to arrive at a fairly clear picture of what must have happened.

The general outline of the story is as follows: Jesus is invited to a feast in his honor at a place called Bethany, which becomes the scene of strange if memorable event. A woman approaches him with an alabaster jar of expensive perfume and pours it over his head. She then kneels beside him and begins to weep, using her long hair to wipe the falling tears from his feet. This episode produces an outcry that the woman has wasted her money on the perfume — money that might have been better spent on "the poor," as members of the Ebionite resistance movement called themselves. Jesus himself was the leader of this movement. Yet instead of objecting to the woman's behavior, he endorses it as not only appropriate but necessary.

In the Lukan account, this strange encounter concludes with his simple admonition to the woman.

"Go, Salome."

What exactly is happening here?

And who is this mysterious Salome?

The answer to both questions lies in the symbolism surrounding the woman's action. Jesus explains its significance by telling those present that she has anointed him for burial, and this is the very task later undertaken by Mary Magdalene and Salome. But there is something even more afoot. According to the gospel accounts, the perfume used to anoint Jesus was of a particular type called spikenard.[313] It was often included in a woman's dowry.[314] And it is mentioned in only one other canonical book — the Song of Songs, which places these words in the mouth of the bride-to-be: "While the king was at his table, my spikenard spread its fragrance." [315]

Now here sat Jesus, the man who would be king, at the table as this woman poured spikenard over him. Can there be any doubt that she, like the woman in the ancient canticle, was a bride-to-be? If there is, further evidence may be found in the reports that she anointed him by pouring the perfume over his head. This action was highly sensual and loving, simulating the ritual lubrication of the phallus to facilitate intercourse on the wedding night.[316] Jesus would recognize the tenderness of this gesture when he commented that "she loved much." [317]

One cannot help but believe that the feeling was mutual.

His task, as in the tale of the woman with the issue of blood, would be to interrupt the menstrual flow by fathering a child upon this woman. In the poetic language of *Leviticus*, "if any man lie with her, and her flowers be upon him, he shall be unclean seven days." [318] The flowers symbolized her menstrual flow. It was the man's obligation to take her flowers, hence the commonly used reference to deflowering a virgin and the tradition of giving one's true love red roses — stained by the color of the menses. There is also the widespread custom that calls for a bride to toss her wedding bouquet over her shoulder, thus signifying that she is about to be deflowered and her virginity is literally behind her.

All this symbolism would seem to indicate that the story of Jesus' anointing is merely an expansion on the tale of the wedding at Cana. There is, however, a problem with this conclusion, involving geography. The wine-from-water incident is clearly described as taking place at someplace called Cana, whereas the anointing is set in a town identified as Bethany. But what if these references are not, in fact, geographic in nature? What if they are meant to be taken symbolically? The name Bethany is familiar because it also identifies the place where John baptized those who came to him. This makes sense, as the baptismal ceremony has already been identified as a ritual union with the dove goddess involving purifying water. This imagery clearly recalls the water pots used for purification at the wedding in Cana, a name that means "reed." And from this name arises the second connection, for Jesus would describe John the Baptist specifically as a reed shaken in the wind.

What it all comes down to is simply this: The baptism, wedding at Cana and anointing at Bethany were all part of a single ritual process presided over by John the Baptist.

Any remaining confusion as to the identity of the bride at this particular wedding are answered by the author of *John*, who refers to the woman who anointed Jesus explicitly by the familiar name of Mary. The author of *Luke* adds even further insight in labeling her a sinful woman. When taken together, these descriptions can point to only one person: Mary Magdalene, out of whom seven demons had been cast.

These seven demons were guardians of the seven underworld mansions through which the star Sirius passed after it sank below the horizon. They were the seven spirits who demanded that the goddess Inanna shed one article of clothing, or veil, each time she passed through one of these gateways during her descent into the netherworld. One of Inanna's titles was Ningeshtina, or "Lady of the Vine of Heaven." [319]

Jesus was the vine, and Mary was his lady, the incarnation of Inanna. And it is the myth of this goddess' descent through the seven gates of the underworld that is believed to have inspired the striptease known as the dance of the seven veils, which tradition ascribes to a woman with another familiar name.

Salome.

Match Made in Heaven

In an apocryphal but nonetheless ancient tradition, a person named Salome first appears in the guise of a midwife attending to Jesus' birth.[320] Given the time frame, this woman obviously cannot have been Mary Magdalene (who was not even born yet), and it is therefore apparent that her presence is meant symbolically. Yet the ahistorical character of the tale scarcely detracts from this symbolism, which identifies this fictional Salome quite clearly with the Sumerian "lady of the mountain," Ninhursag. This goddess was known specifically as the "opener of the womb," possessor of the special divine gift that ushered the unborn infant into the world.[321] It also identifies her with Artemis — the Greek name for the goddess Diana — who supposedly served as the midwife for her twin brother, Apollo. Even though she herself had been born just one day earlier, it seems that she had sprung from the womb fully mature and therefore able to assist in the birthing of her brother. Apollo was a sun god like Horus, and Diana/Artemis was a moon goddess, marking them as not merely brother and sister but celestial consorts in the manner of Jesus and Salome.

Salome was, like Inanna, the royal throne upon which the ruler was seated. The lap of the goddess.

Such titles reflected the fact that the Sumerian tongue recognized no distinction in the words for lap, womb, vulva ...

And, perhaps most significantly, sheepfold.[322] This is nothing less than revelatory, when one recalls the Hebrew title *migdal-eder* — or "watchtower of the flock" — that was invoked by the prophet Micah and which bears such a close resemblance to the name Magdalene. It also casts new light on the words of Jesus, who at one point declares that anyone wishing to enter the sheepfold must do so through the gate or be condemned as a thief. He then goes on to identify himself as the gate, but subsequently develops his discourse by further claiming the role of good shepherd — all of which seems quite confusing in modern terms.[323]

To those who familiar with Sumerian lore, however, the mixed metaphors would have made sense. In this context, the shepherd *was* the gate to the sheepfold. For it was the shepherd king Dumuzi or Tammuz whose phallus provided access to the sheepfold of the goddess, the divine womb or grail of plenty from which sprang all good things. In identifying himself both as shepherd and gate, Jesus was claiming for himself the legacy of Tammuz as divine king — the person through whom the land would be made whole again. And his partner in this endeavor, the personification of the goddess on earth, was none other than Mary Salome, otherwise known as the Magdalene.

In spite of what one might gather from her out-of-context presence as the midwife to Jesus' birth, Salome was still a young woman when she met and married her shepherd king.

But she was not a virgin.

She was the daughter of Herodias, a woman of royal lineage whose name identified her clearly enough as a member of the Herodian line. In fact, she was a granddaughter of Herod the Great, having been born to his son Aristobulus about a year before the unfortunate heir was put to death for treason. Herodias, however, survived and married her uncle. A man likewise named Herod.

The Herodian family tree can be difficult to follow, considering the number of marriages (some of them incestuous) and the proliferation of similar-sounding names. The exercise, however, is worth the effort — particularly in this case. For the Herod in question here is none other than the great king's eldest son by the second Mariamne, more familiar as the mother of Jesus. He had been written out of his father's will when Mariamne was accused of plotting the king's assassination, but had managed to live comfortably enough and maintain his ties to the royal house through his marriage to Herodias. Until, that is, she got a better offer.

The offer in question came from another of Herod's sons, and one with considerably more influence than the disowned son of Mariamne. Specifically, it came from Antipas, who *had* been included in the old king's final will and, after the downfall of Archelaus, enjoyed preeminent status among the Herodian clan for a good many years as tetrarch of Galilee. He was, to put it plainly, quite a catch. And Herodias knew she could not afford to let him get away, so she made arrangements to divorce her first husband with the intention of marrying the man Jesus would nickname "that Fox."

That was the easy part.

The trick came in disentangling Antipas from *his* marriage, a proposition that proved to be considerably more problematic. The difficulty lay in the fact that Antipas had entered into a political marriage with the daughter of the Nabataean king, Aretas (the fourth Arab monarch by that name). Herodias refused to marry him unless he divorced her, but such a move entailed tremendous political risk on Antipas' part. To divorce the Nabatean princess would be tantamount to dissolving his alliance with Aretas, a grossly offensive gesture that was likely to inflame tensions between the two rulers. But Antipas, who had fallen hopelessly in love with Herodias, must have felt that he had no choice. He therefore did as she requested and sent his first wife back to Nabataea, marrying Herodias in her stead. It was a decision that would come back to haunt him (literally, he believed) in the years ahead.

But what of Salome?

In the meantime, it seems, she had married as well. Though only a teenager, it had been arranged that she should follow in her mother's footsteps and wed a member of her own Herodian clan. In this case, the lucky man was her uncle Philip, who like Antipas had been named a tetrarch in his father's final will.

The union certainly seemed to be a propitious one. With Salome wed to Philip and her mother married to Antipas, the two women found themselves in the proverbial catbird's seat — in bed with the two most powerful men in the region, two half-brothers who between them controlled the northern half of Palestine. (The southern half, originally bequeathed to Archelaus, was now under direct Roman rule.) Not everything was coming up roses, however. Salome's marriage to Philip, a man many years her senior, may have been fine in some respects. But one crucial facet of their relationship was lacking: They were unable to conceive a child. As it turns out, the problem was not Salome's, for she would eventually marry yet another member of the Herodian clan and give birth to three sons.[324] However, that prospect was nowhere on the horizon during her time with Philip, and when he died, he left her a childless widow. In other words, she still had an issue of blood.

Salome's condition made her the perfect candidate for a levirate or "brother-in-law" marriage. Under the Hebrew code, a brother of the deceased was obligated to marry his widow and raise up children in his name. If Jesus was Philip's half-brother, he would have been required to fulfill the levirate command by taking Salome as his wife and welcoming her to his bed. Such an arrangement was not only mandated by the law of Moses, it was to Jesus' full advantage. By marrying Salome, he strengthened his ties to the Herodian clan so that even those who dismissed him as an illegitimate pretender would have to acknowledge his status. He also gained a partner of no mean substance, well-positioned to help finance his movement with the wealth she had accumulated through her family and previous marriage. The woman's possession of the extravagantly priced spikenard is evidence enough of her wealth, but there is also a reference by the author of *Luke* to a group of women who accompanied Jesus and "were helping to support him out of their own means."[325] Foremost among these women was Mary Magdalene.

Also numbered among them was a certain Joanna (whose name is the feminine form of John), further identified as the wife of the official responsible for overseeing Antipas' household. This is extremely significant, for it confirms that Jesus had ties with Antipas or someone close to him. That someone could very well have been his new wife, Herodias.

The woman had every reason to know about Jesus. His claim to be the daughter of Herod and the second Mariamne made him the full brother of her first husband. And his subsequent levirate marriage to her daughter would have only strengthened this connection. But why should Herodias have married her daughter off to a man widely regarded as a bastard and a rabble-rouser? Why should she even have associated with such a person?

One possibility is that they had a common goal.

A common enemy.

And his name was John.

XIII

The Bethsaida Incident

It had always been an uneasy alliance.

John and Jesus had been thrown together by circumstances beyond their control, each needing something from the other, but neither able to fully trust the situation. John needed a successor, and Jesus needed the Baptist's seal of approval to claim the mantle of messiah. But that mutual dependence only seems to have bred mutual suspicion. John for his part would publicly second-guess himself for picking Jesus as his successor, sending emissaries to ask him point-blank: "Are you the one who was to come, or should we expect someone else?" [326] Jesus, meanwhile, walked a tightrope that required him to honor the man who had anointed him as messiah, while at the same time emphasizing that he himself was somehow superior. This tension was reflected in what appears to be a an enigmatic statement: "I say to you, among those born of women, there is no one greater than John; yet the one who is least in the kingdom of God is greater than he." [327]

But Jesus' point would have been clear enough to his audience. John had been born of a woman, but he had *not* been born again. And those who had not been born again could not inherit the kingdom.

John was not the messiah. Jesus was.

End of discussion.

It is no wonder that the Mandaean sect, which did (and still does) view John as the savior, took a dim view of Jesus in its literature, bitterly dismissing him as a fraud and a charlatan.

Jesus needed John's anointing to legitimize his status as messiah. Once he had this, he had no further need of John. He was the new Horus whose duty was to overthrow the old fisher king John, who played the part of Seth in the tanist ritual. This ritual was played out in symbolic terms during the forty days in the desert; now it was about to be played out in real life.

After receiving John's anointing, Jesus broke ranks with the Baptist almost immediately. At first, he continued to repeat John's mantra: "Repent, for the kingdom of God is at hand." But he made it clear from the outset that he was not about to play second fiddle to anyone. Having accepted the Baptist's sanction, he at once began recruiting followers away from the older man, drawing a man named Andrew and his brother Simon into his nascent movement. No sooner was this accomplished than Jesus set up shop near the Jordan, baptizing those who came to him in direct competition with John. This obviously concerned those who had remained loyal to John, who proceeded to question him about the propriety of Jesus' activity: "Rabbi, the man who was with you on the other side of the Jordan — the one you testified about — well, he is baptizing and everyone is going to him." [328]

It is here that John is quoted as responding that he himself must decrease, while Jesus must increase. This was certainly the tanist way. But whether John actually spoke these words is doubtful. The author would have his readers believe that John, being a prophet, meekly accepted his position as the tanist Seth and saw his downfall as inevitable. Yet this was not the usual way of things. Seth was not known for having calmly surrendered his position to Horus; on the contrary, he had put up an epic battle to protect his position. Any suggestion that John would have stepped aside willingly is most likely the product of wishful thinking by the author, who was after all a follower of Jesus and was at pains to present him in the best possible light. As the avatar of Seth and *kher heb* priest of the sacred garden, John was expected use his flaming sword to guard the tree of life from all comers — Jesus included.

John was supposed to fight, and he was nothing if not a fighter. He brandished the fiery rhetoric of his oratory like the flaming sword of the cherub, captivating the crowds with his call to revolution and striking fear into the hearts of his enemies in the establishment. John was never shy about confronting his enemies and accusing them to their faces. They were, in his words, no better than a brood of vipers. And among them were the client rulers Rome had installed to do her bidding.

The Death of Philip

The Slavonic version of Josephus' *War of the Jews* contains an account of an encounter with one such ruler, the tetrarch Philip. According to this narrative, the tetrarch had a troubling dream in which an eagle tore out both of his eyes. He summoned all the sages in his service in an attempt to discover its meaning, but their interpretations merely conflicted with one another. At this point, John burst upon the scene without being asked and offered his exposition: "The eagle is your venality, because that bird is violent and rapacious. And this sin will take away your eyes, which are your dominion and your wife." [329]

John said no more and stalks away, leaving Philip to brood on his words. He didn't have long for contemplation, though — the scene ends with the statement that the tetrarch was dead before nightfall.

What was the point of this odd episode?

The symbolism that John used in confronting Philip makes it clear that his tirade was meant as a condemnation of Rome. The eagle was, after all, the symbol of the empire. And the Jewish opposition had long focused its attention on the venality of Rome — the empire's willingness to reward its favorites on the basis of bribes, and its insatiable urge to collect more than it needed in taxes. It would therefore seem that John was accusing Philip of acting as a creature of Rome, a greedy and corrupt ruler who would get his just reward: The empire would turn on him and rip out his eyes, making off with his wife and his dominion. All this would have made perfect sense. The kicker, however, was the ending: Strangely enough, the prophet's prediction did *not* in fact come true. The empire played no part in taking away Philip's dominion, nor did it make any move to dissolve his marriage.

He simply died.

End of story.

This would have been a clear embarrassment to John, whose reputation as a prophet would have been damaged by the failure of his prediction. If someone had a motive to embarrass the Baptist in such a manner, not to mention an interest in dispatching the tetrarch, it would have been a simple matter to pre-empt John's prophecy by arranging for his demise. The question is whether such a person in fact existed. Was there someone who had an interest in doing away with Philip, and whose position would likewise have been furthered by knocking John down a few pegs? In fact, there was. And his name was Jesus.

Indeed, Jesus had an even broader motive. With Philip dead, he would be free — indeed, obligated under levirate law — to marry Philip's widow, Salome. This would make him the husband of the former tetrarch's wife and give him a claim on Philip's holdings. The fact that Jesus' followers sought to proclaim him king during an episode that took place in Philip's territory (on the far side of the Sea of Galilee) would seem to bolster the case against him. But such evidence is highly circumstantial, and one would never convict a person of plotting an assassination based on motive alone. The fact of the matter is, however, that a record of Philip's death and Jesus' connection to it is preserved very neatly in perhaps the last place one might expect to find it — *The Gospel of John.*

It is there that a series of events unfolds that traces the progress of Jesus' peculiar relationship with the tetrarch from their first meeting through Philip's death.

The tetrarch is introduced in a rather perfunctory manner, during a narrative that describes how Jesus' first followers became attached to his movement. It begins with Andrew and another disciple of John the Baptist taking notice of Jesus and deciding to join his group. They, in turn, find Andrew's brother Simon — a.k.a. Peter — and recruit him to the movement. All this is presented in such a way as to suggest that these people sought out Jesus and latched on to this charismatic new leader. But it is here that the tone of the narrative changes profoundly: "The next day, Jesus decided to leave for Galilee. Finding Philip, he said to him, 'Follow me.' " [330]

The narrator introduces Philip without any embellishment. He is not described as a disciple of John, a brother of some other disciple or in any other terms. He is simply Philip. It is as though the author expects his readers to know full well whom he is talking about, as though the Philip in question were easily recognized by his first name alone as a significant player on the historical stage. Adding to this impression is the fact that, whereas Jesus passively accepted the allegiance of his other disciples, he actively went out to find and recruit Philip to his cause. Jesus, too, apparently thought this Philip was important and made an concerted effort to contact him.

Obviously, Philip the tetrarch was an important man.

And the sense of similitude between the Philip in *John*'s narrative and the tetrarch is only heightened by what the author of *John* reveals next: "Philip ... was from the town of Bethsaida." [331]

This is significant because, to begin with, Bethsaida was within the borders of Philip's tetrarchy. But beyond this, it was particularly notable as a town that Philip rebuilt from the ground up. Its name meant "house of the fisherman," a suitable title for a fishing village on the northeast shores of the Sea of Galilee.[332] By the time Philip was finished with it, however, it was much more than a village.

During his nearly four decades as tetrarch, he had it greatly enlarged — both in terms of its population and amenities — and rededicated it in honor of the emperor's wife. He was so proud of it that he decreed that he was to be buried there and that a funeral monument should be constructed in his honor. This decree proved prophetic, for the tetrarch in fact died in the Bethsaida.[333]

And this brings us to an interesting episode recorded by the author of *John* a short time later in his narrative. The author places his account of this episode immediately after an incident in Cana, involving a certain royal official whose son lay sick at Capernaum — a city on the northern shore of the Sea of Galilee, within walking distance of Bethsaida. In this tale, Jesus does not actually go to see the man's son but merely sends the official on his way with the assurance that the boy has been healed. The scene ends at this point, to be followed immediately by an odd disjuncture, in which the author appears to skip over a certain period of time as he transports Jesus to Jerusalem for "a feast of the Jews." [334]

The narrator then launches into his account of an incident involving a paralyzed man and a pool that was said to contain miraculous healing properties. In the story, a large number of "the blind, the lame and the paralyzed" have gathered around the pool in hopes of being healed. According to some translations, their hope rests in an angel of God who would descend periodically to stir up the waters, whereupon the first person who found his way into the pool would be healed of his affliction.

Among those present is a man who has been an invalid for thirty-eight years, and who never manages to make it to the pool because he needs someone to assist him. That someone, he believes, might be Jesus. But when he entreats Jesus to provide him the assistance he needs, he is told instead to stand and pick up his bed (or mattress) and walk away. Amazingly, he succeeds in doing so. The episode concludes with an encounter between the man and some of Jesus' detractors in the temple.

There is much of interest in this tale. For one thing, the pool itself sounds very much like another manifestation of the sacred well of life or fountain of youth that so often accompanies the serpent priestess and living tree. But what is more interesting is the *name* of the pool, which is reported in some translations as Bethesda but which is referred to in others by another, similar-sounding name.

Bethsaida.

This is an interesting coincidence, if coincidence it is. The author has gone to a great deal of trouble in relocating Jesus from the Sea of Galilee to Jerusalem, only to have him wind up at a pool that just so happens to share the name of a Galilean town located not ten miles from the spot where he was last seen. And not just any Galilean town, but the one where Philip died.

The next order of business is to identify the paralyzed man, whose name is never stated.

He is, however, *described*.

The man in question is said to have been "an invalid for thirty-eight years." This is quite a precise statement. The word translated here as "invalid" more specifically indicates feebleness or lack of strength, a connotation driven home by fact that the man is unable to reach the pool without assistance. He is, to put it bluntly, lame in his lower extremities. Such a description should at once conjure up images of the Fisher King, who was likewise rendered lame by his wounded thigh. And the connection is only strengthened by the fact that this particular invalid happens to be lying by a pool called Bethsaida, literally "house of the fisherman." This is, of course, very closely analogous to the grail myth, where the ultimate destination is the castle of the fisher king.

Moreover, the invalid in John's narrative is associated with a bed or mattress, just as the Fisher King is commonly depicted as lying or reclining on a bed. As these pieces begin to come together, it becomes obvious that the invalid is no mere peasant but in fact a fisher king who has been afflicted with a wounded thigh — in other words, he is unable to father a child.

Such a description would certainly have applied to Philip the tetrarch, who not only rebuilt the city of Bethsaida but was also unsuccessful at conceiving a child with his wife, Salome. Like the Fisher King, he was impotent.

The Fisher King in the grail myths must remain in his suffering state until a true champion arrives to "heal" him. But the remedy in question is hardly what one might expect. It does not, in fact, involve healing the king himself; rather, it constitutes a healing of his *lands*, which have been fated to share in his afflictions — his infertility — until one comes along who can replace him. A supplanter. A tanist jack. One who is, in fact, capable of fathering a child and thus restoring the land to its full health and verdure. In doing so, the new champion must depose his predecessor, slaying the impotent Fisher King so that he might take his place. This is the nature of the "healing" in such a motif.

And this is precisely what Jesus had every motive to undertake when it came to Philip. By "healing" him in this fashion, he could claim Philip's wife under the levirate law, establish a legitimate claim to the tetrarchy and further marginalize John the Baptist. In two of these goals, he succeeded, but the empire was not about to leave the tetrarchy in the hands of a royal claimant with ties to the Jewish independence movement. Instead of appointing Jesus to replace his dead half-brother, the emperor Tiberius chose the safer course and annexed Philip's lands to the province of Syria, thereby depriving Jesus of the political legitimacy he seems to have coveted. Though he at one point gathered a following of some five thousand people near Bethsaida who were intent on making him king, this was hardly enough of a following to threaten the will of Rome. Indeed, the size of the turnout must have been disappointing, for Jesus would later rail against Bethsaida for refusing to embrace his movement. "Woe to you, Bethsaida!" he would declare. "For if the miracles that were performed in you had been performed in Tyre and Sidon , they would have repented long ago in sackcloth and ashes. But I tell you," he continued bitterly, "it will be more bearable for Tyre and Sidon in the day of judgment than for you!" [335]

On that level, the endeavor was clearly a disappointment. Even so, it appears to have paid off in other respects: Mary Salome (who had probably abandoned Philip and attached herself to Jesus' movement some time before), became Jesus' wife, and John the Baptist was embarrassed when his eagle prophecy failed to reach its proper fulfillment. Motive and evidence, when taken together, present a compelling case against Jesus in the death of the tetrarch.

And any doubt about the identity of the invalid in *John*'s story should be erased when one final clue is presented.

The author of *John* specifically states that the man in question had been in his state of lameness for thirty-eight years. This is a very specific statement. The number is not one that is commonly used in any symbolic sense, unlike such figures as three, seven and forty. On the contrary, it appears to be an actual reference to that specific number of years. And one might expect it to correspond either to the number of years the fisher king had either been impotent or to the duration of his reign — how long he had in fact been a fisher king. Or, perhaps, both.

As it turns out, the number fits Philip perfectly. He was born about 20 B.C.E. and came into possession of his tetrarchy sixteen years later upon the death of his father. As this was shortly after he must have reached puberty, it could well have been about this time that he was found to be impotent. But more importantly, it marked the beginning of a tenure that lasted until his death 34 C.E. — precisely thirty-eight years later. This being the exact duration of the invalid's lameness, it would seem a simple matter to conclude that this invalid was in fact Philip. The invalid was "healed" (i.e., killed) at a place called Bethsaida; Philip himself died at Bethsaida.

The presence of the royal official who, in the preceding incident, asks Jesus to come and heal his son may further illuminate matters. His station indicates that he must have been connected with one of the two tetrarchs (royal scions from the Herodian clan) who were in power at the time — Philip or his half-brother, Antipas. Neither of these men had any authority over Jerusalem, which was then under direct Roman sovereignty, a fact that makes the author's sudden change of scenery from Capernaum to the pool of Bethsaida at "Jerusalem" all the more suspect.

It appears, in fact, that this artificial transition has been inserted to break up what was once a continuous narrative, thereby obscuring the original nature of the story.

The likelihood that these two scenes were originally a single entity is strengthened by the author of *Matthew*, who relates an alternate version in which:

➢ Jesus is once again asked by an official to heal someone — in this case, the man's servant — and does so simply by sending the man on his way with an assurance that the healing has been accomplished.

➢ The servant is specifically described as suffering terribly because he is *paralyzed*.

This account links elements from each of the two artificially separated incidents related in *John*, presenting an account in which the official is asking Jesus to heal a lame or paralyzed figure. This, therefore, must have been the original nature of the scene. The characterization of the paralytic as a suffering servant in *Matthew* further indicates his stature, for the prophet Isaiah had spoken of a just such a person whose "form (was) corrupted beyond human likeness." [336]

Such a phrase could certainly describe a badly disfigured paralytic.

Yet there is even more to be discovered from this passage, for the Hebrew term that is translated here to indicate corruption is derived from a root with two parallel meanings. The root in question is *shachath*. And, as with its English equivalent, it could be taken in two different senses — corruption in the sense of physical decay, or corruption in terms of a propensity toward depravity (specifically the buying and selling of influence). The latter was the very sin of which Philip had been accused by John the Baptist in his interpretation of the eagle dream. Philip's venality was blinding him, and that venality was a direct result of his willingness to bow to Rome.

It is fitting, therefore, that the man described in *John* as a royal official appears in *Matthew* as a Roman centurion.

It is as a result of this Roman official's pleas that the paralytic is "healed."

Or killed.

Gradually, the picture of what seems to have happened begins to form. Philip had a disturbing dream in which an eagle plucked out his eyes, and he let it be known that he wanted an interpretation. John got wind of this and hurried off to deliver his prophecy. In the meantime, however, Jesus had co-opted a member of Philip's household into his movement. This royal official agreed to act on Jesus' behalf in "healing" or assassinating Philip at the proper moment. (Perhaps as a result of the Baptist's prediction that Rome would be the tetrarch's undoing, the author of *Matthew* depicted this person as an imperial centurion.) The official's willingness to do Jesus' bidding is indicated in the speech attributed to him by the author of *Matthew*: "Just say the word, and my servant will be healed. For I myself am a man under authority, with soldiers under me. I tell this one, 'Go,' and he goes; and that one, 'Come,' and he comes. I say to my servant, 'Do this,' and he does it." [337]

The man's words indicated that Philip was completely in his power; and the official in turn was at Jesus' disposal. All Jesus had to do was say the word, and it would be done.

The healing would be complete.

The assassination would be carried out.

Off With His Head

With one obstacle out of the way, Jesus turned his attention once more to his rivalry with John.

The Baptist, not content with railing against Philip, had set his sights on the other Herodian ruler in the region, Antipas. But whereas he had accused Philip of corruption, he targeted his half-brother with a different accusation — and one that hit somewhat closer to home. It involved his marriage to Herodias, which the Baptist claimed was unlawful in light of her divorce from Antipas' half-brother. According to the author of *Matthew*, Antipas responded to John's tirade by locking him up.

Josephus, however, tells a slightly different story. Nowhere does he refer to a confrontation involving Antipas' new wife; instead, he states that the tetrarch arrested John for purely political reasons. According to Josephus, Antipas "feared lest the great influence John had over the people might put it within his power and inclination to raise a rebellion — for they seemed ready to do anything he should advise." [338] This statement only serves to reinforce the picture of John as a revolutionary figure. But it does not negate the possibility that Antipas' marriage to Herodias played some role in his arrest and subsequent execution.

Indeed, this appears to have been the case, for Josephus introduces the story of John in the context of a subsequent conflict between Antipas and the Nabatean king Aretas. During these hostilities, the tetrarch suffered a severe setback when most of his army was destroyed — a development that, the historian says, many viewed as divine punishment for Antipas' execution of the Baptist. And, as it turns out, the very same event served as both the impetus for John's criticism and the excuse for Aretas to declare war.

That event was the tetrarch's marriage to Herodias.

In order to marry her, he had been forced to divorce his previous wife, who just happened to be Aretas' daughter. As might have been expected, the Nabatean king took great offense at this; indeed, he responded by dissolving his alliance with Antipas and declaring an open state of war between the two realms. All this made for quite a mess, from which Antipas was fortunate to extricate himself. And from start to finish, the Baptist was at the center of it all.

When he waltzed in and declared Antipas a sinner for stealing his half-brother's wife, this immediately put him on the wrong side of both the tetrarch and his new bride. Herodias probably would have wished him dead then and there, but Antipas was not so quick to act. John had attracted a huge retinue of adventurers, nationalists, religious purists and hangers-on, a group that was probably considerably larger, at that point, than the crowds that were following Jesus. If Antipas killed him on the spot, he might only succeed in infuriating his followers and further galvanizing the support of those who believed in him. This is why he took such great pains to see that John was kept locked safely away in the Dead Sea fortress called Machaerus. In this remote location, he posed little threat to anyone. But he was still alive. And as long as he remained alive, no one could make him into a martyr.

Such a stalemate was perfect for Antipas' needs, but it was not enough to satisfy Herodias, who was still seething (and perhaps a bit guilt-ridden) over the Baptist's denunciation of her divorce and remarriage. And it didn't help Jesus' position, either. As long as John remained alive, the Baptist would still be considered the rightful high priest by most of those in the opposition. But certainly he wasn't doing anybody any good in prison, leaving the movement at a standstill for lack of leadership. Jesus saw himself as the person to step into the void, but he could not do so with the Baptist still alive. Fortunately for him, he had the kind of connections that could facilitate John's departure and his own elevation to the status of opposition high priest. These connections would enable him, finally, to complete the inevitable tanist ritual that he had played out on a symbolic level with John in the desert. Now, however, he was playing for keeps.

His connections came in the form of family ties. He was, specifically, the husband of Salome — who in turn was the daughter of Herodias, with whom he now had common cause. Both of them wanted the Baptist dead; now all that remained was to come up with a plan to accomplish it. That plan, in its final form, revolved around the one person Jesus and Herodias had in common: Salome. This young beauty was to be the focal point of an elaborate deception to be played out on the occasion of Antipas' birthday feast. Herodias would arrange for Salome to provide some entertainment, the sacred striptease known as the dance of the seven veils. She would wait, however, until Antipas had swallowed his share of liquor. Then, once the tetrarch was drunk, he could be counted upon to offer her some extravagance for her trouble.

It was at this point that she would demand her price: "I want you to give me, right now, the head of John the Baptist on a platter." [339]

This is, in fact, exactly how events played out.

Antipas was so pleased with the young woman's dance that he offered here anything she might desire, up to half his kingdom. And Salome took this as her cue to demand the Baptist's head. The tetrarch knew that it was a heavy price to pay, as he feared that news of the popular leader's death would spark widespread rioting and perhaps even a full-fledged revolt. Yet there was no help for it. He had pledged himself to Salome with an oath in front of a large assembly, and he could not afford to be seen as a man who went back on his word. He therefore ordered John's execution in an event that would become, in some ways, the prototype for the grail procession with its disembodied Baphomet head displayed upon a platter borne by a beautiful maiden.

Of course, there is no way to prove that Jesus had a direct hand in the Baptist's demise. But there can be little doubt that he had both the means and the motive to help carry out such a scheme. And when one considers that his own wife appears to have been the catalyst in the entire drama, it can scarcely be denied that, at the very least, he knew what was about to unfold.

XIV

The Seeds of Revolution

John's death signaled a turning point for Jesus. With his longtime rival consigned to the grave, he was now free to advance his claims to leadership of the movement. But his hopes for legitimacy had been dashed when the emperor chose to ignore his claim to Philip's former tetrarchy and instead annex it to Syria. It was a development that forced Jesus to rethink his strategy and shift direction, abandoning his efforts to score political points with the elite and turning instead to a more reliable — and malleable — source of support. The masses.

Many of John's former supporters, finding themselves leaderless, gravitated toward him. And he gained still more as he began to speak out loudly against the empire, casting himself as the Baptist's natural successor and a champion of the common man in impassioned speeches laced with inflammatory language. He concentrated his efforts around the region known as Galilee, where he already had an active following to build upon.

At a Sabbath assembly in the local synagogue, he opened the scroll of the prophet Isaiah and read: "The spirit of the lord is on me, because he has anointed me to preach the good news to the Poor. He has sent me to proclaim freedom for the prisoners and recovery of sight for the blind, to release the oppressed and to proclaim the year of the lord's favor." [340]

His mission was clearly laid out.

- ➢ The Poor were the Ebionites, the self-styled children of the revolution.
- ➢ The prisoners were political prisoners (perhaps an appeal to the followers of John the Baptist, who had been imprisoned and killed by the Romans).
- ➢ The blind were those who blindly acquiesced to Roman rule.
- ➢ The oppressed were the Jews under the Roman occupation.

Within a year, Jesus promised, the situation would be changed. The time was now. *This* was the year of the lord's favor. "Today," he declared, "this scripture is fulfilled in your hearing." Jesus was doing nothing less than inaugurating the first phase of the Jewish revolution. Predictably, his words enraged the members of the establishment, who drove him out of town toward a precipice and sought to throw him to his death. Jesus managed to escape, but this would not be the last attempt on his life by his enemies.

From there, he took his message to the Sea of Galilee. He spent much of his time in the towns that ringed the shoreline of the inland "sea," also known as Lake Gennesaret. Thirteen miles long by eight miles wide, it would serve as a base of operations for Jesus in the north. Capernaum. Bethsaida. Chorazin. All would bear witness to Jesus' provocative message.

The words of the prophet Isaiah would be fulfilled: The kingdom of God was at hand.

"Then will the eyes of the blind be opened and the ears of the deaf be unstopped. Then will the lame leap like a deer and the mute tongue shout for joy." [341] Later writers would attribute all these miracles to Jesus during his sojourn in Galilee. But his listeners would have understood Jesus' words as highly charged political rhetoric. The coming of the kingdom, he promised, would usher in a new age of healing and prosperity for those who had been so long afflicted by Roman rule.

Jesus may have gained a reputation as a miracle worker. But when asked to produce a great sign to prove his identity as the messiah, he refused outright.

"This is a wicked generation," he declared. "It asks for a miraculous sign, but none will be given except for the sign of Jonah. For as Jonah was a sign to the Ninevites, so will the Son of Man be to this generation.... The men of Nineveh will stand up at the judgment with this generation and condemn it, for they repented at the preaching of Jonah, and someone greater than Jonah is here!" [342]

God had chosen Jonah, the legendary ark hero, to declare the impending downfall of Nineveh some seven centuries earlier. Nineveh, a massive city of more than a hundred thousand people, was the capital of the Assyrian Empire — the same empire that had conquered northern Israel and dominated the region for nearly three hundred years. It represented the pinnacle of power in the ancient world. Yet Jonah had declared that it would fall within forty days if it failed to repent.

Now, God had chosen Jesus to declare the impending downfall of another imperial oppressor, Rome. The men of Nineveh had listened to Jonah, but the men of Rome were turning a deaf ear to "someone greater." Jesus. Those who caught the nuances of his words must have nodded knowingly at his reference a prophet named Jonah. The name was, of course, a subtle reference to the similarly named prophet John. The Baptist. Just as Jesus was "greater" than Jonah, he was also claiming to be greater than John — the heir to a double portion of his prophetic spirit, just as Elisha had been the recipient of Elijah's.

Those who recognized such nuances were those who had been cured of their deafness, having developed "ears to hear" the message of Jesus.

This was the nature of Jesus' healings.

Some who had been blind to the oppression around them were having their eyes opened. Some who had been mute were speaking out against the corruption of the empire. And some who had been lame were taking action, responding to Jesus' call. Jesus made it clear that people were not "healed" by any miraculous effort on his part, but based on their own ability to hear, understand and act on his message. It was their faith, not any action on his part, that produced results. They were blind and deaf by choice, not because of any physical ailment. And he could only heal them — literally, make them whole — if they *first* abandoned their blindness and deafness. Again, he quoted the prophet Isaiah:

"This people's heart has become callused. They hardly hear with their ears and they have closed their eyes. Otherwise, they might hear see with their eyes, hear with their ears, understand with their hearts and turn. And I would heal them." [343]

Some people Jesus healed in just this manner.

From others, he cast out evil spirits.

Such "evil spirits" could make one blind or mute. They could cause a man to close his eyes to the empire's oppression, and fear to speak out against it. When such spirits were removed, the man's sight and speech would be restored. It was no miracle. It was a political conversion. Jesus was simply recruiting men to his cause. Seeing his success, some people asked, "Could this be the son of David?" Could this man be the anointed one destined to occupy the throne of David and expel the Roman forces from Israel?

Jesus assured them that the answer was yes.

He had come to cast out the evil spirit of Rome's influence from Israel, a spirit named for the Roman legions that occupied the land. "My name is legion, for we are many," this spirit would tell him. It implored Jesus not to send it out of the area — as Jesus sought to expel the Roman occupation forces from Israel. A large herd of pigs was feeding on the hillside nearby, and the spirits begged him: "Send us among the pigs; allow us to go into them." Nothing could have been more appropriate. The pigs were unclean animals, just as the Romans were an unclean presence in the land. They were totem animals of Seth, the current ruler or emperor whom Jesus was bent on overthrowing. He therefore granted their request, and the pigs plunged headlong down an embankment into the lake below, where they were drowned.

The entire episode seems to have been based upon an initiatory ceremony into the greater mysteries of Eleusis in Greece. These rites began with a call for the youths involved to rush into the sea for ritual cleansing, each carrying under his arm a young pig to wash in preparation for sacrifice.[344]

This makes it obvious that Jesus, too, was practicing a sort of ritual initiation into his movement, a variation on the baptismal rite with mystical and revolutionary overtones. Those from whom the demons had been cast out were the initiates; the pigs were the animals to be sacrificed as part of the ceremony; and those who tended the pigs were the enemy — Roman sympathizers who opposed Jesus' movement. It was they who, according to the gospel account, spread the word about what had happened and stirred up the surrounding community against Jesus, so that they with him to leave the area.[345]

Their concern?

They didn't want to be around when the Romans found out about the incident and returned to investigate.

Those sympathetic to the resistance were eager to see the Roman influence cast out of Israel. But, as one would expect, those who supported the Roman occupation saw things differently. For them, Jesus was the one possessed by an evil spirit. And he was acting on the authority of Beelzebul, the prince of evil spirits who took his name from the god Baal.

Jesus heard this charge frequently, and he was ready with an answer. If he recruited followers by the authority of Beelzebul, on whose authority did the Romans recruit their supporters? But if he did so on the authority of God, it was a sign that the kingdom of

God had come upon them. And if this was true, Jesus warned, the Romans' downfall was imminent.[346]

"When a strong man, fully armed, guards his house, his possessions are safe," Jesus told them. "But when someone stronger attacks and overpowers him, he takes away the armor in which the man trusted and divides up the spoils." [347]

The Roman army was strong and well armed. But the kingdom of God, Jesus assured them, was stronger, and it was gaining strength with each passing day. As Jesus traveled throughout Galilee "healing the sick and casting out demons," he was actually recruiting new citizens for this kingdom — people who would fight to bring Isaiah's vision of a new age to fruition. Jesus was the vine, and his followers were the branches. Those that did not bear fruit would be tossed aside to wither up and die. In due course, they would be cast into the fire and burned. When the kingdom was established, Jesus would have no mercy on those who had deserted him.[348] But those that bore fruit would produce a crop many times the size of what had been planted.

Jesus told his followers to be bold in proclaiming his message.

"Do you bring in a lamp to put it under a bowl?" he asked them. "Instead, don't you put it on its stand?" [349]

Jesus would not act alone in spreading his message. On the contrary, he would build his movement around an inner circle of three trusted cohorts who also served on a council of twelve leaders. Beyond this, there would be a group of seventy with a lesser degree of authority who were nonetheless empowered to carry out certain tasks on behalf of the exiled kingdom. These numbers were not chosen at random; each carried a particular significance. Jesus appears to have based his hierarchy on a model he obtained from or at least shared with Qumran. *The Community Rule* in force there declared: "In the council of the community, there shall be twelve men and three priests, perfectly versed in all that is revealed of the law, whose works shall be truth, righteousness, justice, loving-kindness and humility." [350]

As Jesus' brothers/cousins were all sons of the high priest Joazar, they qualified to fill the roles of the three priests. The gospels identify the members of this inner circle as Peter, James and John, once again reserving a place for the Baptist long after his death. In reality, the third place was probably taken by the only one of the four brothers *not* included in the list — Judas. The gospel writers likely used their pens to strike him from the his rightful position, judging him unfit to have held such a place of honor in light of his later reputation as a traitor. This, even though they retained the memory that he had been chosen as keeper of the group's finances, a position of the highest possible trust.

The larger council of the twelve, who would became known as apostles, was almost certainly meant to represent the twelve tribes of Israel.

Seventy, meanwhile, is familiar from its significance as the number of days Sirius spent below the horizon during its annual descent into the underworld. More importantly in this context, however, it was also the number of elders who served on the national council that governed Israel, known as the Sanhedrin. This council could consist variously of seventy members, or seventy-one if the high priest were included in their number. Beyond this, there are also instances in which it seems to have been composed of seventy-two members.[351]

The latter number is familiar from the myth of Thoth and the creation of the five epagomenal days, in which he won a fraction of the moon's light in a game of draughts. In order to fashion these five extra days, Thoth needed exactly one seventy-second of the moon's light each day. The possibility that the higher number of elders on the Sanhedrin dates back to this myth is not to be discounted, especially in light of a rabbinic tradition that Jesus had not twelve but five disciples.[352]

Both these numbers have clear lunar connections, with the former signifying the number of months (or moons) in a year and the latter a collection of the extra moonlight contained in the solar annum. But regardless of these connections, it is clear that Jesus' council of seventy was meant to represent a sort of opposition Sanhedrin, a government in exile ready to take the reins when the kingdom of heaven was established.

While out of power, however, this anti-Sanhedrin served a somewhat different function. The first order of business for the nascent movement was to increase its numbers, in the hope of forming a popular groundswell against the empire that could finish what the Galilean's tax revolt had started. If the masses rose as one and God himself sanctioned their effort, not even the Roman legions could stand in the way of their success.

This, at least, was the thinking.

And it was with this in mind that Jesus sent members of his council of twelve and his broader group of seventy out in teams of two, blanketing the countryside with his message that the kingdom was at hand.

He sent them out with specific instructions that closely resemble the rules by which the Essenes were said to live. A comparison between the language of Jesus as reported in *Matthew* and that attributed by Josephus to the Essenes is instructive:

Provisions:

- They carry nothing with them when they travel to remove areas, though they still take their weapons with them — Josephus
- Do not take gold or silver or copper in your belts — Jesus

Clothing:

- Nor do they allow a change of garments or shoes, until they are entirely torn to pieces or worn out by time — Josephus
- Take no bag for your journey or extra tunic or sandals or staff — Jesus

Accommodations:

➤ There is, in every city where they live, one appointed to take care of strangers and to provide garments and other necessities for them — Josephus [353]

➤ Whatever town or village you enter, search for some worthy person there and stay at his house until you leave — Jesus [354]

Josephus made it clear that members of the Essene movement dwelt in every city and were, as a condition of membership in the group, obligated to open their homes to others of the sect: "If any of their sect come from other places, what they have lies open before (the visitors), just as if it were their own. And they go into such as they never knew before, as if they had ever so long been acquainted with them." [355] Jesus' followers seem to have made considerable use of this loose network of Essene safe houses during their travels across the countryside. But they had to be careful: Not every householder could be trusted to support their radical mission, and it was therefore necessary to use a sort of code at the outset to ensure their safety. "As you enter a home," Jesus told them, "give it your greeting."

This greeting was probably a sort of password known by both the visitors and their prospective hosts, establishing their common goals in support of the opposition. If, however, the greeting was not accepted — or the password was not properly acknowledged — the emissaries were to depart at once: "If anyone does not welcome you or listen to your words, shake the dust off your feet when you leave that home or town." [356]

As it turned out, there appear to have been few such instances during this initial mission. Indeed, the inaugural endeavor proved to be an overwhelming success: When Jesus' followers returned, they declared that "even the demons submit to us in your name."

Jesus was elated, and the initial response to his recruiting drive emboldened him to step up his efforts. His confidence soared: "All things have been committed to me by my father," he boasted.

"Blessed are the eyes that see what you see, for I tell you that many prophets and kings wanted to see what you see but did not see it, and to hear what you hear but did not hear it." [357]

Nothing, Jesus felt, could stop him now. The kingdom of God was in ascendance, and more would join as the recruiting drives continued. Jesus instructed his disciples to go first to the "lost sheep of Israel," but their mission would not be limited to ethnic Jews. The kingdom of God might start with Israel, but it did not end there. Foreigners had a place in the revolution — as long as it was *on Jewish terms*. The messianic vision went far beyond the borders of Israel. According to the prophets, it included the whole world. The son of David would restore the kingdom of David and expand it, just as the legendary Solomon had done, establishing the law of God throughout his creation. Gentiles were bound to be included sooner or later. If they joined the movement voluntarily at the outset, so much the better.

They would, of course, have to obey the laws of Moses. And they would have to be circumcised. The resistance would not compromise with the Gentiles, but neither would it exclude them based on simple prejudice.

Jesus followed this policy consistently. Re-establishing the kingdom was the first step. Expansion would come next. Hence, Jews — the lost sheep of Israel — would hear the message first. In launching a revolution, one had to be careful about whom one trusted. Pearls should not be cast before swine, and bread meant for the children of Israel should not simply be tossed to the dogs. Yet even the dogs were allowed to eat the scraps that fell from the table. Even the Gentiles had their place in the resistance, if they were sincere. Against Rome, Jesus needed all the help he could get.

"Whoever is not against us is for us."

Tax-gatherers, sinners and prostitutes who wished to join the movement were not the enemy. The empire was. Jesus was always aware of this distinction, even if his opponents were not. The kingdom of God, like any other kingdom, had its foreign policy and its domestic policy. Jesus could, on the one hand, advocate the violent overthrow of Rome while at the same time teaching his followers to turn the other cheek. There was no contradiction in this. Within the kingdom, peace was crucial — a kingdom divided against itself, Jesus observed, could not stand. But in order to establish and preserve the kingdom, one might have to wage war against external enemies.

When Jesus told his followers to love their enemies, he wasn't referring to Rome. He was referring to personal enemies within the kingdom. Love your neighbor as yourself.

"And who is my neighbor?" someone asked him.

It was the man lying in the middle of the road, left for dead by robbers and shunned by two holy men. Jesus spoke of a priest and a Levite who showed no mercy to the fallen man.[358] Yet a despised Samaritan took time to bandage the man's wounds and find a place for him to stay until he recovered. The first two men were members of the establishment, priests appointed by the friends of Rome. The third man was a pariah — a half-breed from a bastard race. Yet it was he who showed the man mercy, and doubtless gained his gratitude in return. It was just such an approach that Jesus advocated for the kingdom.

It was a message of solidarity.

Again, a kingdom divided against itself could not stand. The people of Palestine had their differences, but these would have to be set aside for the common good. Anyone who was so much as angry with his neighbor would be subject to judgment. Slander would be cause for legal action. Any disputes were to be resolved before sacrifices were made, and lawsuits were to be settled before they reached court.[359] Solidarity was crucial if war with Rome was imminent. And each of these directives was designed to foster such solidarity.

Jesus called for peace within the kingdom of God and war against those who stood against it. That was the distinction between the kingdom's domestic and foreign policies — a distinction that has been drawn in virtually every nation throughout history. He simply believed, like many rulers, that peace could neither be achieved without sacrifice nor maintained without solidarity. And in consequence, he called on his followers to supply both.

Such qualities would be crucial. Jesus warned those he sent out that, because they were revolutionaries, they would be targets for the Romans and their collaborators.

"I am sending you out as sheep among wolves," he announced. "Therefore be as shrewd as snakes and as innocent as doves." He warned them to "be on guard against men. They would hand you over to the local councils and flog you in the synagogues. On my account, you will be brought before governors and kings to give evidence against the foreigners (i.e. the Romans). But when they arrest you, do not worry about what to say or how to say it. At that time, it will be given what to say, for it will not be you speaking but the spirit of your father speaking through you."

Jesus knew it was not a matter of *if* members of the resistance would be arrested, but *when*. The war between the sons of light and the sons of darkness, he believed, was rapidly approaching.

And in the coming conflict, no one could be fully trusted.

"Brother will betray brother to death, and a father his child," he warned. "Children will rebel against parents and have them put to death. All men will hate you because of me, but he who stands firm to the end will be preserved. When you are persecuted in one place, flee to another. I tell you the truth: You will not finish going through the cities of Israel before the son of man comes." [360]

The meaning of this last reference was clear to anyone who knew the Jewish scripture. When the so-called son of man arrived, the kingdom of God would be established. The revolution would begin.

Jesus believed he was this son of man, foretold by the prophet Daniel.

In a vision, Daniel had foreseen the coming of the messiah, whom he had referred to as "one like a son of man coming with the clouds of heaven." This son of man, he prophesied, would be led into the very presence of God and "given authority, glory and sovereign power. All peoples, nations and men of every language will serve him. His is an everlasting dominion that will not pass away, and his kingdom will never be destroyed." [361]

The vision was not to be taken literally, but symbolically. The son of man was not actually expected to descend out of heaven in the clouds. The imagery was used to depict the messiah's unique standing before God, his role as the phoenix descending out of heaven and his ability to call upon the heavenly host to do battle alongside the forces of the resistance movement, guaranteeing a glorious victory. And ushering in the kingdom of heaven.

"You will battle against them from heaven above, for the multitude of holy ones in heaven and the hosts of angels in your holy realm give you praise," the Qumran scribes promised. "By the hand of your anointed (literally, *messiah*) who sees your decisions, you have announced to us the time of battle." [362]

This battle, Jesus knew, was drawing near. The kingdom of heaven, he promised, was at hand. But it would not come easily. If the revolution were to succeed, people would have to be willing to fight. From the moment John the Baptist established his mission to free Israel, Jesus declared, men of violence had been seeking to take the kingdom of God by force.[363] "Do not suppose that I have come to bring peace to the earth," Jesus admonished his followers. "I have not come to bring peace, but a sword. I have come to turn a man against his father, a daughter against her mother." Indeed, he declared, "a man's enemies will be the members of his own household!"

Under such circumstances, Jesus knew he must demand unquestioning loyalty from anyone who enlisted in his cause: "Whoever acknowledges me before men, I will acknowledge before my father in heaven," he promised. "But whoever disowns me, I will disown him before my father.... Anyone who loves his father or mother more than me is not worthy of me. Anyone who loves his son or daughter more than me is not worthy of me." [364]

This was, he realized, a fight to the death. And, as in any war, there would be casualties. Men would be crucified — the standard penalty reserved for revolutionaries and enemies of the Roman state. And others, he knew, would lose their lives on the battlefield. These, he promised, would be martyrs in the holy cause of the kingdom: "Whoever (seeks to) find his life will lose it, but whoever loses his life for my sake will find it." [365]

Not all would be martyrs, he promised: "I tell you the truth," he declared. "Some of you who are standing here will not taste death before they see the kingdom of God come with power." [366]

Urgency

Time was indeed running out. Unlike John, Jesus could not afford to stay put and wait for recruits to come to him; if he did so, he would risk being captured himself. Moreover, time was of the essence if the kingdom of God were to be inaugurated. It was therefore necessary to seek recruits while on the move. No long initiation process was needed. All that was necessary was a quick invitation to "sell all your possessions and give (the money) to the Poor, so you may have treasure in heaven. Then come and follow me." [367]

If he was to challenge the empire, he needed numbers.
Fast.

He likened himself to a farmer scattering seeds, speaking to anyone who had "ears to hear." Some of the seeds were tossed onto the rocks, others onto shallow soil and still others among the thorns. These seeds, of course, produced no fruit. But others found fertile ground. And these, he said, had produced a crop thirty, sixty or even a hundred times what was sown. As evidence, he had only to point to the fruits of his labor. As he stood on the shore of the Sea of Galilee, the crowds pressed in upon him to such an extent that he was forced to address them from a boat. It was then that he told the parable of the seeds.[368]

The seeds of revolution.

Jesus promised that the kingdom of God would be like a mustard plant, which started out as "the smallest of all your seeds. Yet when it grows, it is the largest of garden plants and becomes a tree (so large) that the birds of the air come and perch upon its branches." [369]

Jesus was aware of the fact that such rapid growth would allow enemies the opportunity to infiltrate his group. It was, however, the price that had to be paid. If he did not have time to spend separating the good soil from the bad, neither did he have time to weed out the bad seeds scattered by his enemy. "While you are busy pulling the weeds, you may pull up some of the wheat with them," he told his followers. That process would have to wait, he said, for the harvest that was soon to come. Then, the weeds would be gathered into bundles and burned.[370]

Jesus did take some precautions. For one thing, he spoke in parables — codes that his closest followers would understand, but his enemies would be unable to decipher. This practice was followed at Qumran, as well, where the scrolls of the resistance movement never mentioned their enemies by name. The Romans were the *Kittim*, and specific figures were referred to by such pseudonyms as the "Wicked Priest" or the "Righteous Teacher." Even the ancient Jewish texts were viewed as codes to be deciphered in light of the current struggle. Hence, the scribes of Qumran composed *peshers*, or interpretations, of the sacred scrolls and attached them to the texts themselves. If such information fell into the wrong hands, it would be invaluable to an enemy. For this reason, it was coded. And, in the case of the Qumran documents, it was carefully hidden in desert caves near Qumran, where it remained undisturbed for centuries until the mid-twentieth century.

"The knowledge of the kingdom of heaven has been given to you, but not to them," Jesus told his followers. "This is why I speak to them in parables: 'Though seeing, they do not see; though hearing, they do not understand.' " [371]

Jesus had no intention of placing important information in the hands of his enemies if they were within earshot, as he knew they must be. Indeed, the Pharisees and other imperial cronies dogged his every step as he moved through the towns of northern Israel. Time and again, they sought to catch him in some hypocrisy and discredit him. How could he claim to be a pious Jew if he ate with tax gatherers and sinners? And how could he do so if he failed to observe the Sabbath — the Jewish holy day of rest?

When a group of Pharisees saw Jesus' disciples picking heads of grain as they walked through the fields on the Sabbath, they did not miss their opportunity to denounce him.[372]

"Look!" they accused. "Your disciples are doing what is unlawful on the Sabbath."

According to legend, however, had done so.

And Jesus was claiming the throne of David.

"Haven't you read what David did when he was hungry?" he asked them. "He entered the house of God, and with his companions ate the consecrated bread — which was not lawful for them to do, but only for the priests."

The Hebrew scriptures related the tale of how this had happened before David was king.[373] At the time, they said, the throne was still in the hands of Saul, Israel's first monarch. David, however, had begun to make a name for himself as a military hero by defeating the Philistine champion Goliath in single combat. As David's popularity grew, so did Saul's resentment. The king began to view David as a political rival, and he responded to the threat by ordering David's arrest and execution as a traitor.

Jewish legend would portray Saul as paranoid, egotistical and even mentally unstable. The popular slogan "Saul has killed his thousands and David his ten thousands" supposedly rang in his ears and threw him into a jealous rage. In fact, however, Saul had good reason suspect David of sedition. David lost no time in confirming his worst fears, going into exile and forming an army of his own. About six hundred men joined forces with him, and he began moving like a political fugitive from one town to the next — just as Jesus would be forced to do many centuries later. Eventually, David made his headquarters in the caves of the Judean desert, by the western shore of the Dead Sea.

Caves in the same desert, a few miles to the north on the shore of the same inland sea, would serve as headquarters to another resistance movement a thousand years later — the movement at Qumran.

David had been an exile waiting to claim the throne, just as Jesus was now. And when asked for permission to eat the consecrated bread, he was out gathering supplies for his band of revolutionaries. There can be little doubt that Jesus was doing the exact same thing. He was not violating the Sabbath out of choice, but out of necessity. Time was short, and he was preparing to launch a revolution.

Jesus, as the messiah — the man who would be king — had the right to bend the rules.

"The son of man," he declared, "is lord of the Sabbath."

Taxing Questions

When Jesus' enemies weren't denouncing him for violating the laws of Moses, they were accusing him of breaking Roman law — specifically, the empire's policy of taxation.

Opposition to Roman taxes had been a cornerstone of the resistance movement since the days of Judas the Galilean. If confronted on the question, Jesus would be placed in a no-win situation. If he were to endorse the taxes, he would lose all credibility with his followers. If he were to oppose them, he would give his opponents grounds to arrest him as a political agitator.

Jesus was forced to walk a fine line.

On one occasion, a tax collector at Capernaum approached Simon Peter and demanded to know whether Jesus had paid the temple tax.

"What do you think, Simon?" Jesus asked him. "From whom do the kings of the Earth collect duty and taxes — from their sons or from others?"

"From others," Simon answered.

"Then the sons are exempt," Jesus responded. The implication was clear. Jesus and the members of his movement were sons of the great king. God. They were therefore exempt from paying Roman taxes. The kingdom of God superseded the Roman Empire. This had been the stated position of Jewish resistance movement since the time of Judas the Galilean, and Jesus was not about to oppose it. But he was not about to oppose the empire directly, either — not yet. So he instructed Simon to pay the tax.[374]

Still, the matter would not go away.

On another occasion, the Pharisees asked him point-blank whether it was appropriate to pay taxes to the emperor. Jesus' response was ingenious. He told them to show him a coin and then asked them whose portrait and insignia it bore. The answer was obvious: Caesar's. Then, Jesus said to them, "give to Caesar what is Caesar's and to God what is God's." [375]

The answer confounded his opponents. On its surface, it appeared that Jesus was endorsing Roman taxation. But his followers knew better. The pious Jew believed that *all things* belonged to God. Had not the psalmist said, "The earth is the lord's, and everything in it — the world, and all who live in it"? That, of course, included the Roman emperor. A portrait of Caesar on a coin counted for nothing. If anything, it was a violation of the Mosaic law forbidding graven images — the same law that had triggered the eagle incident in the temple under Herod.

Jesus had, in fact, challenged Rome's right to tax the Jews. But he had done so without giving the emperor's cronies any grounds to arrest him — at least for the moment. Despite his attempts to deflect the charge that he opposed Roman taxation, it would resurface as one of the primary complaints against him at his arrest and trial.

Sons of Abraham

When attacks on Jesus' teachings failed, his enemies would often resort to personal attacks. The most scathing accusations involved the rumor that he was an illegitimate child. If Jesus was laying claim to the throne of Israel, his opponents would do their best to portray him as unfit to hold it. And certainly no bastard son of an Egyptian woman, even an ethnic Jewess of high priestly stock, was qualified to rule the sons of Abraham.

"Abraham is our father," his opponents declared.

They appear to have boasted of this repeatedly, not only in confronting Jesus but also in their dealings with John the Baptist. Indeed, the latter had warned them of their folly in doing so: "Do not begin to say to yourselves, 'We have Abraham as our father.' For I tell you that out of these stones, God can raise up children for Abraham!" [376] For John, and for Jesus, it was not one's heritage that mattered, but one's dedication to the kingdom of God.

"If you were Abraham's children," Jesus said, "you would do the things Abraham did."

As it was, however, his enemies wanted him dead, just as Saul had wanted David out of the way. Jesus knew their intent and called them on it, branding them implicitly of sons of the devil. "As it is, you are determined to kill me, a man who has told you the truth I heard from God. Abraham did not do such things. You are doing the things your own father does!"

The response was equally scathing: "We are not illegitimate children."

The implication: Jesus was.

Jesus understood them well enough, but they had failed to understand him. It didn't matter whether they were sons of Abraham or bastards. What mattered was their conduct before God — and his. "Can any of you prove me guilty of sin?" he asked. If they had a specific charge, he wanted to hear it. "If I am telling the truth, why don't you believe me? He who belongs to God hears what God says. The reason you do not hear is that you do not belong to God."

There. He had made an accusation of his own. His opponents were rejecting his message not because he was a bastard and they were sons of Abraham, but because he had submitted himself to God's ways and they hadn't. It was a harsh accusation, and predictably brought an equally harsh response. Again, however, his opponents refused to charge him with any specific offense. Rather, they resumed their personal attacks: "Aren't we right in saying you are a Samaritan and demon-possessed?"

Jesus left the first charge unanswered; it was just another way of branding him a bastard. The Samaritans were considered a half-breed race, not full-fledged Jews. Now the same charge was being leveled against Jesus. He ignored it, undoubtedly weary by this time of defending his birthright to men who had no intention of listening. The second charge was a feeble attempt by his opponents to turn his own words against him. He had accused them of being the devil's spawn; now they fired the charge right back at him. He denied it: "I am not demon-possessed."

Despite such attempts to discredit Jesus' movement, it continued to grow. At one point, some five thousand people were counted among the resistance, many of them likely on its fringes — disgruntled taxpayers looking for someone to save them from the oppressive policies of Rome. These were the seeds that fell on shallow soil, springing up suddenly but withering just as quickly in the sun because they had no root. When it came, however, to laying down one's life for the cause, many balked. They were looking for the son of David to be their champion — someone to face down the Goliath of the Roman imperial army in their behalf. They could not stomach the prospect of taking up arms themselves.

Yet this was exactly what Jesus would ask them to do.

He spoke of bringing not peace, but a sword. "I have come to cast fire upon the earth," he declared, "and how I wish it were already kindled!" [377] He demanded unyielding loyalty, to the point of being crucified as traitors or dying in battle for the kingdom of God.

Jesus warned that "kingdom would rise against kingdom" — the kingdom of God against the kingdom of Rome. The revolution would be launched, and the empire would retaliate by arresting Jesus' followers, who would be "persecuted and put to death … because of me." [378] It would be a violent revolution: Bodies would be broken and blood would be spilled. Jesus himself was willing to die for the cause, and he expected the same from others. "Unless you eat the flesh of the son of man and drink his blood, you have no life in you," he declared.[379]

This was no enigmatic saying; it was a call to arms for the revolution. His followers understood exactly what he Jesus was telling them. He expected to offer himself as a possible martyr in the cause of the kingdom, and he expected his followers to willingly do the same. "Can you drink of the cup I am going to drink?" he would ask. "You will indeed drink from my cup." [380]

The cup of blood.

This cup was the symbol of the sacred bloodline of kings, the vaginal well of wisdom and immortality. It was the well from which Odin would drink the sacred mead; the cup from which Enki and Inanna had partaken in their great feast; the lake watched over by Arthur's lady. It was the womb of the earth, from which one must be born again. But in order to be so reborn, one must first endure the tribulations of death: "Unless a kernel of wheat falls to the ground and dies, it remains only a single seed. But if it dies, it produces many seeds." [381] Those who died amid the struggle would return to the womb of the earth, but they would not be forgotten. They would become martyrs and a source of inspiration to those who came after them, thus ensuring their immortality because they had given their lives for this great cause. Jesus had seen how the Baptist's death had galvanized the people; death, he realized, was not an end but a new beginning. It was, in fact, the key to the kingdom of heaven.

The cup of blood — in Hebrew, the *dam koce* — become the emblem of the Jewish resistance against Rome, symbolizing the inevitable war with the empire. As the prophet Amos had predicted, Yahweh had punished the Jewish nation for its apostasy.[382] The

Roman occupation had made the Jews exiles in their own land. And they would remain exiles until they repented and drank the blood of the cup. When they did so, the revolution would begin.

The Qumran scribes by the Dead Sea spoke of it in a scroll titled *The Document of the New Covenant in the Land of Damascus*. This scroll, known as *The Damascus Document* for short, has nothing at all to do with the Syrian city of Damascus. Rather, it deals with the *dam koce* — the blood of the cup. The old covenant had been established in blood, as well. That covenant, between God and Abraham, had been sealed in the blood over every male child circumcised on the eighth day after birth. The new covenant, likewise, would be sealed in blood — the blood of the cup. Those who drank of this cup committed themselves to a new covenant (or testament) for the land (Israel).

A covenant in blood.

A covenant of war.

A covenant of death and rebirth.

It is no coincidence that coins minted during the Jewish uprising three decades after Jesus' death were inscribed with the image of a cup. The government of the revolution knew of the deep symbolism associated with the cup.

So did Jesus.

The kingdom of God was at hand. Ushering it in meant war — a willingness to drink of the cup of the new covenant in blood.[383]

To those on the fringes of the movement who had expected deliverance, not war, such language must have been disturbing — even alarming. From the time Jesus began talking about the prospects of "drinking blood" in war, the author of *John* reports, many of his disciples turned back and no longer followed him.[384] Were they able to drink of the cup Jesus had placed before them?

For many, the answer was no.

It was a setback for the kingdom of God.

XV

Sponsors and Spies

Jesus must have known the grass-roots support he had gained could not overcome the strength of the empire.

One day, he would address five thousand followers beside the Sea of Galilee and they would attempt to take him by force and make him their king.[385] The next, many of these same followers would desert him because they were unwilling to die for the kingdom of God. This was to be expected. When a farmer scattered seed to the wind, much of it would land on rocky soil. But Jesus needed firmer ground on which to plant a revolution.

He needed connections within the establishment itself.

"In my father's house are many dwelling places," he told his disciples.[386] "I have other sheep that are not of this fold. I must bring them, also. They, too, will listen to my voice, and there shall be one flock with one shepherd." [387]

These other sheep were members of the establishment. They were tax collectors like Matthew and a certain Zacchaeus, who had renounced their posts to follow Jesus. They were women with connections, like Joanna, whose husband was the manager of

Antipas' household. And they were members of the Roman-controlled Jewish national council, a largely judicial body known as the Sanhedrin. Two of these last are known by name: Nicodemus and an enigmatic figure named Joseph of Arimathea. Such people provided the resistance with two important commodities — financial support and information. They were, to be blunt, sponsors and spies.

Matthew and Zacchaeus likely contributed large sums of money to the resistance coffers, as did Joanna, one of several women who provided financial support to the movement. Through her position in Antipas' household, she almost certainly provided intelligence, as well. So did a man named Nicodemus, a member of the Sanhedrin who visited Jesus secretly at night and came to his defense when others on the council wanted to arrest him. But perhaps the most important contact Jesus forged was with a man named Gamaliel, the grandson of the famed Jewish teacher Hillel. It was Hillel who, a generation earlier, had founded the most influential school of his day. From humble beginnings, he rose to found his own academy and was eventually chosen to lead the Sanhedrin as *nasi* — literally, prince or patriarch, a title culled from the same root that produced the term Nazirite and one that, as we may recall, seems to have been applied to Jesus himself. His colleague and chief rival, a teacher named Shammai who had founded a school of his own, served as vice president, a position known as "father of the court." Over the years, Hillel and Shammai engaged in a series of debates over issues raised by the Jewish law. In almost every case, Shammai took a more conservative approach, while Hillel preferred a looser interpretation of the law. And in almost every case, Hillel prevailed.

One example was their debate over how strictly to observe the Sabbath. The Jewish law banned most activity on this day of rest, which lasted from sundown on Friday until sundown the following day. Shammai argued that the law should be interpreted strictly, but Hillel maintained that certain exceptions should be granted. For instance, when the Passover festival fell on a Sabbath, the duty to sacrifice must take precedence over Sabbath proscriptions.

Both Hillel and Shammai were Pharisees, and their interpretations — though often at odds with one another — both gained widespread respect among their contemporaries and successors. During his time as leader of the Sanhedrin, Hillel especially gained an unmatched reputation for compassion and insight. After his death, his school continued to be regarded as the foremost in Jerusalem and his descendants sat in his place as ruler of the Sanhedrin. If anything, his influence continued to grow after his death and was felt across Israel in Jesus' day.

Certainly, it had a profound effect on Jesus himself. Jesus' relaxed approach to Sabbath regulations reflected Hillel's view on the subject. And Jesus' insistence that "he who is least among you is the greatest" may have owed something to Hillel's saying that "a name made great is a name destroyed." [388] The two men shared a concern for the poor and a disdain for the arrogant. But it was Hillel's emphasis on love that was most apparent in Jesus' teachings. Hillel urged his followers to "be disciples of Aaron, loving peace and pursuing peace, loving your fellow creatures and drawing them near to the Torah." [389]

On one occasion, a Gentile came to Shammai and vowed that he would convert if the teacher could teach him all of Judaism while standing on one foot. Shammai rudely rebuffed the man, who went off and presented the same proposition to Hillel. This time, he was not turned away. Hillel answered promptly: "What is hateful to you, do not do to anyone else. All the rest is commentary. Go and learn it!"

Jesus agreed. When asked to name the greatest commandment, he replied: "Love the lord your God with all your heart, soul and mind. This is the first and greatest commandment. The second is like it: Love your neighbor as yourself. All the law and the prophets depend on these two commandments." [390] He also passed on a slight variation of Hillel's instructions: "So in everything, do to others what you would have them do to you, for this sums up the law and the prophets." [391]

Perhaps he learned this saying from Gamaliel.

In Jesus' lifetime and for several years afterward, Gamaliel enjoyed a reputation as one of the nation's foremost rabbis. Like Hillel, he was a Pharisee who ran his own academy in Jerusalem and had inherited his grandfather's mantle as leader or prince of the Sanhedrin, holding a rank that was in many ways comparable to that of the high priest.

He also appears to have been sympathetic to the resistance: Like Nicodemus, he was a spy. An early Ebionite document called *The Recognitions of Clement*, which includes a good deal of material comparable to that in *The Acts of the Apostles*, described Gamaliel in the following terms: He was "of our faith, but ... by a dispensation remained among (our enemies), so that if they should attempt anything unjust or wicked against us, he might either check them by skillful counsel or warn us to be on our guard." [392]

This arrangement seems to have begun with Jesus, whose teaching owed so much to Gamaliel's grandfather Hillel. Unlike the core members of Jesus' group, Gamaliel was not a revolutionary. He and those like him were waiting to see whether a revolt could succeed before committing themselves openly to such a cause. Secretly they might support the resistance, but in public they struck a pose of cautious neutrality. When members of the resistance were brought before the Sanhedrin, Gamaliel would speak in their behalf, admonishing the council to "Leave these men alone!" and "Let them go!" But he would not claim their cause as his own, nor would he endorse their methods and objectives publicly. "If their purpose or activity are of human origin," he reasoned, "it will fail. But if it is from God, you will not be able to stop these men. You will only find yourselves fighting against God." [393]

This approach was typical of the moderate element within the Jewish culture of Palestine. While the Roman collaborators supported the empire and conservatives cried out for revolution, the moderates were content to sit and wait — on the fence, so to speak. It was not their responsibility to pass judgment, but God's. Which side would prevail? That question had yet to be answered. And only when it was could God's position in the matter be known for sure. Until then, it was better not to declare for either side.

Such an approach must have frustrated Jesus, who had instructed his followers to speak out openly for their cause. What was whispered in their ear, they should proclaim it from the rooftops. "No one lights a lamp and then hides it in a jar or under a bed," he told them. "Instead, he puts it on a stand so that those who come in can see the light. For there is nothing hidden that will not be disclosed and nothing concealed that will not be brought into the open." [394]

Yet even Jesus understood the need for secrecy, withdrawing to secret places when necessary and often using coded parables to convey his message to those who had "ears to hear." And he was not one to turn away help where he could find it. Whoever was not against the resistance was for it — and that included the moderates. But whereas Jesus saw an alliance with Gamaliel as a means of expanding his base of support to include them in the kingdom, his followers saw it as a compromise. Gamaliel was, after all, a Pharisee. And the Pharisees had cooperated with the Romans time and again in their efforts to undermine the resistance. To complicate matters, Gamaliel's son had been spearheading these efforts.

This man would later assume his father's role as a leader on the Sanhedrin, but little information about him would be passed down in the rabbinic texts. Only his Hebrew name, Simon, and a few isolated traditions remain. Fortunately, however, quite a bit is known about him through another, much more personal source — a series of several letters from his own hand, in which he would refer to himself by exclusively using his Roman name.

Paul.

In the Flesh

It has long been assumed that Paul did not know Jesus personally, a conclusion based largely on the fact that Paul discloses very little about the person of Jesus in his letters; when he does make some assertion about his master, he is likely to rely upon esoteric visions as the source of his authority. Yet despite this, Paul's first letter to his followers at Corinth confirms the exact opposite: that he *did* in fact know Jesus. "Am I not an apostle?" he asks at one point. "Have I not seen Jesus our lord?" [395] He makes no reference to any vision in this context, thereby implying that he had been acquainted with Jesus in the flesh. If there is any doubt as to the truth of this, he erases it in his second letter to the Corinthians with an even more direct assertion: "Though we have known Christ according to the flesh, we know him (thus) no more." [396] In this statement, Paul does not hesitate to classify himself among those who had known Jesus during his lifetime.

In the flesh.

He also clearly identifies himself as the son of the famed rabbi Gamaliel, the same man known from rabbinic sources by the Hebrew name Simon. Never one for modesty, Paul was not about to hide his connection to such an esteemed figure. On the contrary, he openly boasted about having been "brought up" by Gamaliel — a phrase connoting a much closer relationship than one of simply teacher and student.[397] The implication is that Simon was raised by Gamaliel, who assumed the sort of role usually ascribed to a father. Simon was, in his own words, "a Pharisee, the son of a Pharisee." [398]

That Pharisee was Gamaliel.

As most Pharisees were, he started out as a steadfast opponent of the resistance movement. "For you have heard of my previous way of life in the Jewish religion, how intensely I persecuted God's assembly," he wrote. "I was advancing in the Jewish religion beyond many Jews of my own age and was extremely zealous for the traditions of my fathers." [399]

His fathers.

Gamaliel and Hillel.

As the latest in a line of respected teachers, Simon (who would not adopt the name Paul until a later date) could justifiably brag that he was a "Hebrew of Hebrews; in regard to the law, a Pharisee zealously persecuting the assembly" of Jesus — just as the other Pharisees were doing during Jesus' time.[400] Simon took a position at the forefront of these efforts, even as his father was secretly forging a tentative alliance with Jesus.

For this alliance to succeed, Jesus knew, he would have to enlist Simon as well. But in this regard, he almost certainly faced stiff opposition from within his own ranks. Others in the resistance never could bring themselves to welcome Simon into the fold. As revolutionaries, they were suspicious by nature, especially of someone who had made it his business to oppose them openly. Their later distrust and outright rejection of Simon indicates that they probably never accepted him, despite Jesus' efforts to win him over to their cause. Jesus may well have argued cogently about the advantages of having contacts within the establishment, but one can imagine his followers countering that argument by making an equally persuasive case against recruiting someone like Simon. Espionage was a two-edged sword. Contacts on the "inside" could unearth valuable information, but if one trusted the wrong spy, it could undermine everything. What if the so-called spy was actually working for the other side? The entire security of the resistance movement could be compromised.

The risk was simply too great. Simon might join the resistance, but he would always be viewed with a suspicion that bordered on outright contempt. He could not be trusted. His ties to the empire — he was a Roman citizen — were simply too close. And his liberal view of the Jewish law clashed resoundingly with the legal precision demanded by the Qumran community with which they maintained such strong ties. If Simon were accepted into the movement, they were convinced he would turn out to be a double agent planted by the empire to undermine the resistance.

Jesus, however, was determined in his purpose. He was convinced that the potential benefits of an alliance with Simon outweighed the dangers, however great the risk. And as the leader of the resistance, he had the last word on such matters. He would not even have to bother finding a way to approach Simon — his sources had apprised him that the man was intent upon coming to him. Already, Simon had obtained letters from the high priest, Joseph Caiaphas, authorizing him to pursue and arrest members of the resistance.[401] But Jesus, aware of his plans, was one step ahead of him, already baiting his trap as the oblivious Simon set about assembling a group of men and set out on his mission to take the rebels into custody.

His destination?

Somewhere called "Damascus."

As in *The Damascus Document*, however, this could not have been the city in Syria. Letters from the high priest would have held no legal authority there. The city of Damascus was under the direct jurisdiction of a Roman governor. Like such ephemeral locations as Cana and Bethany, this "Damascus" was not so much a place as a state of being. It was, once again, a reference to the *dam koce*, the cup of blood.

What could this have meant? Perhaps it referred to Jesus himself, who might have been regarded as the earthen vessel containing the royal bloodline. In this sense, he would have been the cup of blood. More likely it was his consort, Mary Magdalene, the feminine vessel — or cup — destined to carry the royal bloodline forward to future generations. The gospels explicitly mention that Mary and her sister Martha had a home, with their brother Lazarus.

Most likely, Simon Paul had received information that Jesus (code word: *dam koce*) was in Judea, at the home of Mary. As we shall see, he was intimately acquainted with this particular residence and its occupants. He knew it well.

What he didn't know is that Jesus had intelligence of his own — he may even have allowed the information about his whereabouts to leak out as an inducement to draw Simon out. Once this was accomplished, Jesus went out to meet him while he was still on the road.

The confrontation took Simon by surprise. No doubt Jesus had his own group of men with him, probably his personal bodyguard and an otherwise intimidating collection of ruffians sufficient to overwhelm whomever happened to be accompanying Simon. Suddenly, the tables had been turned. Instead of confronting Jesus, the son of Gamaliel found himself suddenly on the defensive, ambushed in the middle of the road and completely taken by surprise.

"Why are you persecuting me?" Jesus asked.

An Orderly Account

The author of *Acts* would take this story out of context and transform it into an encounter between Paul and a phantasmic vision of Jesus. Such a literary device seems strange in light of the author's stated intention to produce an "orderly account" of the events he was describing. This very goal was laid out clearly in the introduction to his two-volume work: "Many have undertaken to draw up an account of the things that have been believed among us, just as they were handed down to us by those who from the first were eyewitnesses. ... Therefore, since I myself have carefully investigated everything from the beginning, it seemed good also to me to write an orderly account for you ... so that you may know the certainty of the things you have been taught." [402]

The author as much as admitted by implication that he himself was not one of the first eyewitnesses, but a later investigator whose task was to sift through any number of more primitive sources before him and synthesize them into a cohesive whole. By the time he wrote, there seem to have been any number of accounts floating around, and the author wanted to create the definitive version. It was not an easy undertaking, especially considering the scope of the project. By the time it was finished, the author had produced a two-volume set spanning about six decades. The first volume, known to us as *Luke*, dealt with the life of Jesus. The second, later titled the

Acts of the Apostles, focused on the activity of his followers after his death.

The fact that the author had several sources at his disposal only compounded the problem. "Many" had drawn up similar accounts in the past, but these accounts did not always mesh. Some traditions were difficult to reconcile with one another, while others appeared to be outright contradictions. One group claimed Jesus had said or done one thing, yet another group disputed it. So-called "secret" words of Jesus were also circulating along with more well-known sayings attributed to him. Even today, several separate sources can be identified running through the body of the work:

- Hebrew prophecies
- Traditions concerning Jesus' birth and childhood
- Sayings derived from a source he shared with the author of *Matthew*, called Q
- Sayings derived from a second source
- A compendium of miracles attributed to Jesus
- The account of Jesus' death
- Traditions about Jesus' followers supplied by his family
- Similar traditions supplied by Paul and his followers

These he endeavored to combine into a cohesive package — an "orderly account" as he put it — of the events described therein. But it was not orderly in a chronological sense. Indeed, his narrative was not so much concerned with historical accuracy as it was with eternal truth. He was writing the books of *Luke* and *Acts* for a purpose — to serve as a sort of two-volume instruction manual for new converts. His work was undertaken, he said, "so that you may know the certainty of the things that you have been taught." [403]

The author, like many other teachers, felt that a student would learn best by repetition, so he designed each of his two volumes to reinforce the other. When read concurrently, events described in one book would shed light on events at a similar point in the other, and vice versa. The spirit descended upon Jesus near the beginning of *Luke* just as it descended upon the apostles in the opening pages of Acts. Near the end of *Luke*, Jesus went to trial before the Sanhedrin, the Roman prefect and a member of the Jewish royal family — the same three authorities that tried Paul near the end of Acts. Each book also featured a single key event near the middle of the volume that defined its theme. And again, the two were remarkably similar.

➢ In *Acts*, "a light from heaven flashed" around Paul and he heard a divine voice addressing him. He was to be commissioned as God's spokesman on earth.

➢ In *Luke*, Jesus' clothes became "as bright as a flash of lightning" and a divine voice issued forth out of a cloud. He was, likewise, commissioned as God's spokesman on earth: "This is my son whom I have chosen. Listen to him."

The two events were meant to complement one another as the student read through their pages. In fact, virtually every significant event in Acts mirrors a similar event in *Luke*. Below is a closer look at how this was accomplished, with a description of each incident followed by the reference in *Luke*, then the reference in Acts.

Incident	**Luke**	**Acts**
Spirit descends	On Jesus, 3:21	On disciples, 2:4
Crippled man healed	By Jesus, 5:17-26	By Peter, 3:1-10
Foundation speech	By Jesus, 6:17-49	By Peter, 3:11-26
Followers anointed	Twelve, 9:1-2	Seven, 6:3-7
Death of righteous man	The Baptist, 9:7-9	Stephen, 7:1-60
Supernatural appearance	Moses, Elijah, 9:28-36	Jesus, 9:1-7
Criticized on Torah	Jesus, 11:37-52	Peter, 11:1-7

Arrests/tribulations	Predicted, 12:1-11	Fulfilled, 12:1-19
Death of rich fool	In parable, 12:13-21	Agrippa, 12:20-23
Delivered to Gentiles	Jesus, 18:31-32	Paul, 21:11
Welcome in Jerusalem	Jesus, 19:35-40	Paul, 21:27-29
Riot and arrest	Jesus, 22:47-53	Paul, 21:27-36
Sanhedrin trial	Jesus, 22:66-71	Paul, 23:1-11
Roman trial	Jesus-Pilate, 23:1-4	Paul-Felix, 24:1-22
Herodian trial	Jesus-Antipas, 23:6-11	Paul-Agrippa, 26:1-30
Accused of rebellion	Jesus, 23:5	Paul, 24:5-6
Declared innocent	Jesus, 23:13-16	Paul, 26:32
Death overcome	Crucifixion, 24:1-8	Snakebite, 28:1-6
Final destination	Jesus-heaven, 24:50-51	Paul-Rome, 28:11-16

Clearly, the two works were not meant to be "orderly" in a chronological sense. On the contrary, they were designed to be repetitive, reinforcing each other in the student's mind. If this produced discrepancies that were difficult to explain historically, it was a small price to pay.

One such discrepancy occurs when the voice from heaven identifies itself as that of Jesus and asks Simon (a.k.a. Paul), "Why are you persecuting me?" The problem is that Simon could hardly have been persecuting a voice or a vision. And, if the voice is to be believed, Simon was not merely persecuting Jesus' followers, but Jesus himself. This exchange, therefore, could not have taken place after Jesus' death but must have occurred during his lifetime. Once this is understood, the context becomes clear: The Pharisees had begun a campaign to have Jesus arrested, and Simon (independently of his father Gamaliel) was spearheading the effort.

As a result of this confrontation, Simon was won over to the cause of the resistance movement. He saw a light from heaven and was struck blind, whereupon he fell to the ground. This was, of course, not actual blindness but the spiritual blindness that would be healed at the messiah's coming. Isaiah had foretold it. And Jesus, as the messiah of Israel, was healing it by recruiting a new member to the cause of his kingdom. The blind would see.

For three days after this experience, Simon neither ate nor drank. Probably he abstained to fulfill a vow of commitment. He was taken to the house of Judas — Jesus' brother — where he encountered the man who would restore his vision. "Jesus, who you saw on the road as you were coming here, sent me so that you may see," the man announced.

The man's name was Ananias.

Jesus' Alter Ego

Ananias was obviously a high-ranking member of the resistance movement. For one thing, he had access to the house of Judas and claimed to have been sent by Jesus himself. Moreover, he was a miracle worker — one of only a few mentioned in Acts. Usually, such wonders are associated with well-known personages such as Peter and Paul; Ananias, by contrast, is mentioned nowhere else in the accounts of the gospel writers.

Or is he?

In Hebrew, this man's name was Hananiah, a name that had been worn six centuries earlier by a man claiming to be a prophet. His full name was Hananiah the son of Azzur (yet another variant of Asir, the Egyptian name for Osiris), and he lived in a time when the Babylonian Empire was in its ascendancy and stood poised to conquer Jerusalem. Recognizing this, the prophet Jeremiah had fashioned a wooden yoke of straps and crossbars and placed it around his neck. This was to be the symbol of what was about to happen: Jerusalem would be enslaved in the Babylonian yoke.

Hananiah, however, did not see things quite the same way. Indeed, he promised in equally dramatic fashion that the situation was temporary. Removing the wooden yoke from Jeremiah's neck, he broke it and declared, "This is what the lord says: In the same way will I break the yoke of the king of Babylon. I will remove it from the neck of the nations within two years."

The crowd cheered, but Jeremiah was not impressed.

"Listen, Hananiah," he admonished. "The lord has not sent you, yet you have persuaded this nation to trust in lies. Therefore I will remove you from the face of the earth. This very year, you are going to die, because you preached rebellion against the lord!" [404]

It was a scene from six centuries earlier, but it played like a scene from Jesus' own life. In Jesus' day, little had changed. An empire still oppressed Jerusalem, and it is probably no coincidence that Rome was often compared to Babylon. Like Hananiah, Jesus had promised rest for the weary who were oppressed by the yoke of the empire. As a member of the resistance, he had preached rebellion to any who would listen. They could, he told them, exchange the yoke of the empire — with its heavy taxes and odious pagan customs — for the yoke he offered them. "My yoke is easy," he promised them, "and my burden is light."[405]

And like Hananiah, he was wrong.

Jeremiah's scathing condemnation of Hananiah still rang forth from the scrolls of the prophets that were read in the synagogues. And how easily it could have been directed at Jesus by those who watched his spectacular failure. Despite his promises, the empire would not be overthrown. History would bear witness to the emptiness of Jesus' promises; he had not been sent by God, and the soothing words he had used to entice the nation were nothing short of empty pledges. Rome's yoke, like that of Babylon, would endure, weighing more heavily than ever because of those who had sought to cast it off at the instigation of Jesus and his co-conspirators. And Jesus himself? He would die a criminal's death on the cross, accused of treason against the empire for attempting to foment rebellion.

Such parallels make it seem possible that the Ananias mentioned in the account of Simon's healing was, in fact, Jesus himself — a name perhaps adopted by the Jewish scribes who condemned his movement and simply incorporated by the author of *Acts* into his narrative without realizing the irony of it. These scribes would speak of Jesus elsewhere in their literature, as well, referring to him by the name of Hanina (a shortened version of the name Hananiah) ben Dosa.

Hananiah meant "the lord has mercy."

Jesus meant "the lord saves."

But more than their names were similar. Hanina, like Jesus, was a Galilean. Like Jesus, he was known to be "poor," a description that linked him with the resistance movement. Like Jesus, he was esteemed as a rabbi, but stood aloof from the Jerusalem establishment. And like Jesus, he had a reputation for working miracles — some of them strikingly similar to those performed by Jesus.

On one occasion, Hanina's neighbor was building a house and found that the beams were not long enough. At a word, he lengthened them so that they reached from wall to wall.[406] The story closely parallels a legend associated with Jesus. According to this story, Jesus was helping his father "Joseph" (note the phonetic similarity to the name "Dosa") build a bed. One piece of wood, however, was too short to match its corresponding beam. So Jesus took hold of the shorter one and miraculously stretched it until it was even with the longer piece.[407]

In another legend, someone told Hanina about a poisonous lizard that lived nearby. In response, the rabbi went out and stepped on the lizard's hole. Predictably, it bit him. But what happened next was anything but predictable. Instead of Hanina getting sick, the lizard died. Hanina then put the lizard on his shoulder and used it as an object lesson: "See, my children, the lizard does not kill. It is sin that kills." [408]

Paul himself would later echo this teaching in his own writings, warning his friends in Rome that "the wages of sin is death." [409] And it is probably no coincidence that a similar legend grew up around

Paul himself. While shipwrecked on the island of Malta in the central Mediterranean, he was bitten by a poisonous viper. Although everyone expected him to fall ill and die, he simply shook it off and suffered no ill effects.[410]

Just as Hanina had done.

The implication in the legend of Hanina and the lizard was clear. It was sin that killed. But because Hanina was without sin, he had remained unharmed. Paul would make the same claim about Jesus, that he "had no sin."[411] Had not Jesus himself spoken of the ability to step on poisonous animals without being harmed? Indeed, he had promised to pass this ability on to his followers: "I have given you the authority to trample on snakes and scorpions.... Nothing will harm you."[412] Paul was simply taking him at his word.

The similarities do not end there. Hanina and Jesus were both masters of the storm. Jesus, for his part, calmed a tempest that raged on the Sea of Galilee, causing his followers to exclaim in wonder, "Who is this that commands even the wind and the water, and they obey him?"[413] Hanina, likewise, calmed a storm. In his case, he was caught in a downpour while walking down the road with a basket of salt on his head. "Master of the universe," he complained, "the whole world is at ease, but Hanina is in distress." At his word, the rain stopped.[414]

Such mastery over the elements was the mark of a wizard. Moses had parted the sea, and Elijah had called down fire from heaven. A century before Jesus' time, Honi had drawn a circle and brought rain that ended a drought. This had earned him the grudging praise of his rival Simeon ben Shetah, who was forced to acknowledge that Honi had invoked divine assistance in a manner not unlike that of a son who ingratiates himself with his father.[415]

This father-son relationship would serve as a model for Jesus' own view of his relationship with God.

And Hanina's.

According to legend, each day a divine voice would go forth and declare, "The whole world is supplied with food only on account of my son Hanina, while my son Hanina is satisfied with four pints of carobs from Sabbath eve to Sabbath eve." [416] The specific mention of carobs is, of course, significant in that it bespeaks Hanina's status as *kher heb* priest — a position that Jesus likewise claimed. And just as a divine voice claimed Hanina as a son of God, so a similar voice is said to have proclaimed of Jesus, "You are my son whom I love. With you I am well pleased." [417] Jesus, too, was satisfied with little to eat. According to the legend of his temptation in the wilderness, he resisted the urge to transform stones into bread on the grounds that man did not live by bread alone.

Both Jesus and Hanina were also known as healers.

Among the best-known stories of Jesus' miraculous powers was his healing of the Roman centurion's son. As legend had it, a Roman centurion asked Jesus to heal his servant, who lay paralyzed at the centurion's home a short distance away. The centurion told Jesus not to trouble himself to come in person, but to merely "say the word, and my servant will be healed."

Jesus did so, and the centurion returned to find that his servant had been healed at that very hour.[418]

As already noted, this legend seems to have been a veiled reference to the death of Philip the tetrarch, the paralyzed fisher king whose fortuitous passing cleared the way for Jesus to marry the man's widow.

What does this have to do with Paul?

The answer is somewhat complicated, but the anatomy of this particular legend can, in fact, be reconstructed with a little effort. The stories of Paul's conversion and Philip's death in fact share several common themes.

➢ Paul is struck blind; Philip has a dream in which an eagle tears out both his eyes, blinding him.

➢ Paul is healed and baptized; Philip is "healed" when he bathes in the waters of Bethsaida.

➤ Paul dies symbolically through his baptism; Philip dies in reality as a result of his "healing."

In light of such shared motifs, it is not surprising to find that the rabbis — writing many years after the fact — appear to have confused the two stories in recalling the same miracle and attributing it to Jesus' alter ego, Hanina. In their version of the tale, an important rabbi in Jerusalem sent two scholars to Hanina in Galilee, bearing the message that the rabbi's son was ill. The messengers implored Hanina to have mercy on the rabbi's son, and Hanina responded by withdrawing to an upper chamber and praying to God for mercy. When he emerged, he told the men, "Go, the fever has left him." The messengers made note of the exact moment when Hanina had told them of the healing, then returned to Jerusalem. He told them excitedly, "The time you put down is not an instant before or after what happened! At that very moment, the fever left my son and he asked me for a drink of water." [419] (Perhaps this was the living water of which Jesus spoke.) The story of this miraculous, long-distance healing so closely parallels that of Jesus and the Roman centurion that there can be little doubt they are derived from a common source.

But one piece of evidence has yet to be revealed — the name of the rabbi who sought Hanina's help in healing his son.

It was none other than Gamaliel.

His son, of course, was Simon, otherwise known as Paul. The account has brought us full circle. Hanina healed Simon the Pharisee, son of Gamaliel, just as Ananias (Hananiah) had healed Paul and Jesus had healed the centurion's servant. The three stories are, in fact, varying accounts of the same event, which is familiar from *Acts*. Paul was the "centurion's servant" in a metaphorical sense. The centurion represented the might of the Roman Empire. And Paul, a Roman citizen, had been seeking to exert that might by working on behalf of the empire's allies to arrest Jesus and others in the resistance.

Jesus performs only one miracle in the book of *Acts*: He blinds Paul.

Ananias, likewise, performs only one miracle: He restores Paul's sight.

When it happened, according to the author of *Acts*, "something like scales" fell from his eyes.[420]

The Leper

The Greek word for scales, used nowhere else in the canon, is *lepis* — the root word for leprosy. Years later, Paul would write of a "thorn in his flesh" that tormented him. Three times he prayed that it might be removed, but his prayers were never answered.[421] This thorn may well have been "leprosy," a term applied to any one of several skin conditions common in the first century. Most of them were minor physical ailments, not the chronic and progressive disease by that name that eats away at the extremities and is ultimately fatal. But this sort of leprosy was, even so, debilitating in another sense. Lepers were regarded as ritually unclean under Jewish law. Those who associated with them were also unclean, so lepers were routinely shunned from society. A leper had to wear a bell around his neck to warn others he was coming. When they heard the bell, it was a signal for them to get out of the way.

Such a condition would have been more than an embarrassment to one in Paul's position. It would have been an outright disgrace. Here he was, a person of great status as the son of Israel's most famous teacher, yet he was shunned and labeled unclean by his own countrymen. It was perhaps this painful paradox that led Paul to pursue a life of unquestioned piety. He was, in his own words, "faultless" in obeying the law of Moses.[422] Yet no matter how hard he strove to fulfill this law spiritually, his own physical condition — over which he had no control — doomed him to failure.

"I find this law at work," he would lament. "When I want to do good, evil is right there with me."

He could not escape it.

This was not some moral failing. Paul was, by his own

declaration, faultless in this respect. Something else was keeping him from fulfilling the law — something involving his body.

"For in my inner being I delight in God's law," he said. "But I see another law at work in the members of my body, waging war against the law of my mind and making me a prisoner of the law of sin at work within my members. What a wretched man I am! Who will rescue me from this body of death? Thanks be to God through Jesus, the messiah, our lord." [423]

It appears to have been Jesus' willingness to overlook Paul's "unclean" condition — his thorn in the flesh — that convinced Paul to join the resistance movement. Unlike others, Jesus did not turn his back on lepers, but accepted them. In doing so, he symbolically removed their uncleanness.

The author of *Luke* refers to ten such men being cleansed by Jesus, though only one of them returned to thank him.[424] Another man cleansed of leprosy immediately went out and began talking freely about Jesus.[425] Perhaps this account referred to Simon Paul himself — known elsewhere as Simon the Leper.[426]

After Simon's experience on the road to *dam koce*, he was baptized and began to eat again.

His initiation was complete.

Though perhaps not healed of his leprous condition, he was at least no longer spiritually blind. The author of *John*, indeed, may well have been referring to Simon in recounting the story of an unnamed man born blind. This tale is fascinating for the intricate detail it provides in describing Jesus' method of healing the man: He spit in the dirt, using his own saliva to produce a muddy paste that he rubbed into the man's eyes. He then sent him away to wash in a pool called Siloam, which we have identified as a miraculous well associated with Salome. The author of *John*, however, provides a different explanation for the name, declaring that it means "sent." The man's sight was then restored, and he went on his way.[427]

The man born blind was Simon Paul, "a Pharisee the son of a Pharisee" who had been born in spiritual blindness. He was instructed to wash in the pool, a metaphor for the baptism that Paul underwent. He was sent, strangely enough, to a pool called *sent*. This might appear at first glance to be gibberish, but the author knew exactly what he was saying. He was merely repeating it for emphasis. The word in Greek is *apostello*, signifying one set apart and sent out on a mission.

An apostle.

The unnamed man born blind was, in fact, being commissioned as an apostle.

The apostle Paul.

His blindness was never meant to be taken literally. "For judgment I have come into the world," Jesus declared, "so that the blind will see and those who see will become blind." This was allegorical. Jesus had no desire to see people lose their physical eyesight, any more than he had the ability to restore it. The blind would see as they gained understanding of God's kingdom. Those who believed they already had such understanding would be left in the dark. The blind would see; those who saw would be struck blind. The Pharisees, who prided themselves on their knowledge of the Jewish law, fell squarely into the latter category.

And they knew it.

"What?" they asked, incredulous. "Are we blind, too?"

"If you were blind, you would not be guilty of anything," Jesus responded. "But because claim you can see, your guilt remains."

Simon Paul, on the other hand, had recognized his own blindness and seen the light. He had joined the resistance movement and, for the time being at least, was working to restore the kingdom of God.

The Lazarus Link

The story of Paul is intertwined with that of a man named Lazarus.

Paul, of course, was a real person. But Lazarus was not. He was actually a fictional character — a beggar who served as the focal point of a parable recounted by the author of *Luke*. This Lazarus was laid at the gate of a rich man. There he sat, allowing the dogs to lick his sores and longing for an opportunity to eat whatever might fall from the rich man's table. It was an opportunity that never came his way. Instead, his would-be benefactor ignored him, until the beggar finally died in misery and the angels carried him away to join Abraham in heaven.

The rich man eventually died as well, but he was consigned instead to eternal torment in hell. He pleaded for mercy, but was told he could not escape his plight. As he had ignored the poor beggar, now he himself was being ignored.

Finally, convinced he could do nothing for himself, he turned his attention to the members of his family who were still living. "I beg you, father," he said to Abraham, "send Lazarus to my father's house, for I have five brothers. Let him warn them, so that they will not also have to visit this place of torment. ... If someone from the dead goes to them, then they will repent."

Abraham, however, would not allow it.

The man's brothers already had Moses and the prophets to warn them, he argued. "If they do not listen to Moses and the prophets, they will not listen even if someone rises from the dead." [428]

It would do them no good.

Lazarus never rose from the dead — at least not according to the author of *Luke*. But when the author of *John* put pen to parchment, he performed his own literary resurrection. In his account, he transformed a fictional beggar who never rose from the dead into a real person who did. Lazarus was given a hometown, two sisters and an extensive personal history. He was no longer the subject of a parable, but a close personal associate of Jesus himself. All these details couldn't have simply appeared out of thin air, so where did they come from?

Was Lazarus a real person, after all?

Yes.

And no.

The author of *John*, for some reason, merged the fictional story of Lazarus the beggar with another familiar narrative — the account of Simon Paul's encounter with Jesus.

The result is a study in self-contradiction.

Upon learning of Lazarus' affliction, Jesus assures the man's family that his illness will not end in death. Almost immediately, however, Lazarus dies. This leaves Jesus' credibility seriously in doubt. "If you had been here," his distraught sister Martha declares, "my brother would not have died." Jesus, it seems, had failed. How could he have assured her that this illness was not life threatening? Plainly, he had been wrong. And now, her brother was dead.

Lazarus, the beggar from Jesus' parable, died. But Paul was only struck blind. Jesus would have been quite right in declaring that his "illness" would not end in death. He was spiritually blind in his opposition to the kingdom of God, and his sight would be restored. His plans to arrest members of the resistance movement would not end in their death, but in Paul's awakening.

Jesus tells his disciples: "Lazarus has fallen asleep."

He had closed his eyes, just as Paul's eyes had been closed after he saw the blinding light on the road.

Upon learning of Lazarus' affliction, Jesus speaks in terms of blindness, not death. "Are there not twelve hours of daylight?" he asks his disciples. "A man who walks by day will not stumble, for he sees by this world's light. It is when he walks at night that he stumbles, for he has no light." [429] The account of Paul's so-called journey to Damascus could not have been more faithfully reproduced.

- Paul walked by day (it was about noon).
- He saw a brilliant light.
- He was struck blind.
- He stumbled and fell to the ground.

The words also closely parallel those Jesus spoke when describing the plight of the man born blind — so closely, in fact, that the two sayings are nearly identical. Both share the same theme, contrasting the activity of daylight hours with the restrictions imposed by the blinding veil of night. In the story of the blind man, Jesus states that "as long as it is day, we must do the work of him who sent me. Night is coming, when no man can work." And in addressing the blind man's condition, he declares that "this has happened so that the work of God might be displayed in his life." [430] Compare this to what Jesus is said to have uttered upon learning of Lazarus' illness: "It is for God's glory, so that God's son might be glorified through it." [431] The author is merely repeating these sayings in a slightly altered form.

In similar fashion, the story of Paul's blindness merely repeats the entire story of the man born blind, also in a slightly altered form. The only difference: Jesus' parable of Lazarus has been superimposed on it.

This blending created a rather absurd dilemma for the author. The story of Lazarus would have to be turned on its head. Jesus' credibility had already been damaged in the process. He had assured Lazarus' family that the man would not die, yet the character of Lazarus in the parable *did* die. This had to be an embarrassment to the author, who had backed himself into a corner. In order to salvage Jesus' reputation, Lazarus would have to be raised from the dead, spoiling the very point of the original parable — that raising a man from the dead would be of no avail in convincing the members of Lazarus' family to repent.

Why would the author of *John* create such confusion?

The answer lies in another event associated with the story of Paul's encounter with Jesus — his baptism. It is reported in Acts as well as in the account of the "man born blind" who was "sent" to wash (or be baptized) in the Pool of Siloam. In the story of Lazarus, however, there is no mention of it.

Or is there?

Paul, writing three decades later, would recall the significance of the event: "All of us who were baptized into Christ Jesus were baptized into his death. We were therefore buried with him through baptism into death, in order that, just as Christ was raised from the dead through the glory of the Father, we too might have new life." [432] For Paul, baptism was the equivalent of death and resurrection, the two key events associated with Lazarus in *John*. Lazarus remained in the tomb for four days. Likewise, Paul remained blind and abstained from food for three days — four if one counts the day he encountered Jesus on the road. He was, symbolically, as good as dead.

When Lazarus finally emerged from the tomb, he was wrapped in linen clothing similar to the ceremonial cloth used for baptism. The symbolism, stated explicitly by Paul in his writings, was left implicit in *John*: Baptism was "death," just as opposition to the resistance movement was "blindness." One died figuratively when one went down into the waters and was reborn upon re-emerging. This was symbolic of the repentance that John the Baptist had demanded. Unless one was born of the water (baptized) and the spirit, one could not enter the kingdom of God.[433] One could not join the resistance.

The Feast

Simon Paul appears elsewhere in the gospel records under a couple of predictable names, both of which are worn by a man who appears to have been intimately involved in Jesus' wedding feast. The authors of *Mark* and *Matthew* refer to him as Simon the Leper, a fitting title considering the Paul's apparent affliction with leprosy. The author of *Luke*, meanwhile, does not allude to his physical condition, but instead identifies him merely as a Pharisee; he also quotes Jesus addressing the man by name as Simon. This fits equally well with Paul's identity a "Pharisee, the son of a Pharisee."

In the first two accounts, the man plays a relatively passive role as the host for the banquet at which a woman (whom we know to be Mary Magdalene) anoints Jesus with a jar of expensive perfume. In this capacity, Simon is placed in the same position occupied by

Lazarus in the fourth gospel: He is the owner of the house, who has offered his home to Jesus for this important event. According to the author of *John*, the anointing took place "where Lazarus lived."[434] This reference further identifies Simon the Leper or Pharisee with the semi-fictional Lazarus, whom we have already revealed as Paul's alter ego.

In *Luke*'s version, however, Simon the Pharisee takes a more active role. When the woman (here nameless) anoints Jesus with the perfume from her alabaster jar, it is Simon who objects to her action on the grounds that "she is a sinner." This is just the sort of puritanical protest one might have expected of Paul, whose boasts of being perfectly righteous in regard to the Hebrew law would make their way into his subsequent correspondence.

Simon's objection provides a segue into a parable by Jesus involving a pair of debtors who owed a certain moneylender money — one five hundred denarii and the other only fifty. Seeing that neither man had the money to pay, the lender had compassion on them and canceled both their debts. Which of these two men, Jesus asked, would be more grateful that his debt had been forgiven?

"I suppose the one who had the bigger debt canceled," Simon answered.

Jesus responded that he had judged correctly and went on to apply this principle to the sinful woman, whose great love matched the magnitude of her forgiveness for her many sins. His rebuke of Simon makes it clear that the son of Gamaliel was not an easy fit with the resistance; he still had much to learn, and he faced a bumpy road ahead. But even so, he would become a vocal advocate for the resistance movement. He took Jesus' admonition to heart, making forgiveness a central feature of his message in subsequent years. And in doing so, he would become a target of the authorities — just as he himself had once targeted Jesus on their behalf. The author of *Acts* reports that he immediately began speaking in the synagogues on Jesus' behalf. This subversive activity drew the attention of his former allies in the establishment, who responded by plotting to kill him.[435] Like Jesus, the man called Lazarus now had a price on his head: "The chief priests made plans to kill Lazarus, as well, for on account of him many were going over to Jesus and putting faith in him." [436]

The plan nearly succeeded. The authorities put a guard on the city gates and ordered his arrest. But Simon was fortunate enough to elude them with the help of some friends in the resistance movement, who lowered him in a basket through an opening in the city wall.[437]

Jesus, too, found himself more heavily watched than ever. He decided to stop moving about publicly and instead withdrew to the desert, where the resistance had its greatest support. He had no intention of allowing himself to be arrested, at least not just yet. When he re-emerged, it would be on his own terms. He was already planning what those terms would be, and one thing was certain — when the time was right, he would take the stage in a manner befitting the man who would be king.

XVI

Hosanna in the Highest

By allying himself with the house of Gamaliel, Jesus had raised his stature to a new level. No longer was he a provincial rabbi followed by a few hundred utopians and frustrated nationalists. He was now squarely in the mainstream, married to a Herodian princess and allied with the most powerful family in Israel. Through a series of shrewd maneuvers, he had overcome the questions about his messianic claims to become a major player on the political stage. Now all eyes were upon him, eager to find out what he would do next.

He would not disappoint.

It was mid-September, time for the annual feast of Sukkot. The city would be at its busiest during this weeklong celebration. Thousands of Jewish pilgrims would be making their way to Jerusalem for the festival, a celebration of the harvest and the new year. According to custom, they would erect temporary shelters or tabernacles in the streets and on the rooftops, shading them with palm branches and other greenery. Such shelters, they believed, had been used when their ancestors, the remnants of the once-great Hyksos empire, traveled up from Egypt in search of a promised land "flowing with milk and honey."

If Jesus wanted an audience, he had one.

He also had the perfect setting to announce his arrival.

The focal point of the feast was a ritual procession in the temple. It was traditional for pilgrims to join in this procession around the altar, waving palm branches as they shouted the words of the psalmist, "Hosanna!" — literally, "Save us!" — "Blessed is he who comes in the name of the lord!" [438] If Jesus wished to send a message, he would have no better opportunity. He was the one who came in God's name to save the city and the nation from the fetters of Roman oppression.

With this in mind, he sent one of his contacts in Jerusalem ahead of him to prepare for his entrance into the city. This person, unnamed by the gospel writers, was to obtain a colt and tie it up in plain view at Bethphage, just east of the capital. When this had been done, Jesus instructed two of those traveling with him to "go into the village ahead of you. Just as you enter it, you will find a young donkey tied there which no one has ever ridden. Untie it and bring it here. If anyone asks you, 'Why are you doing this?' tell him, 'The master needs it and will send it back here shortly.'" [439]

Jesus wanted to send a message. According to the prophet Zechariah, the messiah would enter the city on a donkey's back: "See, your king comes to you, righteous and having salvation, gentle and riding on a donkey — on a colt, the foal of a donkey." But that wasn't all. The prophecy declared that Israel's enemies would be expelled from Jerusalem, and the nation's sovereignty would be restored. A clearer challenge to the authority of Rome could not have been imagined:

"I will take away the chariots ... and the war horses from Jerusalem, and the battle bow will be broken. He will proclaim peace to the nations. His rule will extend from sea to sea and from the (Euphrates) River to the ends of the earth."

The Roman Empire would give way to the kingdom of God — a kingdom not merely restored, but expanded. Just as the bridegroom king Solomon had expanded the kingdom of his fathers, so Jesus would follow his example as the bridegroom newly incarnate. Solomon had arrived at his coronation ceremony on the back of a mule; now, Jesus would do likewise on the back of a donkey. His entry into the city would signify his conquest of the donkey god Seth, the proud and braying old order that was destined to give way before the new kingdom. The kingdom of this world, established by the emperor in Rome, was passing away; the kingdom of heaven, to be ushered again by the heavenly sun king, was at hand. Jesus was the young solar champion Horus, whose role it was to subdue Seth and inaugurate this new kingdom. In doing so, he would fulfill the covenant made with Abraham so long ago, the creation of a kingdom so vast that its subjects would be as the sands of the sea. It was a covenant sealed in blood by the circumcision of every male child born in Israel.

This was the covenant of blood.

For the sake of this covenant, Jews had willingly died in the time of Judas Maccabee. For the sake of this covenant, they had endured ridicule from their Roman conquerors, who considered circumcision a crude practice unworthy of a civilized people. And for the sake of this covenant, they would enter into a new covenant of blood — blood spilled on the battlefield, through which they could be born again to eternal life as heroes for the ages.

"As for you, because of the blood of my covenant with you, I will free your prisoners from the waterless pit," the prophet Zechariah had promised. "Return to your fortress, O prisoners of hope; even now I will announce that I will restore twice as much to you." [440]

Sukkot, or the Feast of Tabernacles, was the time when Israel would escape its waterless pit. With the last harvest came the first rains, bringing with them salvation to the land of Israel. As part of the celebration, the priests would draw water from the pool of Siloam and pass it from one hand to the next up to the altar for a libation. This ceremony would be followed by a night of celebration.

Their salvation had come.

Coinciding as it did with Sukkot, it is no wonder that Jesus' arrival in the city caused such a stir. Upon hearing that he was approaching the city, his followers who were participating in the ritual procession at the temple came out to greet him, still waving the palm branches they had been holding during the ceremony and shouting the words central to the psalmist-inspired liturgy: "*Hosanna*! Blessed is he who comes in the name of the lord!" The palm branches were particularly appropriate in this context, as the date palm was sacred to the phoenix — the reincarnation of the messianic sun king Horus.

In Jesus' arrival, they saw the fulfillment of Zechariah's prophesy: "Never again will an oppressor overrun my people." [441] This man riding into Jerusalem on a donkey was promising to deliver them from their Roman oppressors and establish a kingdom that could never again be subdued. "Blessed is the coming kingdom of our father David!" they cried out. "*Hosanna* in the highest!" [442]

Cleansing the Temple

Upon entering Jerusalem for Sukkot, Jesus went directly to the temple area. According to the author of *Mark*, he "looked at everything, but since it was already late he went to Bethany with the twelve." [443]

Bethany.

The house of heaven.

This was likely a reference to Jesus' personal residence, wherever it happened to be — a dwelling place for the lord of heaven. After spending the night there, probably with his wife and family, Jesus rose the next morning and set out again for Jerusalem. He was hungry and apparently in an ill temper. Things must not have been going as well as he had hoped. He may have foreseen a popular uprising at his arrival — perhaps he had even tried to orchestrate such an event through his contacts in Jerusalem. If he had, those plans had gone awry. The crowds had greeted him with enthusiasm, but they had not risen up to follow him.

Whatever the reason for his frustration, he vented his anger against a fig tree on the road from Bethany to Jerusalem: "Seeing in the distance a fig tree in leaf, he went to find out whether it had any fruit. When he reached it, he found nothing but leaves, because it was not the season for figs. Then he said to the tree, 'May no out ever eat fruit from you again.'" [444]

This episode seems to have involved a play on the name of the town Bethphage, which was on the road to Jerusalem. The name, in fact, meant something like "house of the unripe fig." Beyond this, however, the fact that it was not the season for figs exposes the gospel writers' error in associating Jesus' triumphal entry with the Passover feast. The ceremony of the palm fronds was associated with Sukkot, not the Passover. And beyond this, figs would not have been in season during autumn, the season of Sukkot; they would have been plentiful during the springtime Passover ritual.

Having cursed the fig tree, however, Jesus' anger remained unassuaged. He therefore went on to Jerusalem and headed straight for the temple area, where he flew into a rage. He formed a whip of cords and began using it to drive out the merchants and moneychangers whose tables were set up in the outer Court of the Gentiles. These men would have been doing a particularly brisk business during a festival, when pilgrims from across the empire descended upon Jerusalem. Many of them, too poor to offer a lamb on the altar, purchased doves to be sacrificed at the temple. Others, arriving from abroad, did not have the proper currency to pay the annual temple tax — which had to be paid using Tyrian silver shekels coins.

In order to obtain the proper coinage, travelers relied on the moneychangers who set up shop in the temple. This service was not free. On the contrary, the moneychangers would charge a hefty fee for the exchange — up to five percent of the transaction. It was yet another financial demand on the already strapped Jews. Every Jewish farmer was obliged under the law of Moses to turn over a tenth of his produce to the temple. His firstborn livestock and the first fruits of his harvest were sent there, as well, to serve as sacrificial offerings. Moreover, every adult male was responsible for paying a yearly temple tax of one-half shekel, which was used to maintain the temple and its environs. And on top of all this, the Romans imposed their own taxes — levies on land, slaves and certain goods. The property tax alone accounted for twenty percent of the harvest produced on the land.

Then there were the tax collectors, typically local ruffians under contract with the empire. These men would travel about, bullying farmers and peasants into paying what they owed. In exchange, they were empowered to charge their victims an additional fee, the extent of which was often limited only by the scope of their greed. A great many Jews were reduced to living at or below the subsistence level as a result. So it is no wonder that imperial taxation remained the focal point of the resistance movement for more than a century, beginning with the revolt of Judas the Galilean. And it is equally clear why the tax collectors themselves became so universally despised in Jesus' time. Jewish rabbis even permitted their followers to break the law of Moses in their dealings with these men. According to the legal interpretations contained in the Mishnah, it was acceptable for a man to swear falsely if he was dealing with "publicans and robbers." [445]

Like the tax collectors, the moneychangers were charging an additional fee — a levy dictated, more than anything else, by avarice.

Why should a poor farmer have to *pay* someone to take his money?

The principle was the same whether that someone was a tax collector or a moneychanger. Such people were, in effect, getting something for nothing by charging interest — a practice strictly forbidden in the law of Moses, especially when it came to dealings with the poor.[446]

To the "poor" in Jesus' time, the Ebionites, the burden was the intolerable. Jesus himself once saw an impoverished widow place two very small coins into the temple treasury. In doing so, she must have bypassed the moneychangers, for her coins were not the standard Tyrian shekels but nearly worthless Greek lepta. They were, in fact, all she had.

"I tell you the truth," Jesus said on that occasion, "this poor widow has put more into the treasury than all the others. They gave out of their wealth. But she, out of her poverty, put in all she had to live on." [447]

This was the level to which many Jews had been reduced. By people like the "robbers and publicans." By people like the moneychangers.

Seeing their activity in the temple area drove Jesus into a fury. "Get these out of here!" he shouted at the men selling doves. "How dare you turn my father's house into a market! It is written, 'My house shall be a house of prayer.' But you have turned it into a den of robbers!" [448]

"Robbers" was the same epithet the rabbis used to describe the imperial tax collectors. Jesus knew he dared not criticize Roman taxes directly without risking arrest, so he did the next best thing: He attacked the most visible symbol of financial injustice in Jerusalem — the tables of the moneychangers. The temple itself had become a symbol, not of Jewish piety, but of Roman corruption. Imperial cronies, the Sadducees, dominated temple service, while the true Zadokite priesthood embodied by the resistance was excluded. And corrupt bankers defiled the temple courts, their trade an affront to the law of Moses.

This temple, to all intents and purposes run by a foreign power, was no more holy than an outhouse. This was Jesus' view. He related it to one of his followers, a man named Jacob (Greek: James), who retold the story a generation later. Eventually, the account found its way into Jewish folklore. In it, Jesus was asked whether it was lawful for the temple to accept a prostitute's donation. His answer was "yes." Quoting from the prophet Micah, Jesus said: "Since she gathered her gifts from the wages of prostitutes, as the wages of prostitutes they will again be used."

It was a powerfully political statement.

The prostitutes were the temple priests, puppets of the empire, who had sold their bodies and their loyalties to the Romans. At their head was the high priest, a man appointed not for his piety but for his loyalty to the empire. This man's name was Caiaphas, and he had made no secret of the fact that he wanted Jesus dead (though his true motive in this is not so obvious as it might at first appear). It is therefore hardly surprising that, when asked about the prostitute's donation, Jesus sarcastically suggested it could be used to build an outhouse for the high priest. "Since it originated in filth, it can be applied to filth." [449] He wasn't just talking about the outhouse, but the high priest himself, a Roman collaborator who was usurping a role that should have belonged to the opposition Zadokites. Jesus regarded himself as the rightful high priest. Caiaphas should, as a pretender, be relegated to the outhouse. As long as he presided over the temple, it *was* an outhouse!

The temple was the seat of Caiaphas' power, and Jesus represented a threat of the worst kind. If this troublesome revolutionary were not dealt with, Caiaphas warned the Sanhedrin, the Roman forces might intervene and "take away both our place and our nation." [450]

Our place.

The temple.

Eventually, the Romans would in fact destroy the temple that Herod had begun as a monument to the Jewish God and his own splendor. But Jesus was ready to beat them to it. "I will destroy this house," he declared, "and no one will be able to build it again!" [451] When his followers marveled at the temple's beauty, Jesus responded: "As for what you see here, the time will come when not one stone will be left on another. Every one of them will be thrown down!" [452] It was not a prophecy, but a threat. As far as Jesus was concerned, the dwelling place of God had been hopelessly polluted by interlopers and charlatans. He foresaw a time when the holy of holies itself would be utterly defiled, as it had been when the Roman general

Pompey invaded a century earlier and brazenly entered the sacred chamber.

Jesus knew that, if he launched a revolution, history would likely repeat itself. Like Caiaphas, he was a realist. He knew that the Romans would move to quash the rebellion, and that they would probably try to seize the temple — the single most powerful symbol of Jewish sovereignty. He also knew that they would almost certainly succeed. The rebels were fiercely determined, but their training and armaments were no match for the empire's legions. Any imperial assault on the temple would likely end the same way it had a century before, with the Roman general standing victorious in the holy of holies, where only the high priest was permitted to set foot. Jesus, however, was willing to sacrifice the temple. The sanctuary had already been defiled by a series of corrupt high priests. What difference would it make if a Roman general did the same?

Indeed, Jesus already had proclaimed that, "something greater than the temple is here" — the kingdom of God.[453] The day was coming when God would be worshipped not in any temple made by human hands, but in spirit and in truth. Even King Solomon was said to have declared as much upon dedicating the first temple: "The highest heaven cannot contain you. How much less this temple I have built!"[454]

The imperial cronies in charge of the temple had already expelled the righteous priests, the sons of Zadok. Caiaphas and his supporters had sold their freedom for Roman riches, and they had sold the temple itself into the hands of salesmen and moneychangers who were no better than thieves. The prophet Micah had foreseen such a time, when the rulers of Israel would become slaves of corruption: "Her leaders judge for a bribe, her priests teach for a price and her prophets tell fortunes for money," the prophet had written. "Yet they lean on Yahweh and say, 'Is not Yahweh among us?' No disaster will come upon us. Therefore, because of (them), Zion will be plowed like a field, Jerusalem will become a heap of rubble, and the temple hill a mound overgrown with thickets."[455]

Jesus never specifically invoked this prophecy, but he may well have had it in mind when he foretold that the temple would be laid waste and the entire land would face upheaval. He warned his followers, "When you see Jerusalem being surrounded by armies, you will know that desolation is near." [456] Those armies — imperial armies — would storm Jerusalem and capture the temple, just as they had during the time of Pompey. The sanctuary would be violated by an "abomination that causes desolation," a sign that the war had begun. The rebels were to scatter and begin fighting a war they could win, a guerrilla war from the hill country east of Jerusalem, where Qumran and the other resistance strongholds lay.

"When you see the abomination that causes desolation standing where he does not belong, then let those who are in Judea flee to the mountains," Jesus said. " Let no one on the roof of his house go down or enter the house to take anything out. Let no one in the field go back to get his cloak." [457]

Jesus was, indeed, a realist. He knew that declaring war on Rome would mean great peril and sacrifice. Women and nursing mothers would endure great hardship, which would be compounded if the revolt broke out in winter. A guerrilla war would be difficult to orchestrate. Communication would be tricky, and there was always the danger that rival factions would arise and turn the conflict inward, away from their common enemy. Jesus warned that opportunists, false claimants to the title of messiah, would arise. Unity would be essential. A kingdom divided against itself could not stand, and that kingdom had one leader, Jesus.

But Jesus was also an idealist. He believed that great battle scripted in the *War Scroll* at Qumran would end in victory because God would fight alongside the sons of light. The heavenly host would join the son of man, God's anointed, in the battle to free Israel from her oppressors. These angels, at his command, would ride the four winds to the ends of the earth, gathering his chosen followers to join the battle. "When these things begin to take place," he told his followers, "stand up and lift up your heads, because your redemption is drawing near." ⁴⁵⁸

Indeed, it was already drawing near.

Jesus believed that the time of distress would be cut short by God's decree, and he vowed that "this generation surely will not pass away until all these things have happened." ⁴⁵⁹

XVII

Betrayal

Jesus remained elusive.

Prior to entering Jerusalem for Sukkot, he had stayed for a time in a village called Ephraim about fifteen miles north of the capital. According to the author of *John*, Jesus was able to keep the place secret while the chief priests searched for him and gave orders "that if anyone found out where Jesus was, he should report it so that they might arrest him." [460]

But nobody did find out. Jesus stayed out of the public eye until the feast, when he could count on protection from the crowds.

The disturbance at the temple was well planned. It had to be. Jesus must have known he was taking a great risk. When the rabbis Judas and Matthias had torn down the golden eagle above the temple gates, they had been arrested at once. Jesus must have been prepared for a similar reaction. Had he acted alone, he certainly would have been detained for trying to incite a riot. He must have had help from supporters who shielded him from the temple police, then provided cover for a quick exit. The crowds of pilgrims who had arrived in the capital for Sukkot also must have insulated him from the authorities.

The crowds were crucial to his strategy. For most of the year, he would remain in hiding, at a safe distance from the authorities. But during the feasts, he would emerge, counting on the crowds to protect him. Hundreds of thousands of people descended upon Jerusalem during these festivities, many of them pilgrims, pious Jews who had traveled great distances to observe the holy days. These men took their faith and their heritage seriously. They were devoted Jews, the sort of men likely to respond to Jesus' call for independence.

With such men around, the Romans dared not move against him.

When the Sukkot feast was over, the crowds dispersed and Jesus went into hiding once again. He would remain in seclusion for some six months until the crowds began to return for the next major Jewish holy day, Passover. This was perhaps the most significant festival on the calendar, recalling the exodus from Egypt some fifteen centuries earlier. According to legend, God had delivered the Jewish slaves from their Egyptian oppressors by sending a series of plagues, each punctuated with Moses' demand to the pharaoh: "Let my people go!" Gnats, flies, frogs and locusts had swarmed the land. First hail, then darkness had blanketed the countryside, and the water of the River Nile had turned to blood. Yet each time, the Egyptian king stood firm: He would not release the Israelites.

The final plague, however, was the worst. It would strike down the first-born male in every household. Only the Israelites would be spared. They were to slaughter a year-old lamb at twilight and smear its blood on the doorframes of their houses. The occupants of every house so marked would not perish — God would "pass over" the doorway and those inside would be spared.

The symbolism of the Passover was keenly relevant in Jesus' day, though the facts behind the Theban expulsion of the Hyksos from Egypt had been muddied and glossed over. To the Jews living in Jesus' time, the expectation was simple: Just as God had, according to legend, delivered the Jews from their Egyptian masters, many believed he would save them from the Romans. For those who chafed under imperial rule, the festival was a source of hope that they might somehow be released from their servility, just as their ancestors had been freed. All they needed was a leader, someone like Moses, to invoke God's judgment against their oppressors. Someone chosen by God, as Moses had been. An anointed one — a messiah.

The *War Scroll* at Qumran proclaimed that "by the hand of your anointed … you will deal with them as with Pharaoh and the commanders of his chariots in the Red Sea." [461]

Jesus boldly cast himself in that role.

"Just as Moses lifted up the snake in the desert, so the son of man must be elevated." [462]

When confronted with venomous snakes, Moses had invoked the power of God by crafting the image of a snake in bronze. When those who had been bitten looked upon the snake, they were saved from the effects of the venom. In the same way, the people of Jesus' generation found themselves amidst a "brood of vipers" — the Romans and their allies. Those who looked to Jesus as their leader, raising him up to a position of power as Moses had raised the bronze snake, would likewise be saved.

The Cornerstone

Upon returning to Jerusalem for the Passover, Jesus headed straight for the scene of the disturbance he had caused during Sukkot — the temple.

He was ready to force the issue.

He was met, not by the temple guard, but by members of the Sanhedrin itself. To them, Jesus was no simple troublemaker, he was a force to be reckoned with. He had started a near riot in the temple courts the previous fall and walked away a free man; the people's support for him was so strong that the temple guard dared not arrest him, as they had Judas and Matthias, for fear of triggering a full-scale uprising. The situation was delicate, at best. If Jesus' enemies confronted him openly, they might spark an open revolt. Yet if they failed to do so, they would be perceived as weak and Jesus' followers might seize the moment to move against them.

"By what authority do you do these things?" they demanded. "Who gave you this authority?"

"These things" were, most likely, his flamboyant arrival in Jerusalem for Sukkot and his subsequent attack on the merchants and moneychangers in the temple. These events were doubtless still the talk of Jerusalem. With the first, he had practically laid claim to the throne of Israel. With the second, he had vowed to destroy the temple. On whose authority, they wanted to know, was he acting?

The question was a trap. There were only two recognized sources of authority in Jerusalem: Caesar and Yahweh. Jesus could hardly maintain that he was acting on Caesar's authority. Any such claim was patently absurd and would damage his credibility among even his most devoted followers. If, on the other hand, he were to claim Yahweh's sanction, he would expose himself as an outlaw and revolutionary. Was it lawful to pay taxes to Rome or not? The choice was the same in both questions: God or Caesar. It was a no-win situation.

Jesus, however, turned the tables on his accusers.

"I will ask you one question," he responded. "If you answer me, I will tell you by what authority I am doing these things. John's baptism — where did it come from? Was it from heaven or from men?"

Now it was his enemies who were trapped. If they admitted that John's message had come from God, they would be exposed as hypocrites for failing to heed it. On the other hand, if they denied his baptism. ... "We are afraid of the people," they reasoned. "For they all hold that John was a prophet." These same crowds that had followed John were now following Jesus. They were waiting for a reply. And they were looking for an excuse to start a revolution. No matter how humiliating the answer, they could give no other: "We don't know."

One can easily picture this reply drawing hoots of laughter and cries of derision. Here were the most learned men in Israel, unable to answer the simplest of questions. Not only had Jesus escaped the snare they had lain for him, he had discredited them as well. His purpose accomplished, he threw salt on the wound by scoffing, "Neither will I tell you by what authority I do these things." [463]

And he continued to do them.

Not content with having put his opponents in their place, he went on the offensive. He told a parable of a man who planted a vineyard, then rented it to a group of tenant farmers. When the owner sent men to collect his share of the harvest, the tenants seized them. They beat one, killed another and stoned a third, even put the man's son to death.

The analogy was unmistakable. God had, in effect, rented the land of Israel to the Romans and their allies, who had abused their rights as tenants by mistreating and murdering his servants. Now they were seeking to kill his son, the incarnate Horus who had been anointed as messiah.

Jesus promised that the owner of the land would return and "bring those wretches to a wretched end." God would have his vengeance on the Romans for mistreating his servants.

"Have you never read in the scriptures? 'The stone that the builders rejected has become the cornerstone. The lord has done this, and it is marvelous in our eyes.'"

Herod had built his temple, but he had done so by compromising with the empire. The Romans and their allies rejected the true Zadokite priests who should have been serving there. These men, however, would be restored to their proper place. Indeed, they would serve as the cornerstone for the reconstituted kingdom of God. As for the men who had risen to power by cooperating with the Romans, they would come to a wretched end. "Therefore I tell you that the kingdom of God will be taken away from you and given to a people who will produce its fruit. He who falls on this stone will be broken to pieces, and he on whom it falls will be crushed."

It was a chilling threat, and nothing less than a declaration of war. Jesus' meaning was crystal clear. The author of *Matthew* reports that "when the chief priests and the Pharisees heard Jesus' parables, they knew he was talking about them. They looked for a way to arrest him, but they were afraid of the crowd because the people held that he was a prophet." [464]

Again, the crowds had saved him.

But the Passover celebration had just begun, and he would have to be careful. It would last a full two weeks, and Jesus' enemies would have plenty of time to seize him in the days leading up to the feast. In the meantime, he spent his days in full view of the crowds that so effectively shielded him from the authorities. Early every morning, vast crowds would flock to the temple to hear him speak, but each night he would leave the city and go into hiding on the Mount of Olives, a secluded location just outside Jerusalem proper.

In public, his enemies continued to hound him.

Was it right to pay taxes to Caesar or not?

What was the greatest commandment?

And Jesus, for his part, continued to castigate them. They were hypocrites, a brood of vipers and whitewashed tombs. As the rhetoric escalated on both sides, so did the stakes. Two days before the Passover feast was to be celebrated, the high priest assembled his allies on the Sanhedrin with one purpose in mind: They would come up with a plan to arrest Jesus and have him killed. "But not during the feast," they said, "or there may be a riot among the people." [465] They would have to act quickly, before the Passover itself and the Feast of Unleavened Bread.

Jesus knew the situation was coming to a head. Just two days remained until the feast, and he had reason to believe that his enemies would try to arrest him as he entered the city. The crowds would be dispersed, the pilgrims busy preparing to celebrate the Passover, and Jesus would be vulnerable. Caution was essential. Accordingly, he resolved to keep his own plans for the Passover secret. Where would he eat the Passover? He refused to disclose the details to even his closest followers until the last possible moment. Only two men would know of his plans: the owner of the house they were to use and a messenger carrying a water jar. No directions were given, no names were used, and a code phrase was to be employed.

"As you enter the city," he told his followers, "a man carrying a jar of water will meet you. Follow him to the house that he enters and say to the owner of the house, 'The teacher asks: Where is the guest room, that I may eat the Passover with my disciples?' He will show you a large upper room, all furnished. Make preparations there."

The Passover itself was still two days away, but Jesus planned a meal of his own that was even more important for that evening. He would convene a council of his closest associates and announce his plan to launch the revolution.

For some time, Jesus had been fueling the nation's appetite for a revolt. His every move had been deliberately provocative. His high-profile arrival in Jerusalem for the Feast of Tabernacles, the disturbance in the temple and his public confrontations with the authorities had all been designed to set the stage for an explosion. Now, all he needed was someone to light the fuse.

That someone, it turned out, was his brother Judas.

The Last Supper

When his disciples arrived on that fateful evening, they had no idea what to expect. The meal would, no doubt, be served in the traditional manner. The Scroll of the Rule at Qumran outlined the procedures to be followed whenever at least ten people were present for a meal: "Let no man stretch out his hand over the first fruits of bread and wine before the priest. For it is he who shall bless the first fruits of bread and wine, and shall first stretch out his hand over the bread. Afterward, the messiah of Israel shall stretch out his hand over the bread. Then, all the congregation of the community shall bless it, each according to his rank." [466]

The bread and wine were symbolic of Israel's independence. The prophet Isaiah had declared: "The lord has sworn by his right hand and by his mighty arm: 'Never again will I give your grain as food to your enemies, and never again will foreigners drink the new wine.' " [467]

The ritual signified a declaration of independence. The grain used to make the bread belonged to Israel, not the Romans; the wine, also, was Israel's possession. Jesus had warned that this new wine would cause the old wineskins of Roman rule to burst and be ruined. The chasm separating Jew and Roman could not be covered over with a patch; a whole new wineskin — the kingdom of God on earth — was needed.[468] And God's messiah would provide this new wineskin.

According to the ritual, the messiah of Israel would stretch out his hand over the bread, just as God had sworn by his right hand and mighty arm. His messiah stood waiting at his right hand to deliver Israel from those who had stolen her grain and her wine. When Jesus stretched out his hand to bless the bread and the wine, he identified himself as both messiah and high priest. A hush must have fallen over the room as he took the cup and declared the revolution had begun. "This is my blood of the new covenant. I tell you the truth, I will not drink again of the fruit of the vine until I drink it anew in the kingdom of God!" Jesus' meaning could not have been clearer. He was taking a Nazirite vow, swearing that he would not taste the fruit of the vine again until the kingdom had been established.

The kingdom of God was, indeed, at hand.

War had been declared, and blood would be spilled. In this blood, God would establish his new covenant with the people of Israel. He had established his covenant with Abraham in the blood shed at circumcision. Now, he would establish a new covenant with Jesus and his followers through the blood shed liberating Israel from her oppressors — perhaps the blood of Jesus himself. Simon Paul must have been among those present at the war council, for he remembered having "received" instructions directly from Jesus: "For what I received from the lord," he would write to his followers in Corinth, "I also passed on to you. The lord Jesus, on the night he was betrayed ... took the cup, saying, 'This cup is the new covenant in my blood.' " [469]

Similarly, he also broke the bread and distributed it to his followers, declaring that it was his body. The Greek word used here for "body" is *soma*, which curiously is the same word used to denote a mystical draught of some sort that had been given to the Indian god Indra. Its effect? Upon drinking it, Indra was elevated to the head of the pantheon, claiming kingship among the gods.[470] This myth quite clearly equates the royal office with the corporeal manifestation of the greatest god — the very foundation for pharaoh worship in Egypt, where each king was looked upon as the incarnation of Horus. Jesus himself had expressed this principle succinctly in regard to himself when he declared: "I and the father are one." Horus the son, upon his death, would be transformed into Osiris the father. There was no distinction.

Now, as his day of reckoning approached, Jesus understood the need to pass his royal authority on to his followers. Should he fail to survive the ordeal ahead of him, the fate of everything he had worked so hard to achieve would be left squarely in their hands. They would partake of the *soma*, thereby becoming heirs to the throne he hoped to establish in his new kingdom.

They would become, literally, the "body of Christ" — the *soma* of the messiah.

Once Jesus had appointed his followers to their royal mission, all that remained was to prepare them for the task ahead, the great war they would have to fight. In the midst of the meal, Jesus stood and removed his outer garments, wrapping a towel around his waist. Pouring water into a basin, he beckoned his followers to step forward and, one by one, began to wash their feet. It must have seemed a bizarre gesture to those who failed to understand its significance, and indeed Peter is said to have objected that Jesus should humble himself in such a way.

But Jesus stood firm: "Unless I wash you, you have no part of me."

Peter then asked that Jesus wash his hands and head, as well. But he had missed the symbolism of Jesus' action: "A person who has had a bath needs only to wash his feet." [471] The members of the resistance had been cleansed, symbolically, at their baptism. But they had not yet been prepared for war. This was, in fact, what Jesus was doing — preparing their feet to march forth into battle. If they refused to take part in the coming battle, they could have no part with him. He had come not to bring peace, but a sword. And the time had come to wield it.

Earlier, Jesus had sent his disciples out without a purse, bag or even sandals.

"But now," he told them, "if you have a purse, take it. And if you don't have a sword, sell your cloak and buy one." [472]

The time to fight was at hand.

"One of you," he announced, "will betray me."

The Plan

The announcement took Jesus' followers off guard. One by one, they stared back at Jesus incredulous and insisted, "Surely, not I."

How could Jesus be so sure?

The members of his inner circle were beyond reproach. Many were members of his own family, and all had dedicated their lives to his cause; Jesus had chosen them himself. None of the people in the upper room that night would dare to betray him — unless, of course, he ordered it. And there can be no doubt that this is exactly what happened.

Jesus' plan demanded someone willing to sacrifice himself for the cause, and Judas was the natural choice. Jesus needed someone he could trust implicitly, and he could have asked for no better choice than one of his own brothers. Judas was both reliable — he served as the group's treasurer — and skilled, as illustrated by his title. Judas must have been known for his cunning and his stealth, for he was the Iscariot, the Sicarii assassin. Until now, Jesus had not had any need for an assassin. But now, the war had begun. He had told his followers to purchase swords; the small, curved knives for which the Sicarii were known would also come in handy.

Did Jesus order Judas to assassinate someone? And if so, who?

Such a move would have made sense. Jesus wanted to trigger a revolution, and a high-level political assassination would have done just that. But Jesus had something more in mind: He wanted Judas to betray him. He was convinced that his brother's actions could trigger the fulfillment of the ancient prophecies that, he believed, would set in motion a domino effect leading inexorably to the manifestation of the kingdom.

Anyone who doubts that Judas acted on the express instructions of Jesus need only look at the gospel accounts, which leave little doubt as to the nature of the interaction between these two key figures. Having informed his disciples that one of them would betray him, Jesus would turn to Judas and address him directly: "What you are about to do, do quickly." [473] Jesus clearly knew exactly what Judas had in mind, and that he was actually encouraging him to get on with it. The flavor of the brief exchange is unmistakable: The two men had obviously formulated a plan and discussed it at some length ahead of time. All that was needed was a cue to carry it forward — a cue that Jesus now provided.

The nature of the arrangement between Jesus and Judas is further illuminated by the author of *John*, who attributes to Jesus a quote first uttered by the psalmist: "He who shares my bread has lifted up his heel against me." [474] Jesus then proceeds to hand Judas a piece of bread. A portion of the psalmist's quote, however, is omitted in the gospel reference; these few words further identify the man in question as "my close friend, whom I trusted." [475]

The Hebrew word *reya*, translated here as "friend," can also carry the connotation of a brother. It also may be related to various words for "king" discussed earlier, such as Ra, *rey* and *roi*.

Judas was, of course, Jesus' brother.

But the reference goes much deeper than this. To understand its significance, one must again step back across the centuries and recall the myth of Seth and Osiris, two brothers who likewise shared a last supper. It was at the end of this meal that Seth betrayed his twin brother the king (or *rey/roi*) by handing him over to his enemies, the seventy-two men who had conspired with him to carry out the murder. In the very same way, Judas would betray Jesus, turning his brother, a claimant to the throne, over to the authorities, identified as the "chief priests" — members of the Jewish council known as the Sanhedrin, which could include as many as seventy-two members. Osiris would end up dead, imprisoned in a tree; Jesus would likewise meet his fate upon a "tree." The cross.

This myth may have served as the source of a peculiar tradition that Judas was in fact not only Jesus' brother, but his twin.

Just as Seth had been a twin to Osiris.

According to at least one ancient source, Judas was known by another name as well: Thomas.[476] This much can be gleaned from the opening words of *The Gospel of Thomas*, a collection of sayings that many believe to be on a par with the canonical gospels in terms of antiquity; the closest thing there is to a fifth gospel. It is attributed to someone named Didymus Judas Thomas, or Judas Thomas the twin. All these names are highly significant.

The name Judas is the Greek form of Judah — the name of the patriarch who fathered the line of Jewish kings. But it is also similar to the name Jeoud, which is significant for the fact that it was worn by the sons of Phoenician kings. The Phoenicians, or people of the phoenix, were descendants of the Hyksos who had fled Egypt and colonized the Syrian coast. As such, they were closely related to another group of Hyksos refugees that had settled farther to the south, in the area that would come to be known as Judah. This second group of refugees had wreaked havoc across the region, mercilessly slaying men, women and children in a bloodthirsty series of sieges and invasions worthy of Viking raiders. Their conquests would pave the way for the foundation of a new kingdom around the ancient city of Jerusalem — the kingdom of Judah.

Their northern cousins the Phoenicians were known for some equally bloodthirsty behavior. It was their custom, for example, to offer a human sacrifice to their war god in times of great distress. But not just anyone could be sacrificed. The blood that was spilled had to belong to the divine son of the king himself, the man named Jeoud. He was, symbolically speaking, the firstborn son of the nation. And his death therefore corresponded to the Hebrew mandate that every firstborn child or animal would be set aside for the war god Yahweh. This was, in fact, the heritage of the Hyksos when they left the land of the Nile: "When I struck down all the firstborn in Egypt, I set apart for myself every firstborn in Israel, whether man or animal. They are to be mine. I am Yahweh." [477]

The fact that this exodus was commemorated each year during the feast known as the Passover would be highly significant.

It was at this feast that Jesus, the firstborn son of God, would die.

The sacrifice, though recorded in connection with the Egyptian conflict, probably had its origins in prehistoric times. It embodied an ancient superstition that a war god such as Yahweh could be appeased by such an act. This belief could go a long way toward explaining Yahweh's peculiar reaction to Cain's murder of his brother Abel in the *Genesis* account: Instead of invoking his own law of "an eye for an eye" and striking down Cain in retribution, the lord of hosts actually appears to *reward* the guilty party, bestowing upon him a mark of personal protection.

An even clearer example of how such a sacrifice played out, however, may be found later in the same Hebrew text. The Phoenician ceremony of Jeoud is in fact eerily reminiscent of the famed story involving the patriarch Isaac, who is said to have come within a split second of being sacrificed to Yahweh in a bizarre episode that is characterized even today as an act of extreme piety on the part of his father, Abraham. This scene in *Genesis*, interestingly, follows immediately upon the report of a conflict between Abraham and a rival king. The sacrifice therefore fits into the Phoenician pattern quite well, following as it does upon a period of distress that could have caused Abraham to call upon the war god for succor — and to sacrifice his son in exchange for such assistance. The idea of the Phoenician ceremony, as related by the ancient writer Philo of Byblos (not to be confused with Philo of Alexandria) was a simple one: "It was an ancient custom in a crisis of great danger that the ruler of a city or a nation should give his beloved son to die for the whole people, as a ransom." [478]

These words are remarkably similar to those placed in the mouth of the high priest Caiaphas by the author of *John*. His purpose? To convince the seventy-two member Sanhedrin that it was necessary to sacrifice another man claiming to be the son of a king. "You do not realize that it is better for you that one man die for the people than that the whole nation perish?" [479]

Under the Phoenician model, one might have expected this person to be Judas, whose name corresponds rather nicely to the title Jeoud — meaning literally "only begotten." [480] Yet ultimately it was not he, but his brother Jesus who was destined to take the fall. There may have been several reasons for this, not the least of them being that Jesus (not Judas) was the one claiming to be the son of the king. Even so, it is quite interesting to note an alternate version of the story developed under which Jesus *did not*, in fact, die on the cross. Instead, this strongly persistent tradition maintained, a surrogate was crucified in his place.

A lookalike. A twin.

Which brings us back, once again, to Judas Didymus Thomas.

The very name Didymus meant "twin," and the name Thomas carried the same connotation. It was, however, significant for another reason as well: It appears to have been derived from the name of the old Babylonian god Tammuz, who was in turn a later form of the Sumerian god Dumuzi. This was the great shepherd king and husband of Inanna, whose name sounds at least a bit like Didymus. It was Dumuzi who was consigned to the underworld for a portion of each year, only to rise again from the fertile earth in the springtime. Dumuzi, like Jeoud, was killed as a surrogate — in this case for Inanna, who forcibly enlisted him to take her place in the land of the dead after being trapped there herself.

The motif of Dumuzi as the shepherd king marks yet another point of contact with the myth of Abraham, wherein Isaac is ultimately spared his intended fate by the fortuitous appearance of a ram whose horns had become entangled in a thicket. Abraham takes this as a sign and spares his son the knife, instead taking the ram and sacrificing it as a surrogate. This represents an interesting doubling of the theme, as Isaac himself was originally meant to be sacrificed as a Jeoud-like surrogate for the entire nation — the "great nation" that God had promised would issue forth from the loins of Abraham. The ram is the lamb of God — a title later applied to Jesus, who was likewise said to have been a substitute sacrifice for "the whole nation." And the animal's predicament associates it even more closely Jesus' situation, as both are caught and held against their will by something made of wood.

In one case, a thicket; in the other, a cross.

One might therefore expect the pattern of the double surrogate established in the legend of Isaac to be applied in Jesus' situation as well:

- The nation
- Jeoud — first surrogate
- Lamb or ram — second surrogate

And indeed it is.

But before exploring this further, it would behoove us to ask one question: Why was there a need for *two* surrogates?

Once again, the answer lies in the symbolism of ancient ritual — in this case, the ritual carried out each year on the Day of Atonement. One goat was chosen to be sacrificed on the altar; a second goat was released into the wilderness of Seth to become the scapegoat. In order to perform the ceremony as intended, both goats were needed; in the same way, both Jesus and Judas were needed to carry out the roles assigned to them in their human re-enactment of this drama. The goat sacrificed on the altar was Osiris, the lamb of god; the goat sent into the desert was Seth, a figure known to mythology as the mature king but demonized in later tradition under the name Satan.

Hence, we find Jesus sending Judas away just as the high priest sent the scapegoat out into the wilderness.

"What you are about to do, do quickly."

When Jesus quoted the psalmist in reference to Judas, he implied that the latter was a close friend worthy of his trust. And indeed he must have been: He was the only one Jesus trusted enough to carry out the plan he had conceived.

It was a complicated plan, one that many others in his inner circle had failed to grasp. Still convinced that Jesus was destined to expel the Roman legions and ascend the throne of Jerusalem in glory, they were unwilling to accept the necessity of what must happen first: The son of man must die.

In order to live again.

Unlike these others, Judas understood the importance of fulfilling the prophecies to the letter. He was fully committed to the plan that Jesus had concocted and willing to play his part without question; hence, he did not hesitate to follow his brother's lead when things were set in motion, leaving on cue to betray him to the authorities.

Upon doing so, the author of *John* states, "Satan entered into him." [481] But this is not what it appears. One is almost certainly confronted with images of Judas being possessed by a malevolent daemon intent upon using him to some ill purpose. But in fact, nothing could have been further from the truth. He had agreed at Jesus' behest to play the role of Satan — or rather Seth — assuming the identity of the betrayer in the elaborate passion play that was about to unfold.

Jesus had chosen the words of the psalmist carefully: "He who shares my bread with me has lifted up his heel against me."

He had found a prophecy that perfectly expressed Judas' role in his plan, that of a betrayer who was nonetheless a close and trusted friend. Jesus did not accuse his brother of raising his hand against him, but of lifting his heel. Such language indicated that this was not a physical confrontation; on the contrary, a person who lifts his heel against another can only be *walking away* from that person. And had not Jesus sent Judas *away* as a human scapegoat?

The heel signified not strength, but weakness. It was the single vulnerable spot on the body of heroic Achilles, the key to his ultimate undoing. It also played a prominent role in the *Genesis* account of creation, during which man and serpent are pitted against one another for all eternity: "He will crush your head, and you will strike his heel." [482] This sheds further light on Judas' role, for it is said that Satan entered into him when he lifted his heel against Jesus. Satan (and Seth) was specifically associated with the serpent of the *Genesis* myth, an animal with long, sharp fangs that could inject a deadly dose of venom into the heel. Its victim would sweat, perhaps convulse or writhe in agony, and develop a high-grade fever that could lead to death. It would indeed appear to the onlooker as though a spirit had entered into the person's body to possess it — the spirit of the serpent, a.k.a. Satan or Seth.

No snake ever bit Judas, and Jesus' words were never meant to be taken in any but the figurative sense. Yet the symbolism they contained reveals the exact nature of the task Judas was called upon to carry out. He was to play the role of the first surrogate, turning himself over to the authorities in the first phase of the eternal ritual. He, in turn, would then "betray" Jesus to the Romans, thereby earning his own release just as Isaac had been released when Abraham saw the lamb of god entangled in the thicket. Now it was Jesus' turn to be the lamb of God, the goat destined to be sacrificed on the altar while the scapegoat (Judas) went free.

The plan was risky, to say the least. Judas would allow himself to be arrested and then lead the authorities to Jesus. Once Jesus was arrested, his public trial and sentencing would cause the sort of outcry he had failed to ignite with his ostentatious arrival in Jerusalem at Sukkot. The penalty for opposing the empire was crucifixion, a form of punishment that would identify Jesus as the dying tree king Osiris.

More than this, however, he would be the royal son being sacrificed to the war god, Yahweh, thereby enlisting his aid in the uprising that was to follow. His blood would cry out to God from the earth, forcing the divine hand to obey his purpose in launching a crusade against the oppressor. Jesus would be the Passover lamb of God in the flesh, his blood spilled for the good of the people.

This symbolism, Jesus believed, would fire the hearts of the faithful to rise up and begin the revolution he had been so meticulously planning. His supreme sacrifice would inspire the crowds that had surrounded him for the past two weeks; they would rise up in righteous fury against the Romans, and not even the imperial forces would be able to stand in the path of a people so inspired by the spirit of God's holy vengeance. And Jesus would be there to watch everything unfold.

It is difficult to believe that Jesus planned to actually end his life — and well-nigh impossible when one begins to consider the kind of planning that went into the crucifixion. The man was simply a master at orchestrating events to suit his purpose, and this was no exception. His plan, in this case, was exceptionally daring and ambitious in the extreme. His goal was to use the potent symbolism of baptismal ceremony as a basis for an actual, physical death and rebirth. In a dramatic tour de force, Jesus *would* in fact be born again.

He would enact the journey of the arker, surviving the perilous waters of death just as Jonah and Noah had done. Yahweh would deliver him, just as he had delivered the great king David:

The torrents of destruction overwhelmed me...
He reached down from on high and took hold of me
He drew me out of deep waters
He rescued me from my powerful enemy
From my foes who were too strong for me [483]

Those foes were his captors, the imperial forces who were indeed too strong for Jesus.

But not too smart for him — not by a long shot.

In the same psalm, the ancient scribe had spoken of David's triumph over and the grave.[484] The king had felt the cords of death tightening around him, but Yahweh had sent a great earthquake to deliver him from the grave. (The author of *Matthew* would make use of this symbolism in invoking an earthquake of his own to coincide with Jesus' resurrection.) Then the great God himself had descended from the heavens, smoke rising from his nostrils and a consuming fire issuing forth from his mouth in a striking bit of imagery that reveals him to be nothing less than a fire-breathing dragon. A comet, perhaps. A flying serpent, to be certain.

The phoenix.

Jesus was the son of the dragon, the Ben Dragon or Pendragon like the pharaohs before him who had been anointed on the back of the fearsome crocodile. He was the son of the phoenix, and he was therefore also the phoenix itself — for the legendary bird was reborn from its own ashes. Jesus himself had declared it: "I and the father are one." The phoenix was about to land on its eternal perch, the cross, whereupon it was appointed that he should rise from the dead after three days. The ancient myth was coming to life: Like the phoenix, Jesus would rise up and ascend to the clouds of heaven. This was his destiny. If he failed to do so, all his effort would have been wasted; the entire enterprise would, in the blunt language of Paul, be exposed as altogether "useless." [485]

The question was, how to pull it off?

How could he possibly hope to die without dying?

As always, Jesus had the answer. He had planned everything down to the most minute detail, calculated what he would need to do in order to survive the waters of death. To this end, it was essential that his crucifixion take place on the day before the Passover: Jesus knew that Jewish sensibilities would never allow the Romans to keep anyone hanging on a cross once during the holy day itself — which actually began at sunset the day before. They would have to remove such a one or risk a violent backlash, especially if the person in question was a charismatic leader with a significant following such as Jesus. But there could be complications. What if the Romans chose to defy Jewish tradition and risk a riot? Or what if they sought to hasten Jesus' demise by brutalizing his body to such an extent that he no longer had the strength to resist death? This, he knew, was a very real possibility. The prophet Isaiah had declared that the messiah must suffer excruciating torment, and Jesus was certain that such oracles must be fulfilled to the letter. Nevertheless, their fulfillment required that he walk a fine line, beckoning death with one hand and shunning it with the other.

Jesus would have to allow for such eventualities, and in the final accounting, he was well to heed his own admonitions. His captors would indeed think to hasten his death by breaking his legs — a move that would keep him from holding his body weight up, hastening the collapse of his lungs and ultimate death. But Jesus, it turned out, was one step ahead of them, for when they arrived, it seemed to their eyes that the prisoner was already dead.

What had happened?

The answer lies in a passage that describes what appears, at first blush, to be an insignificant event. According to the author of *Mark*, "one man ran, filled a sponge with wine vinegar, put it on a stick and offered it to Jesus to drink." [486] The author of *Luke* attributes this action to some Roman soldiers who were taunting him, yet his account is universally acknowledged to be dependent upon that in *Mark*. And two things stand out about the earlier version. First of all, the man is unnamed and appears to be in something of a hurry to carry out this task. Why? Perhaps because time was of the essence and Jesus had asked that he do so at a specific point in time, perhaps even signaling him from the cross with the exclamation "*Eloi, Eloi, lama sabachthani.*" These words opened a psalm that began in the depths of despondency, yet concluded in a triumphant affirmation of Yahweh's power.

Jesus hoped for a similar triumph of his own.

The second crucial piece of information in the Markan passage is the reference to wine vinegar. The allusion leaves one with the nagging feeling that something is not quite right. Had not Jesus vowed to abstain from the fruit of the vine until such time as the kingdom of God was inaugurated? He was, in essence, taking a Nazirite vow — a vow that explicitly included not only wine but also *wine vinegar*.[487] The kingdom had clearly not been inaugurated as he hung upon the cross: Rome remained firmly in control of Palestine, and Jesus himself was at his most vulnerable. That meant only two conclusions were possible. On the one hand, it might have meant that Jesus was breaking his vow, having come to accept the futility of his mission — an unlikely inference given the level of his determination to this point. Which leaves only one other possibility: The liquid contained in the sponge was not, in fact, wine vinegar at all.

But something else.

The suggestion that Jesus was given some sort of sedative is not new, but it is nonetheless quite compelling. It is certainly the kind of thing that might have been expected under the circumstances. Jesus wanted to simulate death for two very important reasons — first, for symbolic purposes that he might "die" before rising again; second, for much more practical considerations. Put simply, he did not want to die in actuality. And with every minute that he remained on the cross, the chances of this happening became magnified that much more.

Jesus certainly had access to the kind of expertise that would have enabled him to partake of such a potion. He had close ties to the Essene fraternity, which in turn was closely connected to an Egyptian group whose members called themselves the Therapeutae. Literally, the healers or doctors. It may have been a connection to this group that earned *Luke* his nickname, "the physician." However this may be, it seems likely that these Therapeutae had the wherewithal to produce the sort of powerful sedative Jesus had in mind.

Having partaken of this potion, there would be nothing to do but wait. One of his contacts on the Sanhedrin would approach the

Roman prefect and remind him of the need to remove the bodies before nightfall; he would volunteer to undertake the task himself, an offer that Pilate would have no reason to refuse. This insider would then take Jesus quickly to his own private tomb, where he could receive other medicine to counteract the effects of the sedative and stimulate the hoped-for recovery.

He would then re-emerge from the tomb after three days, fulfilling his role as the phoenix and amazing all who had doubted that it was possible. But with God, all things were possible. If a man could conquer death, a nation could throw off the shackles of her oppressor. Most thought death was invincible; he would prove otherwise. Most thought the imperial armies unconquerable. Again, he would prove them wrong. Having emerged from the grave, he would set about orchestrating a full-scale revolt to crush the Romans and establish the kingdom of heaven on earth.

But everything would have to work perfectly. In turning himself over to the authorities, Judas was running a tremendous risk. As a Sicarii assassin and a leading figure in the resistance, he was a wanted man; Jesus was gambling that he could regain his freedom by striking a bargain with the establishment to deliver an even bigger fish — Jesus himself. Yet there was every possibility that the authorities would refuse such a bargain. Jesus made it clear that Judas could very well be going to his death. "Woe to the man who betrays the son of man," he declared. "It would be better for him if he had not been born." This was not a threat. It was a realistic expectation of what the Romans might do to Judas once they caught him.

Yet he had to take that chance.

There was no time to spare. The Passover feast would begin shortly, and Jesus wanted to force his enemies' hand. If Judas were caught in an assassination attempt, they would have to arrest him. This would offer him the perfect opportunity to implicate Jesus and "betray" him, again leaving the authorities with little choice but to move against the accused ringleader.

But if they arrested or tried him on the Passover itself, they would be playing right into Jesus' hands. In such a scenario, he could invoke the most powerful sort of symbolism: Just as Moses had ordered the Egyptian pharaoh to "let my people go," so now Jesus could make the same demand of the Roman governor, Pontius Pilate. And he could do so on the Passover, the day that, more than any other, epitomized Israel's deliverance from oppression. His actions would set in motion God's deliverance; after his miraculous resurrection, the crowds who had followed him would rise up and the imperial forces would be put to flight. If worse came to worst, he reasoned, he would die upon the cross.

But even if the Romans were to succeed in executing him, it would be as a martyr, not a criminal. The belief was strong among many Jewish nationalists that God would avenge the blood of his martyrs, and Jesus had warned his enemies that this very thing would happen: "This generation will be held responsible for the blood of all the prophets that has been shed since the beginning of the world, from the blood of Abel to the blood of Zechariah." [488]

The blood of Abel (whose name was yet another variation on the name of the dying god Baal) had cried out from the ground, and God had answered — driving his murderous brother Cain from the land.[489] In the same way, the blood of Jesus would cry out to God, and he would respond by banishing the Romans and their fawning allies from the land of Israel.

Arrest

After Judas departed, Jesus led his followers to a place called the Gethsemane — literally "the oil press" — on the Mount of Olives. It had been his custom in the days leading up to the Passover to retire here, outside the city.

It would be easy for his enemies to find him. The Passover was celebrated at the first full moon of springtime, so there would be plenty of light. Instructing the rest of his followers to stay behind, he went on farther with only his brothers, James and Peter. Together, they would face the inevitable as they watched his daring plan unfold. His brothers must have been unsure what lay ahead — he had confided his plans to Judas alone.[490]

But Jesus himself knew.

And he was, understandably, nervous.

"My soul is overwhelmed with sorrow to the point of death," he told them. Then he fell to his knees and prayed earnestly, "My father, if it is possible, may this cup be taken from me. Yet not as I will, but as you will." [491]

This cup. The cup of blood. The *dam koce*.

Jesus knew that the events he had set in motion were beyond his control now. He knew the Romans would come to arrest him, would charge him with seeking to foment an insurrection and nail him to the cross as a traitor. It was all but inevitable. Yet despite his determination to carry through with what he had started, he still prayed that there might be some other way. His prayer may have been a frantic exercise in last-minute brainstorming, a struggle for some wondrous illumination that could save him from his destiny. If this is what he was searching for, it did not come. Even the greatest minds must sometimes admit they are out of ideas, and it had come to that for Jesus as he knelt there in the garden.

His mind was probably also consumed with worry: Judas still had his part to play in the unfolding drama. Could something have gone wrong?

It wasn't long before he had the answer.

Judas arrived, as planned, accompanied by a large crowd. Some, sent from the "chief priests and elders," were armed with clubs. Others were Roman soldiers. Indeed, a full cohort of six hundred men armed with swords arrived on the scene to confront Jesus.[492] After witnessing the huge crowds that had followed Jesus in the days leading up to the feast, they were taking no chances. This was no minor troublemaker. This was a serious threat.

Given their precautions, they must have been surprised by what they saw. Before them stood a small group of men, armed only with two swords. Peter — apparently still unaware of Jesus' plans — drew one of them and lunged at the high priest's servant, cutting off his ear. But otherwise, they offered no resistance. "Put your sword away," he commanded. "Shall I not drink of the cup the Father has given me?" [493]

Jesus was acting as though he *wanted* to be arrested. And of course, this was exactly what he did want. When Judas greeted him, he did so with a traditional kiss, likely a sign between them that all had gone as planned. Then, when the soldiers moved to seize him, he played the part of the innocent victim.

"Am I leading a rebellion, that you have come out with swords and clubs to capture me?" he asked them.

Of course, he *was* leading a rebellion. To all appearances, however, he was nothing more than a simple rabbi being harassed by a gang of bullies. And appearances were important. It was early evening, and the commotion may well have drawn a crowd of curious onlookers. To them, the scene must have seemed absurd: a huge, well-armed contingent of Romans and temple guards marching out to confront a handful of men, most of whom were unarmed. Even an impartial observer would have seen the authorities as villains and Jesus as their unfortunate victim.

The Romans were cowards, afraid to confront him in broad daylight, waiting until nightfall to seize him: "Every day I sat in the temple courts teaching, and you did not arrest me."

The soldiers ignored his protests, as he knew they would. The words were not meant for their ears, anyway.

Trial and Error

As they led him away, those who had come with him fled, fearful of sharing his fate. Two of them may have been captured, and two others attempted to follow Jesus at a distance. One of them was Peter, and the other was an unnamed "young man" — literally, someone younger than forty — wearing nothing but a linen garment.

According to the author of *Mark*, the soldiers attempted to seize him, but were able to catch only his shirttails. They were left with the linen garment in their hands as their would-be prisoner fled naked.[494]

Who was this young man?

A passage in the so-called *Secret Gospel of Mark* provides a clue. The disputed document, which survives only in two second-century quotations from Clement, a bishop of Alexandria in Egypt, was supposedly a different version of the gospel attributed to *Mark* that was being circulated at that time. Its author refers to a "young man … clothed only in a linen cloth on his naked body," a description that would seem to match that of the young man who fled at the time of Jesus' arrest. According to the author of *Secret Mark*, Jesus had raised this young man from the dead, an obvious variation on the story of "Lazarus" — otherwise known as Simon the Pharisee.

Simon Paul.

He must have found some replacement garment and rejoined Peter, however, who had been following Jesus at a distance. The author of *John* reports that "Simon Peter and another disciple were following Jesus. Because this disciple was known to the high priest, he went with Jesus into the high priest's courtyard, but Peter remained at the door. The other disciple, who was known to the high priest, came back and spoke to the girl on duty there. Then he brought Peter in." [495]

This disciple could well have been Simon the Pharisee. As Gamaliel's son, he would have been known to the high priest and had a certain amount of influence with him. Before aligning himself with Jesus' movement, he had obtained letters from the high priest authorizing him to arrest members of the resistance. It was therefore natural that he should be allowed to witness what was about to take place. Peter, on the other hand, was a known revolutionary with a Galilean accent — he would hardly have been welcome. He therefore tried to remain inconspicuous as he sat in the courtyard, listening in on the proceedings, but a servant girl noticed him and confronted him with the unwelcome observation that she had seen him with

Jesus.

He denied it and moved away, but she pressed the issue, repeating the charge in front of several others: "This fellow is one of them."

Again, he denied it.

"Surely you are one of them," they pressed. "You are a Galilean."

It was a dangerous assertion. Not only was Peter being linked with Jesus, but now he was being called a revolutionary — a man aligned with the movement begun by Judas the Galilean. He began cursing and denied it with an oath: "I don't know this man you're talking about!" Apparently, his denial was convincing, because no one moved to arrest him.

Meanwhile, several members of the Sanhedrin had gathered inside the high priest's residence. Accounts vary as to whether they had been summoned by the high priest, Joseph Caiaphas, or by his father-in-law and predecessor in that position, Annas. Most likely it was Caiaphas, who was the acknowledged high priest at the time.

This Sanhedrin normally convened in the inner court of the temple at a place called the Hall of Hewn Stone, but Caiaphas had his reasons for avoiding a formal daylight trial — reasons that will become clear soon enough. The truth of the matter is that the so-called trial at the high priest's palace was not, in fact, a trial at all. It was a gathering to prepare a case against Jesus that could be sent with their prisoner to the Roman prefect, Pontius Pilate.

Why didn't the Roman soldiers present at Jesus' arrest simply take him directly into custody themselves? Perhaps because they wanted nothing to do with the case against Jesus. The prefect, while better equipped to handle a riot than the Jews, had no more wish than they to risk such a disturbance by taking him into custody or making him a martyr. He had seen how the Baptist's death had provoked the masses, and he had no desire to provoke things in a similar manner this time. Indeed, he ultimately tried to foist the situation off on Antipas, who had ordered John's execution and — he hoped — would be willing to take this problem off his hands.

Jesus was a political hot potato.

He went first to Caiaphas, then to Pilate, then to the Galilean tetrarch Antipas, who sent him back to Pilate. Finally, Pilate symbolically washed his hands. No one wanted to be held responsible for condemning this charismatic man, deemed by some to be the messiah. No one wanted to feel the wrath of the masses who had gathered around him and hailed him as their liberator.

Those political maneuvers, however, were still ahead. On the night in question, Jesus stood before the high priest and listened as a series of "witnesses" rehearsed their statements in an attempt to coordinate their accusations against him. The task was apparently an arduous one. The so-called witnesses contradicted one another, but gradually a strategy began to take shape: Jesus would be accused of plotting to destroy the temple. Jesus would be cast as a man committed to a militant revolution who would stop at nothing to achieve his goals and was willing even to desecrate Israel's holiest site. Jesus, of course, maintained that the temple already had been profaned. But such a drastic plan would certainly shock more moderate Jews, who preferred the hardship of Roman rule to the prospect of war.

Still, even if the witnesses were able to coordinate their stories, the case against Jesus would be complete only if they could gain a confession from the accused. And so, they questioned him. Did he, in fact, intend to lead an uprising against Rome? Was he claiming to be the messiah, the anointed one, the rightful king of Israel? If they could get him to admit to this, the Romans would have no choice but to execute him.

When the high priest began to question him, however, Jesus gave no indication that he was about to cooperate.

He was combative.

Confrontational.

Evasive.

"I have spoken openly to the world," he answered. "I always taught in the synagogues or at the temple, where all the Jews come together. I said nothing in secret" — not exactly a truthful assertion, if one considers his coded parables and private discussions with his followers explaining them. "Why question me?" he scoffed. "Ask those who heard me. Surely they know what I said."

The response earned Jesus a cuff across the face from an official standing nearby. "Is this the way you answer the high priest?" he demanded.

But Jesus was unbowed. "If I said something wrong, testify as to what is wrong," he demanded. "But if I spoke the truth, why did you strike me?" [496]

He got no answer, but another question: "Are you the messiah, the son of the blessed one?" The blessed one, in this case, was David, who had been blessed by God, and whose son (or descendant) the prophets had declared would deliver Israel and establish the kingdom of God. When Jesus had entered Jerusalem for the Feast of Tabernacles, the masses had proclaimed him the son of David, the new Solomon. He could hardly deny the charge.

"I am," he answered finally. "And you will see the son of man sitting at the right hand of the mighty one and coming on the clouds of heaven." [497] It was, in the language of Qumran, a declaration of war by the sons of light against the sons of darkness. It was Jesus' firm belief that God's heavenly host would deliver him from his imprisonment and Israel from its unlawful subjugation to the empire. He would lead the assault himself. "For you will battle against them from heaven above," the author of the *War Scroll* declared. "The powers of the host of angels are among our numbered men.... And our horsemen are the clouds." [498]

This was all the high priest wanted to hear.

Then and there he tore his clothes and adjourned the meeting. He had enough evidence to take his case to the Romans, even without the help of witnesses. Jesus' words, he said, were tantamount to blasphemy. True, he had not actually spoken against Yahweh, but one could just as easily be guilty of blaspheming (literally, defaming) other holy things, such as Moses or the temple.[499] Jesus was, in fact, accused of the latter. But although he had not specifically blasphemed Yahweh, he had presumed to speak in his behalf. As a result, the high priest saw him as a false prophet. And a false prophet was worthy of death under the law of Moses.

According to the law, if a prophet arose and claimed he could perform miracles, yet urged the people to follow other gods, he was not to be believed — even if the miracles he announced should come to pass. "This prophet or dreamer must be put to death, because he preached rebellion against the lord your God. ... He has tried to turn you from the way the lord your God commanded you to follow. You must purge the evil from among you." [500]

Jesus fit the profile almost perfectly. He had not explicitly urged his disciples to follow other gods, but his threat to bring down the temple constituted an attack on the very heart of Jewish religious life. This was evidence enough that he had "preached rebellion" against God. He had, in the judgment of the Sanhedrin, taken God's name in vain.

He had blasphemed.

And the law was unequivocal.

"A prophet who presumes to speak in my name anything I have not commanded him to say, or a prophet who speaks in the name of other gods, must be put to death." [501]

The fact that Jesus was condemned as a false prophet is confirmed by the action taken against him after the high priest announced his decision. Placing a blindfold over his eyes, they struck him and mockingly demanded: "Prophesy to us, messiah! Who hit you?" [502]

Jesus did not answer.

King of the Jews

Pontius Pilate probably knew a good deal about Jesus before the rebel leader was brought before him.

The leaders of the Sanhedrin had identified Jesus as the man responsible for starting a near riot in the temple. Now they claimed he had threatened to assemble a force powerful enough to seize and even destroy the holy structure. Empty threats, Pilate must have judged. How could this man muster an army large enough and disciplined enough to challenge the empire? Yet such threats, even if empty, had to be taken seriously. Some thirty years earlier, the rebel Judas had seized the palace in Sepphoris and plundered it completely. This Jesus, identified like Judas as a "Galilean," might have similar designs on the temple.

If so, an example would have to be made of him.

Pilate may have heard other tidings of Jesus, as well. The Galilean tetrarch Antipas apparently feared that this man posed a threat comparable to that of John the Baptist, who had drawn large crowds with his message of piety and its nationalistic overtones. Antipas had wisely executed the man as a revolutionary. But the crowds that had followed him had simply transferred their allegiance to this Jesus.

Now, Jesus was in custody, having been brought by the Sanhedrin to Pilate's residence, the Praetorium.

The question was what to do with him.

When Antipas had ordered John's execution, the Baptist had been imprisoned in the remote fortress of Machaerus on the eastern shore of the Dead Sea. Away from the crowds that had followed John, Antipas had been able to order his execution quietly without risking an uprising. Perhaps, Pilate may have reasoned, Antipas could take similar action with Jesus. Sentencing a charismatic opposition leader in Jerusalem on the eve of the Passover could trigger mass chaos, especially with the city's population having swollen to three or four times its normal size. The situation was volatile, to say the least. And as luck would have it, Antipas was in Jerusalem at the time to celebrate the feast, and Pilate found it convenient enough to send Jesus to the tetrarch.

Antipas sent him right back.

The tetrarch, already widely condemned for having slain John, had no wish to add Jesus' blood to his resume.

Neither did Pilate.

Creating a martyr, the prefect knew, would only provide a focus for nationalist resentment of the empire. He wanted Jesus dead, to be sure. But he did not want to be the man's executioner. Accordingly, he tried to foist responsibility back off on the Jewish leaders. They had, after all, brought Jesus to him on purely religious charges — that he was a blasphemer and a false prophet. Such accusations, even if true, were hardly grounds for imposing the death sentence.

"Take him yourself and judge him by your own law," he told Caiaphas.[503]

The high priest and his supporters, however, were not so easily persuaded. They, like Antipas and Pilate, did not want Jesus' blood on their hands. This was a matter for imperial justice, they charged. Only the empire could carry out a capital sentence. And only the empire could consider the other accusations they were bringing against Jesus. This man was not only a blasphemer and a false prophet, he was a revolutionary as well. As such, the chief priests characterized him as a threat to "our nation."

The meaning behind these words could not have been lost on Pilate. The Jewish establishment was pledging its loyalty to the empire — and questioning his own if he failed to act. The Romans and the Sanhedrin were in this together, and if Jesus posed a threat to the Jewish establishment, he was an equal danger to the empire. "We have found this man subverting our nation," they charged. "He opposes payment of taxes to Caesar and claims to be the messiah, a king." [504]

These were serious charges, and when Pilate himself questioned Jesus, he found nothing to refute them. As he had been with Caiaphas and Antipas before, Jesus was defiant and uncooperative.

"Are you the king of the Jews?"

"You have said so," Jesus mocked. "Is that your own idea, or did someone else tell you about me."

Pilate was not amused.

"Am I a Jew?" he asked contemptuously.

The exchange ended inconclusively, with Jesus using the language of Qumran to assert that he was indeed a king, and that his kingdom was not of this world. Indeed, it had been sanctioned by God himself. Jesus, the messiah, would lead God's army of heavenly hosts into battle against the Romans and overthrow the imperial order. It is unlikely that Pilate understood the nature of Jesus' threat, but he did understand one thing:

Jesus was claiming to be a king.

And that was enough.

Before the prefect stood a claimant to the throne of David. If the high priest was correct in accusing him of opposing Roman taxation — and Pilate had no reason to doubt it — Jesus was a successor to Judas the Galilean. He was a rebel, a troublemaker and a would-be usurper.

His accusers had it right: "Anyone who claims to be a king

opposes Caesar." [505]

Outmaneuvered by his own allies, Pilate resigned himself to imposing the death sentence. But the situation was no less delicate than it had been. He still had to find a way to impose the death sentence on this man without inciting a riot. He had to order an execution, yet at the same time appear to be innocent of doing so — and give the volatile masses of anti-Roman nationals something of what they wanted. Fortuitously for the prefect, he had not one but two revolutionaries in custody. Another man had been arrested for murder about the same time and was likewise awaiting a decision on his fate.

In this person, Pilate held the key to an incredible series of events that was about to unfold — a key that, unbeknownst to him, had been handed to him by Jesus.

Give Us Bar Abbas!

When Pilate led Jesus out into the courtyard of the praetorium, the prisoner found everything just as he must have expected it. An angry mob had gathered below and was milling about, demanding to know what was going on.

So far, so good.

He may have taken comfort in the psalmist's words, which described his mission in terms the Qumran scribes had emulated:

Why do the nations conspire
And the peoples plot in vain?
The kings of the earth take their stand against Yahweh and his messiah.
The one enthroned in heaven laughs;
Yahweh scoffs at them.

Then he rebukes them in his anger
And terrifies them in his wrath saying,
"I have installed my king on Zion, my holy hill."

MESSIAH IN THE MAKING

I will proclaim the decree of Yahweh:
"You are my son. Today, I have become your father."

Jesus was the son of the Father — literally, Jesus bar Abbas.

The prophecy was about to turn events in his favor. God in heaven laughed at the machinations of his enemies as he prepared to confront them with his heavenly host. They would come on the clouds of heaven and submit themselves to the leadership of God's messiah, the son of the dragon. With them at his side, he would shatter the nations like pieces of pottery. They would become his possessions, even to the ends of the earth. And the kingdom of God would be established.[506] Even as he stepped out onto the portico, he could hear his supporters calling for him. "Give us Bar Abbas!" they cried. Give us the son of the Father.

The scene was mass confusion.

Pilate had two men in custody, and the gospel writers assert that it was his custom to release a single prisoner as a token of goodwill at the Passover. The situation once again recalls the ritual from the Day of Atonement, in which one goat would be sacrificed on the altar as the "lamb of God" and a second animal would be released into the wilderness as the scapegoat. Pilate's two prisoners now found themselves in these roles — one fated to die and the other destined to be released. One of these men was Jesus, but who was the other?

The gospel writers name the scapegoat figure as Barabbas. This, however, was obviously a name for *Jesus*, who had become known for describing himself as the "son of the father" — the literal meaning of Bar Abba(s). The Caesarean text of *Matthew* even acknowledges that Barabbas' first name was Jesus.[507] It is as though the motif of the twins, so intimately linked with the Atonement ritual, is being introduced once again at this moment in the narrative. The writer of *Leviticus* had described this ceremony as calling for two goats that were "alike in appearance, in size and in value, and have been brought at the same time." [508] In other words, twins.

Once this motif is recognized, it becomes easier to determine the true identity of the second prisoner: He can only have been Judas. One subtle clue to this can be found in the Greek verb *paradidomi*, which generally means "to yield up" but is translated using different English equivalents depending on the context. When used in connection with Judas, it is usually rendered to indicate betrayal; yet in other circumstances, it is given the more neutral sense of handing someone (or something) over. One such circumstance involves Barabbas directly: The author of *Mark* relates that Pontius Pilate, in an attempt to satisfy the crowd, "released Barabbas to them. He had Jesus flogged and handed him over to be crucified." [509] In this instance, the release of Barabbas leads directly to Jesus being handed over — in the same way that Judas' release from the table at the last supper leads directly to Jesus being betrayed. The words may be different in English translations, but in each case the Greek word used was *paradidomi*.

If this linguistic connection is insufficient, one need only refer to the common symbolism involved in the roles played by Judas and Barabbas. In the earlier portions of the narrative, it is Judas who plays the part of the scapegoat, being sent forth into the spiritual wilderness of Seth (or Satan) to accomplish some nameless task at Jesus' behest. It has been conjectured here that this task involved a political assassination, the specialty of the Sicarii guild to which Judas belonged. The idea would have been for Judas to assassinate some unnamed target and make sure he was caught in the process. Judas would then agree to betray Jesus to the Romans, thereby allowing him to become the lamb of god — the second surrogate for the nation in the royal sacrifice to Yahweh. Judas, the initial "Jeoud" surrogate, would be allowed to go free.

Just as Isaac had gone free when the ram fortuitously appeared, caught in the thicket.

Just as "Barabbas" was ultimately released.

The charges against the second prisoner held by Pilate appear to confirm this scenario. According to the author of *Mark*, he was "in prison with the insurrectionists, having committed murder in the uprising." This murder was most likely the mysterious task assigned to Judas, the Sicarii assassin. The "uprising" must have referred Jesus' nascent rebellion, which he had launched in the hope of inaugurating the kingdom of God.

Rebellion was a key theme in the atonement ceremony, as well. When it came time to release the scapegoat into the wilderness, the high priest was instructed to "lay both hands on the goat's head and confess over it all the wickedness and rebellion of the Israelites." Judas, into whom Satan had supposedly entered, became the embodiment of the entire nation's wickedness and rebellion. This is not because he was a traitor to his brother's cause, but because he was so unwavering in his dedication to it: He agreed to play his part, even though it involved becoming the embodiment of everything that he had been fighting against. Wickedness. Sinfulness. He and his compatriots had been plotting to eradicate such things from Israel, in the hope that by doing so they might succeed in establishing a kingdom of righteousness. Judas became the personification of the sins of the people his name represented, the people of the ancient kingdom of Judah. "The goat will carry on itself all their sins to a solitary place; and the man (appointed to the task) will release it in the desert." [510]

Later generations would misunderstand the symbolism involved in this bold act, accusing both Judas himself and the Jewish nation as a whole of perpetuating a great crime against Jesus.

Both accusations were, and are, patently unjust. Judas may well have realized that, in carrying forth Jesus' plan, he was destined to become a pariah, his very name synonymous with treachery and deceit. As odious as this prospect was, Judas would have recognized that his task was infinitely easier than the one his brother had chosen for himself.

Like the other goat, Jesus would be sacrificed on Yahweh's altar to atone for the sins Israel, cleansing the conscience of the nation and obligating the great war god to intervene on its behalf against the mighty Roman legions.

Now, both Jesus and Judas were being held in custody. One would be sent away to freedom; the other would be crucified.

Bethany Revisited

Before moving on, it is worth taking a moment to explore an alternate explanation of the name Barabbas. A commentary by the early church apologist Jerome quotes a gospel text (no longer extant) as translating it in different terms: Barabbas was, he said, "interpreted in the so-called *Gospel of the Hebrews* as 'son of their teacher.' " [511] This explanation may be based in part upon a variant form of the name, which appears in some places with an extra "r" as Barrabbas. When this form is broken down into its component parts, the result is Bar Rabbas — the suffix closely resembling rabbi or rabban, denoting a teacher.

One tradition names the first person to bear this title in a formal sense as none other than our good friend Gamaliel.[512] This interpretation of the name would therefore seem to suggest some connection between Barabbas and the son of Gamaliel, the man known to us as Simon Paul. Making such a connection based solely on this tradition would be a foolhardy endeavor, but a closer look at the gospel narratives reveals that this is not an isolated instance; indeed, the names and traditions of Judas and Simon are linked to one another repeatedly in the canonical accounts.

To begin with, the author of *John* identifies Judas specifically as a kinsman of someone named Simon.[513] The latter is usually identified by translators as Judas' father, but the term in question can just as easily connote another sort of blood relative. Simon was, of course, an extremely common name, so this by itself is anything but conclusive. Yet there is another connection to be considered — one that links Judas much more closely with the character referred to variously in the gospel chronicles as Simon the Pharisee or Simon the leper — the man we have identified as the son of Gamaliel.

The narrative in question is the sequence involving Jesus'

anointing by the woman with the jar of expensive perfume. In three versions of this story, it takes place at the home of Simon, who plays a direct role in the tradition preserved by the author of *Luke*. This is the passage in which Simon himself objects to the woman's action on the grounds that she is a sinful woman, unworthy of coming into contact with Jesus. This exchange serves as an introduction to Jesus' example of the creditor who forgives his loans to two debtors — one of whom owed a much larger amount than the other. Jesus uses the story to illustrate the principle that the person who is forgiven much will be more grateful than his fellow man who is forgiven little.

The financial theme of Jesus' analogy is carried forward in *John*'s narrative, but with a twist. The author dispenses with the parable itself but retains the fiscal theme by altering the nature of the complaint against the woman. One of the disciples objects that the perfume used to anoint Jesus might have been sold to produce revenue for the Poor. And, as it turns out, this objection is raised by none other than Judas Iscariot, the same disciple who subsequently responds to the entire incident — according to the authors of *Matthew* and *Mark* — by making up his mind to betray Jesus.

There seems to be a good deal of overlap here.

One author writes of an objection raised by Simon, while the other attributes a complaint to Judas. Both complaints have some connection to money. And two writers conclude the incident by referring to Judas' sudden decision, apparently on the basis of what has just transpired, to deliver Jesus into the hand of his enemies. The author of *Luke* does not link the incident explicitly with Jesus' betrayal, but the words he attributes to Jesus seem to imply a certain connection. In concluding his tale of the two debtors, he compares the sinful woman to the man who owed the larger amount. Like the destitute man in his parable, she had been forgiven much; as a result, she had displayed her gratitude in extravagant fashion.

"Do you see this woman?" Jesus asked, addressing Simon. "When I came into your house, you did not give me any water for my feet, but she wet my feet with her tears and wiped them with her hair.

You did not give me a kiss, but this woman, from the time I entered, has not stopped kissing my feet." [514]

Judas, would, of course, kiss Jesus in the famous betrayal scene at the garden of Gethsemane. In fact, these are the only two instances in the canonical gospels that allude to the act of kissing. If we are correct in concluding that Judas was acting on orders from Jesus when he delivered the kiss of betrayal, Simon's refusal to kiss Jesus provides an interesting contrast. In this case, it is not Judas but Simon the Pharisee who is the real traitor; whereas Judas is loyal even to the point of turning his beloved brother over to the authorities, Simon is unwilling even to show him the appropriate hospitality.

This contrast is carried even further by the author of *John*, who opens his account of the last supper by stating that "the devil had already prompted Judas, kinsman of Simon, to betray Jesus." [515] This revelation provides an introduction to the writer's report — unique to his narrative — of the distinctive ritual in which Jesus washed his disciples' feet. This is the very ritual that Simon the Pharisee is chided for having failed to perform upon Jesus: "You did not give me any water for my feet." Once again, it is remarkable to find such a juxtaposition of events involving Judas and Simon. The author even goes on to report that another Simon (in this case Peter) initially refuses to take part in the foot-washing, providing another parallel to the negligent behavior on the part of Simon the Pharisee.

The significance of such parallels is not to be taken lightly. Clearly, there was some sort of identification between Judas and Simon the Pharisee, both of whom in turn seem to have had some sort of connection with an accused murderer referred to as Barabbas.

How is it, we must ask, that the figures of Judas and Simon became so intertwined? Perhaps the answer lies in an accusation of betrayal against Simon the Pharisee that was later glossed over by his followers. Simon, under the name Paul, would eventually reshape the movement Jesus had founded to serve his own purposes, shunting aside those who had followed in Jesus' footsteps — people such as his brothers, James and Peter. And Judas. These men would display little tolerance for some of Paul's ideas. In fact, they would seek to relegate him to the margins of their community as part of a power play that would end up backfiring against them. Paul was not the sort of person to take such an insult lying down; he was a proud man with more than his share of ambition, and he did not like to take "no" for an answer. He would therefore respond by lashing out violently against the men who had sought to ostracize him. He would even lead a personal attack on James in the temple courts, an assault that paved the way for James' eventual execution. As a result, Simon Paul would be castigated by the mainstream of the resistance movement as a murderer.

The same charge leveled against Barabbas.

More will be said about the friction between Simon Paul and the family of Jesus in the pages ahead. For now, however, it is sufficient to relate that Paul and his successors would ultimately succeed in wresting control of the movement from Jesus' brothers. And having done so, they would be in a position to rewrite history by obscuring any connection between Paul and his alter ego, Simon the Pharisee. Those who were loyal to Jesus' family would come to view Paul as a traitor to the cause, a man who pursued financial gain above all else and had set out to achieve his own personal agenda at the expense of whatever might stand in his way. Such views had begun to circulate in the form of oral tradition and in certain manuscripts written by these loyalists. When Paul's followers got hold of them, they simply shifted the blame onto the most logical candidate.

Judas.

Suddenly it was Judas who was portrayed as the money-grubbing traitor, a lover of mammon who made a habit of pilfering from the common fund. Where he had once been revered as Jesus' closest confidant, the man he trusted above all others to carry forth his ambitious plan, Judas was now transformed into a simple thug who betrayed Jesus for nothing more than the promise of thirty pieces of silver (a fictional bit of information borrowed from the Hebrew prophet Zechariah).[516] It is the winners who write history, and those loyal to Paul did an admirable job in telling their side of the story. The echoes of the other side, however, remain just beneath the surface. Those who care to get their hands dirty with a bit of digging will be rewarded with their discovery.

On this, there is more to come.

For now, however, we must return to the matter at hand — the account of Jesus' final days.

Crucify Him!

Jesus' supporters knew just what to expect. They had been briefed about the events that were about to unfold and the part they would be required to play; they had been told it was Pilate's custom to release a single prisoner at the Passover, and they now seized on the occasion to hold him to his word. For his part, Pilate must have realized he was being manipulated, though there was little he could do about it. Custom demanded that he release someone; the only question involved which prisoner would be set free. It was a question to which he doubtless thought he knew the answer. One prisoner was militant assassin of considerable notoriety within the resistance and, as such, was a fine catch. The other, however, was the real prize: Jesus was the leader of the resistance movement, the man who claimed to be not only the true king of Israel but the legitimate high priest as well. Certainly, Pilate must have thought, the crowds would demand that he release their leader, the man they hailed as the king of the Jews. And this is exactly what he *wanted* them to do. Executing Jesus at this point would only inflame the massive crowds that had gathered for the feast, and a riot was the last thing he needed. If, on the other hand, he released Jesus, Pilate could always order him arrested again at some future date when the situation was less volatile.

But the crowd, to his surprise and dismay, had other ideas. Instead of calling for Jesus' release, they began shouting for Pilate to emancipate the other prisoner. The murderer.

Pilate was taken aback. Things were not going the way he had anticipated, and he was suddenly on the defensive. Certainly they didn't want him to crucify their leader, did they? Seeking clarification, and perhaps uncertain he was hearing them correctly, he shouted above the din: "What shall I do, then, with the one you call the king of the Jews?" [517]

This time, the answer left him with no doubts.

"Crucify him!"

"Shall I crucify your king?" Pilate asked, incredulous.

They shouted back: "We have no king but Caesar!" [518]

The scene must have struck the prefect as surreal. Certainly these men who had so consistently scorned the empire and called for independence could not now be pledging fealty to the emperor. Something was terribly wrong here, and if Pilate had ever doubted he was being manipulated, all those doubts were by this time washed away. There was nothing else to do but to admit he had been beaten and walk away. If these rebels wanted their leader crucified, so be it, but he would not take the blame for it — this was their doing, not his. According to the author of *Matthew*, the prefect turned aside and dipped his hand in a water basin, washing his hands of the entire affair. Whatever madness the rebels were up to, he wanted no part of it.

The murderer was released and Jesus was sent away to be crucified beneath a sign declaring him "The King of the Jews."

The Jeoud cycle was running its course.

The lamb of god was about to be slain.

Yet even as he approached the place of his execution, the crowds of disenfranchised Jews who had seen him as their champion did not abandon him. They followed him through the streets of Jerusalem, the women among them weeping and wailing at what they knew lay ahead. Even these women were playing the part assigned to them, taking upon themselves the role of the weeping widow Isis as her husband was bound over for death and carried away. The prophet Ezekiel had foreseen this very episode in a vision. A heavenly guide had taken him to the north gate of the temple, where he saw "women sitting there, weeping and mourning for Tammuz." His guide then said to him: "Do you see this, son of man? You will see things more detestable than this." [519]

Now, Jesus — who was taking upon himself the role of the good shepherd Tammuz — virtually echoed these words.

"Daughters of Jerusalem," Jesus told them, "do not weep for me. Weep for yourselves and for your children." Indeed, more detestable things than this would they see. Whether or not he would manage to survive the horrible ordeal that lay ahead of him, he was prescient enough to understand that others would suffer even greater hardships — and for far longer. If he succeeded in igniting a revolution, he would call down upon Jerusalem the full fury of Rome and her legions. True, he was confident of victory, yet he also knew that it would come at a great price. Thousands would die by the sword; widows and orphans would be left to beg for their lives — if they survived at all. Famine would envelope the countryside as once-fertile fields lay fallow, abandoned by those who would otherwise have tended them, men engaged on the field of battle. And in the wake of famine would come plague. "The time will come," Jesus predicted, "when you will say, 'Blessed are the barren women, the wombs that never bore and the breasts that never nursed!' Then, they will say to the mountains, 'Fall on us!' and to the hills, 'Cover us!' For if men do these things when the tree is green, what will happen when it is dry?"

Before he was led to be crucified, Jesus was scourged and taunted by the Roman soldiers, who mocked his claim to be a king. They dressed him in a purple robe and pressed a crown of thorns firmly down upon his head. This was yet another aspect of the ancient Phoenician Jeoud ceremony: Philo of Byblos reported that the only-begotten son of the king would be "dressed in royal robes" before being sacrificed.[520] Pilate reinforced this imagery when he ordered a sign made that read "The King of the Jews" and ordered it affixed to the cross upon which this pretender should be hanged. The prefect, however, was sending a different message: This was what happened to anyone who dared to challenge the authority of Rome. Indeed, the Jews could have no king but Caesar.

Two other men were to be crucified with Jesus. Like him, they were rebels, most likely members of his movement arrested along with him. Their names were not recorded, but their last words were. They held a tone of desperation that must have come with the realization that there would be no escape from the cross. They had given their lives in the hope of establishing a new and shining kingdom of Israel; now, they would not live to see its realization. Indeed, the sight of Jesus on the cross between them probably caused them to mistrust that such a kingdom would ever appear.

The crushed and broken body of their leader seemed to testify quite clearly that his movement had been defeated; that there would be no new Davidic kingdom established by this failed pretender of a messiah.

Angry and disillusioned, one of his fellow victims shouted at Jesus: "Aren't you the messiah? Save yourself — and us!"

But the other man, though resigned to his fate, had not yet lost all hope: "Don't you fear God, since you are under the same sentence?"

The same sentence. All three men had been branded revolutionaries. All three were condemned to die. The hopeless situation they found themselves in echoed the words of the psalmist:

> *O my God, I cry out to you by day but you do not answer,*
> *by night, and am not silent*
> *Yet you are enthroned as the holy one;*
> *you are the praise of Israel.*
> *In you our fathers put their trust;*
> *they trusted you, and you delivered them.*
> *They cried to you and were saved;*
> *in you they trusted, and were not disappointed.*
> *But I am a worm and not a man,*
> *scorned by men and despised by the people.*
> *All who see me mock me;*

they hurl insults, shaking their heads:
"He trusts in the lord, let the lord rescue him.
"Let him deliver him, since he delights in him."

I am poured out like water,
 and all my bones are out of joint
My heart has turned to wax;
 it has melted away within me.
My strength has dried up like a potsherd,
 and my tongue sticks to the roof of my mouth;
 you lay me in the dust of death.
Dogs have surrounded me;
 a band of evil men has encircled me;
 they have pierced my hands and feet.
I can count all my bones;
 people stare and gloat over me.
They divide my garments among them
 and cast lots for my clothing.

Those who chronicled the death of Jesus turned to the twenty-second psalm for inspiration. Many of the details of their hero's final hours had been forgotten, so the psalmist's words were used to fill in many of the blanks. The Roman soldiers cast lots for his garments, just as the psalmist had predicted. His enemies scorned him and gloated. They pierced his hands and feet — though in a crucifixion, the victim's wrists, not his hands, were pierced in order to support his weight upon the cross. The author of *John* further invoked the prophet Zechariah in as the backdrop for his report that one of the Roman soldiers in charge of Jesus' crucifixion had pierced his side with a spear. Zechariah had proclaimed that "they will look upon the one they have pierced." [521] This oracle, the author declared, was fulfilled when the soldiers arrived to hasten the deaths of the three men who had been crucified. Their purpose was quite practical: They wished to make sure the prisoners could be removed from their crosses before nightfall, when the Passover itself would begin.

The soldiers began by breaking the legs of two men, but then discovered that Jesus already seemed to be dead. The sedative contained in the sponge that had been offered to him apparently had done its job well. But not well enough, for one of the soldiers took it upon himself to be sure — taking a spear and piercing Jesus' side, thereby eliciting a flow of blood and water. This act was extremely significant in symbolic terms, and not merely because it fulfilled the oracle of Zechariah. In fact, each of the elements involved in this tale is particularly potent in terms of the message it conveys.

A message of death and rebirth.

The blood and water have already been identified with the dual elements of the womb and conception. Their presence in this context further affirms the nature of the crucifixion as a process of divine rebirth, the fulfillment of Jesus' own command that one must be born again. Both are emblems of the feminine principle; which are united with the masculine spear (or phallus) for the purpose of conceiving new life amid the ruins of mortality. What is at first surprising, even jarring, is the realization that Jesus has taken on the blatantly feminine role as keeper of the womb and vagina in relation to the phallic or masculine "spear."

Could it be that the original role model for the passion ritual was not a man at all, but a woman? And is Jesus therefore to be regarded as heir to the widespread (and, strangely enough, somewhat romanticized) ancient tradition of sacrificing a young virgin on the altar to appease the gods?

Instead of answering such questions directly, it would perhaps behoove us to examine a spear incident involving a divine figure other than Jesus. The episode in question appears in the myth of the Norse god-king Odin, who is said to have been pierced through by a spear as he hung upon a tree.[522] The parallel to Jesus' experience on the cross is obvious. But what may not be so obvious, and is worth repeating here, is the fact that Odin appears to have been originally a feminine character. His name appears to have evolved from that of

Lotan or *lwtyn*, the sea serpent slain in the ancient myths of Syria and Palestine.

And such sea serpents were almost always female.

It is therefore not surprising to find that, while much of the material used as the basis for Jesus' passion narrative may be found in Hebrew prophecy, it is in fact older than that.

Much older.

The trail of clues takes us back once again to the ancient myth of Inanna, the Sumerian queen goddess who was brazen enough to mount a campaign against the netherworld for the purpose of annexing the land of death. Her descent into this ghostly realm parallels Jesus' supposed assault upon the gates of hell, which he predicted could never withstand an offensive by the kingdom of heaven. But this is only the tip of the iceberg when it comes to parallels between the two legends.

Perhaps the most interesting of these parallels involves the measuring rod and line with which Inanna is equipped before her departure for the underworld.[523] This corresponds to the staff placed in Jesus' hand by the Roman soldiers shortly before his crucifixion. The purpose of Inanna's measuring rod is not stated in the legend, but the most reasonable explanation is that the goddess needs a way to mark her progress in the depths of the underworld — and a means of finding her way out again once her mission is completed. The journey to the grave was one from which no one had ever returned, and it was therefore easy for the ancients to assume that the deceased simply "lost their way" in the dark recesses of the earth and were unable to find their way back. Anyone who has ever become lost while exploring a cave will understand this analogy at once. To the superstitious mind of primitive man, the grave was an entryway to a maze of hidden doors and secret passages so complex that it could confound the mind of all but the most gifted and resourceful hero.

Such a hero was a man named Theseus, who in Greek myth braved just such a labyrinth to slay a beast known as the minotaur and thereby free the island of Crete from its curse. This monster had the body of a man and the head of a steer, the product of an unnatural union between the queen of the island and a "bull" with whom she had lain. Considering the bull's position as symbolic of kingship in Egypt and elsewhere, the story was probably not meant to be taken quite so literally. Perhaps it even contains the distant echo of an actual event in history, involving the birth of a deformed or insane child to a royal couple on the island. Ashamed of this disfigured child, the king renounced it and ordered the "beast" locked away where it could not be an embarrassment to him. In his fury, he then ordered that seven boys and seven girls from Greece be sacrificed to the minotaur each year.

Here the number seven, associated in Sumerian myth with the seven gates of the underworld, comes to the fore again — as does the theme of human sacrifice. And these themes are amplified by the mechanism that is created to isolate the beastly child from society at large.

A labyrinth.

The word literally means "house of the double ax," an interesting association that links the entire story to the familiar motif of the tanist ritual.[524] Recall that the cherubim (*kher-heb* priests) appointed to guard the tree of life in Eden were equipped with a flaming sword that flashed back and forth, thereby creating a two-edged effect.[525] This gives new meaning to the familiar but perhaps somewhat obscure saying that the word of God is sharper than a two-edged sword.[526] It indicates, quite simply, that God has the power by the force of his decree to overwhelm the very weapon that separates mankind from the tree of life.

The idea of all this is that death can in fact be conquered, and that the tanist ritual is the means by which to do so.

The hero of the Greek myth, Theseus, resolves to brave the labyrinth and slay the minotaur, thereby ending the curse that requires a regular yearly sacrifice of seven boys and seven girls. It is no accident that Jesus' death was viewed in similar terms, as negating the need for any further sacrifice on the temple altar. In Theseus' case, he had the invaluable help of his lady love Ariadne, who provided him with a ball of twine that he unrolled as he ventured into the labyrinth. Once he had completed his journey and slain the minotaur, he returned from the realm of the dead (i.e., was resurrected) by using the twine as his guide. In doing so, he freed the other youths who had been sent there as sacrifices, in much the same way that Jesus was said to have freed the souls of the righteous when he descended to the underworld and assailed the gates of hell: "The tombs broke open and the bodies of many holy people who had died were raised to life." [527]

There is no explicit mention of twine in the story of Jesus, but the word itself gives one pause because it generally refers to a *double strand* of rope and stems from an Anglo-Saxon term that expressed the same concept using a slightly varied spelling: Twin. This word is identical to the modern word for, well, twin. Is this accidental? Or is it possible that the dual strands of twine inspired a comparison to the relationship between twins, whose lives and fates seemed similarly intertwined? In answering this question, it is helpful to recall that the twin sons of Tamar, who identified one son as the firstborn by tying a piece of scarlet thread to his wrist, thus signifying that the royal bloodline was to be manifest in him.[528]

This brings us back to the story of Theseus, wherein the twine is obviously to be identified with the same measuring rod and line given to Inanna in preparation for her descent into the underworld. The motif of the twins may well have grown out of this legend, as well, for it is almost instinctive to use one twin as a standard by which the other is measured.

Gwydion's Trumpet

This brings us to yet another legend — one that involves a figure whose name closely corresponds to that of Theseus' lady love, Ariadne. This is the legend of Llew Llaw Gyffes, a divine sun king whose name translates as "Lion with the Steady Hand" (the name

Llew being closely related to Leo).[529] It is a name that at once identifies him as both a solar figure and a king.

Llew is the son of a wonder-working monarch named Math, a name that means "gift." One may be reminded that the holy spirit is referred to in similar terms by Jesus, who instructed his disciples to "wait for the gift my father promised." [530] If this association is correct, it would indicate that Math was in fact the holy spirit by which Llew Llaw Gyffes was conceived, just as Jesus himself was said to have been conceived by the holy spirit. In light of all this, there can be little doubt that a miraculous birth is right around the corner.

And so the tale proceeds. A maiden is brought in to Math, who asks her whether she is the one destined to be his wife. She answers that she knows not, and so he puts her to the test: Producing his magic wand, he bends it and bids her to step over it. The sexual imagery is not to be missed, for the wand is clearly a euphemism for the king's phallus, which the maiden "steps over" in the sense that she straddles his organ, allowing it to penetrate her. The bent wand indicates the penis in its relaxed state; the implied test is whether she can arouse the king to an erection and thereby conceive his child. It is a test that she passes with flying colors, for there appears at once a boy-child whose yellow hair betrays him as an avatar of the sun.

But something peculiar occurs at the same time: As the boy cries, his mother moves toward the door and those present catch a fleeting glimpse of a small form. Yet before anyone can get a second look at it, the wizard Gwydion snatches it up and conceals it in a velvet scarf, whereupon he hides it in the bottom of a chest at the foot of his bed. This is obviously a second child, or twin, born after the first one. And he is just as obviously an ark figure, for he is immediately wrapped in material like a mummified corpse and placed in a chest. Or ritual casket.

It is this second child who will be the focus of the story, just as the younger twin Jacob supplants his elder brother Esau in their legend.

Before considering his fate, however, two other prominent

figures in the tale should be addressed. The first of these is the yellow-haired child, who is baptized under the name Dylan, meaning "son of the wave." Here we have an interesting point of contact with the Arthurian saga, whose primary female character was named the queen of the white wave, Guinevere. *The Romance of Llew Llaw Gyffes* gives the reason for Dylan's name as follows: "So that day they had the boy baptized; as they baptized him, he plunged into the sea. And immediately when he was in the sea, he took its nature and swam as well as the best fish that was therein. And for that reason he was called Dylan, the son of the wave. Beneath him no waves ever broke. And the blow whereby he came to death was struck by his uncle Giovannion. The third fatal blow was it called." [531]

It would seem that Dylan, like Oannes (Jonah) before him, was a solar fish man and ark hero, just like his twin brother. The narrative speaks of his death as a sort of epilogue to the story of his baptism, once again linking these two incidents symbolically with one another. His death at the hands of an uncle would indicate that, unlike Horus — who defeated his uncle Seth in tanist combat — Dylan was unsuccessful in his tanist challenge to an elder lord and hence died an early death. It would be left to the other child, the twin ark hero hidden away in the chest at the foot of the wizard's bed, to succeed to the throne.

This brings us to the second prominent figure, that of the wizard himself.

His name is Gwydion, which appears somewhat similar to that of the Norse-Germanic king god Odin or Woden. The latter's role as a wizard or Seth figure has already been established and matches perfectly the role played by Gwydion in the Celtic tale. Moreover, both figures are particularly associated with two trees prominent on the European landscape, the oak and the ash. It would be appropriate at this point to examine each of these two trees in greater detail.

The very name of the ash tree links it to the ancient Asherah pole that served as the prototype for the maypole, so it should come as no surprise that the ash tree was used in May Day rituals.[532] It was, according to Norse myth, the tree at the center of the world. Its wide-spreading roots burrowed deep into the soil while its branches extended to touch the sky, thereby uniting the underworld and the world of men with the heavens. The ash was often depicted as embracing the entire world, as a mother does her child. Its great root system reached out protectively to enfold the terrestrial sphere, much as the ocean was shown encircling the world like a great serpent.

This ocean serpent was none other than the primordial sea mother Tiamat or Rahab or Leviathan, embracing her children, the sons of men. The resulting figure resembles nothing so much as an egg within the waters of the womb, and the very word "egg" seems to be born of the same linguistic root as the Norse name for the great ash tree at the center of the world, Yggdrasil. The god Woden himself was also known as Yggr, a name that has been linked to a Greek word for sea, *hygra*.[533] And the Irish had an even more revealing name for the ash.

They called in the *nin*.[534]

This is the very same word the Sumerians used to designate a lady.

Through all this, it is becoming clear that the ash tree was viewed in a very real sense as the archetypal mother of mankind, the primeval dragon lady who appears time and again under such guises as Isis, Eve, Asherah and Inanna to name but a few.

In Norse myth, the great ash tree Yggdrasil was attended by a serpent that was said to gnaw perpetually at its roots. Since the tree itself was in some sense a serpentine or "dragon lady" figure, this other serpent must have been her consort — the Seth wizard or *kher heb* priest-king who served as her constant guardian and companion. Such a figure was Woden/Oden or Gwydion, whose role as such neatly explains his close association with the ash tree.

But there is also the association with the oak to consider.

The oak has been seen across many cultures and traditions as the Sethian tree of kings. Its very nature identifies it closely with the storm god who came to reign supreme in so many cultures across the western world. When the god vented his fury in a flash of lightning, it was most likely to strike the oak tree.[535] Rainmaking wizards such as Merlin and Honi served the storm god with their staves, which in some cases were doubtless made of oak. One custom known from Arcadia (yet another name containing the word ark) required a priest of Zeus to dip an oak branch in a mountain spring during time of drought. By so stirring the waters, he produced a mist that floated skyward and was believed to form the basis of a raincloud.[536]

This sounds suspiciously similar to Odin's act of casting his eye into the well in exchange for wisdom. The eye was in fact the single eye of his penis, which was on the end of a "staff" that approximated the oaken staff used by the priests of Zeus at Arcadia. Zeus, of course, was a storm god as well. So was his Roman counterpart Jupiter, whose name probably was originally Zeus-pater, literally "father Zeus" and who in turn served as an archetype for the person who would succeed him as the god of Rome.

St. Peter.

Or the pope.

Literally, the father.

The oak's acorns appear quite similar to the head of the penis, adding to its phallic quality. And its broad and sturdy trunk make it a natural emblem for the father god in his form as a stout and upright pillar, symbolism readily traceable to that of the mummified Osiris. A small insect found in the tree produces a scarlet dye that must have resembled wine or blood to the ancients' eyes.[537] This is perhaps the origin of the "bleeding-tree" legend found in the legend of Solomon's ship, and it also bespeaks the royal bloodline that issued forth from this royal tree — the vine that sprouted from the bones of Osiris and the sprout that came forth from the stump of Jesse. The stump, it would seem, of the oak tree.

The druid priests might have reverenced the ash tree, but they most often held court beneath the oak. And so, too, did the eminent men in Hebrew legend, who appear to have held the tree in similarly high regard. When Jacob sought to purify his household of all its "gods," he collected the idols and buried them under an oak tree.[538] This is because the oak tree was a symbol of the supreme storm god, in this case known as Yahweh, who ruled supreme over all the other gods. But he had other names as well. In Hebrew, the word for oak tree is *alla*, almost certainly the root of the Islamic name for the supreme being, Allah.

There are indications that tradition called for royal figures to be buried beneath an oak tree. Jacob's instructions to his sons concerning his own burial were explicit: "Bury me with my fathers in the cave in the field of Ephron the Hittite, the cave in the field of Machpelah near Mamre in Canaan…. There Abraham and his wife Sarah were buried; there Isaac and his wife Rebekah were married, and there I buried Leah."[539] On more than one occasion, this traditional place of burial is associated with a grove of great trees. Mamre may have been a place name, but it was also a Hebrew word meaning "strength." These trees were thus the great trees of strength, a description that applies most fittingly to the oak.

Hence the legend of the oaks of Mamre.

The Boaz pillars that likewise signified strength. In burying the symbols of other gods beneath the oak tree, Jacob was probably in fact burying the bones or sacred artifacts of his own forefathers. In committing them to the earth, he was allowing them to become the new Osiris, beneath the pillar of the great tree that stood over them — the pillar of the storm god Yahweh, or Jehovah or Jove, a contraction of the Hebrew name that was adopted by his alter-ego storm god Jupiter.

Even the name Machpellah may have significance. In Celtic terms, the prefix *mac* meant "son of," while the suffix pelah may be derived from a root that also served as the basis for the Latin *pila* — meaning "pillar." It seems therefore at least possible, as well as quite fitting, that the name Machpellah means "son of the pillar."

Perhaps most revealing among the Hebrew myths is the tale of a heroic personage who was confronted beneath an oak tree by a messenger from Yahweh. In this story, the messenger appears under the sacred oak belonging to a certain Jo-ash, whose name bespeaks the union of the storm god and his consort, Asherah. From this union sprang the hero of the tale, who first appears threshing wheat in a winepress, thereby combining the sacred bread and wine in his own person. Upon finding him there, the messenger announces that he is a mighty warrior destined to deliver his people from their oppressors. Such a description would certainly have been fitting for the war god Odin or Woden, and it applied just as well to this man.

His name was Gideon.

The similarity to the name Gwydion is striking, and it quickly becomes clear that the legends of the two men draw from more than a little common material. The story of Gideon is perhaps most famous for its account of his victory over the Midianites, a nation that perhaps corresponds to the Norse realm of Midgard — meaning simply the middle plain and corresponding to the world of men. The Norse gods lived in their own distinct realm called Asgard, a name formed from the suffix *gard*, the equivalent of our word "yard" but denoting more specifically a plain or estate, along with the prefix *as*. The latter was a shortened form of the word *ass*, which referred to a pole holding up the roof of a structure. In other words, a pillar. Odin and the other gods, therefore, lived in a place called the land (or estate) of pillars — probably referencing a temple gateway to the afterworld.

And indeed, Gideon's biblical exploits are worthy of the battle god Odin, king of Asgard. In the end, he achieves victory using a scant three hundred men who storm the enemy camp after nightfall sounding trumpets and causing all manner of confusion. It is not a victory of strength, but one of craft and cunning — just the sort of victory one might expect a wizard to engineer. And indeed, Gwydion himself uses a nearly identical tactic in accomplishing his purposes: "In the early twilight, Gwydion arose. And he called unto him his magic and his power. And by the time that day had dawned, there resounded through the land uproar and trumpets and shouts." [540]

This language might as well have been lifted directly from the story of Gideon. As in that story, the sound of trumpets and the great ruckus is accomplished not by a great army but by Gwydion's magic and power — in other words, his cunning. Just as Gideon's army is an illusion, numbering a scant three hundred men, so Gwydion's army is nonexistent. It is nothing more than a product of his prowess as a wizard.

Gwydion is described in the Welsh legend as the son of a certain Don, whose name appears to be a masculine form of the goddess name Dana or Diana. He was her *kher heb* consort, the high priest of the grove. And there is a strong indication that Gideon was also a high priest. Shortly before his death, he asked each of his soldiers to give him an earring taken as plunder from his slain enemies. These he melted down, using the resulting gold to fashion something called an ephod. This was a garment specifically fashioned for high priests in the line of Aaron, an ornamental shoulderpiece perhaps similar to those worn by generals. The ephod certainly seems to have been imagined in military terms, being accompanied by such accouterments as a waistband, breastplate and braided chains (chain mail?)[541]

Here, too, is another point of contact with the tale of Gwydion, who conjured up his imaginary army in order to procure for his protégé *a suit of armor*. More about that shortly.

In the meantime, it is important to point out one more point of contact between the oak tree and the storm god. The Irish name for the oak was the *dair*, a word closely related to the modern word "door." This is sensible enough, given the age-old practice of using the oak's heavy wood to fashion doors capable of resisting assault by an enemy. But the association goes deeper than this. The name of the Norse storm god was Thor, whose sacred tree was the oak. Can it be mere happenstance that the name Thor sounds an awful lot like the word door, with the letters D and T (or Th) being commonly exchanged for one another in many ancient tongues? As a storm god, Thor also shared his name with the high and rocky hills, each of which was known in Anglo-Saxon parlance as a *tor* or *torr*. And this word in its turn is related to the Latin *turris*, whence come such words as turret... And tower.

If it seems like we are approaching familiar ground, this is no accident. The tower was the *migdol*, the artificial mountain or ziggurat that served as the bridal chamber and final resting place of the king. It was this king who, in the final years of his life, had served as the storm god personified. And it was this mountain temple that served as the first mansion in the series of seven through which he would pass in the afterlife, the gateway to the otherworld.

The door.

When Jesus said, "I am the gate of the sheepfold," the Greek word for gate attributed to him was *thyra*. Again, the resemblance of this word to the name Thor and the word door is apparent. Jesus believed that he was opening the way to the afterlife for those who dared to follow him, and that as such he was the door. Literally. He was also the *dair*, the oak tree or pillar of the dying Osiris, the father through whom all things were possible.

In light of all this, the character of Gwydion becomes extremely significant as a gatekeeper in his own right to the secrets of eternal life, as envisioned by the ancients. And there is still one more figure in the old Welsh story able to shed light on the beliefs of so many in both the ancient and the modern world.

The Blood Wedding

The twin brothers in the court of Math were his sons (or according to some traditions Gwydion's) by the maiden, whom we have allowed to remain nameless to this point. But her name is crucial to the understanding of the story, for it reinforces the idea of the twin as a measuring rod. The narrator gives the maiden's name as Arianrod, a name that sounds similar to the Ariadne of the minotaur legend. The supposed meaning of the name is "silver wheel," an interesting epithet to say the least, for it links her to the spinning of thread that signifies the royal bloodline. This silver wheel can be none other than the heavens themselves, dotted with a dazzling array of silver stars that appear to move in a circle around the earth. Arianrod is therefore yet another manifestation of Inanna, the original queen of heaven who took up a rod and line as she descended into the underworld.

This underworld was, in Egyptian terms, the abode of the dead king Osiris — who was associated with the constellation known as Orion. A close inspection of this name will reveal the source of the Arianrod legend, for it reveals the name to be the personification of the very rod used by Inanna — Arianrod, or Orion's rod. This, again, can be nothing but the phallic wand of Math, which the maiden "steps over" as a prerequisite for conceiving her twin sons. And who could also fail to notice the connection to Aaron's rod in Hebrew tradition, the one that brings forth flowers, nuts and other bounty?

Hence, the measuring rod that is taken into the afterworld is the same rod that holds the secret of fecundity and regeneration. It is the phallus that enters the vagina, just as the dead body returns to the womb of the earth by way of the grave and the kernel of grain is planted in the field. All are destined to bring forth new life. This explains why Horus was supposedly conceived miraculously after the death of his father Osiris. It simply had to be this way.

The legend of Llew Llaw Gyffes bears other striking similarities to familiar material that further connect it to its Egyptian and Sumerian sources. As the tale continues, the hero grows to manhood but is hindered by several curses placed upon him by his mother. The most important of these, for the purpose of the narrative, is her decree that he will never have a human wife. This, however, only serves as an opportunity for Math and the wizard Gwydion to fashion a woman by magical means, using the blossoms of several flowering plants to create the most beautiful creature ever beheld.

In this regard, the connection between flowers and the menstrual flow should be remembered. It is strongly confirmed by her name, which is given as Blodeuwedd and has the apparent meaning "flower aspect." [542] This is all very interesting, as the narrator is obviously using the name as a cue to the observant reader: Watch for the symbolic import of this woman. Though such symbolism may be less apparent to the modern reader, it is far from being obscured altogether. For example, if the prefix *blode* indicates a flower, this only serves to reinforce the connection to the menstrual *blood*. Indeed, the word "blood" stems from an Anglo Saxon verb indicating the act of blooming. And this in turn probably explains why the modern English exclamations "bloody" and "bloomin' " are virtually interchangeable.

The suffix *wedd*, meanwhile, seems to have some connection to the idea of a wedding. On the wedding night, as previously noted, the virgin's hymen was broken, producing a flow of blood.

But though virginal and gorgeous, Blodeuwedd is not faithful. Like Guinevere, she marries the good king Llew only to fall in love with another suitor after the fact. In the more civilized version of the tale, Lancelot remains altogether virtuous and loyal to Arthur in spite of his love for Guinevere. This, however, seems to be a later gloss on the original form of the story found in the legend of Llew, wherein the rival suitor has no loyalty to the hero at all — in fact, he schemes with Blodeuwedd to do away with the unsuspecting Llew in a tanist ritual. As it turns out, Llew is nearly invulnerable, but the beautiful Blodeuwedd seduces him into revealing the only manner in which he may be killed. If all this sounds very much like the legend of Samson and Delilah, it is worth mentioning that Samson was a solar figure associated with lions in very much the same way Llew was. And like Samson, the unfortunate Llew allows his hormones to get the better of him and reveals his only weakness.

He may be killed, he tells his beloved, only if he first bathes in a cauldron by the side of the river, then emerges from it and stands with one foot on the cauldron and the other on the back of a buck. (How he could accomplish this without falling off is a miracle in itself, but one must remember that we are dealing in the realm of symbolism.) When in this position, he still may only be slain if he is pierced by a spear that is a year in the making. Here again the solar nature of the myth is clear, for the new sun king born at the winter solstice will have become the old and feeble Fisher King of the darkened days after a year's time.

Horus will have become Seth.

And it was Seth, in his guise as a hippopotamus, who was pierced by a spear in the Egyptian myth, just as Jesus was pierced by a spear or lance upon the cross. (Incidentally, this is probably the origin of Lancelot's name in the grail saga.)

Blodeuwedd then asks the rather gullible hero to demonstrate exactly how he might be slain, a request he is only too eager to grant out of love for her. She thereupon instructs her lover to lie in wait for poor Llew by the riverside, where he will be able to slay him with the spear at the appropriate time. All proceeds exactly according to plan, and Llew is in fact slain. But at the moment of his demise, he takes on the form of an eagle and ascends, uttering a piercing cry — just as Jesus did on the cross — after which he is seen no more. The eagle, of course, represents the spirit of the phoenix born again from the dead king and ascending to the heavens.

Llew Llaw Gyffes is eventually restored to mortal form with the help of a song by the wizard Gwydion, which causes him to descend from an oak tree in which he has been perched, phoenix-like. Having recovered his true nature, he then sets about confronting his murderer and demands that the vile man undergo the same punishment at *his* hands. In due course, the unfortunate lord is taken out to the exact same spot by the river and is himself impaled by a spear. Here again is convincing proof that, although Llew himself has died, his spirit has passed into a new body in the form of a young challenger who continues the eternal tanist cycle by slaying the old *kher heb* priest of the sacred garden.

And what of poor Blodeuwedd?

She is, appropriately enough, transformed by the wizard into an owl, identifying her as both the incarnation of sophia or wisdom and the latest manifestation of our old friend Lilith.

Yet she is allowed to retain one thing — her name. For it was this name that identifies her as the keeper of the bloodline, the onetime holder of Aaron's magical flowering rod and therefore merely another manifestation of the original matriarch of the tale, Arianrod.

The silver wheel.

Aaron's rod.

The measuring rod and line became the inspiration for the archetypal lifeline or bloodline spun by the divine seamstress for her king. It is the scarlet cord of Rahab the harlot and Tamar. And it is the thread-like straw in the tale of Rumplestiltskin, spun by the beleaguered maiden into gold at the behest of the king. The tale bespeaks her ability to create for him the most valuable gift of all, eternal life — which is later granted to him in actuality when she marries him and gives birth to his son.

The lifeline theme even found its way into the popular children's tale of Hansel and Gretel, two youngsters who are abandoned him the woods and nearly eaten by a witch, only to escape and find their way home by following a line of pebbles they had dropped on their way out. Hansel and Gretel are the descendants, thematically speaking, Theseus and Ariadne; the minotaur merely has been transformed into a witch, while the ball of twine has become a line of stones. The basic plot of the two stories, however, is the same.

And both, like the story of Jesus, owe a great deal to the legend of Inanna. Some more parallels between the Sumerian narrative and the gospel accounts are worth mentioning in this regard:

➢ Inanna prepares for her descent by placing the "crown of the steppe" upon her head.[543] The reference to the steppe is noteworthy because this particular region is known for its generally arid character, supporting few leafy plants and instead giving rise to thin and prickly vegetation such as cacti and thorn bushes. It would seem that Jesus was adorned with this very same crown when his captors placed upon his brow a crown of thorns.[544]

➢ The Sumerian text relates that Inanna "wrapped a royal robe around her body" in preparation for her descent into the netherworld.[545] Jesus' enemies, likewise, clothed him in a robe of scarlet — the color of royalty.[546]

➢ The writer of an early text known as *The Gospel of Nicodemus* reports that a voice spoke out when Jesus arrived at the gates of hell, loosely quoting the psalmist: "Open thy gates, that the king of glory may come in." [547] Inanna makes the same demand upon arriving in the netherworld: "Open the doors, gatekeeper." [548]

➢ Inanna is stripped of her clothes as she passes through the seven gates of death; Jesus is likewise deprived of his garments, which are divided among the soldiers in charge of his crucifixion.[549]

➢ Jesus dies by hanging and is eventually born again as he is raised to life; Inanna undergoes the very same sort of death and resurrection.

Just as Jesus was playing the part of a surrogate sacrifice, so Inanna forced a surrogate to take her place — her husband Dumuzi (Tammuz), who shared Jesus' title, the good shepherd. Despite this, however, the feminine nature of the initial sacrifice was retained. Even though a masculine surrogate had replaced the feminine dying goddess, the male figure was still treated as though he were female: He was pierced by the spear, just as the vagina is pierce by the penis, bringing forth the blood of the torn hymen and clear fluid, or water. The fact that this piercing is in the side confirms the feminine origins of this sacrifice. In the same way that Adam's side had been opened up to remove his rib, thereby engendering the creation of his consort, so Jesus' side was similarly opened up as he hung upon the cross.

Adam meant, in some sense, "man," and Jesus was the son of man.

Paul called him the last Adam.[550] In doing so, he was expressing his belief that Jesus had managed to put right what had gone dreadfully wrong in the primordial garden paradise by substituting himself for the first Adam. The original Adam had been a hermaphrodite of sorts, containing within himself both the masculine and feminine principles. But the latter had been stripped from him during the process by which the first woman, or *issa*, was formed.

Jesus' task was to restore the spiritual wholeness that had been forfeited at the fall, but more specifically at the point when the feminine principle was removed from the man's physical being. The spear in the side symbolized the restoration of this principle, with Jesus taking on a decidedly feminine role and thereby restoring the wholeness that had been lost in the garden — lost with the dawn of the tanist era, in which sexual intercourse between two beings replaced the individual wholeness that had come before. Or so the mythmakers believed.

It is perhaps for this reason that Jesus is depicted today, incorrectly, as a celibate. He is believed to have restored humanity to its perfect state by taking upon himself the image of the complete Adam *before the fall*. Priests who seek to follow his example in this regard likewise commit themselves to celibacy with a vow that may well stem from this same tradition.

Jesus was not only the last Adam, the archetypal man, but he was also — according to the Quran — Issa.

The woman.

The Hebrew word *issa* deserves at this point another examination. As mentioned earlier, it combines the word *is*, signifying a man, with the suffix *sa*, most likely of Egyptian origin. As we have seen, the latter word could be expressed using several different hieroglyphs containing various meanings. Some of these are directly relevant to this stage of our investigation:

➢ *Hidden* — This could reflect that the feminine principle was hidden in the body of the first man before being exposed when the woman was removed from his side. In this sense, the word *issa* would have meant "hidden (in) man."

> *Side or back* — This reveals that the word could well have signified the "side of man." Recall that one of the names for the archetypal woman was Side, the consort of Orion. It was from Adam's side that the first woman was taken, and it was Jesus' side that was pierced.

> *Son* — This meaning creates the phrase "son of man," a title that Jesus used repeatedly in referring to himself.

Jesus himself is said to have touched on the idea of male-female reunification at death. "When the dead rise," he said, "they will neither marry nor be given in marriage; they will be like the angels in heaven." [551] The clear implication is that sexuality will be abolished and the human spirit will become, in a sense, androgynous at death.

This idea takes us back once more to the myth of the dying king Osiris, whose corpse was cut into pieces by Seth and scattered across the land of Egypt. The only piece not recovered was the phallus. For this reason, he served as the archetypal Fisher King of the pierced thigh (actually genitalia) or *morddwyd tyllion*. This act of mutilation robbed Osiris of his sexual identity at death, in a sense making him *female* — in the same way that Jesus took on a feminine role at *his* death. He had become, in a sense, a eunuch by undergoing an extreme form of circumcision in preparation for his marriage to the queen of heaven. As in *Genesis*, the two would become one, and he would symbolically become her.

Apparently, some people sought to achieve this androgynous state before death, thereby hoping to enter into the kingdom of heaven while still alive. Jesus spoke of their actions as controversial, though he did not explicitly condemn them. If anything, he gave his tacit blessing to the procedure, while acknowledging that it wasn't for everyone: "Not everyone can accept this word," he told his followers, "but only those to whom it has been given. For some are eunuchs because they were born that way; others were made that way by men; and others have made themselves eunuchs for the kingdom of heaven." [552]

They were doing so in imitation of Osiris, Jacob and the other heroes of the *morddwyd tyllion*. It is instructive to note that the Hebrew word denoting a eunuch is *saris*, found in variant form in Arabic as *srys* — referring literally to impotence or sterility.[553] These words both sound very much like the name Osiris, who was of course a eunuch himself after his death. They also sound like the name of the star Sirius, associated with Osiris' consort Isis, the queen of heaven *with whom he became one*. How? Certainly not by the traditional means of sexual intercourse, for he had been deprived of his phallus. The only other means available was by merging his identity with her and thereby returning to the androgynous condition that was humanity's original state — the state of being "like the angels" to which Jesus referred.

The spear used to pierce Jesus' side is a key factor in all of this. It is intriguing to find that the Hebrew word for spear or lance is *romah*, a name that evokes the name for the great city of Roma (Rome). Could it have been this play on words that caused the narrator to portray a Roman soldier as the culprit who thrust the spear into Jesus' side?

There is another apparent linguistic connection worth mentioning as well, hearkening back to the opening passages in *Matthew*. It is in this context that the author quotes the prophet Jeremiah as declaring: "A voice is heard in Ramah, weeping and great mourning; Rachel weeping for her children and refusing to be comforted, because they are no more." [554] The passage is invoked in reference to the so-called slaughter of the innocents, Herod's supposed campaign to murder all the young boys in the region as he sought to eliminate the threat of a new messiah. But it is perhaps even more appropriate in this context. And although the author of *Matthew* does not go so far as to invoke it a second time, several manuscripts of his work hint at its influence on his description of Jesus' final hours.

These manuscripts include an extra verse that brings the account into conformity with the narrative of *John* — to a degree. After describing the incident wherein someone offered him wine vinegar to drink, these texts insert the following bit of information: "But another, having taken a lance, stabbed at his side, and there came out water and blood." [555]

One might suspect at first that this material is a late addition, borrowed from the work of *John* and inserted into this narrative. Yet one piece of information mitigates against this. Here, the piercing of Jesus' side takes place before his death, whereas it occurs *afterward* in the work attributed to John. Certainly, the scribes could not have been so reckless as to have put it in the wrong place, could they? The most likely answer is that they didn't — that the material is in fact original to the text and was later removed, perhaps because it didn't conform to the information supplied by the author of *John*.

In these variant texts of *Matthew*, the piercing takes place immediately prior to an important event: "And when Jesus had cried out again in a loud voice, he gave up his spirit." [556] Without the spear incident, this loud cry seems to come out of nowhere. Yet when the information about the spear is included, it makes perfect sense — certainly someone would cry out loudly after being pierced with a spear. And it also makes better sense as a fulfillment of Jeremiah's prophecy: The voice of lamentation that is heard in Ramah is now given actual utterance as the voice of despair issuing forth from the cross in response to the spear, or *romah*. Once again, it is intriguing to point out that the original voice belonged to Rachel and was therefore feminine, further hinting at the roots of the crucifixion ceremony as a sacrifice of Inanna. Yet despite the gender gap, Rachel was a natural choice as a model for Jesus: Her name meant "ewe," while Jesus was the lamb of god.

According to the Torah, none of the Passover lamb's bones were to be broken when it was slain.[557] This was the commandment that was fulfilled through the spear, which succeeded in bringing about the death of the ultimate Passover lamb — Jesus — without breaking a single bone.

Despite the many layers of symbolism contained in the account of the spear, however, one must still wonder whether there is an actual historical component to the tale. Piercing the body of a crucified prisoner appears to have been an actual practice under such circumstances.[558] And although the author of *John* refers to the event as a fulfillment of the Zechariah oracle, he is emphatic in insisting that this particular occurrence is historical: "The man who saw it has given testimony, and his testimony is true." [559]

What are we to make of this? And what of the variant account in some texts of *Matthew*, which places the piercing before Jesus' death?

The symbolism involved in the blood and the water cannot obscure the possibility that the piercing actually took place, and that bodily fluids did in fact issue forth from the resultant wound. If this did happen, it would seem to indicate that Jesus' vital fluids were still circulating within him — in other words, that *he was not dead*. This would help explain, on a purely practical level, why the alternate versions of *Matthew* include this account before Jesus' death in contrast to the version supplied by *John*. This would be consistent with the hypothesis that Jesus was somehow drugged to appear dead when he was offered the "wine vinegar." If he were in fact alive but unconscious when the soldiers came back to check on him, they might well have assumed that he was dead but pierced him with the spear just to be sure. Such an act would have naturally roused Jesus from his drug-induced stupor and caused him to utter a loud cry. Jesus was obviously still alive; the question at this point was how long he would remain that way. If the spear had punctured his vital organs, he would not have long to live; if such were the case, no amount of restorative work by the Therapeutae or anyone else would be able to revive him.

Jesus was dying.

But he was not dead yet.

The Caiaphas Connection

Despite his apparent plans to somehow survive the crucifixion, it would seem that Jesus died shortly after his ordeal on the cross. Most records of him afterward portray him as a supernatural, often unrecognizable caricature of the man who had so boldly defied the

Roman Empire. Even the account in which he appears most human seems somehow contradictory. Jesus challenges one of his disciples (Thomas) to reach out and touch his wounds, thereby "proving" that he is not an apparition. Yet the narrator, in this case the author of *John*, contradicts this impression by stating that Jesus somehow entered the room unannounced even though the doors had been locked. Such activities are, in fact, the very stuff of apparitions.

In most other scenes, it is peculiar to find that his closest associates fail to even recognize him. For example, this odd condition afflicts some members of Jesus' inner circle when he appears to them during a fishing expedition on the Sea of Galilee. According to the author of *John*, "Jesus stood on the shore, but the disciples did not realize it was Jesus." [560]

The entire episode, however, is highly suspect. It is virtually identical to a scene related by the author of *Luke*, who places it not after Jesus' death but during his lifetime.[561] In both episodes, the disciples are fishing in their boats when Jesus directs them to a particular location. When they follow his instructions, their nets become so full of fish that it is impossible to haul them in without breaking them. In each instance, this miracle elicits a declaration from Peter concerning Jesus' identity as the messiah. There can be little doubt that these two narratives are based on a common tradition, and one that was not included in the original version of John's work.

Anyone reading *John*'s narrative is likely to be struck by the fact that it appears to conclude *before* the account of the fishing expedition, with the author declaring that "Jesus did many other miraculous signs in the presence of his disciples that are not recorded in this book." [562] This is obviously meant as a final statement intended to summarize the works of Jesus. It is therefore puzzling to find it followed by the account of yet another sign — the miraculous haul of fish. Obviously, an editor has been at work here (and not a very good one, at that). The awkwardness of the transition is only compounded when he attempts to summarize the material he has added in the least original manner possible: by repeating the conclusion supplied by the original author almost verbatim. "Jesus did many other things as well. If every one of them were written down, I suppose that even the whole world would not be able to contain the books." [563]

There is another instance in which Jesus is not recognized by his own followers. This is the famous scene from the road to Emmaus, preserved by the author of *Luke*, in which "Jesus" joins two disciples as they are walking along the road and engages them in a rather intense conversation as he travels with them for some distance. They eventually invite him to dine with them, but they still are unable to recognize him until he breaks bread with them.

At which point he vanishes.[564]

Again, Jesus appears to be little more than an apparition — or an exercise in wishful thinking. And this is probably exactly what he was. But there seems to have been something fueling the hopes of those who believed they had seen him, a certain undeniable fact that allowed them to imagine a set of circumstances whereby Jesus might have somehow survived the crucifixion. The fact in question was, of course, the empty tomb. According to all the gospel accounts, Jesus' followers arrived at the grave where he had been buried to find the body missing and the stone rolled away from the entrance. Later versions of this tale, preserved by the authors of *Matthew* and *Luke*, added drama to the episode by introducing an angel or two into the narrative. The presence of two such supernatural beings in *Luke* was likely meant to convey a symmetry conforming to that of the twin cherubim surmounting the casket that was the ark. In *Matthew*'s version, only one angel appears, and in the earliest version of the tale — reported by the author of *Mark* — no angels are involved at all. There is merely a single young man dressed in a white robe, who informs visitors to the tomb that Jesus "is going ahead of you into Galilee." [565]

Who was this young man? His white robe may well have marked him as a member of the Essenic brotherhood or the Therapeutae. The youth reports that Jesus has been raised, a term with several possible connotations. It might have meant, on the one hand, that he had been awakened; or it might simply have indicated that he had been lifted — that his body had been moved to his home region of Galilee for permanent interment. In either case, the account is at odds with those preserved in *John* and *Luke*, where the authors contend that Jesus appeared to his disciples not in Galilee but in Jerusalem. Indeed, there are so many disparities and outright contradictions among the four accepted accounts that it is nearly impossible to determine with any certainty what occurred.

Despite such incongruities, however, the gospel writers were able to agree on a few things. Among them was the identity of a key player in the drama, a man whose name surfaces here and nowhere else.

He was, it would appear, the ultimate insider.

His name: Joseph of Arimathea.

Another Voice from Ramah

Joseph was the man who asked Pilate for permission to take custody of Jesus' body after the crucifixion. He then placed it in his own personal tomb, apparently located in a garden not far from Jesus' place of execution. According to the author of *John*, he was accompanied by a member of the Sanhedrin named Nicodemus who had supported Jesus and now undertook to prepare his body for burial along with Joseph. The other three gospel writers, however, report that Joseph acted alone. It therefore seems quite possible that this enigmatic figure was the only person to have seen Jesus between the time of his crucifixion and his removal from the tomb.

And this raises the question: Just who was he?

The first important piece of information to consider is his status in the community. He was, according to the author of *Mark*, a member of the Sanhedrin — and not just any member, but a *prominent* member.[566] This would seem to indicate that he enjoyed a level of influence beyond that of an ordinary council member. It would also explain why one writer would refer to him as a friend of Pilate, one of sufficient personal and professional standing to secure the body of Jesus from the prefect. Yet he was also, according to this same author, a friend of Jesus who therefore had a vested personal interest in claiming the body.[567] By assuming this dual role, he was walking a fine line, courting the empire on the one hand and consorting with a subversive individual on the other. He was walking an extremely fine line, and it is therefore no surprise to find the author of *John* describe him as someone who kept his association with Jesus secret out of fear.[568]

This is, most likely, the reason that he seems to appear out of nowhere in the gospel narratives. Here was a man of some considerable influence who had been very careful to obscure his connection to the opposition movement. It is therefore doubtful that the writers should have known his true identity — or if they did, that they would be willing to reveal it by referring to the man by his given name.

But perhaps the name they gave him contains some sort of clue that might be useful in identifying him. It is perhaps significant that, unlike many figures in the gospel accounts who are introduced only by a single name, Joseph is known by two. He is identified specifically as being from the town of Arimathea, a village about twenty miles to the northeast of Jerusalem. The town's name means little until one realizes that it is the Greek form of a much more familiar Hebrew name.

Ramah.

This is, of course, the very same Ramah mentioned in the prophecy of Jeremiah quoted by the author of *Matthew*. But it was significant for another reason, as well: It was the hometown of a singular luminary in Hebrew lore, the prophet-priest Samuel, who according to legend had anointed David as the nation's greatest king. By identifying Joseph with this particular village, the author was linking him strongly to this tradition. And an interesting tradition it was.

Samuel was said to have been the product of a miraculous union between his father Elkanah and his mother Hannah, who had been unable to conceive a child for several years. She finally became pregnant, but only after a heartfelt prayer during which she vowed that no razor would ever touch the head of her hoped-for son — in other words, that he would be a lifelong Nazirite. The familiar motifs of the miraculous birth and Nazirite dedication certainly help identify the story as more legendary than historical, but it is the names of Samuel's parents that serve to make its mythical nature abundantly clear. The name Hannah is a slight variation on Anna, the queen of heaven, and her husband's name is even more revealing. It translates into Hebrew as *el qanah*: El, the highest god in the Canaanite pantheon, coupled with the familiar-sounding word for a reed or cane — a word that signifies (in its most basic form) erection. Elkanah is therefore the god of the erection, the dead Osiris in his ithyphallic form, while his wife Hannah is the queen of heaven.

Isis.

When it comes right down to it, the story of Samuel's conception is nothing more than a thinly veiled rewrite of Egyptian myth, in which Horus was the product of a miraculous union between Isis and Osiris. And just as Horus became priest-king of the Egyptian people, so Samuel assumed this role in Hebrew legend. In his later years, he underwent the customary transformation from Horus into Seth, from the young prince into the wise old king. And in this capacity, he anointed a successor.

His first choice, Saul, failed in his tanist challenge to Samuel. When he attempted to usurp Samuel's role as high priest too quickly by offering a sacrifice in his stead, he was rebuked and stripped of his authority. The old king, it would seem, was still very much in control of things. He remained too strong for this particular young challenger, who was summarily dismissed from his position in favor of a more worthy heir named David. And it is Samuel's anointing of David, the man who ended up succeeding him, that is particularly germane to the story of Joseph.

In the same way that Samuel had anointed David, so now Joseph of Arimathea would anoint the "son of David" and heir to the

Davidic throne. According to the author of *John*, he and Nicodemus brought with them a mixture of myrrh and aloes for just this purpose, then mummified the body by wrapping it in linen strips. It would therefore seem likely that Joseph was a priest like Samuel, and a very important one at that. Not only is he described as a prominent member of the Sanhedrin, but the name Arimathea — or Ramah — was derived from a word that designated something as lofty, high or exalted. Indeed, the name could easily have been read as Joseph the High.

High what?

High priest, perhaps?

As Joseph was a prominent member of the Sanhedrin and appears to have been a priest, such an identification would seem plausible. Yet historians are unanimous in attesting that this position was held by a man named Caiaphas during the period in question. Certainly this would seem to negate any possibility that Joseph of Arimathea served in this capacity — at least on the surface. But before reaching such a conclusion, one would do well to recall that Joseph was an insider, a secret follower of Jesus who would have put not only his position but his life at risk by revealing the nature of his ties to the rebel leader. As a result, it is highly improbable that he should have used his true name when dealing with the opposition. Is it just possible, therefore, that his true name was Caiaphas?

This would be something of a stretch without the invaluable testimony of the historian Josephus. Whereas the gospel writers refer to the high priest by the single name Caiaphas, Josephus is somewhat more complete. It would seem that the man in question had two names, and the historian was not shy about committing the high priest's other name to paper as well.

That other name was Joseph.

Joseph of Arimathea was, according to the author of *Mark*, the person who rolled the stone across the entrance to the tomb, thereby sealing it and setting the stage for the resurrection that was to follow. In this, he performed a function identical to that of Joseph Caiaphas, who had sealed Jesus' fate in similar fashion by prompting the Sanhedrin to condemn him to death. He had even rent his garments at the moment the decision was reached, thereby foreshadowing the rending of the temple veil reported later in the narrative.

Joseph Caiaphas, however, is portrayed in the canonical writings as anything but a friend of Jesus. It was he who provided Paul with the letters of authorization he needed to arrest Jesus on the road to the *dam koce*. And it was he who suggested to the Sanhedrin that Jesus be killed. According to the author of *John*, some members of the council were dismayed that Jesus' movement was growing to such an extent that the Romans were bound to see it as a threat. Then, they warned, the empire would arrive with its legions to occupy the temple and revoke whatever small measure of independence the Jewish people enjoyed.

Caiaphas' response was both chilling and pragmatic: "You know nothing at all," he told them. "You do not realize that it is better for you that one man die for the people than that the whole nation perish." [569]

On its surface, this statement would appear to indicate a high degree of hostility toward Jesus. Caiaphas was, in essence, suggesting that Jesus be killed as an atoning sacrifice for the nation's sins. Yet isn't this exactly what Jesus wanted? In fact, Caiaphas' words were in perfect harmony with Jesus' mission to orchestrate his own death and resurrection as a prelude to inaugurating the kingdom. The tone of Caiaphas' monologue seems to indicate that he was at odds with others of the council, whom he condemned as a bunch of know-nothings. It was his blistering speech that persuaded them to pursue the very course Jesus had set for himself.

This sounds very much like the action of a man acting in Jesus' interests, or even in his behalf.

With this in mind, the nighttime trial before the Sanhedrin can be seen in a whole new light. Even the gospel writers depict it as a dress rehearsal of sorts for Jesus' presentation to the Romans on charges they could accept. Caiaphas and Jesus both wanted to ensure that these charges would stick; they were united in this purpose. Yet Caiaphas' support of Jesus was still very much a secret, and there were those on the council who opposed the idea of turning him over to the Romans. Jesus therefore had to appear combative when addressing Caiaphas, obscuring their cooperative effort while at the same time strengthening the case for delivering him into Roman hands. It was a masterful acting job.

Caiaphas was probably also acting on Jesus' behalf when he handed Paul the documents ostensibly authorizing his arrest. It is worth remembering that Jesus appears to have known about Paul's intentions ahead of time, allowing him to surprise the man as he traveled along the road. And if he knew, someone must have told him. Certainly, that someone wasn't Paul, who at that point was quite hostile toward Jesus' movement; and considering the covert nature of the operation, it is unlikely that many others knew about his mission. Indeed, the only other person who *must* have known was the high priest himself. Caiaphas.

If Caiaphas were, in fact, in league with Jesus, it stands to reason that he set the whole thing up and then alerted Jesus to Paul's intentions, enabling the would-be messiah to intercept his foe along the way.

Caiaphas, who had held the position of high priest for eighteen years, was relieved of his duties within a year or so of Jesus' death. Though this may be pure coincidence, the clear possibility exists that someone found out about his connection to the failed revolutionary and alerted the Romans, who took it upon themselves to remove him from office. His family ossuary was discovered in a park just outside the old city of Jerusalem; containing the bones of a sixty-year-old man and some younger relatives, it bears the name "Yosef bar Caifa."

It is indeed highly ironic that Joseph's remains have been discovered, whereas the remains of the man he buried in his tomb are still unknown.

The Rock

The name Caiaphas itself is interesting in itself. One possible derivation is a Chaldean word meaning "the dell" — commonly applied to a small wooded valley or, perhaps, a garden. The author of *John* refers to Joseph of Arimathea burying Jesus in just such a place, while the apocryphal *Gospel of Peter* even goes so far as to name it as the "Garden of Joseph." In light of this, it is intriguing that the name Joseph Caiaphas might very well mean Joseph of the Garden.

But there is another linguistic connection that is perhaps even more tantalizing. One can hardly fail to notice the similarity between the names Caiaphas and Cephas, the latter being the Greek form of the name Peter, meaning "rock." Indeed, the two words are identical save for a minor variation in their vowel structures. Was Caiaphas, like Peter, therefore associated with a rock of some sort? As high priest, he convened the Sanhedrin in a place called the Chamber of Hewn Stone in the temple, a location of great significance that served as the seat of power for the Jewish aristocracy.

The fact that this chamber was in the temple itself is of significant import, given the symbolism surrounding the great sacred structure. The temple, after all, originally functioned as a resting place for the dead king and was considered a gateway to the afterlife, whereby the departed "father" Osiris might gain access to the paradisical garden planted at the beginning of time. It was for this reason that the original temple of Solomon is said to have been adorned with images of fertility and vegetation, the doors to the inner sanctuary decorated with carvings of palm trees (the symbol of the phoenix) and open flowers, overlaid in gold.[570] Images of gourds appeared elsewhere, while pomegranates and lilies adorned the capitals of pillars that were themselves designed to resemble sturdy trees.

The temple's symbolic character as a garden reveals a striking parallel with the garden belonging to Joseph of Arimathea. This latter even had its own chamber of hewn stone, the "tomb cut out of rock" in which Jesus' body was lain. And in each case, the chamber was presided over by someone named Joseph.

The author of *Matthew* cements the parallel between temple and garden even further. In a bit of dramatic storytelling that appears nowhere else in the gospel accounts, he reports that a great earthquake occurred at the moment of Jesus' death, causing rocks to split in two and tombs to be opened. He further contends, in a detail repeated elsewhere, that the veil of the temple's inner sanctuary was rent down the middle. These events set the stage for a *second* earthquake a short time later, coinciding with Jesus' supposed resurrection. This second cataclysm causes the stone to be rolled away from the entrance to the tomb in Joseph's garden, in much the same way that the first temblor uncovered the temple's holy of holies. Such a vivid parallel is certainly not to be missed, and it becomes all the more potent upon recalling that the temple's inner sanctuary was originally designed to function as a tomb — the final resting place of the casket, or ark, that contained the dead king's remains.

It was, in fact, a garden tomb.

On the ark itself were perched two cherubim, so it was only natural that the authors of *Luke* and *John* should place two angels (or men clothed in glowing raiment) in the garden tomb. This symbolism is clearest in *John*, which place the angels "where Jesus' body had been, one at the head and the other at the foot." [571] It is a description that corresponds perfectly to that of the ark casket, upon which the cherubim were situated at either end. Now, in the same way that the ark itself had disappeared, so Jesus' body was missing.

Though the author of *Matthew* only mentions one angel in connection with the tomb, it is clear that he took much of the inspiration for his dramatic description from the eighteenth psalm, in which the cherubim and an earthquake both play prominent roles. The context? David was being rescued from the "cords of the grave," just as the son of David was now being similarly delivered from the tomb. According to the psalmist, "the earth trembled and quaked, and the foundations of the mountains shook." [572] Yahweh himself then descended on the wings of the cherubim, manifesting himself as the storm god he was, cloaked in rainclouds and sending forth hailstones and bolts of lightning. This imagery was not missed by the author of *Luke*, who declared that the two visitors to the tomb were clothed in garments that flashed like lightning.[573] Nor was the psalmist's declaration that Yahweh cloaked himself in darkness ignored by the author of *Matthew*, who used it as a basis for the solar eclipse that appears in his account in the hour of Jesus' death.

This dramatic eclipse was accompanied by another, similarly telling sign — the rending of the veil in the temple's inner sanctuary. The darkness bespoke the union of the sun god and the moon goddess, the celestial circumcision that marked their coupling and accompanied the death of the sun solar hero, thereby paving the way for his rebirth as the phoenix. The rending of the veil held similar import, for it represented the tearing of the goddess' hymen and signified that the god was re-entering the womb of Mother Earth, whence he would be born again.

The prophet Amos had foretold the darkening of the solar disk: "I will make the sun go down at noon and darken the earth until in broad daylight," he had declared. "I will turn your religious feasts into mourning ... like mourning for an only son." [574] There could have been no better framework for the story of Jesus' death than this prophecy. The man who had called God his father had been crucified on the eve of the Passover — the greatest of Jewish feasts.

The Passover lamb had been slain, but what would happen now?

The Empty Tomb

Once the Sabbath was over, Mary Magdalene did not waste any time.

At daybreak, she hurried out to the tomb with the intent of preparing Jesus' body for burial. But when she arrived, she found that someone else had gotten there first. The stone that had been laid across the entrance to the tomb had been rolled away, and she realized in a flash that she was not alone.

But who was there with her?

According to the oldest account of the incident, preserved by the author of *Mark*, it was a single young man clothed in white. But the author of *John* introduces a mysterious figure that Mary initially identifies as "the gardener." This would seem at first glance to indicate the owner of the garden, Joseph of Arimathea. Such an identification is reasonable, for Joseph had, according to this same author, visited the tomb after nightfall to embalm the body. He was also the owner of the property, and was therefore the person most likely to be there. Yet the author confounds this natural supposition by throwing in a strange twist, equating the so-called gardener with Jesus himself. This is a jarring assertion that leaves the reader scratching his head. Even Mary herself is reluctant to entertain the idea and proceeds to speak on the assumption that she is talking to the gardener.

According to the author of *John*, Mary "turned around and saw Jesus standing there, but did not realize that it was Jesus." [575]

On its surface, this appears to be yet another case in which a close associate of Jesus (in this case his wife) inexplicably fails to recognize him. But on closer inspection, it becomes clear there is something more at play. Recall that Osiris himself was identified as "the gardener." Here, Jesus was cast in the role of the risen Osiris, having been mummified in very much the same manner that described in the story of Lazarus.

But Joseph of Arimathea, the actual gardener, was probably also present, along with the young man in white. The account in *John* is garbled and confusing, but it is possible to make some sense out of it.

According to the narrative, Mary then begins a short dialogue with someone who asks her why she is crying and whom she is seeking. The way the passage is written, it appears she is talking to Jesus, but these questions would have made no sense at all on the lips of Jesus himself; this was his wife, after all. The object of her search would have been patently obvious, and one can scarcely imagine

Jesus taunting her by pretending to be someone he was not — then compounding the cruelty by asking her such a question. Certainly the question must have been posed by someone who did not in fact know the answer. And that someone could not have been Jesus. It must have been either Joseph or the young man in white.

Mary responds that she wants to know where Jesus' body has been taken, but the exchange is cut short by a single word.

According to the author of *John*, Jesus then speaks her name. "Mary."

Whereupon the woman turns toward Jesus in sudden recognition and cries out. She seems to have run up to him, as one might expect in such a situation, making as if to throw her arms around him. She would have been overjoyed. Relieved. Ecstatic to find that her husband was in fact alive. Yet the author reports that he stopped her short, cautioning her not to touch him because he had not yet ascended to his father.

The author's poorly structured narrative makes it seem as though this is the second time Mary is speaking to Jesus. But as we have seen, the she must have been speaking to someone else. This is confirmed by a doublet in the narrative that would not otherwise make sense: When Mary first sees Jesus, she turns toward him and fails to recognize him. She then engages someone else in a brief dialogue, whereupon she hears her name and *turns toward Jesus again*. This implies that she had turned away after seeing him the first time, focusing her attention instead upon the second person. Not Jesus. Probably Joseph of Arimathea. Joseph's identity as the owner of a garden plot and Jesus' identity as Osiris "the gardener" may have confused the author into creating an incoherent narrative.

Once this is clear, however, we can disentangle the threads and make some sense of it.

Joseph and the white-robed man have been attending to Jesus, preparing him to assume the guise of Osiris and ascend to the father. He is obviously on the point of death, so badly battered and drained from his ordeal that he is barely recognizable. Indeed, he is so weak he is only able to utter a single word: the name of his beloved.

"Mary."

This is what causes her to turn again and face him, as recognition suddenly dawns. It is the first time Jesus himself has spoken to her, the previous exchange having involved someone else. At once, she recognizes his voice and rushes to him. She had seen him there before but had failed to recognize him, not because she had mistaken him for someone else but simply because of his physical appearance. The scars on his face, the wound in his side, the bruises all across his body ...

She wants to hold him, to comfort him. But he cannot allow it. He has not yet ascended to the father, and his body is failing. In a short time, he knows, he will be dead, and he has one thing yet to do. When Mary had come upon him at the tomb, he had been in the midst of an ancient and sacred ceremony that was crucial to the kingdom of God. This was the ceremony of the opening of the mouth, during which the mummified dead king Osiris was *raised* into a standing position. In other words, resurrected. One man who claimed to have taken part in such a ceremony was the infamous sorcerer Simon Magus, who thereafter claimed as his title the Standing One. (More will be said about this enigmatic figure shortly.) In this light, it is probably no accident that Jesus is described as "standing there" when Mary first notices him.

In point of fact, it would have been impossible for him to stand on his own, having suffered two broken legs during the crucifixion. He would have required two men to hold him up. Two priests, one representing Seth and the other Horus, holding him upright just as Aaron and Hur had held Moses' arms upright just before his death. In this case, the two men in question would have been Joseph of Arimathea and the enigmatic young man in white mentioned by the author of *Mark*.

This opening of the mouth ceremony required the participation of two priests, the *kher heb* and another priest identified as Horus — the princely successor to Osiris who is identified in the Egyptian

Book of the Dead as the *sem* priest. This designation is entirely fitting, for the word *sem* meant nothing more than "son." [576] It is identical to the name of the patriarch Shem, whose named served as the basis for the word "Semitic" — literally, people of the son. It may also be related to "semen," the seed of Abraham. And the son, or seed, was none other than Horus, incarnation of the eternal heavenly father and keeper of the throne.

The messiah.

The opening of the mouth ceremony involved, as the name implies, the opening of the dead pharaoh's mouth. A distant echo of this tradition may be present in the account of John the Baptist's birth preserved by the author of *Luke*. In this narrative, the Baptist's father Zechariah is struck dumb by an angel for doubting that his aged wife would be able to conceive a child. Zechariah further protests that he himself is an old man and therefore, by implication, no longer able to father a child. Yet his name would seem to indicate otherwise. In Hebrew, *zekar-yah* was said to mean "Yahweh remembers," but this is something of a euphemistic gloss on the actual source of the name. Actually, Zechariah seems more closely related to the Arabic word *zakar*, which refers to the phallus and also appears related to the Egyptian god Seker, whom we have already met briefly.

This god was considered a guardian of tombs and was, as mentioned earlier, identified in many respects with the dead king Osiris — sometimes depicted with an erect phallus.

There was even explicit mention of this particular god in the opening of the mouth liturgy, wherein the *kher heb* priest declares: "I have pressed your mouth for you, even as your father has pressed it in the name of Seker." [577] John the Baptist was, of course, a *kher heb* priest. And his father, whose name apparently meant either "phallus of Yahweh" or "the god Seker manifest through Yahweh," was the dead king Osiris whose erect phallus was the instrument for continuing the royal line. This is doubtless why the author of *Luke* reported that Zechariah's "mouth was opened" on the day that John was circumcised and given his name.[578] John was the *sem* priest Horus, receiving his royal name upon succeeding his dead father to the throne — in this case the high priesthood at the temple in Leontopolis.

In Jesus' case, the opening of the mouth may have corresponded to the opening of the tomb wherein he had been placed. The Egyptian ceremony traditionally took place at the entrance to the tomb, just as the ritual involving Jesus was carried forth before the opening to the garden gravesite.[579] As mentioned earlier, this ceremony centered on the opening of the dead king's eyes and mouth through the intervention of his son Horus, represented by the *sem* priest. The purpose of opening the mouth was two-fold. First, it ensured that the heavenly father's voice could issue forth: The *sem* priest is made to declare in the liturgy that the dead king "shall speak again." Second, it allowed the deceased pharaoh to be nourished again. The ceremony specifically called for the *sem* priest to make an offering of grapes, which he stepped forward to place in the mummified king's mouth once it was open.

Grapes were symbolic of the lifeblood and source of the wine that inspired men with its intoxicating effects. The word "inspired" is appropriate here, for it stems from the ancient belief that men under the influence of alcohol and similar drugs were experiencing the effects of a *spirit in* them. This is likewise the origin of the phenomenon referred to as demon possession, for the word daemon means nothing more or less than "spirit." By feeding the mummified king grapes, the *sem* priest was attempting to re-animate the corpse by providing it with the sacred blood of life.

There is no direct reference to this grape ritual in connection with Jesus' resurrection, but there is a tantalizing prediction from Jesus himself, already referred to here, that seems to imply that it would take place: "I tell you the truth, I will not drink again of the fruit of the vine until that day when I drink it anew in the kingdom of God." Grapes were, of course, the fruit of the vine. It certainly seems conceivable that Jesus was referring to his future participation in the opening of the mouth ritual, in which he would be fed the fruit of the vine by his *sem* priest successor.

Indeed, both the *sem* priest and the other primary figure in the opening of the mouth, the *kher heb*, seem to have been present in the gospel narratives at the empty tomb. The high priest Joseph of Arimathea plays the latter role, while the young man in the white garment who is introduced by the author of *Mark* serves as the *sem*. This man, too, must have been a priest. And though he is not identified by name in the gospel accounts, his identity can be deduced from other sources with a reasonable degree of certainty.

In the ceremony, he is Horus, the successor to Osiris — Jesus.

And we know without question who succeeded Jesus as the leader of the Jewish nationalists. He was a man known specifically as a righteous priest, a son of Joazar who was therefore Jesus' brother/cousin.

A man named James.

The Gospel of Thomas is unequivocal in proclaiming James as heir to Jesus' mantle, quoting Jesus himself as designating his kinsman as the man to follow in his footsteps: "Wherever you have come, you will go to James the Just, for whose sake heaven and earth have come into being." [580] This is quite a ringing endorsement. It identifies James without question as the man destined to inaugurate the kingdom of heaven on earth. His status as head of the nationalist movement is confirmed by the author of *Acts*, where he is depicted as the man who has the final word in decisions made by the resistance leaders.[581] It is also clearly implied by Paul in his epistles: He names James first among the "pillars" of the leadership and reports an incident in which James appoints a delegation to act on behalf of that group.

A fragment from the so-called *Gospel of the Hebrews* indicates that James was perhaps the first to actually see Jesus after he had "risen," which would make sense if James was the unnamed young man in white at the tomb. (Though he was not in fact particularly young, his role as heir to the throne rendered him youthful in a symbolic sense.)

Appropriately enough, a tradition was preserved that James used to wear linen robes.[582]

The Gospel of the Hebrews also makes reference to such a garment. It maintains that Jesus appeared to James when he "had given the linen cloth to the servant of the priest." The high priest at this point in time was Joseph Caiaphas, a.k.a. Joseph of Arimathea, who was present during the opening of the mouth ceremony; James, likewise, would serve as a high priest, though he would serve in that capacity for the opposition (perhaps at the temple in Leontopolis). The identity of the servant himself is left a mystery in the brief passage, but it is irrelevant to the writer's purpose in establishing James as the chosen successor of Jesus. The *sem* priest. The author relates that James had taken an oath to eat no bread until he should see the risen Jesus. It then describes his encounter with the resurrected messiah, who invites him to break his fast because "the son of man has risen from among those who sleep." [583]

This scene is almost certainly symbolic, for Jesus appears to have died shortly after being "raised."

The narrative does, however, draw a distinct parallel between Jesus and James. The former had vowed to abstain from the fruit of the vine until he might taste it again in his father's kingdom. James, in similar fashion, had pledged to take no bread. The wine represented the spirit of a man that coursed through his veins and gave him life; the bread was his body, his physical presence in this world. When Jesus was given the fruit of the vine during the opening of the mouth ceremony, it was so that he could be transformed into a spirit and thereby ascend to the heavens; when James partook of the bread, he became the new incarnation of the divine presence. He was the *sem* priest or son. He had become Horus in the flesh, having inherited this mantle directly from Jesus — indeed, at his express invitation.

The tradition that James succeeded Jesus as leader of the group would seem to argue against the persistent rumor that Mary Magdalene had born a child to the fallen messiah. Though she must have become pregnant at some point, having been cured of her "issue of blood" (i.e. her menstrual cycle was interrupted), it is possible that the child was not carried to term or died in its youth. In an age long before vaccinations and sterile environments, infant mortality rates were high; this would explain why Jesus chose his cousin/brother to succeed him rather than a son. But it was also possible that she had a baby girl — a princess who would carry on the royal bloodline in the ancient matrilineal tradition. Indeed, there was a tradition that just such a girl, Sarah (whose name meant "princess") accompanied the Magdalene to France after the death of Jesus.

The Order of Melchizedek

Jesus was probably barely alive when he took part in the opening of the mouth ceremony. The wounds inflicted upon him had sapped his strength, and the life was rapidly draining out of him. When confronted by Mary Magdalene outside the tomb, he informed her that his departure was imminent — occurring even as they spoke: "I am returning to my father and your father; to your God and my God." [584] This was the message he instructed her to give his brothers, implying that he would not be around long enough to do so himself.

Despite the contention that Jesus remained on earth for forty days and made contact with his disciples after emerging from the tomb, the likelihood is that he departed this world within days or even hours of his resurrection. The forty days mentioned by the author of *Acts* is likely symbolic, corresponding to the forty days he had spent in the desert following his baptism — the symbolic rebirth that was now being played out in much more literal fashion. During those first forty days, he had engaged in the familiar wilderness ritual, a tanist combat with "Satan" in the form of his predecessor, John the Baptist. Now it was he who played the role of Seth, with his successor James taking on the part of Horus. Certain sects among his followers recognized this all too well, depicting Jesus as a man with the head of a donkey (the animal so closely associated with Seth) hanging on the cross. Had Jesus not been pierced with a spear, just as Seth was finally vanquished when his hippopotamus form was harpooned as he stood straddling the mighty Nile? As in the forty-day wilderness ordeal after his baptism, the model of Elijah and Elisha was used to craft the emerging legend of the dying master and the apprentice destined to carry forth his legacy. Elijah had anointed Elisha as his successor, imparting to him a double portion of his spirit and then ascending to heaven in a fiery chariot; John had selected Jesus; now Jesus similarly appointed James. Like Elijah, Jesus would be "taken up into heaven." [585]

At that point, the Elijah metaphor had served its purpose.

Once he had ascended, the risen Jesus took on the aspect of another legendary character from the Hebrew scriptures.

Melchizedek.

The name belonged to a mysterious character from the book of *Genesis* who encountered Abraham and blessed him. According to the *Genesis* account, Melchizedek arrived on the scene shortly after Abraham led his army of retainers to victory over an allied force headed by four kings — men who had kidnapped his brother, Lot, in southeastern Palestine. The initial battle took place in the Valley of Siddim, a word that simply means "the flats" and is described as being "full of tar pits." The reference to the Dead Sea (referred to here as the Salt Sea), with its flat geography and asphalt deposits, is unmistakable. It was a lifeless, barren region filled with salt deposits that left it devoid of fresh water and vegetation. Its fate was attributed, in the language of poetry, to the wrath of the Elohim against two cities that had stood upon the plain.

Sodom and Gomorrah, the legend said, had been destroyed for their wicked deeds. The gods had rained burning sulfur down on them from heaven, destroying everything that lived upon the plain: "all those living in the cities and the vegetation in the land." When Abraham looked out on the plain the next morning, "he saw dense smoke rising from the land, like the smoke from a furnace" — the waves of heat rising off the barren desert. Lot fled the area with his wife, who unwisely looked back in defiance of a divine edict and was transformed into one of the salt pillars that stood along the Dead Sea plain.[586]

Those mythic events, however, were said to have occurred sometime after the battle of Siddim. When the battle took place, according to *Genesis*, the cities of Sodom and Gomorrah were still standing. Indeed, Lot had settled in Sodom and was almost certainly fighting for the Sodomite forces — part of the defeated coalition — when he was taken captive at Siddim.

His captors subsequently transported him to a place called Dan.

This place is not to be confused with the city or region of Dan, which was not so designated until long after Abraham's time. Dan meant, simply, "judge." And the appellation most likely referred to the area where judgment was carried out against Abraham's enemies. It was there that Abraham, upon hearing that his brother had been taken prisoner, organized a night raid against his captors to obtain Lot's release. It was a huge success. According to *Genesis*, Abraham routed his enemies, "pursuing them as far as Hobah, north of Damascus."

It is startling to find the name Damascus in an account of events associated with the Dead Sea. Certainly, it seems out of place. The city of Damascus was nowhere near the salty inland lake — indeed, it lay well over a hundred miles from its extreme northern tip. Yet more than two thousand years later, the scribes at Qumran on the shores of that same body of water would similarly write about the new covenant in the land of Damascus, not referring to the city of Damascus in Syria, but to the *dam koce* — the blood of the cup. The cup of sacrifice, bearing the blood spilled by martyrs in a great struggle against oppression.

A holy war.

And Abraham, like the Dead Sea freedom fighters, was at war.

It was a long way from the desolate hills and arid wasteland by the lakeside to the city of Damascus. Abraham might have pursued them that far, but it is more likely that he put them to flight near the site of the initial battle, on the Dead Sea plain, chasing them as the retreated to a place called Hobah — a Hebrew word that means "hiding place." There were plenty of hiding places in the region of the Dead Sea. It was there, among the crags and caves of En Gedi on the lake's western shore, that the fugitive general David was said to have hidden from King Saul.[587] And it was there that the Qumran revolutionaries would make their headquarters, hiding their precious writings in caves just to the north of where David reportedly took refuge.

The terrain would have provided a natural *hobah*, or hiding place, for the men fleeing Abraham.

Yet if this hiding place was north of "Damascus," that must have meant Damascus was somewhere nearby — not in Syria, but on the shores of the Dead Sea. It was in this very place that the Qumran scribes would write of their new covenant in the land of Damascus, their new covenant in the cup of blood — the *dam koce*. It was the place where they would prepare for war, planning strategy for the coming apocalyptic clash between the sons of light and the sons of darkness.

The military watchtower at Qumran and the words of the *War Scroll* they buried in the caves there testify to their intentions. Just as their progenitor, Abraham, had routed his wicked enemies on the plain of Sodom and Gomorrah, the sons of light would rout the sons of darkness in the final apocalyptic conflict.

It was foreordained.

That first battle had set the stage for Abraham's encounter with Melchizedek, a shadowy character who would become the resistance movement's most powerful symbol. His name included the familiar suffix -*zedek*, or *zadok*, meaning "righteousness" or "justice" that served as the cornerstone concept for the movement. The full name meant "king of righteousness," yet another case in which a name is actually a description.

Melchizedek was indeed a king. He is described as the king of Salem, an early name for Jerusalem that also happens to mean "peace." And he was also a priest of the most high God. In the latter capacity, he declared: "Blessed be Abram by the most high God, creator of heaven and earth. And blessed be the most high God, who delivered your enemies into your hand."

The allegorical nature of the passage is unmistakable: After a cataclysmic battle between the forces of good and evil, a figure arrives representing peace and blessing. According to the writer of *Genesis*, Melchizedek "brought out bread and wine" to Abraham. Here was the origin of both the ritual meal at Qumran and the so-called last supper of Jesus. It is also the model for the account in *The Gospel of the Hebrews*, wherein it is said that the risen Jesus instructed James to "bring a table and bread." According to this passage, James had vowed not to eat bread "from that hour in which he had drunk the cup of the lord until he should see him risen from among them that sleep." Jesus would now assure him that this vow had been fulfilled. When James had brought the table as instructed, it is related that Jesus "took the bread and broke it, giving it to James the Just and saying to him, 'My brother, eat your bread, for the son of man is risen from among those who sleep.'" [588]

The absence of wine might seem problematic, but it is easily explained in light of James' status as a Nazirite who had pledged never to consume the fruit of the vine. This pledge left the author in something of a quandary, for he could not very well depict James drinking wine, yet at the same time he wished to preserve the complete imagery of body *and* blood. He ended up walking a tightrope by conceding on the one hand that James had in fact "drunk of the cup of the lord" while carefully omitting any reference to its contents — the wine.

By eating the broken bread, James was in fact partaking of Jesus' broken body in symbolic fashion. The disciples had reportedly done likewise at the last supper, when Jesus broke bread and declared: "This is my body, which is broken for you." [589] They had thereby become his successors, the body of Christ.

But where did this tradition come from?

The earliest reference to it occurs in Paul's first letter to his followers in Corinth, and it therefore reflects his thinking on the matter. It was Paul who came up with the idea that the full assembly constituted the new body of Christ, a concept he referred to extensively in his writings.

This was a natural extension of his background as a Roman citizen well acquainted with the democratic ideals of Hellenistic society, a man who would fight tooth and nail to include ethnic Greeks at the very heart of the movement begun by Jesus. His goals would bring him into direct conflict with James, who viewed the movement first and foremost as means of restoring the kingdom of heaven and doing away with everything the Greeks and Romans had brought in to pollute the purity of Israel. If Paul's leanings were toward inclusion, James' were firmly in the camp of tradition — a tradition that embraced the concept of a monarchy headed by the one true God and his incarnate son on earth. Until now, that had been Jesus; now it was James himself.

James was the new Horus, the one who claimed against Paul's assertions that he, personally, was the body of Christ. This was the meaning of the tradition contained in *The Gospel of the Hebrews*, which depicted James alone as partaking of the bread that represented the body of Jesus.

It was James, not the assembly at large, who was to become the incarnation of the father on earth.

The new Horus.

When the followers of Paul, with the help of the Roman legions, ultimately managed to defeat James' faction, they lost no time in suppressing the legends surrounding the man Jesus had chosen to succeed him and substituting their own traditions in their place. But in fragments of such documents as *The Gospel of the Hebrews*, along with certain references in the canonical accounts (even Paul's own letters) portions of the James' story were preserved so that it may now be reconstructed with a fair degree of accuracy.

In serving the bread to his brother, Jesus was playing the part of

Melchizedek while James took the role of Abraham. The point of the *Genesis* account was to portray Melchizedek, the king of Salem (Jerusalem) passing his authority to Abraham and thereby conferring upon his descendants the right to rule his holy city. Jesus, who had been crucified as king of the Jews, was now conferring the same honor upon his brother James.

It was a promise that, although Jesus was dying, his dream was not. James would carry it forward in his behalf, leading the sons of light to victory over their enemies on earth while Jesus himself ascended to command the armies of heaven. The psalmist had foreseen this day and sung its praises:

> *The lord says to my lord:*
> *"Sit at my right hand*
> *Until I make your enemies a footstool for your feet."*
>
> *The lord will extend your mighty scepter from Zion.*
> *You will rule in the midst of your enemies.*
> *Your troops will be willing on the day of battle.*
> *Arrayed in holy majesty from the womb of the dawn,*
> *You will receive the dew of your youth.*
> *The lord has sworn and will not change his mind:*
> *"You are a priest forever,*
> *In the order of Melchizedek."*

James became the new Abraham, carrying out the divine mandate on earth. Like Abraham, he would go to war in the cause of righteousness on the Dead Sea plain. Like Abraham, who had established the old covenant in blood of circumcision, he would establish a new covenant in the blood of the cup.

And like Melchizedek, Jesus would return when the war was over to bless him.

Throughout ancient literature, Jesus would be portrayed as seated at the right hand of power, waiting for the chosen moment to return.

With James' own dying words, he would answer those who asked him about Jesus: "Why do you question me about the son of man? I tell you, he is sitting in heaven at the right hand of the great power, and he will come on the clouds of heaven." [590]

Those at Qumran believed that it was Melchizedek who would carry out Yahweh's judgment and deliver the captives from their enemies. God would allow them to share in the inheritance of Melchizedek, who would return "and proclaim them liberty, forgiving them of all their iniquities." [591] This was, of course, exactly the role ascribed to Jesus in ancient texts. According to the gospels, Jesus had declared forgiveness of sins and announced that he had come to proclaim liberty to the captives.[592]

The Epistle to the Hebrews made the connection explicit. According to the author, Jesus "became a source of eternal salvation for all who obey him and was designated by God as high priest in the order of Melchizedek." [593]

The resistance clearly considered the legend of Abraham and Melchizedek a model for the apocalypse and its aftermath.

➢ Once again, there would be a great battle on the Dead Sea plain.
➢ Once again, God would rain down judgment upon the sons of darkness.
➢ Once again, God would choose a favorite (Abraham/James) to lead his forces into battle and uphold a divine covenant of blood.
➢ And once again, God would send a mysterious divine agent (Melchizedek/Jesus) at the conclusion of that battle to declare peace and inaugurate a new era of blessing.

This model has endured for two thousand years. The resistance movement was ultimately crushed, and the empire that defeated it is long dead. Yet many continue to believe that a final, cataclysmic battle will take place, signaling the return of Jesus from heaven to usher in a new era of peace and blessing. An apocalypse followed by a golden millennium. The images are powerful — indeed, so powerful that the hope they engender has long outlived the events that inspired them in the first place.

Are they still relevant in this modern age?

That is a question only the individual can answer.

The Sorcerer

And so, it would seem, we have come full circle. We began with an account of Isis mourning her dead husband Osiris, and we conclude with the tale of Mary Magdalene grieving over Jesus.

We would be remiss, however, not to at least briefly examine where this has brought us. What happened in the years following Jesus' death that transformed a messianic movement into a universal faith? Who was responsible for this fundamental change, and just what occurred to make it possible?

The answers to these questions may be found in a struggle that took place during the three decades after Jesus' death, a bitter confrontation between imperial Rome and the independence movement in Judea. The conflict had been simmering since Pompey's invasion of the temple a century before the crucifixion. It had flared under Judas the Galilean, and again under John the Baptist and Jesus. But now two new and compelling figures took the stage to test one another in a battle of wits and wills, and the stakes were higher than ever. In the end, the winner would determine the course not just of the Roman Empire but of western civilization as a whole.

On one side stood James, Jesus' chosen successor to the

independence movement; on the other stood a man whose aspirations clashed fundamentally with those of his opponent. We have met the man in question under the name of Simon the Pharisee or Simon the leper, a man who would eventually come to be known under a different name altogether.

Paul.

The fact that he used this name exclusively in referring to himself speaks volumes. It indicates clearly that he preferred to think of himself as a product of Greek and Roman culture, downplaying his status as an ethnic Jew. The editor who compiled the *The Acts of the Apostles*, in telling his story, does not refer to him as "Paul" until midway through his work — the first such reference occurring during an episode on the island of Cyprus, an island governed by a man named Sergius Paulus. The implication is that Paul perhaps adopted this man as a sort of patron, taking his name in a gesture of respect for the proconsul.

The *Roman* proconsul.

His decision to associate himself so closely with an agent of the empire is emblematic of the starkly divergent paths followed by James and Paul in the wake of Jesus' death. For both, this event had been a milestone of tremendous import. Yet the two men drew radically different conclusions about its significance. For James, it was a sign that Israel had not yet succeeded in attaining the degree of piety necessary to force God's hand in inaugurating his kingdom. He therefore set about implementing a program notable for its austerity and conservatism. Whereas Jesus had reached out to court allies in the mainstream, James took the opposite tack and formed a tightly knit community known for its rigorous standards of piety rather than its openness.

Under James' leadership, the group met regularly in a place known as Solomon's Portico, a colonnade on the eastern side of the temple complex. But though they gathered openly, the author of *Acts* reports that "few dared to join them, even though they were highly regarded." [594]

The source of this apprehension can be determined readily enough. The opposition movement under James was no place for the faint of heart. Strict rules of conduct were followed, analogous to those in effect at the Qumran community on the Dead Sea, and these rules were enforced with a ruthless certitude that made men understandably wary.

At Qumran, members of the community were required to "eat in common, bless in common and deliberate in common." [595] James now established a similar program, under which "all the believers were together and had everything in common. ... Every day, they continued to meet together in the temple courts. They broke bread and ate together with glad and sincere hearts, praising God and enjoying the favor of all the people." [596]

James laid a great deal of emphasis on the ideal of poverty. These were, after all, the Ebionites — the Poor. At Qumran, anyone admitted to the community was expected to hand over his property to the common fund (Jesus had reportedly demanded the same thing of a wealthy man he came across during his travels).[597] Now, this practice was followed in James' community: "No one claimed to have any possessions of his own, but shared everything they had. ... None among them was needy. From time to time, those who owned lands or houses sold them, brought the money and put it at the apostles' feet. It was distributed to anyone as he had need." [598]

The punishment for failing to do so was swift and severe.

A member of the Qumran community caught lying about his property would be banned from eating the common meal for one year. He would also have his food rations cut by one quarter.[599] Banning such a person from the common table may have amounted to declaring the offender figuratively "dead" to the community for a period of time, and it appears that just such a fate befell a certain man and his wife in Acts. The couple, Ananias and Sapphira, sold a piece of property and handed over part of the profits — while secretly holding back the rest for themselves. When Simon Peter confronted them with the truth, they both reportedly "fell down and died." [600]

It is hard to believe that they actually expired on the spot. More likely, they simply were declared ritually impure and ostracized from the common table fellowship, thereby rendering them dead in a symbolic sense. There could be no compromise when it came to the laws of God; every violation hindered the advent of heaven's kingdom, and therefore could not be tolerated. James, as a Nazirite and an ascetic purist, held to this principle above all others and set about crafting the opposition movement in this image.

"What good is it," he is said to have written, "if a man claims to have faith but has no deeds? Can such faith save him?" [601]

In James' mind, the answer was clearly no.

But while James was setting up a community based on rigorous adherence to the Torah and an unstinting dedication to good deeds, Paul was embarking on an altogether different journey. Jesus' death had affected him as well, but it had led him to conclusions that were diametrically opposed to those of James. On the issue of faith and deeds, for example, Paul believed that James was fundamentally mistaken. The kingdom of heaven could never be established by following the law, he insisted. Indeed, the pursuit of righteousness had been *hindered* all these years by Jews who "pursued it not by faith, but as if it were by deeds." [602] His position was simple: "We maintain that a man is justified by faith, apart from observing the law."[603]

Ironically, however, it was James who still had faith. He was convinced, in spite of past failures and the empire's overwhelming military superiority, that God would deliver Israel from her oppressors if only the nation demonstrated its resolve. Its purity. Its dedication to the law.

Paul, on the other hand, operated under no such illusion. He was a pragmatist who had reached the conclusion that it was impossible to keep the entire law. All had sinned, he declared, and therefore had fallen short of God's glory. It was a game that simply could not be won, so the only alternative was to rewrite the rules and start over. This is what Paul sought to do, not only theologically but in a political sense as well. The same sort of pragmatism that had led him to argue against the notion of perfect piety also brought him to the inevitable conclusion that James refused to accept: Rome could not be beaten. If it was impossible to keep the law without faltering, it was equally impractical to hold out any hope of defeating the imperial armies.

In a way, it was natural that Paul should have chosen this course. Unlike James, a man born into a tradition of Jewish nationalism, Paul was a Roman citizen who had spent a portion of his life in the highly cosmopolitan city of Tarsus. His father Gamaliel was a pragmatist as well, who thought it best to see which way the wind blew before committing himself to one side or the other. If a person's activity were of human origin, it would crumble; if it was from God, no one would be able to stop it. All one had to do was sit back and wait to see who prevailed — this would indicate which side was favored by heaven.

Paul understood this principle all too well, but he also knew there was no reason to sit back and wait in this case. It was already quite apparent that a band of ill-equipped insurgents was no match for the military might of the empire. To align himself with such a movement would be akin to suicide, and Paul certainly had no wish to die. Yet neither did he have no wish to abandon the movement Jesus had championed; it would be far better, he believed, to transform it from a party of radical revolutionaries into a spiritually oriented group whose aims were fully compatible with those of the empire.

He would, once again, change the rules.

"Everyone must submit yourself himself to the governing authorities," he wrote his followers in Rome, for whom the authorities could only have been duly appointed agents of the empire. Paul stated flatly that all authority came from God, so any governing body must therefore have earned his sanction. The implication was that an imperial decree was tantamount to the word of God.

Such pacific acquiescence to the governing regime paved the way for the Roman church's successful effort to establish itself as the unquestioned master of the Mediterranean in the coming centuries. It is no wonder that the church came to include so many of Paul's writings — both authentic and disputed — in its canon. But this meek acceptance of the status quo would have sickened men such as the Maccabees who had fought so valiantly for independence in the belief that God was with them. Paul's philosophy was hardly the stuff of revolution, and it can only have stoked the tensions between Paul and James, who doubtless viewed himself as heir to the Maccabean cause. Indeed, a brief reference by the historian Suetonius may well indicate that the two men were working at cross purposes in the imperial capital. The single sentence refers to a group that was fomenting rebellion in Rome, the very city to which Paul wrote in counseling obedience to the authorities. According to Suetonius, the emperor Claudius at one point ordered all Jews expelled from the capital because they "caused continuous disturbances at the instigation of Chrestus." [604]

This name or title appears to be a variation on the word Christus, the Greek word for messiah. And the reputed messiah at this point was none other than James, whose rebel movement had ample motive to stir up trouble against the Romans. The rebels in Judea still wanted their independence, and they were willing to use guerrilla tactics to achieve it, striking even at the heart of the capital itself. It is probably no accident that a group of so-called Christians (followers of Chrestus?) was blamed for another, far more serious attack on Rome more than a decade later under the emperor Nero — the infamous fire that gutted much of the city. It is quite possible that this brazen assault on the capital was meant as a message to the empire: Relinquish sovereignty over Judea and withdraw your troops.

Now.

Paul, on the other hand, believed that such provocative acts against the empire could only backfire against the agitators. Like Gamaliel, he wanted to end up on the winning side. And it was to this end that he set about forging ties with imperial figures of note such as Sergius Paulus, the governor of Cyprus who seems to have become his sponsor early in his career.

Other connections followed.

For example, he appears to have had some influence with Gallio, proconsul of the Greek province known as Achaia. Gallio was in office when Paul arrived in Corinth during the course of his travels, one of several journeys abroad upon which he embarked to drum up support for his movement. Upon his arrival, he drew the attention of certain opponents (identified as ethnic Jews), who hauled Paul into court on charges that his manner of worship somehow violated imperial law.

They clearly expected Gallio to throw him in jail for his actions.

But midway through the hearing, the unexpected occurred: Just as Paul was about to answer the charges, Gallio abruptly dismissed the case. He ejected Paul's opponents from court and had the leader of the synagogue that had brought the case flogged.

The proconsul was clearly favorably disposed toward Paul.

One must ask why.

Paul would later reveal that he had contact with "those who belong to Caesar's household." [605] This group could well have included the philosopher Seneca, who served as Nero's adviser — and also just happened to be Gallio's brother. Later tradition linked Paul with Seneca through a series of letters that reportedly passed back and forth between the two men. And although the letters themselves are probably not genuine, the tradition underlying them is quite plausible. It was not uncommon for members of a given community to forge letters or other documents in support of various strongly held oral traditions.

And if Paul did, in fact, know people in the emperor's household, Seneca may well have been have been among them.

If Paul did, in fact, know Seneca, it would explain why the philosopher's brother Gallio was so quick to dismiss the case brought against him by "the Jews." The identity of his accusers is nowhere stated more specifically, but it is tantalizing to consider the possibility that these Jews were somehow connected to those who had stirring up trouble a short time before in Rome at the instigation of Chrestus.

By this time, James' group in Jerusalem was openly at odds with Paul's rival faction and had a better motive than anyone else for trying to undermine his actions.

Of course, there is no way of proving that James was behind Paul's arrest in Corinth, but considering the growing enmity between the two men at this stage in their careers, one thing is certain.

He would have approved.

The Circumcision Debate

Perhaps Paul's most open break with James came over the issue of circumcision. This was no small matter for the Jewish people; on the contrary, it was the defining symbol of their national identity and ethnic pride, a custom the Hyksos had brought with them from Egypt and had made the hallmark of their culture. Circumcision was the original covenant of blood, symbolizing the royal house and its sacred line of inheritance. As long as the rite of circumcision continued, the bloodline of the king — and by extension, that of his people — would be preserved. And so, in like manner, would Jewish sovereignty.

It is for this reason that the men who conquered Judea had sought to discourage the practice, hoping to suppress nationalist sentiment and facilitate acceptance of the ruling order. Under the Seleucid ruler Antiochus, it had been outlawed altogether on penalty of death, as the emperor sought to integrate Judea fully into Greek society at large.

His efforts, however, had only produced a backlash that resulted in the Maccabean revolt — an uprising that, in many ways, served as a precursor for the resistance movement headed successively by Joazar, John the Baptist, Jesus and now James. All these men belonged to the same family, which they regarded as the keeper of the messianic bloodline. It was through circumcision, the rite that prepared a man (and a woman) for the mystical union of the bridal chamber, that this bloodline was protected and preserved.

One can therefore only imagine James' reaction when Paul embarked on a campaign to discredit the practice altogether. Striking at the heart of ancient tradition, he told his followers that "circumcision is nothing" and had a particularly venomous message for those who continued to advocate the practice: "As for those agitators, I wish they would go the whole way and emasculate themselves!" [606]

Paul would come back to this issue time and again, the level of his rhetoric demonstrating quite clearly that this was no trifling effort at reform. It was, to his way of thinking, fundamental. The messianic movement had long held to Egyptian notions of a royal bloodline, whereby the spirit of the king passed from one generation to the next. In denigrating circumcision as unnecessary, Paul was effectively repudiating this very principle.

And it was on this principle that James' authority rested.

There can be little doubt that Paul sought to supplant James as leader of Jesus' movement. His disdain for James and other members of the leadership is palpable in his writings, where he dismisses them as "those reputed to be pillars." [607] The implication is that Paul himself was not ready to accept them as such. When speaking of "those who seemed to be important," Paul denigrated them further: "Whatever they were makes no difference to me," he declared, boasting that "these men added nothing to my message." [608]

The context of the reference makes it pretty clear he is talking about James and his cohorts, whose "message" was in fact quite different. It was one of works before faith; one of revolution, not obedience to Rome; one that exalted James' authority above that of Paul.

With this in mind, Paul warned his followers against accepting any message but his own. He referred to some of the people spreading such a message as super-apostles, a clear reference to an elite leadership group of some sort. This can only be the pillars to whom he referred to in his letter to the Galatians, the group led by none other than James. Yet Paul adopted a defensive tone in declaring that he was in no way inferior to these men and denigrating their message as lacking.

He characterized such men as false apostles and deceitful workers masquerading as apostles, warning his followers that even Satan might appear in the guise of an angel.[609] Such men, he said, were no angels: "Even if we or an angel from heaven should preach a gospel other than the one we preached to you, let him be eternally condemned," he railed. Such condemnation would have certainly applied to the message being spread by James, which stood in direct contrast to that of Paul on several key points.

One of these points involved the question of whether Gentiles should be permitted to share a meal with Jews. James believed firmly that such a practice was unacceptable, whereas Paul not only permitted but encouraged it. The issue came to a head in Antioch, the Syrian capital where Paul had established his headquarters. The circumstances? A visit by James' brother Peter, a member of the elite Essenic high council of three priests — in Paul's words, those reputed to be pillars.

For whatever reason, Peter took a somewhat more lenient stance toward the idea of sharing a table with Gentiles, initially accepting the practice without complaint. But his stance changed abruptly on the arrival of a larger contingent representing James' conservative party. Peter's sudden about-face took Paul completely by surprise. He was dumbfounded. He would recall the incident in a letter to his supporters in Galatia, a province in what is now Turkey: "Before certain men came from James, he used to eat with the Gentiles. But when they arrived, he began to draw back and separate himself from the Gentiles because he was afraid of those who belonged to the circumcision group."[610]

Paul's blunt assessment of the situation clearly identifies the men from James as those who belonged to the circumcision party.

Now, they were stirring up trouble on another front — denying Gentiles the right to eat alongside ethnic Jews. Such a stance considerably weakened Paul's authority, as most of his support was drawn from the Gentile population. Paul felt he been betrayed. What was Peter's motive in first accepting the common table and then suddenly withdrawing his support for the practice? Was he simply a coward? A hypocrite? Or perhaps he had only feigned support at the outset in order to set a trap for Paul — one that he had obligingly walked right into. Whatever his motives, his sudden change of heart drew a blistering diatribe from Paul, who would report that "when Peter came to Antioch, I opposed him to his face, because he was clearly in the wrong." [611]

It was a clear instance of espionage on the part of James, an effort to catch him off guard and put him in his place. Paul probably had such activities in mind when he wrote his Galatian that "some false brothers had infiltrated our ranks to spy on the freedom we have." [612] The freedom to do things such as share a table with Gentiles, to forgo the circumcision ritual and to eat meat that had been sacrificed to idols.

This last issue was yet another point of contention between Paul and James. The author of *Acts* relates an incident in which a group of men from Jerusalem arrived at Antioch and informed Paul in no uncertain terms that circumcision was mandatory. These were, obviously, members of the so-called circumcision group mentioned in Paul's letter to Galatia. Perhaps the incident referred to in Acts is even identical with that mentioned in Paul's letter, where he derides the men who came from James to undermine his authority. The circumstances certainly appear to be similar.

Whether or not this was the case, the encounter was anything but friendly.

As might be expected, a furious debate ensued between Paul and those in the Jerusalem group — a debate that wound up in a stalemate. Neither side was about to give an inch, and it soon became clear that the only way to settle matters would involve an appeal to a higher authority. That authority in question was, naturally, none other than James. So both parties set out for Jerusalem, intent on presenting their case to the messiah and deciding the issue once and for all. In the end, however, even James was unable to bring about a satisfactory resolution. As things turned out, he didn't even mention the circumcision issue in his ruling, instead issuing a decree that required Gentiles to abide by four simple rules: They were instructed to abstain from sexual immorality, from the meat of strangled animals, from blood and from food polluted by idols. This was a victory of sorts for Paul, who somehow succeeded in avoiding a definitive ruling in favor of the circumcision party.

But Paul had little use for partial victories. In a letter written not long after the decision was rendered, he openly ridiculed the provision banning the consumption of meat polluted by idols. His followers, he boasted, knew better than to worry about such petty rules. An idol itself was nothing, and it was therefore no sin to eat meat that had been dedicated to one. But in a condescending piece of rhetoric, Paul admitted that "not everyone knows this. Some people are still so accustomed to idols that when they eat such food, they think of it as having been sacrificed to an idol. And since their conscience is weak, they are defiled." [613]

These ignorant fools were none other than those who had issued the decree against eating such meat in the first place. James and his followers.

Paul's patronizing language effectively repudiated James' ruling as a concession for weak-willed men such as James himself. The biting sarcasm of his statement was certainly not lost on members of the circumcision party who came across it. James had gone out of his way (uncharacteristically for an ascetic of such strong principles) to forge a compromise with Paul, only to be ridiculed with language that bordered on open defiance.

From this point forward, there would be no further attempt to compromise by either side. Each man would fight tooth and nail for his own personal vision in an attempt to establish himself as the ultimate authority over the movement that would become known as Christianity.

Magus

Perhaps Paul's most important ally in this struggle was a man named Felix, who was appointed procurator of Judea less than two decades after Jesus' death. Felix was yet another member of the Roman establishment with whom Paul managed to ingratiate himself.

How he did it is a matter of no small interest.

The story is preserved by Josephus, who recalls a meeting between the procurator and a certain man named Simon. We have already identified this as Paul's Jewish name, under which he appears in the gospel accounts variously as Simon the Pharisee and Simon the leper. To these epithets a third may now be added: Simon the sorcerer, or Simon Magus. This was probably a moniker imposed upon him by the resistance, a group of ethnic Jews who would naturally have referred to him by his Jewish name.

Simon the appears just once in the canonical accounts, where he is introduced by the author of *Acts* as an independent agent who had "boasted that he was someone great." [614] Subsequently, however, he becomes devoted to Jesus and dedicates himself to the nationalist cause, only to run afoul of the movement's leadership when he offers up an ill-conceived bribe. Having received the leaders' formal commission through the laying on of hands, he immediately asks for the authority to impart the same commission to others at his own discretion. As an incentive, he offers an undisclosed amount of money in exchange for the privilege. He is, however, rebuffed by Peter, who rewards him for his impudence by expelling him from the movement altogether: "May your money perish with you, because you thought you could buy the gift of God." [615]

This is the end of the exchange and the extent of Simon the sorcerer's involvement in the narrative of *Acts*. This brief mention, however, earned Simon a degree of notoriety vastly disproportionate to this short scene. His name itself became the basis for the word "simony," which denotes the sale or purchase of spiritual favors. And beyond this, he became known as the father of all heretics, a sort of arch villain who symbolized the antithesis of all the church represented. Certainly a single act of bribery should not have been enough to engender such a reputation; it appears there is something more afoot here than meets the eye.

As it turns out, that "something" is Simon's identity.

As mentioned earlier, the author of *Acts* drew on a variety of sources in compiling his account. And two of these sources are especially prominent. They are readily identified by their subject matter, with roughly the first half of the document focusing on the original members of Jesus' group and the second half virtually abandoning this theme in favor of a detailed look at the travels of Paul. It is clear not only from the shift in focus but also from the linguistic style that two separate accounts have been somehow grafted together. Much of the latter portion, for example, is written in the first person, with numerous references to "we" that seem to indicate it was produced by a companion of Paul who accompanied him on portions of his travels. These two sections are generally taken to be in chronological order, with Paul's journeys seeming to follow directly upon the events in the earlier portion of the book. Yet as we have seen, the author's idea of an "orderly" account had very little to do with chronology. Thematically, the second volume of his work (*Acts*) was written to parallel — and thus reinforce — the material contained in his first volume (*Luke*).

This raises an intriguing possibility. Is it possible that the two distinct sections of *Acts* are not in chronological order at all? Is it worth considering that perhaps, just perhaps, they parallel one another in some respects, describing at least some of the same events from radically different points of view?

If the second section was written, at least in large measure, by a companion of Paul's, one might expect Paul himself to receive favorable treatment — and to be referred to by the Roman name he clearly preferred. On the other hand, because the first section concentrates on the resistance leaders, one might expect to encounter a narrative promoting *their* viewpoints. No one should look for anything favorable about Paul in this section. The author of this source material would probably take great pains to downplay Paul's role in the events of the day, mentioning him sparingly and then only in a negative light.

Moreover, the Jewish author would be much more likely to use Paul's Jewish name.

Simon.

(The redactor, in an attempt to gloss over this dichotomy, seems to have created another Jewish name for Paul out of whole cloth, referring to him as Saul — a conflation of the names Simon and Paul.)

While the Pauline document lauded him as a hero, the resistance narrative disparaged him as a sorcerer, a charlatan and a braggart who had the gall to offer money in exchange for an apostolic commission. And there is evidence that, in fact, Paul did just that. He is depicted collecting a money from his followers abroad do provide a donation for "the poor" in Jerusalem. Recall that this phrase was a favorite self-designation of those in the resistance, who referred to themselves as Ebionites. Could this collection have been the bribe that Simon the sorcerer was accused of offering Peter?

There are other points of contact between the stories of Paul and Simon, as well. For one thing, both men appear to follow similar paths: Each is initially opposed to the resistance movement, but each subsequently joins it for a period of time, only to eventually break from it once again.

Moreover, when Peter derides Simon for his "boasting," he is criticizing him for something Paul himself was known to do. In defending himself to his followers in the Greek city of Corinth, for example, Paul would declare himself willing to brag about the very same things for which others found reason to boast. These others are left nameless, but it is clear from the context of the letter that he is talking about ethnic Jews:

"Are they Hebrews? So am I. Are they Israelites. So am I. Abraham's descendants? So am I. Are they servants of Christ? (I have to be out of my mind to talk like this.) I am more. I have worked much harder, been in prison more frequently, been flogged more severely and been exposed to death again and again." [616]

It is plain that some people in the Jewish community were refusing to grant Paul the status he believed he deserved — and they were doing this despite the fact that, in Paul's view, he was more worthy than they to claim such status. If all this sounds naggingly familiar, recall that Simon the sorcerer likewise sought to claim a position of authority within a Jewish community, only to be sternly rebuked by Peter. Simon wanted the ability to grant a formal commission of sorts to whomever he deemed suitable, but Peter refused to allow it. This is the very issue over which Paul and the Jewish opposition leaders known as the "pillars" had clashed. Paul wanted the ability to welcome Gentiles into his group, while James and Peter insisted that they were the final arbiters over who would be accepted.

Indeed, the issue of welcoming Gentiles was the very issue over which Paul opposed Peter "to his face" at Antioch.

Paul (or Simon) claimed parity with the "pillars" and firmly believed he should be allowed to accept new members based on his discretion alone.

"Am I not an apostle?" he asked his supporters in Corinth, making it clear that the answer in his own mind was an unqualified yes. But the very fact that he had to raise the subject implies that someone thought otherwise — most likely James or Peter. The fact that Paul considered himself a "pillar" on a par with those revered persons is evident from a tradition according to which Simon the sorcerer adopted the title of Standing One, an apt description for a pillar.

This raises at least the possibility that Simon Paul had gone through some sort of resurrection ceremony patterned on the opening of the mouth ritual and, unlike Jesus, survived. In doing so, he would have become a *djed* pillar, in a symbolic sense. A standing one.

Various legends about Simon the sorcerer focus on his claim that he could rise from the dead. And only one person other than Jesus is known to have undergone such a ceremony — Lazarus, a figure who appears to be nothing more than an alter ego for Simon the Pharisee.

Or Paul.

In his letters, Paul speaks emphatically of his belief that he and others have been symbolically buried with Jesus that they might be united with him in his resurrection. Could such claims refer indirectly to his own experience in a symbolic ritual of death and resurrection? It appears at least conceivable. Moreover, it seems entirely possible that Paul believed he had ascended to heaven in the aftermath of this ritual. In writing to the Corinthians, he clearly implies having been caught up to the third heaven at some point, where he heard things that he was not permitted to repeat. This contention also may have found an echo in the apocryphal literature surrounding Simon the sorcerer, who was said to have enjoyed the ability to fly — in other words, ascend to the heavens. He was undone, however, by none other than Peter, who literally brought him back down to earth during an epic battle of wills in Rome.

According to the legend, Simon would up dead as a result.

Can it be a coincidence that Paul, like Simon, is said to have died in Rome?

And that Paul is also said to have opposed Peter?

Perhaps. But the coincidences are adding up quickly, and as they do they are becoming more and more difficult to ignore. All of which brings us to one final such "coincidence," this one involving the Jewish procurator mentioned earlier — a man named Felix who had not occupied his new post too long before he enlisted the help of a certain sorcerer named Simon.

The Drusilla Affair

Felix's problem was simple: He had fallen head over heels in love with a young woman named Drusilla, the daughter of the late King

Agrippa who reportedly "exceeded all other women in beauty." [617]

There was only one problem: Drusilla was already taken. Her brother (also named Agrippa) had arranged for her to marry a certain Azizus, king of the Syrian city-state of Emesa some distance north of Chalcis. As a condition of the marriage, Azizus had allowed himself to be circumcised — something Drusilla's previous suitor, yet another king, had been unwilling to do. As it turned out, however, his efforts in this regard would be wasted: Felix was determined to have her, married or not.

To this end, he enlisted the help of a "friend of his named Simon, a Jew from Cyprus who pretended to be a magician." [618] This magician can only have been Paul, a.k.a. Simon the sorcerer, who was known to have spent considerable time on Cyprus under the governor Sergius Paulus and was probably for this reason identified with this particular locale. It is worth noting here that Simon the sorcerer was supposedly from a town called Gitta in Samaria, a piece of information that doesn't appear to fit well with the life story of Paul — until one realizes that the name Gitta is just one letter removed from Kitta, a common name for Cyprus in that period. Moreover, members of the Qumran community often referred to the Romans in general as the Kittim. As Paul was a Roman sympathizer, this epithet seems quite appropriate.

Certainly, Paul would have had more than one reason for helping Felix. For one thing, Felix was uncircumcised — and he was not about to let himself be circumcised, either. If Paul could broker a marriage with Drusilla, he could claim a major symbolic victory over those who insisted so vehemently on the necessity of the ritual — the so-called circumcision party of James and his followers. And, most importantly, he could put the newly appointed procurator squarely in his debt.

It was a debt he would soon have occasion to call in.

Showdown in Jerusalem

Something happened in the temple.
Something that would change the course of history.

It began with Paul's visit to Jerusalem where, the author of *Acts* informs us, he stirred up such trouble that he got himself arrested and shuttled off to the provincial capital of Caesarea Maritima. But it is best to start at the beginning.

The author begins by reporting that Paul was received warmly by James and members of the Jerusalem opposition on his arrival, specifically naming James and "all the elders" among the welcoming party.[619] This in itself is suspicious, considering the tension that had been building for some time between the two rivals. The venomous words Paul had written to his followers concerning James can hardly have gone unnoticed, and it is obvious that each viewed the other with an intense level of suspicion. Given their history of conflict, it is highly unlikely that James would have welcomed Paul with anything resembling open arms. The description may therefore be a gloss on the part an author or editor eager to portray the two men as allies rather than enemies; or it may depict a meeting that actually took place, in which each man assumed a deliberately diplomatic posture in the face of a sworn enemy.

Either way, the reference to a genuinely warm welcome rings hollow, as does the contention that James and the others praised God upon hearing of Paul's work among the Gentiles. Paul's letter to the Galatians makes it abundantly clear that James' attitude toward Gentiles was exactly the opposite: He did not want them consorting with ethnic Jews and viewed them as having no place at the common table. The statement in *Acts* about James "praising God" is almost certainly a gloss as well, and it is exposed as such by the material that follows it — material that states in no uncertain terms the general opposition among ethnic Jews to Paul's work with the Gentiles.

Having received Paul (warmly or otherwise), James and the others immediately launch into a speech meant to warn their visitor against pursuing his work with the Gentiles any further. If he insists upon doing so, they tell him, he will be putting himself in imminent danger: "You see, brother, how many thousands of Jews have believed, and all of them are zealous for the law. They have been informed that you teach all the Jews who live among the Gentiles to turn away from Moses, telling them not to circumcise their children or live according to our customs." [620]

In reading a text, it is often difficult to imagine the intonation of the speaker being quoted.

Not so here.

James or his spokesmen is drawing the lines quite clearly, referring to circumcision and the obedience to the law explicitly as *our* customs — those accepted by the speaker and his supporters. It seems from the language employed that James had brought a great number of those supporters with him to "welcome" Paul, for the speaker's words indicate that their visitor can *see* how many thousands of Jews are zealous for the very law Paul has been attacking. One can certainly picture James bringing a large number of men with him to intimidate Paul by showing him just what he was up against. The message was loud and clear: This is my turf — don't try to mess with me here, if you value your life.

"What shall we do?" the speaker asked, his voice no doubt dripping with false concern. The people who opposed Paul would certainly hear of his arrival, and there would be trouble. Of course, it could not have been lost on Paul that the people in question were standing directly in front of him.

The question, meanwhile, was entirely rhetorical. The speaker was not trying to elicit ideas from Paul; he had his own thoughts on the matter. Four men had been rendered impure in some manner after having taken a temporary Nazirite vow. In order to prove his loyalty to the movement and the law of Moses, Paul was instructed to sponsor these four men during a purification ceremony so that they could have their heads ritually shaved in accordance with prescribed custom. Furthermore, he was told that he would have to join them in this ritual, offering himself up for cleansing as well. This was not a suggestion. Paul was not being given any option but to comply — or risk the wrath of the circumcision party.

Furthermore, he was reminded of the edict that James had issued earlier, commanding that Gentiles refrain from sexual immorality, blood, the meat of strangled animals and food sacrificed to idols. They doubtless felt that Paul needed reminding about this in light of writings in which he portrayed the ban on idol-food as a proscription meant for weaklings and simpletons.

Paul knew he was being backed into a corner, but he was powerless to do anything about it. If he wished to leave Jerusalem alive, he would have to go along with the conditions set before him; he would have to sponsor the four Nazirites and accompany them to the temple, so that he might join them in the ritual of purification. This must have seemed an insult of the highest order to Paul, who would have hardly considered himself in need of purification. Yet he was willing to go along with this charade, for it was certainly better than giving the circumcision party an excuse to kill him.

What he didn't know was that they planned to do so anyway.

The conservatives had no intention of letting Paul off the hook, even if he followed their instructions to the letter. They wanted to be rid of him once and for all, so they stacked the deck against him and waited to spring their trap. The idea was simple: Some allies from the province of Asia would spread a rumor that Paul had brought a Gentile into the portion of the temple that was considered off limits to non-Jews. Near the end of the seven-day period allotted for the ritual purification, the Asians would arrive at the temple to confront him. The idea was to start a riot that, they hoped, would result in Paul's demise.

The author of *Acts* reports the incident as follows: "They stirred up the whole crowd and seized him, shouting, 'Men of Israel, help us! This is the man who teaches all men everywhere against our people and our law and this place. And besides, he has brought Greeks into the temple area and defiled this holy place." [621] In short order, the entire city was up in arms and men came running from all directions to answer the call. Paul found himself facing what must have appeared to be certain death. Surrounded and isolated the midst of an angry mob, there was little prospect for escape and nowhere to hide in such a public place. In no time, he found himself being dragged outside the temple (so it would not be defiled by his death) and subjected to a savage beating by his enemies.

The author of *Acts* states plainly enough the goal of Paul's assailants: "They were trying to kill him." [622]

The only thing that stopped them was the timely intervention of the Roman commander, who got wind of the riot and came running with a group of soldiers in time to prevent any further bloodshed.

Thinking Paul responsible for the situation, the commander ordered him arrested, chained and carted off to the soldiers' barracks, but Paul demurred, asking for an opportunity to defend himself to the mob. This was, to say the least, a futile undertaking. These men had no interest in granting an audience to an enemy they were bent on destroying, but Paul was a man of supreme self-confidence that at times crossed the line into arrogance, and he may well have believed his powers of persuasion could carry the day. In addressing the crowd, he first recounted some of his personal history and stated his allegiance to Jesus. So far, so good. But almost as soon as he succeeded in gaining the rabble's attention, he faltered, asserting that he had been appointed by God himself specifically to carry a message to the Gentiles. This was the last thing the ethnocentric nationalists who had gathered at the temple wanted to hear. Immediately, there were rumblings in the crowd and Paul's enemies began to shout him down: "Rid the earth of him! He's not fit to live." [623]

Their reaction at this particular point in Paul's speech only serves to drive home the crux of the conflict: These men were violently opposed to any interaction with Gentiles. Period. Paul's defense of such fraternization must have validated their suspicion that he had brought a Gentile into the temple. They obviously felt that they had heard enough, for they began throwing off their cloaks and flinging dust into the air — giving every appearance of wanting to pick up where they had left off before the Roman contingent arrived.

The commander, seeing no point in allowing the situation to escalate once more, hurried Paul off with orders that he be beaten and questioned. But before these orders could be carried out, Paul asked one of the soldiers a very pointed question: "Is it legal for you to flog a Roman citizen who hasn't even been found guilty?" [624] Of course, Paul himself knew the answer to that question all too well — and so did the centurion. He immediately informed the commander, who was troubled at the fact that he had put a Roman citizen in chains.

The incident would clearly have to be investigated further.

His first inclination was to release Paul from custody and have the Jewish authorities question him. This plan, however, was thwarted by another near riot, and the Roman commander was forced to take Paul back into custody for his own protection: *Acts* reports that "the dispute became so violent that the commander was afraid Paul would be torn to pieces." [625] This is a key point, and it cannot be stressed strongly enough. Paul was not in custody at this point because he was suspected of some crime, but because he was obviously safer under Roman guard than he would have been if released on his own recognizance.

What happened next only serves to highlight the point. The author of *Acts* relates that a group of Jews (obviously James' followers) formed a conspiracy the very next day, pledging not to eat or drink until such time as they had succeeded in killing Paul. They approached their allies on the Sanhedrin, asking them to bring Paul before the body on the pretext of wanting some more information about him. While he was being transferred, they would wait in ambush to kill him.

The plot was only foiled by chance when Paul's nephew somehow learned of it and alerted Paul, who in turn sent him to inform the commander. His orders in response to this news were as follows:

"Get ready a detachment of two hundred spearmen to go to Caesarea at nine tonight. Provide mounts for Paul so that he may be taken safely to Governor Felix." [626]

The situation could not have been any better for Paul. It is obvious that the guards were being provided for the express purpose of protecting him from his enemies. Certainly two hundred men would not have been required to ensure that he remained in custody; such a contingent would only have been necessary to ward off an attack along the way. The great lengths to which the commander went to ensure Paul's safe passage seem to indicate that he now realized his "prisoner" was a man of some considerable importance.

And the destination he chose for Paul may explain how he came to that realization.

Felix, of course, was a friend of Simon the sorcerer — a.k.a. Paul. The most likely conclusion is that Paul or one of his allies had alerted the commander to Paul's friendship with the governor. This would surely clarify why the commander provided him with the sort of escort usually reserved for Roman officials traveling on imperial business. Paul was indeed a very important man — and one who now found himself in the catbird's seat. Not only could he count upon his friendship with the governor to ensure his safety, he could also take comfort in the fact that Felix was heavily in his debt. After all, had not Paul (in his guise as Simon the sorcerer) provided invaluable assistance to the governor in securing the hand of the beautiful Drusilla? If Rome was for him, who could be against him?

So it was that, when his accusers arrived five days later to press their case, Felix heard them politely — and then dismissed them without taking any further action. In fact, he kept Paul in custody for the next two years. The author of *Acts* provides the rather contrived explanation that Felix wanted Paul to offer him a bribe in exchange for his release. But there is no reason why Paul should have *wanted* to be set free. As it was, he had a very comfortable life: Felix "ordered the centurion to keep him under guard but to give him some freedom and permit his friends to take care of his needs." [627] Again, this is not the sort of arrangement that would have been provided to a nefarious criminal; it was, however, just the kind of setup one might have expected from a government seeking to provide safe haven for a marked man.

When, after two years, Felix was replaced as procurator by a man named Festus, Paul found himself suddenly in danger once again. He seems to have had no relationship with the new governor, and his enemies took the opportunity to renew their urgent appeal against Paul. They did not want him in Roman custody. They wanted to deal with him on their own (murderous) terms.

According to the author of *Acts*, "they urgently requested Festus, as a favor to them, to have Paul transferred to Jerusalem, for they were preparing an ambush to kill him along the way." [628]

Festus, upon hearing the charges, appeared inclined to do Paul's accusers a favor and hand him over to them. Turning to Paul, he asked him whether he would be willing to travel to Jerusalem and answer the charges against him there. But Paul, no doubt realizing that he would be signing his own death warrant should he agree, protested that the proper venue to settle these matters was an imperial court. If Festus himself refused to conduct such a proceeding, Paul felt he had no choice but to call upon a higher authority. "If the charges brought against me by these Jews are not true, no one has the right to hand me over to them," he asserted. "I appeal to Caesar!" [629]

It was a masterstroke. By exercising his right as a citizen to demand a trial before Caesar himself, Paul was ensuring himself safe passage as far away from Jerusalem and his enemies as he could get. *The Acts of the Apostles* concludes with Paul once again under imperial protection, this time in Rome itself: "For two whole years, Paul stayed there in his own rented house and welcomed all those who came to see him." [630] Again, this is hardly the sort of treatment that would have been accorded someone suspected of a heinous crime.

The outcome of the trial before Caesar, if it ever actually occurred, is not recorded by the author of *Acts*, who leaves the story unfinished and states only that Paul stayed in Rome for a period of "two whole years." [631] What happened then is left unsaid. This conclusion has long frustrated readers accustomed to stories with tidy summations and happily-ever-afters. Surely the author, writing several years after the events in question, must have *known* what happened next. He had obviously done a significant amount of research into his subject and would scarcely have remained content to simply leave things hanging.

Unless the conclusion was, in some way, embarrassing.

And a perusal of other sources available to us indicates that it most likely was. For something happened in Jerusalem immediately after Paul completed his two-year stay in Rome that indicates his involvement in matters far beneath the dignity of a spiritual giant. Matters involving revenge. Violence.

And murder.

The victim of this murder was none other than James, against whom Paul must have borne quite a grudge. It had been James who had sought to bring about his destruction by luring him into the trap at the temple; he had failed in this, but had managed to engineer his arrest and subsequent exile as one who dared not return to Palestine for fear of his life.

Until now.

Suddenly, there was a political vacuum in the region, and the time was ripe for revenge. The Jewish historian Josephus reports that the procurator Festus had died two years after taking office, while at the same time the high priesthood passed to a certain Ananus — a man with no love for James. Festus' sudden death left Judea without a procurator until such time as a successor could be installed, and this was no simple matter, as the man in question had to travel some distance to reach his new assignment. This gave Ananus the window of opportunity he needed to act on his own against James. He therefore called for the messiah to be stoned to death, an order that was carried out in rapid fashion.

When the new procurator did at last arrive to claim his post, he was none too pleased that his authority had been undermined in this fashion and quickly removed Ananus from the high priesthood for his insolence.

But there is more to this story than Josephus reveals. Most specifically, he mentions nothing at all about Paul, who seems to have played a pivotal role in assuring James' demise.

Those who investigate the death of James will find an unusual wealth of sources referring to this particular event. Foremost among them, perhaps, is the Ebionite counterpart to *Acts* mentioned earlier, *The Recognitions of Clement*, which speaks of a disturbance in the temple that ensued from a clash between James and his party on the one hand, and "one of our enemies" on the other. This enemy was not, as might be expected from Josephus' account, Ananus. On the contrary, a marginal note in one manuscript indicates that he was none other than Paul.[632]

This is a shocking revelation, but it fits very well. Certainly Paul had a motive for wanting to confront James — a better motive than anyone else, in fact. Revenge. And the incident fits well into the chronology of Paul's life story, occurring about the same time that his two-year stay in Rome would have been completed. The picture that emerges would seem to indicate that Paul agreed to act in concert with Ananus to apprehend James and bring about his execution.

The text of the *Recognitions* begins with the so-called enemy (i.e. Paul) and a few of his cronies barging in on James in the temple and interrupting one of his sermons to the crowd. Crying out in a loud voice, he demanded, "What do you mean, men of Israel? Why are you so easily hurried on? Why are you led headlong by most miserable men, who are deceived by Simon, a magician?"

The reference is to no less a personage than Simon the sorcerer, whose sudden appearance at this juncture appears to make little sense — at least at first. After all, it has become quite clear that Paul and Simon are one and the same. Paul's quarrel was with James, and certainly not with himself. Why, then, would he be smearing his own reputation and speaking about himself in the third person? The entire episode seems nonsensical.

Until one considers the possibility that Paul was being sarcastic.

The disadvantage of reading dry text, which lacks the ability to convey emphasis and intonation, is never more apparent than here. If read in a sarcastic sense, Paul's biting comment becomes perfectly intelligible. The men who had sought to denigrate him as a sorcerer and charlatan had refused to listen to him before. Now, they would be forced to hear him. He, the man who had "deceived" so many into accepting the Gentiles and turning away from the law of Moses, would have the last laugh. It was irony, not literal meaning, that provided the force behind his words.

As a rhetorical tactic, this was nothing new for Paul. He had been known to speak of himself in the third person when writing to his supporters, as he did in relating the story of a man who had been caught up to the third heaven — a clear self-reference.[633] He also often resorted to sarcasm in his letters, speaking about himself in a manner that veritably oozed with mock self-deprecation. He referred to himself at various points as a fool and a wretched man, while at the same time asking his followers to trust the wisdom of his words and proclaiming himself blameless according to the law. This pendulum technique of argument, in which he asserted his own supposedly humble nature only to boast about his achievements, was Paul's trademark. In his second letter to the Corinthians, he stated in faux humility that he and his followers would never dream of comparing themselves with others who have boasted about their achievements.[634] Then, however, he proceeded to do just that, ticking off a long list of his own achievements and denigrating his rivals as "deceitful workmen masquerading as apostles of Christ." [635]

The only people claiming to be apostles during this period, as far as we know, were Paul himself and members of James' faction — the men with whom he came into conflict at the temple not once but twice. And it is obvious from the text of the *Recognitions* that it is not Simon the sorcerer (himself!) with whom Paul is at odds, but James. The author makes it clear that James is the one who seeks to refute Paul's arguments in the midst of the tumult, only to be shouted down by Paul and his supporters.

"Why do you hesitate, you sluggish and inert?" he cried out. "Why do we not lay hands upon them and pull all these fellows to pieces?" [636] He then is said to have snatched a stick of some sort and begun swinging it around like a madman, using it to administer a beating to his enemies. Among those enemies was James, who personally fell victim to this attack and found himself thrown headlong down the temple steps by none other than Paul. The narrative goes on to state that James was left for dead, but that his followers carried him away and he somehow managed to survive the ordeal.

Other sources, while confirming many of the details reported in the Ebionite document, appear to contradict this hopeful outcome.

The so-called *Second Apocalypse of James*, for example, provides another account of the temple riot. According to this narrative, a mob of people rose up against James and sought to destroy him. "Let us kill this man," they shouted, "that he may be removed from our midst, for he will be of no use to us at all." [637] From there, the scene plays out as in the *Recognitions*, with James once more cast down from a great height but somehow managing to survive the fall. In this version, however, he is unable to escape his ultimate fate; instead, he is set upon by the rioters, who force him to dig a hole and then proceed to bury him up to his waist. He is then stoned to death in this position, as he offers up a final prayer.

This account appears closely related to a similar tradition preserved by the early church historian Eusebius, who quotes a now-lost document by Hegesippus from the late first or early second century. Here, too, James is accosted in the temple by a crowd of rabble-rousers who throw him down from a high place and immediately begin pelting him with stones. Instead of seeking to escape, however, he kneels before them and cries out to heaven: "I beseech you, lord God and father, forgive them; they do not know what they are doing." [638]

The petition itself is jarring.

It is virtually identical to the entreaty placed upon the lips of Jesus at his crucifixion by the author of *Luke*.[639] This would seem to further confirm James' role as Jesus' messianic successor, perhaps uttering a ritual prayer of forgiveness that was expected under such circumstances. But this prayer is also eerily reminiscent of words attributed by the same author (in *Acts*) to another martyr who was likewise stoned to death at the temple: "Do not hold this sin against them." [640] The sense of the appeal is certainly the same — a pious attempt to procure forgiveness for a bloodthirsty enemy, even in the face of imminent death.

The person to whom these words are credited is a man named Stephen.

More will be said about him shortly.

In the meantime, however, it would behoove us to revisit the account of Hegesippus, who provides one more important bit of information that is crucial in piecing together this historical puzzle: According to his narrative, the killing blow was not administered by those who were stoning James, but by a man with a club. This, of course, recalls the incident in the *Recognitions* involving the use of a stick by the "enemy" (Paul) in attacking James and the members of his party. And this raises the intriguing possibility that Paul himself actually killed James.

Shocking as this may seem, there is still more evidence that points toward exactly this conclusion. According to Hegesippus, the club in question was specifically wielded by a fuller — someone who works with clothing — and was designed for the express purpose of "beating out the clothes." What does this have to do with Paul? Everything, it turns out.

To understand the connection, however, we must return to the story of Stephen and his martyrdom that appears to closely parallel that of James. In this story, Paul plays an important role. According to the author of *Acts*, he was "there giving approval to his death." [641] This could mean, as is usually assumed, that Paul was a bystander who just happened to agree with the actions being taken against Stephen. But it could just as easily mean that he himself had authorized those actions — that he was the one whose approval was necessary for them to be carried out.

The author of *Acts* also provides a curious detail in recounting the events of Stephen's martyrdom, noting that the witnesses laid their clothes at the feet of Paul. Why would they have done this? Could it have been because Paul was carrying a fuller's club? Certainly there is no better explanation. Men who had come to see an execution would have had no reason to spontaneously disrobe in the midst of it all. And regardless of anything else, Paul was certainly taking on the role of a fuller by taking charge of the clothing in question.

The closer one looks, the more the stories of Stephen and James appear to blend together. Indeed, the similarities are uncanny:

- ➢ Both men die in the temple
- ➢ Both are stoned.
- ➢ Each is said to have delivered a long sermon of sorts just prior to his death.
- ➢ Both seek forgiveness for their assailants.

➢ Both are somehow associated with clothing or a fuller's club.

➢ Each is portrayed as being at odds with Paul.

According to *Acts*, Stephen incited the violence against him by declaring, "Look! I see heaven open and the son of man standing at the right hand of God." [642]

And Hegesippus places similar words in the mouth of James at the very same juncture in the narrative: "Why do you question me about the son of man? I tell you, he is sitting in heaven at the right hand of the great power." [643]

Even the name Stephen seems to identify him with James. It is a name that denotes a crowned one, by implication a royal or priestly figure. Such a description would have fit James like no other, for he had inherited the mantle of messiah from his brother/cousin Jesus at his death. Moreover, he was literally a crowned one. As a Nazirite from his mother's womb, he was forbidden to ever cut his hair, which he wore as the crown on his head. It is quite possible that this custom, like so many others, was inherited from the Egyptian pharaohs who wore elaborate headdresses and appear to have bound their hair in long, neatly tied locks. James, as the messiah, was the successor to these pharaohs.

He was the crowned one.

He was "Stephen."

Son of a Star

The death of James was a turning point in the history of his movement as well as the history of the world. Hegesippus was blunt in stating its significance, identifying James' death as the immediate cause of the Jewish revolt — and the subsequent invasion by the Roman general Vespasian to quell the uprising. "Immediately after this," he wrote, "Vespasian began to besiege them." [644] This is a rather truncated view of history, as the Jewish revolt did not actually break out until some five years after James' death, and Vespasian's offensive did not start until after that. But Hegesippus may well be on the mark in contending that the death of James provided the impetus needed to send the nation inexorably toward a full-scale revolution.

Two years after James' death, a fire broke out in Rome that devastated the city, brutally ravaging ten of its fourteen districts. The imperial palace itself was gutted as the blaze burned on unchecked for five whole days before it was finally extinguished. In the end, the emperor Nero charged the crime against the city's community of Christians. But just who were these "Christians"? Most likely, they were the same agitators who had been expelled from the city more than a decade earlier for engaging in riots at the instigation of Chrestus. These were men who believed that a christ or messiah was destined to deliver Israel from her Roman oppression. A Roman operative named Paul had engineered the downfall of their most recent claimant to the title of christ — James. And it seems altogether possible that they did, in fact, ignite the fire that became Rome's worst civil catastrophe as revenge for the death of their leader.

Their christ.

A few years later, freedom fighters in Jerusalem declared independence from Rome in a defiant act that would result in three years of self-rule. But only three years. At the end of that time, it all came crashing down as Roman forces took Jerusalem and eventually succeeded in destroying the temple itself. The last Jewish outpost to hold out, the mountain fortress of Masada, fell a scant six years after the revolt itself had begun. Before the war even began, the remnants of the Jerusalem opposition that had risen to prominence under James unanimously chose Symeon son of Clopas as their leader. This must have been none other than Simon Cephas, or Peter, whose presence in this position maintained the dynastic thread of leadership that had begun with Joazar. And it no doubt accounts for the tradition that Peter was the first leader of the church. The orthodoxy settled on this legend after ruling out any allegiance to James, who had been so successfully demonized by Paul and his followers, and relegating him to the background as much as possible.

Under Peter's direction, what was left of James' movement fled to the city of Pella in the district of Perea, never to be heard from again. It was probably a prudent move given Jerusalem's ultimate fate. Much of the city was damaged during the Roman assault, and the temple that had been considered Herod's crowning glory was reduced to charred beams and broken rubble. The modern "wailing wall" is today all that remains of it.

But that was just the beginning. Sixty years later, the Jewish nationalists launched a second war for independence, this time under the leadership of a charismatic individual named Simon Bar Kochba. The name Bar Kochba meant "son of a star." The star in question referred to a prophecy that was also applied to Jesus — that "a star has journeyed from Jacob." That star was Sirius, the star of Isis, the Queen of Heaven. Her son was Horus. It appears that Bar Kochba was using the same symbolism employed by Jesus and his followers decades earlier.

Could it be that the followers of Jesus — the Ebionites — who had fled to Pella after the first revolution were somehow involved in sponsoring Bar Kochba, as well?

Like the first revolution, the Bar Kochba revolt succeeded in the short term. Bar Kochba succeeded in establishing an independent state that endured for three years, and which he ruled under the title *nasi* or prince ... the same title that Jesus "of Nazareth" appears to have employed. His coinage, further, bore symbols that would have been familiar to those involved in Jesus' movement. One of them was the date palm, symbol of the phoenix (one coin from the period bears an emblem that looks suspiciously like a date palm actually taking the form of a phoenix). Another was the cup or grail — the *dam koce* or cup of blood.

This was the symbol of the sacred bloodline. Could it be that Simon was, in fact, claiming to be descended from Jesus? Was he

laying claim to the prophecy that the son of man would return —
that he was the resurrected Jesus who had come to claim his
kingdom? At the very least, he seems to have been using the same
symbols to claim the role in history that Jesus had assumed: that of
the messiah and liberator of Israel, the one who would establish the
kingdom of God on earth.

The initial success of the uprising, however, gave way to not only
defeat, but a bloodbath and abject humiliation for the Jewish
nationalists. During this period, Bar Kochba apparently took refuge
in the caves beside the Dead Sea — the same area that had served as
a base of operations for the resistance movement associated with
John the Baptist and Jesus. Eventually, however, he was caught and
killed.

And he was not the only one.

According to one account by the Roman consul and historian
Dio Cassius, nearly six hundred thousand Jews were slaughtered, fifty
fortified towns were razed and nearly a thousand villages were all but
wiped off the map.

In the aftermath of this second failed uprising, the emperor
(Hadrian) took the ultimate step in subjugating the Jewish nationalists
once and for all — he placed the city was off-limits to ethnic Jews
altogether and renamed Aelia Capitolina.

The messianic age had ended in a woeful and tragic failure. The
pharaohs were dead and buried beneath the desert sands. The Jewish
state was no more. And only the message of Paul, who had sided
with the empire, lived on. It bore little resemblance to the
revolutionary blueprint adopted by men such as John the Baptist,
Jesus and James. Its goal was eminently more practical — if you can't
beat the empire, join it. And so the radically altered Pauline
movement did just that, co-opting the imperial system so successfully
that the empire itself first sanctioned it and then, eventually, allowed
itself to be consumed by it.

Gone were the Egyptian origins of the Christian faith.

Forgotten were the myths and legends that had served as its

inspiration — forgotten, that is, by all but a few who preserved them in the form of nursery rhymes and faerie tales; faint reminders and distant echoes of an ancient and powerful belief. Though seldom acknowledged, it is a belief that persists today despite all efforts to stamp it out.

A belief not in some literal resurrection or reincarnation, but in a principle of regeneration on a planet where life is constantly renewing itself in the same eternal pattern. A young hero is born, becomes king, weds his beloved and gains wisdom through their joining. He grows old and raises up children to himself — children who will challenge him and inevitably supplant him. Throughout it all the goddess who is both queen of heaven and his consort watches over him, giving birth to him, accepting his seed, and at the end of life welcoming him anew into the bosom of her womb.

There is always the tree of life.

There is always the wizard, the *kher heb* priest in his serpent guise.

There is always his youthful challenger, the tanist jack.

And there is always the priestess of the grove, a serpent herself in whose sacred cup is borne the bloodline that endures beyond death.

As it is renewed, the land is renewed. The old king is healed and laid to rest; a new king is crowned and fathers an heir on the priestess.

There is always the ark.

There is always the stone from heaven.

There is always blood.

This is essence of the Phoenix Principle, renewing itself in myriad forms as it touches heroes and wonder women of myriad names across the millennia. Seth, Esau, Merlin. Solomon, Jesus, Arthur. Isis, Magdalene, Guinevere. Yet always the story stays true to its ancient form — like the sacred bird that returns time and again to remind us of our living story. Churches may bar their doors to it, and preachers may label it heresy, but research will continue to unearth treasures such as the Dead Sea Scrolls and the Rosetta Stone to shed light on a treasure that once seemed obscured forever behind a veil of myth and symbol.

This work has been about rediscovering that lost treasure — nothing more and nothing less. The thrill of the hunt is exhilarating, and joy of this discovery is beyond measure.

"For everyone who asks receives; he who seeks finds; and to him who knocks, the door will be opened." [645]

These are the keys to the kingdom of heaven.

Timeline

Appendix

Ancient period
(dates approximate)
2630 – Accession of Djoser, pharaoh who commissioned the step pyramid
2550 – Accession of Cheops, builder of the Great Pyramid at Giza
1730 – Accession of Hammurabi, lawgiver and king of Babylon
1720 – Hyksos era begins in Egypt
   Abraham pharaoh
   Subsequent Hyksos pharaohs include Jacob, Benjamin and Solomon
1550 – Ahmose defeats Apophis in Theban uprising
   Moses and the exodus to Palestine
   New Kingdom begins
1480 – Thutmose III conquers Megiddo
1350 – Akhenaten institutes monotheistic worship of the Aten

Age of empires
814 – Carthage founded in North Africa as Phoenician colony
776 – Rome founded
586 – Fall of Jerusalem to Babylonian forces
538 – Conquest of Babylon by Persian emperor Cyrus
525 – Persian conquest of Egypt
458 – Return of exiles to Jerusalem under Ezra
410 – Jewish temple at Elephantine destroyed, later rebuilt
404 – Egyptians launch successful war for independence
   Likely date of ultimate destruction for temple at Elephantine
333 – Alexander defeats the Persians
323 – Death of Alexander; empire eventually broken into three parts
   Kingdoms ultimately set up in Macedonia, Egypt and Syria

Maccabean period
202 – Romans destroy armies of Carthage under command of Hannibal
188 – Peace of Apamea, obligating the Seleucids to pay reparations to Rome

175 – Accession of Seleucid emperor Antiochus Epiphanes
174 – High priest Onias III slain
167 – Abomination set up in the temple at Jerusalem
164 – Temple cleansed
161 – Onias IV establishes Jewish temple in Leontopolis, Egypt
160 – Judas Maccabeus killed in battle
152 – Judas' brother Jonathan becomes high priest
134 – John Hyrcanus begins tenure of three decades as high priest
103 – Alexander Jannaeus proclaimed king and high priest

Herodian period

67 – Death of Queen Alexandra sparks civil war for succession
65 – Death of Honi the Circle-Drawer
63 – Pompey enters the temple in Jerusalem
    Beginning of Roman control in Judea
47 – Herod appointed governor of Galilee
44 – Assassination of Julius Caesar
40 – Roman Senate names Herod king
37 – Herod's armies take Jerusalem
Herod marries the first Mariamne
31 – Octavian (Augustus) defeats Antony and Cleopatra at Actium
29 – Mariamne executed on Herod's orders
5 – Divorce of Herod and the second Mariamne
    Mariamne's eldest son, also named Herod, stricken from Herod's will
4 – Joazar appointed high priest for first time
Joazar replaced as high priest
Birth of Jesus
Death of Herod; kingdom partitioned among three sons

Common Era (C.E.)

6 – Archelaus removed as ethnarch; Roman prefect installed in Judea
    Census under Quirinius, governor of Syria
    Tax revolt orchestrated by Judas the Galilean
    Joazar made high priest by acclamation for a second time
    Joazar removed from office
14 – Tiberius succeeds Augustus as emperor

- 18 – Joseph Caiaphas appointed high priest
- 26 – Pontius Pilate appointed prefect of Judea
- 34 – Philip the tetrarch dies childless
  Probable marriage of Jesus to Salome (a.k.a. Mary Magdalene)
- 35 – Execution of John the Baptist at Machaerus
- 36 – Crucifixion of Jesus at approximate age of forty
  Joseph Caiaphas removed from high priesthood
- 37 – Caligula succeeds Augustus as emperor
- 41 – Claudius succeeds Caligula
- 49 – Jews expelled from Rome because of riots at the "instigation of Chrestus"
- 54 – Nero succeeds Claudius
- 58 – Paul arrested after first riot in the temple, placed under Felix's protection
- 60 – Porcius Festus succeeds Felix as procurator
  Paul appeals to Caesar in Rome
- 62 – Martyrdom of James (Stephen), the messiah and brother of Jesus
- 67 – Jews declare independence from Rome
- 69 – Accession of Vespasian to emperor
- 70 – Roman forces retake Jerusalem
- 73 – Fall of Masada, last remaining stronghold of Jewish resistance
- 132 – Bar Kochba revolt begins; Jews declare independence from Rome
- 135 – Rome crushes Bar Kochba revolt

Bibliography

Akenson, David Harmon – *Surpassing Wonder*, Harcourt Brace, New York, 1998

Aldred, Cyril – *Akhenaten, King of Egypt*, Thames and Hudson, London, 1988

Allegro, John M. – *The Dead Sea Scrolls and the Christian Myth*, Prometheus Books, Amherst, N.Y., 1984

Alon, Gedaliah – *The Jews in their Land*, Harvard University Press, Cambridge, Mass., 1980

Baigent, Michael and Leigh, Richard – *The Dead Sea Scrolls Deception*, Touchstone, New York, 1991

Baigent, Michael and Leigh, Richard and Lincoln, Henry – *Holy Blood, Holy Grail*, Dell Publishing, New York, 1982

Baigent, Michael and Leigh, Richard and Lincoln, Henry – *The Messianic Legacy*, Dell Publishing, New York, 1986

Baring, Anne and Cashford, Jules – *The Myth of the Goddess*, Penguin, London, 1993

Barker, Kenneth – *NIV Study Bible*, Zondervan, Grand Rapids, Mich., 1995

Barnstone, Willis – *The Other Bible*, Harper and Row, San Francisco, 1984

Bauval, Robert and Gilbert, Adrian – *The Orion Mystery*, Three Rivers Press, New York, 1994

Begg, Ean – *The Cult of the Black Virgin*, Arkana Penguin Books, New York, 1996

Best, Robert M. – *Noah's Ark and the Ziusudra Epic*, Enlil Press, Fort Myers, Fla., 1999

Bialik, Hayim Nahman and Ravnitzky, Yehoshua Hana – *The Book of Legends*, Schocken, 1992

Black, Jeremy and Green, Anthony – *Gods, Demons and Symbols of Ancient Mesopotamia*, University of Texas Press, Austin, 1997

Bonwick, James – *Irish Druids and Old Irish Religions*, Dorset Press, 1986

Bowersock, G.W. – *Roman Arabia*, Harvard University Press, Cambridge, Mass., 1983

Brown, Raymond L. – *Death of the Messiah* (two volumes), Doubleday, New York, 1994

Bruce, F.F. – *Israel and the Nations*, InterVarsity Press, Downers Grove, Ill., 1997

Bruce, F.F. – *New Testament History*, Doubleday, New York, 1969

Budge, E.A. Wallis – *The Book of the Dead*, Gramercy Books, New York, 1999

Budge, E.A. Wallis – *Egyptian Language*, Dover Publications Inc., New York, 1983

Budge, E.A. Wallis – *Legends of the Egyptian Gods*, Dover Publications Inc., New York, 1994

Bunson, Margaret – *A Dictionary of Ancient Egypt*, Oxford University Press, New York, 1991

Campbell, Joseph – *The Hero With a Thousand Faces*, MJF Books, New York, 1949

Campbell, Joseph – *Occidental Mythology*, Arkana Penguin Books, 1964

Charlesworth, James – *Old Testament Pseudepigrapha* (two volumes), Doubleday, New York, 1993

Clark, R.T. Rundle – *Myth and Symbol in Ancient Egypt*, Thames and Hudson, New York, 1959

Clark, Rosemary – The Sacred Tradition in Ancient Egypt, Llewellyn Publications, St. Paul, Minn., 2000

Coghlan, Ronan – *Book of Irish Names*, Sterling Publishing Co. Inc., New York, 1989

Collier, Mark and Manley, Bill – *How to Read Egyptian Hieroglyphs*, University of California Press, Berkeley, 1998

Collins, John H. – *Apocalypticism in the Dead Sea Scrolls, Routledge*, New York, 1997

Colum, Pedraic – *Nordic Gods and Heroes*, Dover Publications Inc., New York, 1996

Coogan, Michael David – *Stories from Ancient Canaan*, Westminster Press, Louisville, Ky., 1978

Crane, Frank – *Lost Books of the Bible and the Forgotten Books of Eden*, William Collins, 1926

Crossley-Holland, Kevin – *The Norse Myths*, Pantheon Books, New York, 1980

Crosson, John Dominic – *The Birth of Christianity*, HarperCollins, San Francisco, 1998

Crosson, John Dominic – *The Historical Jesus*, HarperCollins, San Francisco, 1991

Crosson, John Dominic – *Who Killed Jesus?*, HarperCollins, San Francisco, 1996

Currid, John D. – *Ancient Egypt and the Old Testament*, Baker Books, Grand Rapids, Mich., 1997

Davidson, H.R. Ellis – *Gods and Myths of Northern Europe*, Penguin, London, 1990

Davidson, H.R. Ellis – *Myths and Symbols in Pagan Europe*, Syracuse University Press, N.Y., 1988

De Boron, Robert – *Joseph of Arimathea*, Rudolf Steiner Press, London, 1990

De Santillana, Giorgio and Von Dechend, Hertha, *Hamlet's Mill*, David R. Godine, Boston, 1977

Doherty, Earl – The Jesus Puzzle, *Canadian Humanist Publications*, Ottawa, Canada, 1999

Durant, Will – *Christ and Caesar*, MJF Books, New York, 1971
Eisenman, Robert and Wise, Michael – *The Dead Sea Scrolls Uncovered*, Element Books, Rockport, Mass., 1992
Eisenman, Robert – *James the Brother of Jesus*, Viking Penguin, New York, 1996
Ellis, Ralph – *Jesus, Last of the Pharaohs*, Edfu Books, Dorset, 1998
Eusebius – The History of the Church, Penguin Books, New York, 1965
Ewing, Upton Clary – The Prophet of the Dead Sea Scrolls, Tree of Life Publications, Joshua Tree, Calif., 1993
Finegan, Jack – Handbook of Biblical Chronology, Hendrickson Publishers, Peabody, Mass., 1964
Finegan, Jack – *Myth and Mystery*, Baker Books, Grand Rapids, Mich., 1989
Fox, Robin Lane – *The Unauthorized Version*, Alfred A. Knopf, New York, 1992
Frazer, James – *The Golden Bough*, Wordsworth, Ware, Hertfordshire, 1993
Freedman, David Noel – *Anchor Bible Dictionary* (six volumes), Doubleday, New York, 1992
Freke, Timothy and Gandy, Peter – *The Jesus Mysteries*, Harmony Books, New York, 1999
Frend, W.H.C. – *The Rise of Christianity*, Fortress Press, Philadelphia, 1984
Fricke, Weddig – *The Court-Martial of Jesus*, Grove Weidenfeld, New York, 1987
Friedman, Richard Elliott – *Who Wrote the Bible?*, Summit Books, New York, 1987
Gadalla, Moustafa – *Historical Deception: The Untold Story of Ancient Egypt*, Tehuti Research Foundation, Greensboro, N.C., 1999
Gardner, Laurence – *Bloodline of the Holy Grail*, Element Books, Boston, 1996
Gardner, Laurence – *Genesis of the Grail Kings*, Element Books, Boston, 2000
Gardiner, Alan – *Egypt of the Pharaohs*, Oxford University Press, New York, 1961
Ginzberg, Louis – *Legends of the Jews* (four volumes), Johns Hopkins University Press, Baltimore, Md., 1998
Goodman, Martin – *The Ruling Class of Judaea*, Cambridge University Press, New York, 1987
Goodrich, Norma Lorre – *The Holy Grail*, HarperCollins, New York, 1992
Goodrich, Norma Lorre – *Merlin*, HarperCollins, New York, 1988
Goodrick, Edward W. and Kohlenberger, John R. III – *Zondervan NIV Exhaustive Concordance*, second edition, Zondervan, Grand Rapids, Mich., 1999
Gould, Charles – *Mythical Monsters*, Senate, London, 1995

Graves, Robert – *The Greek Myths* (two volumes), Penguin, London, 1960
Graves, Robert and Patai, Rafael – *Hebrew Myths*, Greenwich House,
    New York, 1983
Graves, Robert – *King Jesus*, Noonday Press, New York, 1946
Graves, Robert – *The White Goddess*, Farrar, Straus and Giroux,
    New York, 1948
Green, Joel B. and McKnight, Scot and Marshall, I. Howard –
Dictionary of Jesus and the Gospels, InterVarsity Press,
    Downers Grove, Ill., 1992
Green, Roger Lancelyn – *Tales of Ancient Egypt*, Puffin Books,
    New York, 1967
Greenberg, Gary – *The Bible Myth*, Carol Publishing, Secaucus, N.J., 1996
Greenberg, Gary – *101 Myths of the Bible*, Sourcebooks Inc.,
    Naperville, Ill., 2000
Guest, Charlotte E. – *The Mabinogion*, Dover Publications,
Mineola, N.Y., 1997
Hancock, Graham and Bauval, Robert – *The Message of the Sphinx*,
    Three Rivers Press, New York, 1996
Hancock, Graham – *The Sign and the Seal*, Touchstone,
New York, 1992
Harrington, Daniel – *The Maccabean Revolt*, Michael Glazier,
    Wilmington, Del., 1988
Helms, Randel – *Gospel Fictions*, Prometheus Books,
Amherst, N.Y., 1988
Hengel, Martin – *The Zealots*, T&T Clark Ltd., Edinburgh, 1989
Herm, Gerhard – *The Phoenicians*, William Morrow and Company,
    New York, 1975
Herodotus – *The Histories*, Penguin, London, 1996
Holt, J.C. – *Robin Hood*, Thames and Hudson, New York, 1989
House, H. Wayne – Chronological and Background Charts of the
    New Testament, Zondervan, Grand Rapids, Mich., 1981
Jacobs, Joseph – *Favorite Celtic Fairy Tales*, Dover Publications Inc.,
    New York, 1994
Johnson, Paul – *A History of Christianity*, Atheneum, New York, 1980
Jung, Emma and von Franz, Marie-Louise, *The Grail Legend*,
    Princeton University Press, N.J., 1998
Kane, Matt – *Heavens Unearthed*, Golden Egg Books, Altoona, Pa., 1999
Keller, Werner – *The Bible as History*, Barnes and Noble Books, New York, 1995
Kemp, Barry J. – *Ancient Egypt*, Routledge, New York, 1989
Kirsch, Jonathan – *The Harlot by the Side of the Road*, Ballantine Books,
    New York, 1997
Kirsch, Jonathan – *Moses: A Life*, Ballantine Books, New York, 1998
Klingaman, William K. – *The First Century*, HarperCollins, 1990
Knight, Christopher and Lomas, Robert – *The Hiram Key*,
    Element Books, Rockport, Mass., 1998

Knight, Christopher and Lomas, Robert – *The Second Messiah*,
  Element Books, Boston, 1998
Kramer, Samuel Noah – *The Sumerians*, University of Chicago Press, 1963
Layton, Bentley – *The Gnostic Scriptures*, Doubleday, New York, 1987
Leeming, David Adams – *The World of Myth*, Oxford University Press,
  New York, 1990
List, Robert N. – *Merlin's Secret*, University Press of America Inc., Lanham, Md.,
  1999
Lockhart, Douglas – *The Dark God*, Element Books, Boston, 1999
Lockhart, Douglas – *Jesus the Heretic*, Element Books,
  Rockport, Mass., 1997
Loomis, Richard Sherman – *The Grail*, Princeton University Press,
  N.J., 1991
Maccoby, Hyam – *The Mythmaker*, HarperCollins, San Francisco, 1986
Mackillop, James – *Oxford Dictionary of Celtic Mythology*, Oxford
  University Press, Oxford, 1998
Martin, Ralph P. and Davids, Peter H. – *Dictionary of the Later New
  Testament*, InterVarsity Press, Downers Grove, Ill., 1997
  Mason, Steve – Josephus and the New Testament, Hendrickson
Publishers, Peabody, Mass., 1992
Massey, Gerald – *The Historical Jesus and the Mythical Christ*,
  The Book Tree, Escondido, Calif., 2000
Matthews, Caitlin and John – *Ladies of the Lake*, Thorsons, London, 1992
Matthews, John – *The Druid Source Book*, Blandford Books, London, 1997
Matthews, John – *The Elements of the Grail Tradition*, Element Books,
  Rockport, Mass., 1990
Matthews, Victor H. and Benjamin, Don C. – Old Testament Parallels,
  Paulist Press, New York, 1997
Mead, G.R.S. – *Gnostic John the Baptizer*, Kessinger Publishing, Montana
Mead, G.R.S. – *Simon Magus*, Kessinger Publishing, Montana
Meyer, Marvin W. – *The Ancient Mysteries*, HarperCollins,
  San Francisco, 1987
Moffett, Samuel Hugh – *A History of Christianity in Asia*, Vol. 1, Orbis,
  Maryknoll, N.Y., 1998
Morenz, Siegfried – *Egyptian Religion*, Cornell University Press, Ithaca,
  N.Y., 1960
Morford, Mark P.O. and Lenardon, Robert J. – *Classical Mythology*,
  Longman, New York, 1985
Nadich, Judah – *The Legends of the Rabbis*, Vol. 1, Jason Aronson Inc.,
  Northvale, N.J., 1994
Nodet, Etienne and Taylor, Justin – *The Origins of Christianity*, Liturgical
  Press, Collegeville, Minn., 1998
Pagels, Elaine – *The Origin of Satan*, Vintage Books, New York, 1995
Patai, Rafael – *The Hebrew Goddess*, Wayne State University Press,
  Detroit, 1990

Picknett, Lynn and Prince, Clive – *The Templar Revelation*, Touchstone,
    New York, 1997
Pritchard, James B. – *The Ancient Near East*, Vol. I, Princeton University
    Press, N.J., 1958
Quirke, Stephen – *Ancient Egyptian Religion*, Dover Publications Inc.,
    New York, 1992
Rabinowitz, Jacob – *The Faces of God*, Spring Publications,
    Woodstock, Conn., 1998
Redford, Donald B. – *Egypt, Canaan and Israel in Ancient Times*,
    Princeton University Press, N.J., 1992
Regula, DeTraci – *The Mysteries of Isis*, Llewellyn Publications,
    St. Paul, Minn., 1996
Richardson, Peter – *Herod*, University of South Carolina Press, 1996
Roberts, Alexander and Donaldson, James – *The Ante-Nicene Fathers*,
    Vol. VIII, Eerdmans Publishing, Grand Rapids, Mich., 1986
Rohl, David M. – *Pharaohs and Kings*, Crown Publishers Inc., New York, 1995
S, Acharya – *The Christ Conspiracy*, Adventures Unlimited Press,
    Kempton, Ill., 1999
Salibi, Kamal – *Who Was Jesus?*, I.B. Tauris and Co. Ltd., London, 1998
Sarna, Nahum M. – *Exploring Exodus*, Schocken Books, New York, 1996
Schneemelcher, Wilhelm – *New Testament Apocrypha* (two volumes),
    Westminster/John Knox Press, Louisville, Ky. 1991
Schonfield, Hugh – *The Essene Odyssey*, Element Books,
    Rockport, Mass., 1984
Schonfield, Hugh – *The Mystery of the Messiah*, Open Gate Press,
    London, 1998
Schonfield, Hugh – *The Passover Plot*, Element Books,
    Rockport, Mass., 1965
Shaw, Ian – *The Oxford History of Ancient Egypt*, Oxford University
    Press, New York, 2000
Smith, Morton – *Jesus the Magician*, Seastone, Berkeley, Calif., 1998
Spence, Lewis – *Ancient Egyptian Myths and Legends*,
Dover Publications Inc., New York, 1990
Suetonius – *The Twelve Caesars*, Penguin, London, 1989
Starbird, Margaret – *The Goddess in the Gospels*, Bear and Co.,
    Santa Fe, N.M., 1998
Starbird, Margaret – *The Woman with the Alabaster Jar*,
    Bear and Co., San Francisco, 1993
Steiger, Brad – *Worlds Before Our Own*, Berkley Publishing, 1978
Stewart, Desmond – *The Foreigner*, Hamish Hamilton, London, 1981
Stone, Merlin – *When God Was a Woman*, Harvest Books,
    Orlando, Fla., 1976
Strong, James – *Strong's Exhaustive Concordance*, Crusade Bible
    Publishers Inc., Nashville
Tacitus – *The Annals of Imperial Rome*, Penguin, London, 1989

Tacitus – *The Histories*, Oxford University Press, Oxford, 1997
Tatar, Maria – *The Classic Fairy Tales*, W.W. Norton, New York, 1999
Temple, Robert – *The Sirius Mystery*, Destiny Books, Rochester, Vt., 1998
Tenney, Merrill C. – *New Testament Survey*, Wm. B. Eerdmans,
  Grand Rapids, Mich., 1985
Thiering, Barbara – *Jesus and the Riddle of the Dead Sea Scrolls*,
  HarperCollins, San Francisco, 1992
Thompson, R. Campbell – *Semitic Magic*, Samuel Weiser Inc., 2000
Thompson, Thomas L. – *The Mythic Past*, Basic Books, 1999
Tresidder, Jack – *Dictionary of Symbols*, Chronicle Books,
  San Francisco, 1998
Ulansky, David – *Origins of the Mithraic Mysteries*, Oxford University
  Press, New York, 1989
Verbrugghe, Gerald P. and Wickersham, John – *Berossos and Manetho
  Introduced and Translated*, University of Michigan, 1996
Vermes, Geza – *The Dead Sea Scrolls in English*, Penguin,
  New York, 1995
Vermes, Geza – *Jesus the Jew*, Fortress Press, Philadelphia, 1973
Visalli, Gayla – *After Jesus*, Reader's Digest Association Inc.,
  Pleasantville, N.Y., 1992
Von Eschenbach, Wolfram – *Parzival*, Penguin Books, New York, 1980
Walker, Barbara – *Woman's Dictionary of Symbols and Sacred Objects*,
  HarperCollins, San Francisco, 1988
Walker, Barbara – *Woman's Encolpedia of Myths and Secrets*,
  HarperCollins, San Francisco, 1983
Ward, Kaari – *Jesus and His Times*, Reader's Digest Association Inc.,
  Pleasantville, N.Y., 1990
*Webster's Dictionary of the English Language Unabridged, Encyclopedia
  Edition*, Publishers International Press, New York, 1977
Weston, Jessie L. – *From Ritual to Romance*, Dover Publications,
  Mineola, N.Y., 1997
Whitson, William – *The Works of Josephus*, Hendrickson Publishers,
  1987
Willis, Roy – *Dictionary of World Myth*, Duncan Baird, London, 2000
Witt, R.E. – *Isis in the Ancient World*, Johns Hopkins University Press,
  Baltimore, 1971
Wolkstein, Diane and Kramer, Samuel Noah – *Inanna*, Harper and Row,
  New York, 1993
Wylen, Stephen M. – *The Jews in the Time of Jesus,* Paulist Press,
  New York, 1996
Yonge, C.D. – *The Works of Philo*, Hendrickson Publishers, 1997
Young, George M. – *Goddess on the Cross*, Capall Bann Publishing,
  Freshfields, England, 1999

Stephen H. Provost

The author writes about American highways, mutant superheroes, mythic archetypes and pretty much anything he wants. A historian, philosopher, novelist and veteran journalist, he lives on the Central Coast of California. And he loves cats. Read his blogs and keep up with his latest activities at stephenhprovost.com.

[1] Herodotus, *Babylonian Logos*, quoted in Gerhard Herm, *The Phoenicians*, p. 115-6
[2] Herodotus, *Babylonian Logos*, quoted in Gerhard Herm, *The Phoenicians*, p. 115
[3] Deut. 22:29
[4] Gen. 34:25
[5] Tresidder, *Dictionary of Symbols*, p. 61
[6] Gen. 3:20
[7] *Anchor Bible Dictionary*, Vol. 2, p. 676-7
[8] Samuel Noah Kramer, *The Sumerians*, p. 195
[9] Coogan, *Stories from Ancient Canaan*, p. 116
[10] Coogan, *Stories from Ancient Canaan*, p. 104
[11] Coogan, *Stories from Ancient Canaan*, p. 100
[12] Ex. 20:5
[13] Gen. 49:9-11
[14] Coogan, *Stories from Ancient Canaan*, p. 100
[15] Gen. 38:8
[16] Lev. 21:9
[17] Gen. 38:24
[18] Gen. 38:25
[19] Graves and Patai, *The Hebrew Myths*, p. 159
[20] Ps. 89:9-10
[21] Stone, *When God Was a Woman*, p. 92
[22] Prov. 7:10-11
[23] George M. Young, *Goddess on the Cross*, p. 40
[24] Walker, *Woman's Encyclopedia of Myths and Secrets*, p. 937
[25] Graves, *The White Goddess*, p. 101
[26] Lev. 17:11
[27] Walker, *Woman's Encyclopedia of Myths and Secrets*, p. 937
[28] Gos. Peter 5
[29] Kramer, *The Sumerians*, p. 195-196
[30] Kramer, *The Sumerians*, p. 197
[31] Gen. 2:16
[32] Gen. 3:17
[33] Kramer, *The Sumerians*, p. 196
[34] Is. 6:2-6
[35] Kramer, *The Sumerians*, p. 195
[36] Is. 27:1
[37] Ps. 74:14
[38] Graves and Patai, *Hebrew Myths*, p. 32
[39] Gen. 36:20
[40] Gen. 34:31
[41] 2 Sam. 13:15
[42] 2 Macc. 5:13
[43] Bruce, *Israel and the Nations*, p. 137
[44] 2 Macc. 6:10
[45] 1 Macc. 2:27
[46] 1 Macc. 2:33
[47] 1 Macc. 2:40
[48] Josephus, *Against Apion*, 2:5
[49] Hayim Naman Bialik and Yehoshua Hana Ravinitzky, *The Book of Legends*, p. 202
[50] Thompson, Semitic Magic, p. LVIII-LIX
[51] Judah Nadich, *Legends of the Rabbis*, p. 196
[52] Nadich, *Legends of the Rabbis*, p. 195
[53] Nadich, *Legends of the Rabbis*, p. 196
[54] John, 15:1, 5
[55] Jon. 4:7-8

[56] Regula, *The Mysteries of Isis*, p. 76
[57] Picknett and Prince, *The Templar Revelation*, p. 358
[58] Robert Graves, The White Goddess, p. 89, 91
[59] John 10:30
[60] 2 Kings 1:8
[61] Norma Lorre Goodrich, *Merlin*, p. 58
[62] Gen. 17:17
[63] Ginzberg, *Legends of the Jews*, Vol. 4, p. 167-8
[64] Goodrich, *Merlin*, p. 78
[65] Goodrich, *Merlin*, p. 33
[66] Num. 22:4
[67] Num. 22:16-18
[68] John 3:30
[69] James Bonwick, *Irish Druids and Old Irish Religions*, p. 187
[70] Bonwick, *Irish Druids and Old Irish Religions*, p. 170
[71] Bonwick, *Irish Druids and Old Irish Religions*, p. 193
[72] Ex. 17:11
[73] Goodrich, *Merlin*, p. 167
[74] Goodrich, *Merlin*, p. 24
[75] Graves, *The Greek Myths*, Vol. 2, p. 41 (110.d)
[76] Graves, *The Greek Myths*, Vol. 1, p. 57
[77] Diodorus Siculus, 1:17, 24; 3:73, quoted in Graves, *The Greek Myths*, Vol. 2, p. 88
[78] Graves, *The Greek Myths*, Vol. 2, p. 101
[79] H.R. Ellis Davidson, *Myths and Symbols of Pagan Europe*, p. 96
[80] Willis, *Dictionary of World Myth*, p. 151
[81] Tressider, *Dictionary of Symbols*, p. 104
[82] Kramer, *The Sumerians*, p. 329-30
[83] H.R. Ellis Davidson, *Myths and Symbols of Pagan Europe*, p. 26
[84] Willis, *Dictionary of World Myth*, p. 130
[85] Davidson, *Myths and Symbols of Pagan Europe*, p. 77
[86] Gen. 3:6
[87] H.R. Ellis Davidson, *Gods and Myths of Northern Europe*, p. 117
[88] Davidson, *Gods and Myths of Northern Europe*, p. 115
[89] John 12:24
[90] Georgio de Santillana and Hertha Von Dechend, *Hamlet's Mill*, p. 116
[91] Joseph Campbell, *The Hero of a Thousand Faces*, p. 11
[92] Merlin Stone, *When God Was a Woman*, p. 85
[93] Gen. 47:29
[94] Graves and Patai, *The Hebrew Myths*, p. 274
[95] Gen. 34:25
[96] Graves and Patai, *The Hebrew Myths*, p. 164
[97] Gen. 3:15
[98] Graves, *The Greek Myths*, Vol. 2, p. 150
[99] Saxo Grammaticus, *Gesta Danorum*, 7:248, in Davidson, *Gods and Myths of Northern Europe*, p. 49
[100] Davidson, *Gods and Myths of Northern Europe*, p. 142
[101] Davidson, *Gods and Myths of Northern Europe*, p. 143-4
[102] John 3:14
[103] John 3:15
[104] Willis, *Dictionary of World Myth*, p. 123
[105] Walker, *Woman's Encyclopediat of Myths and Secrets*, p. 555
[106] Rev. 20:1-3
[107] Willis, *Dictionary of World Myth*, p. 122
[108] Willis, *Dictionary of World Myth*, p. 175
[109] Padraic Colum, Nordic Gods and Heroes, p. 13-26
[110] Tressider, *Dictionary of Symbols*, p. 15
[111] Kevin Crossley-Holland, *The Norse Myths*, p. 194

[112] Gen. 6:2, 4
[113] Num. 13:33
[114] Gen. 12:4
[115] Gen. 11:6
[116] Gen. 11:7
[117] Morford and Lenardon, *Classical Mythology*, p. 391
[118] Mackillop, *Oxford Dictionary of Celtic Myth*, p. 336
[119] Goodrich, *Merlin*, p. 185
[120] C. and J. Matthews, *Ladies of the Lake*, p. 123
[121] Graves, *The Greek Myths*, Vol. 2, p. 185-6
[122] C. and J. Matthews, *Ladies of the Lake*, p. 122
[123] Didot Perceval, quoted in C. and J. Matthews, *Ladies of the Lake*, p. 117
[124] John 21:22
[125] Tressider, *Dictionary of Symbols*, p. 185
[126] Matt Kane, *Heavens Unearthed*, p. 27
[127] Frazer, *The Golden Bough*, p. 78
[128] Kane, *Heavens Unearthed*, p. 33
[129] Frazer, *The Golden Bough*, p. 78
[130] Frazer, *The Golden Bough*, p. 141
[131] Frazer, *The Golden Bough*, p. 711
[132] Kane, *Heavens Unearthed*, p. 49
[133] Kane, *Heavens Unearthed*, p. 57
[134] Kane, *Heavens Unearthed*, p. 61
[135] Maria Tatar, *The Classic Fairy Tales*, p. 117
[136] Tressider, *Dictionary of Symbols*, p. 100
[137] Tatar, *The Classic Fairy Tales*, p. 119
[138] Rev. 12:1-6
[139] Finegan, *Handbook of Bible Chronology*, p. 19
[140] Tatar, *The Classic Fairy Tales*, p. 121
[141] John Matthews, *The Druid Source Book*, p. 198
[142] Ex. 3:5
[143] Walker, *Woman's Dictionary of Symbols and Sacred Objects*, p. 154
[144] Deut. 25:5-10
[145] John 1:28
[146] Walker, *Woman's Dictionary of Symbols and Sacred Objects*, p. 155
[147] Kane, *Heavens Unearthed*, p. 237
[148] Ginzberg, *Legends of the Jews*, Vol. 4, p. 143
[149] Walker, *Woman's Encyclopedia of Myths and Secrets*, p. 936
[150] Hancock, *The Sign and the Seal*, p. 83
[151] Ginzberg, *Legends of the Jews*, Vol. 4, p. 145
[152] Tressider, *Dictionary of Symbols*, p. 17
[153] Pamela Forey and Cecilia Fitzsimons, *An Instant Guide to Stars and Planets*, p. 96
[154] Forey and Fitzsimons, *An Instant Guide to Stars and Planets*, p. 85
[155] Joseph Jacobs, *Favorite Celtic Fairy Tales*, p. 76-80
[156] Kane, *Heavens Unearthed*, p. 65, 179
[157] Tressider, *Dictionary of Symbols*, p. 137
[158] Willis, *Dictionary of World Myth*, p. 208-9
[159] Walker, *Woman's Dictionary of Symbols and Sacred Objects*, p. 351
[160] Josephus, *Antiquities*, 14:31
[161] Ant. 16:147
[162] Isaiah 11:1
[163] Herod, *Peter Richardson*, p. 162
[164] Josephus, *Jewish War*, 1:22:2
[165] *Antiquities* 15:3:8
[166] *Antiquities* 15:3:9
[167] Josephus, *Antiquities* 15:242
[168] Josephus, *Antiquities* 15:320-321

[169] Jer. 31:15, Matt. 2:18
[170] Young, *Goddess on the Cross*, p. 33
[171] Gen. 29:9
[172] Gen. 29:11
[173] Gen. 21:25
[174] Gen. 21:30
[175] John 10:2-3
[176] 1 Sam. 15:7, Gen. 25:18
[177] Salibi, *History of the Bible People*, p. 109
[178] Salibi, *History of the Bible People*, p. 96
[179] Salibi, *Secrets of the Bible People*, p. 100
[180] Jonah 2:6
[181] *Protevangelium of James* 8:3-9:1
[182] *Gospel of the Birth of Mary* 5:17
[183] Num. 17:1-8
[184] Hayim Nahman Bialik and Yehoshua Hana Ravnitzky, *The Book of Legends*, p. 397
[185] Walker, *Woman's Encyclopedia of Myths and Secrets*, p. 749
[186] Bialik and Ravnitzky, *The Book of Legends*, p. 397
[187] Kamal Salibi, *Who Was Jesus?*, p. 145
[188] John 4:4-42
[189] John 8:48
[190] *Antiquities* 17:339
[191] Matt. 2:2
[192] Strabo, *Porphyre*, quoted in Bauval and Gilbert, *The Orion Mystery*, p. 182
[193] Bauval and Gilbert, *The Orion Mystery*, p. 220
[194] Luke 2:8
[195] Mark 6:1
[196] John 7:41
[197] Micah 5:2
[198] Luke 1:5
[199] Luke 2:2
[200] Quoted in Robert Graves, *King Jesus*, p. 2
[201] Luke 1:39
[202] Quran, 19:23-26
[203] Desmond Stewart, *The Foreigner*, p. 21
[204] Matt. 1:23
[205] Is. 7:16-7
[206] Barbara G. Walker, *Women's Encyclopedia of Myths and Secrets*, p. 23
[207] Walker, *Women's Dictionary of Symbols and Sacred Objects*, p. 227
[208] Gen 1:2
[209] Jeremy Black, Anthony Green, *Gods, Demons and Symbols of Ancient Mesopotamia*, p. 108
[210] *Protev. James*, quoted in Schneemelcher, *New Testament Apocrypha*, Vol. 1, p. 426
[211] Luke 2:37
[212] Ex. 1:22
[213] Walker, *Women's Encyclopedia of Myths and Secrets*, p. 61
[214] Matt. 2:21-22
[215] Gos. Nicodemus 3, quoted in Schneemelcher, *New Testament Apocrypha*, Vol. 1, p. 508
[216] Stewart, *The Foreigner*, p. 17
[217] Black and Green, *Gods, Demons and Symbols of Ancient Mesopotamia*, p. 35
[218] Walker, *Woman's Encyclopedia of Myths and Secrets*, p. 463
[219] Walker, *Woman's Encyclopedia of Myths and Secrets*, p. 767
[220] Deut. 4:16
[221] *Antiquities* 17:6:2, *Jewish War* 1:33:2
[222] *Antiquities* 17:6:2-4
[223] *Antiquities* 17:269
[224] *Antiquities* 14:158-9
[225] *Antiquities* 17:10:2

[226] Antiquities 17:10:10
[227] Antiquities 18:1:1
[228] Antiquities 18:1:1
[229] Matt. 22:17
[230] Antiquities, 18:26
[231] Josephus, *War of the Jews,* Slavonic version, following 2:7:2
[232] Antiquities, 18:23
[233] John 3:30
[234] Judges 13:2-5
[235] Luke 1:11-15
[236] Luke 7:34
[237] Matt. 2:23
[238] Walker, *Woman's Encyclopedia of Myths and Secrets*, p. 429
[239] Regula, *Mysteries of Isis*, p. 24, 79
[240] Pseudo-Matthew 20:2, quoted in Schneemelcher, *New Testament Apocrypha*, Vol. 1, p. 463
[241] *Anchor Bible Dictionary*, Vol. 1, p. 896
[242] Luke 1:78-79
[243] Babylonian Talmud, Sota 48b
[244] Zechariah 3, 7
[245] Geza Vermes, *Jesus the Jew*, p. 21
[246] Matt. 13:55
[247] Baring and Cashford, *Myth of the Goddess*, p. 189
[248] Antiquities 18:2:3
[249] Antiquities 18:56
[250] Antiquities 18:57
[251] Antiquities 18:59
[252] Qumran Commentary on Habbakuk 6:4-5
[253] Antiquities 18:3:2
[254] Luke 13:1
[255] Jewish War 2:8:4
[256] Epiphanius Panarion 29:1:3-5:3
[257] Antiquities 18:1:5
[258] Luke 6:20-21
[259] Luke 6:24-26
[260] James 5:1-6
[261] Mark 10:21
[262] Mark 10:23, 25
[263] Judges 6:12
[264] War Scroll 6:3
[265] War Scroll 11:1-2, 4-6
[266] Community Rule, 8:14
[267] John 1:23
[268] Matt. 3:7
[269] Dam. Doc. 5:14
[270] Community Rule 3:7-9
[271] Matt. 3:4
[272] Community Rule 12:14-15
[273] Luke 3:16
[274] Tressider, *Dictionary of Symbols*, p. 94
[275] John 3:7
[276] John 3:5
[277] Community Rule 4:21-23
[278] Matt. 3:15
[279] Ps. 2:7
[280] Luke 3:22
[281] Randel Helms, *Gospel Fictions*, p. 28
[282] Heb. 1:5

[283] John 3:3
[284] Gos. Thom. 75
[285] Gos. Phil. 125a
[286] 1 Sam. 13:8-14
[287] Community Rule 7:16
[288] Matt. 20:21
[289] John Allegro, *The Dead Sea Scrolls and the Christian Myth*, p. 181
[290] John 1:28
[291] Ginzberg, *Legends of the Jews*, Vol. 4, p. 5
[292] Matt. 11:14
[293] 2 Kings 2:9-10
[294] Matt. 16:17, John 1:42
[295] John 1:35-42
[296] Martin Hengel, *The Zealots*, p. 53
[297] Deut. 8:3
[298] Ps. 91:11-12
[299] Matt. 4:10
[300] John 2:1
[301] Luke 7:24
[302] Walker, *Woman's Dictionary of Symbols and Sacred Objects*, p. 450
[303] Walker, *Woman's Encyclopedia of Myths and Secrets*, p. 452
[304] Lev. 12:2
[305] Diane Wolkstein and Samuel Noah Kramer, *Inanna*, p. 108
[306] Walker, *Woman's Encyclopedia of Myths and Secrets*, p. 637
[307] Wolkstein and Kramer, *Inanna*, p. 39
[308] Wolkstein and Kramer, *Inanna*, p. 40
[309] Mark 16:1
[310] Luke 8:48
[311] Ruth 3:3-4
[312] Ruth 3:9
[313] Mark 14:3, John 12:3
[314] Starbird, *The Woman With the Alabaster Jar*, p. 40
[315] Song 1:12
[316] Walker, *Woman's Encyclopedia of Myths and Secrets*, p. 167
[317] Luke 7:47
[318] Lev. 15:24 (KJV)
[319] Walker, *Woman's Encyclopedia of Myths and Secrets*, p. 502
[320] *Protevangelium of James*, 19-20
[321] Baring and Cashford, *The Myth of the Goddess*, p. 190
[322] Baring and Cashford, *The Myth of the Goddess*, p. 190
[323] John 10
[324] Antiquities, 18:137
[325] Luke 8:2-3
[326] Luke 7:20
[327] Luke 7:28
[328] John 4:7
[329] Josephus, Slavonic *War of the Jews*, after 2:9:1
[330] John 1:43
[331] John 1:44
[332] *Anchor Bible Dictionary*, Vol. 1, p. 700
[333] *Anchor Bible Dictionary*, Vol. 1, p. 692
[334] John 5:1
[335] Matt. 11:21-22
[336] Is. 52:14
[337] Matt. 8:9
[338] Antiquities, 18:118
[339] Mark 6:25

340 Luke 4:16-19, Isaiah 61:1-2
341 Isaiah 35:5-6
342 Luke 11:29-32
343 Matt. 13:15, Isaiah 6:9-10
344 Young, *Goddess on the Cross*, p. 41
345 Mark 5:1-18
346 Matt. 12:22-28
347 Luke 11:21-22
348 John 15:1-6
349 Mark 4:21
350 Community Rule, 8:1-2
351 *Anchor Bible Dictionary*, Vol. 5, p. 977
352 B. Sanh. 43a, quoted in Bialik and Ravnitzky, *Book of Legends*, p. 519
353 Jewish War 2:124-126
354 Matt. 10:9-11
355 Jewish War 2:124
356 Matt. 10:14
357 Luke 10:22, 23-24
358 Luke 10:25-37
359 Matt. 5:21-26
360 Matt. 10:16-23
361 Daniel 7:13-14
362 War Scroll 11:17-12:1, 11:7-8
363 Matt. 11:12
364 Matt. 10:34-37
365 Matt. 10: 39
366 Mark 9:1
367 Mark 10:21
368 Matt. 13:1-9
369 Matt. 13:32
370 Matt. 13:24-29
371 Matt. 13:11, 13
372 Matt. 12:1-7
373 1 Sam. 21:1-9
374 Matt. 17:24-27
375 Matt. 22:15-22
376 Luke 3:8
377 Luke 12:49
378 Matt. 24:9
379 John 6:53
380 Matt. 20:22
381 John 12:24
382 Amos 5:27, Damascus Document 7:15
383 Mark 14:24
384 John 6:66
385 John 6:15
386 John 14:2
387 John 10:16
388 Luke 9:48, Avot 1:13
389 Avot 1:12
390 Matt. 22:37-40
391 Matt. 7:12
392 Recognitions 1:66
393 Acts 6:38-39
394 Luke 8:16-17
395 1 Cor. 9:1
396 2 Cor. 5:16

[397] Acts 22:3
[398] Acts 23:6
[399] Galatians 1:13-14
[400] Philippians 3:5-6
[401] Acts 9:1-2
[402] Luke 1:1-4
[403] Acts 1:4
[404] Jeremiah 28
[405] Matt. 11:30
[406] B. Tal., Taanit 25a
[407] Infancy Thom. 13:1-2
[408] B. Tal., Berakhot 33a
[409] Rom. 6:23
[410] Acts 28:1-6
[411] 2 Cor. 5:21
[412] Luke 10:19
[413] Luke 8:25
[414] B. Tal. Taanit 24b
[415] B. Tal. Taanit 19a, 23a
[416] B. Tal. Taanit 24b
[417] Mark 1:11
[418] Matt. 8:5-13
[419] B. Tal. Berakhot, 34b
[420] Acts 9:18
[421] Acts 12:7-8
[422] Phil. 3:6
[423] Rom. 7:21-25
[424] Luke 17:11-15
[425] Mark 1:40-45
[426] Matt. 26:6, Mark 14:3
[427] John 9
[428] Luke 16:19-31
[429] John 11:9
[430] John 9:3
[431] John 11:4
[432] Romans 6:3-4
[433] John 3:5
[434] John 12:1
[435] Acts 9:20-25
[436] John 12:10-11
[437] Acts 9:25
[438] Psalm 118:25-26
[439] Mark 11:1-3
[440] Zech. 9:9-13
[441] Zech. 9:8
[442] Mark 11:10
[443] Mark 11:11
[444] Mark 11:12-14
[445] Nedarim 3:4
[446] Ex. 22:25, Deut. 23:19
[447] Mark 12:41-44
[448] John 2:16, Luke 19:46
[449] Avodah Zarah 16b-17a
[450] John 11:48
[451] Gos. Thom. 71
[452] Luke 21:6
[453] Matt. 12:6

[454] 1 Kings 8:27
[455] Micah 3:11-12
[456] Luke 21:20
[457] Mark 13:14-16
[458] Luke 21:28
[459] Mark 13:30
[460] John 11:57
[461] War Scroll 11:7,10
[462] John 3:14, Num. 21:4-8
[463] Matt. 21:23-27
[464] Matt. 21:33-46
[465] Matt. 26:5
[466] Rule Annexe 2:18-22
[467] Isaiah 62:8
[468] Matt. 9:16
[469] 1 Cor. 11:23, 25
[470] Walker, *Woman's Encyclopedia of Myths and Secrets*, p. 636
[471] John 13:4-10
[472] Luke 22:36
[473] John 13:27
[474] John 13:18
[475] Ps. 41:9
[476] *Gos. Thomas* introduction
[477] Num. 3:13
[478] Frazer, *The Golden Bough*, p. 293
[479] John 11:50
[480] Frazer, *The Golden Bough*, p. 293
[481] John 13:27
[482] Gen. 3:15
[483] Ps. 18:4, 16-17
[484] Ps. 18:7-9
[485] 1 Cor. 15:14
[486] Mark 15:36
[487] Num. 6:3
[488] Luke 11:50
[489] Gen. 4:11-12
[490] John 13:28
[491] Matt. 26:39
[492] John 18:3
[493] John 18:11
[494] Mark 14:51
[495] John 18:15-16
[496] John 18:19-23
[497] Mark 14:53-63
[498] War Scroll 11:17, 12:8, 9
[499] Acts 6:8, 13
[500] Deut. 13:1-5
[501] Deut. 18:20
[502] Matt. 26:68
[503] John 18:31
[504] Luke 23:1
[505] John 19:12
[506] Psalm 2
[507] Matt. 26:16-17
[508] Yoma 6:1-2
[509] Mark 15:15
[510] Lev. 12:7-22

[511] Jerome, *Commentary on Matthew*, on 27:16
[512] Raymond E. Brown, *The Death of the Messiah*, p. 799
[513] John 13:2
[514] Luke 8:44-45
[515] John 13:2
[516] Zech. 11:12
[517] Mark 15:12
[518] John 19:15
[519] Ezek. 8:15
[520] Frazer, *The Golden Bough*, p. 293
[521] Zech. 12:10
[522] Davidson, *Gods and Myths of Northern Europe*, p. 52-53
[523] Wolkstein and Kramer, *Inanna*, p. 53
[524] Walker, *Women's Dictionary of Symbols and Sacred Objects*, p. 95
[525] Gen. 4:24
[526] Heb. 4:12
[527] Matt. 27:52
[528] Gen. 38:28
[529] Graves, *The White Goddess*, p. 301
[530] Acts 1:4
[531] Graves, *The White Goddess*, p. 305
[532] Mackillop, *Dictionary of Celtic Mythology*, p. 27
[533] Graves, *The White Goddess*, p. 169
[534] Mackillop, *Dictionary of Celtic Mythology*, p. 27
[535] Frazer, *The Golden Bough*, p. 708
[536] Frazer, *The Golden Bough*, p. 77
[537] *Anchor Bible Dictionary*, Vol. II, p. 806
[538] Gen. 35:4
[539] Gen. 49:29-31
[540] *The Mabinogion*, p. 46
[541] Ex. 28
[542] Graves, *The White Goddess*, p. 41
[543] Wolkstein and Kramer, *Inanna*, p. 53
[544] Matt. 27:29
[545] Wolkstein and Kramer, *Inanna*, p. 53
[546] Matt. 27:28
[547] *Gos. Nicodemus* 16:6; Ps. 24:7
[548] Wolkstein and Kramer, *Inanna*, p. 55
[549] John 19:23
[550] 1 Cor. 15:45
[551] Mark 12:25
[552] Matt. 19:12
[553] Salibi, *Secrets of the Bible People*, p. 122
[554] Matt. 17:18, Jer. 31:15
[555] Brown, *The Death of the Messiah*, p. 1065
[556] Matt. 27:50
[557] Ex. 12:46
[558] Brown, *The Death of the Messiah*, p. 1177
[559] John 19:35
[560] John 21:4
[561] Luke 5:1-6
[562] John 20:30
[563] John 21:25
[564] Luke 24:13-31
[565] Mark 16:7
[566] Mark 15:43
[567] *Gos. Peter* 2:3

[568] John 19:38
[569] John 11:50
[570] 1 Kings 6:32
[571] John 20:12
[572] Ps. 18:6
[573] Luke 24:4
[574] Amos 1:9-10
[575] John 20:14
[576] *Anchor Bible Dictionary*, Vol. 5, p. 1194
[577] Budge, *Book of the Dead*, p. 251
[578] Luke 1:64
[579] Budge, Book of the Dead, p. 248
[580] Gos. Thom. 11
[581] Acts 15:13-20
[582] Eusebius, *History of the Church*, 2:23
[583] Gos. Heb. 7
[584] John 20:17
[585] Luke 24:51
[586] Gen. 19:23-28
[587] 1 Sam. 24:1-2
[588] Gos. Heb. 7
[589] 1 Cor. 11:24
[590] Hist. Eccl. 2:23
[591] 11QMelch
[592] Mark 2:5, Luke 4:18
[593] Heb. 5:9-10
[594] Acts 5:13
[595] Scroll of the Rule 6:2
[596] Acts 2:42-47
[597] Matt. 19:21
[598] Acts 2:32-35
[599] Scroll of the Rule 6:24
[600] Acts 5:1-11
[601] James 2:14
[602] Rom. 9:32
[603] Rom. 3:28
[604] Suetonius, *The Twelve Caesars*, Claudius, 25
[605] Phil. 4:22
[606] 1 Cor. 7:19, Gal. 5:12
[607] Gal. 2:9
[608] Gal. 2:6-7
[609] 2 Cor. 11:1-6, 13
[610] Gal. 2:12
[611] Gal. 2:11
[612] Gal. 2:4
[613] 1 Cor. 8:7
[614] Acts 8:9
[615] Acts 8:20
[616] 1 Cor. 11:22-23
[617] Ant. 20:142
[618] Ant. 20:142
[619] Acts 21:18
[620] Acts 21:20-21
[621] Acts 21:28
[622] Acts 21:31
[623] Acts 22:22
[624] Acts 22:25

[625] Acts 23:10
[626] Acts 23:23-24
[627] Acts 24:23
[628] Acts 25:3
[629] Acts 25:11
[630] Acts 28:30
[631] Acts 28:30
[632] Recognitions 1:70
[633] 2 Cor. 12:2-4
[634] 2 Cor. 10:12
[635] 2 Cor. 11:13
[636] Recognitions 1:70
[637] Second Apocalypse of James, p. 61
[638] Eusebius, *History of the Church*, 2:23
[639] Luke 23:34
[640] Acts 7:60
[641] Acts 7:60
[642] Acts 7:56
[643] Eusebius, *History of the Church*, 2:23
[644] Eusebius, *History of the Church*, 2:23
[645] Matt. 7:7

www.ingramcontent.com/pod-product-compliance
Lightning Source LLC
Chambersburg PA
CBHW070732170426
43200CB00007B/502